LIBERALISM AND SOCIOLOGY

L. T. HOBHOUSE AND POLITICAL ARGUMENT IN ENGLAND 1880–1914

LIBERALISM AND SOCIOLOGY

L. T. HOBHOUSE AND POLITICAL ARGUMENT IN ENGLAND 1880–1914

STEFAN COLLINI

CAMBRIDGE UNIVERSITY PRESS
CAMBRIDGE
LONDON NEW YORK MELBOURNE

Published by the Syndics of the Cambridge University Press
The Pitt Building, Trumpington Street, Cambridge CB2 1RP
Bentley House, 200 Euston Road, London NW1 2DB
32 East 57th Street, New York, NY 10022, USA
296 Beaconsfield Parade, Middle Park, Melbourne 3206, Australia

First published 1979

Printed in Great Britain at the
University Press, Cambridge

Library of Congress Cataloguing in Publication Data
Collini, Stefan, 1947–
Liberalism and sociology.
Bibliography: p.
Includes index.
1. Hobhouse, Leonard Trelawney, 1864–1929.
2. Sociology – Great Britain – History. 3. Liberalism –
Great Britain – History. 4. Political science – Great
Britain – History. I. Title.
HM22.G8H63 301′.092′4 78-23779

ISBN 0 521 22304 0

CONTENTS

TO MY PARENTS

ACKNOWLEDGEMENTS

In writing this book, I have incurred intellectual debts of such extent and depth that even to make the conventional claim to responsibility for errors and omissions almost seems to be a presumptuous piece of egotism. Earlier drafts were read, in whole or in part, by John Burrow, Peter Clarke, Peter Gay, Geoffrey Hawthorn, Alan Lee, Ruth Morse, Peter Nicholson, Michael Oakeshott, Gillian Rose, Quentin Skinner, and John Thompson. For all their criticisms and suggestions I am very grateful. In the case of some of these friends, my indebtedness is of long standing, and extends beyond the reading (and rereading) of these drafts. Peter Gay gave me much-needed encouragement and support at an early stage, and has been a source of stimulation ever since. Credit for the merits of the approach adopted in this book belongs to Quentin Skinner, whose counsel and example have, from the outset, been invaluable. At every stage I have benefited from John Thompson's outstanding gift for careful and constructive criticism, always so selflessly exercised. I am particularly indebted to Peter Clarke for much help and sound advice, and for generously sharing ideas and information about many aspects of this period. More recently, I have received an education from the hugely enjoyable conversation of John Burrow. Finally, my greatest debt is to Ruth Morse: we share, among other things, a distaste for the fulsome rhetoric of Prefaces, but the simple truth is that without her support, example, and unfailing intellectual companionship this book would never have been written at all.

I am also grateful to the Master and Fellows of Jesus College, Cambridge, for financial support at an early stage; to the Adjudicators of the Thirlwall Prize and Seeley Medal; to the Master and Fellows of St John's College, Cambridge, for electing me to a Research Fellowship during the tenure of which much of the research for this book was undertaken; to the Arts Faculty Research Fund Committee of the University of Sussex for a grant towards the typing expenses.

I am also indebted to Mrs J. Balme, Hobhouse's granddaughter, for allowing me to consult her collection of her grandfather's papers, for her generous hospitality, and for patiently answering many enquiries. For providing me with information about unsigned contributions to the *Manchester Guardian*, I am grateful to the paper's Librarian, Mr F. B.

Singleton; for providing me with copies of extracts from her mother's diaries, I am grateful to the late May Wallas. For permission to use and quote from manuscript sources in their possession, I am grateful to Mr A. and Mr H. Llewellyn Smith, and to the staffs of the following libraries: the Bodleian Library, Oxford; the British Library; the British Library of Political and Economic Science; the House of Lords Record Office; the Library of King's College, Cambridge; Manchester University Library; the Library of Merton College, Oxford; the Library of University College, London. I am particularly grateful to the exceptionally helpful and friendly staff of Cambridge University Library.

For answering enquiries about possible manuscript sources, I also owe thanks to George Allen and Unwin Ltd; Mr David Ayerst; Mr Samuel Barron; Mr L. J. M. Beighton; Mr Charles Bosanquet; Miss Violet Butler; the Earl of Carlisle; Mr A. E. Davies; Miss Mary Llewellyn Davies; the Rev. R. A. C. Greenland; Professor E. M. Eppel; Mr Paul Hobhouse; the late Mr Harold Hobson; Mr George Howard; Mrs Muriel Hueffer; the India Office Librarian; the Archivist of Keele University; Mr David Marquand; Professor D. M. Mackinnon; Macmillan International Ltd; Professor Donald MacRae; the Librarian of Marlborough College; Professor T. H. Marshall; Dr A. J. A. Morris; Mr David Mitrany; the Librarian of the *New Statesman*; Messrs Pennington, Lewis and Lewis; Miss Margaret Sinclair; Mr A. J. Porteous; Sir Dennis Proctor; the Librarian of St John's College, Oxford; the Archivist of the *Sociological Review*; Messrs Shepherd and Wedderburn.

INTRODUCTION

Liberalism and sociology are not obviously compatible theoretically, and the history of their relationship is generally presumed to be one of antagonism. Much, of course, depends upon definition, but the currently prevailing understanding of these terms does little to mitigate this opposition. As a political theory, Liberalism is generally taken to be characterized above all by its individualism, that is, by its tendency to take the rational individual pursuing the satisfaction of his non-context-dependent wants as both the unit of analysis and the locus of value. A belief in maximizing the individual citizen's freedom from restraint and a corresponding commitment to restricting the role of the state are seen as its typical expressions. It is identified historically with protest against religious and political authority, and sometimes more specifically with efforts to free the begetters and beneficiaries of the Industrial Revolution from the control of and subservience to a class which derived its power and its privileges from pre-industrial society. By contrast, it is its perspective upon society as a whole and on the 'social' as such which is held to be distinctive of sociology. This involves emphasizing the way in which the individual is not merely influenced but constituted by social forces, and how his actions are largely determined by structural constraints, implying, in consequence, that any strictly individualist social or political theory is conceptually incoherent. Like Liberalism, sociology cannot simply be equated with one particular historical statement, but its origins are usually traced to the social theorists of the late eighteenth and early nineteenth centuries; the formative period of the methodological approaches which have characterized its modern practice is most often taken to be that of the critique of the materialist, Idealist and Utilitarian understandings of society at the turn of this century.

Obviously, both concepts are here being treated at a very high level of abstraction, so much so, indeed, that it is doubtful whether any particular historical examples corresponded to these ideal-types in anything like their pure form. I shall certainly argue that they apply to the subject of this book much less well than has been supposed. But for the moment it is worth remarking that even in its own terms this presumption of antagonism, unless buttressed by so many exclusion clauses that it becomes almost tautologous, is open to serious challenge and even reversal. For example, it might be argued (as Sheldon Wolin has ably and ingeniously done) that the rise of Liberalism as a political theory was bound up with the emergence of the concept of the 'social' and of society as a kind of self-regulating system, so that early Liberalism and early social science were mutually reinforcing rather than antagonistic.[1] The working idea here is that the development of an understanding of 'natural' social processes – that is, of how there is a pattern to human social life which is not the outcome of any kind of deliberate collective decision, and of how, if not interfered with, these social forces tend to produce such desirable results as an increase in wealth, an education in virtue, and so on – in itself involved a decline of 'political' categories, and a corresponding tendency to restrict the role of the state and to exalt the freedom of the individual, the very features most characteristic of Liberalism. Once again, of course, matters of definition are crucial: Wolin's assemblage of Liberals, from Locke to the Utilitarians, is a rather motley crew, and the paradigm of social science involved is provided as much by economics as by sociology. Moreover, the force of the example as a counter to the initial contrast may be thought to be fatally weakened by the fact that it concentrates almost exclusively on a period before either 'Liberalism' or 'sociology' (or, for that matter, 'social science') had even been christened, let alone had grown to anything like their mature form.

This objection, however, could not be raised against the example of Herbert Spencer. Here, a sociology, conceived as the study of structural and functional change in social systems, was developed explicitly to justify an extremely individualistic conception of Liberalism. According to Spencer, it was precisely a proper understanding of the beneficial effects of the adaptive mechanism at work in social evolution which demonstrated the unwise and ultimately self-defeating character of any attempt to achieve social goals by deliberate action on the part of the state.[2] Needless to say, the persuasiveness of the demonstration now seems to depend upon granting Spencer a whole cluster of peculiar assumptions and dubious inferences: in particular, as in all such theories, certain aspects of a determinate historical situation are smuggled into the initial premises, and the extent to which the 'environment' to which man adapts is already in part the outcome of (and hence modifiable by) deliberate political action is suppressed. Nonetheless, the fact remains that the relationship between Liberalism and sociology in the work of a writer of central importance for

[1] Sheldon Wolin, *Politics and Vision: Continuity and Innovation in Western Political Thought* (Boston, 1960), Ch. 9.

[2] For a lucid analysis of Spencer's theory in these terms, see J. D. Y. Peel, *Herbert Spencer: The Evolution of a Sociologist* (London, 1971).

the nineteenth century's understanding of those two terms is hardly that demanded by our initial contrast.

It might still be argued, though, that only from the late nineteenth century onwards could this contrast be expected to obtain. Following Parsons (tacitly, for the most part), historians of the social sciences have taken this to be the period in which sociology is supposed to have shaken off the evolutionary and mechanistic trappings of earlier theories, and to have conceptualized the 'social' in a way which revealed its pervasive role in the constitution of human action, and hence its central place in the explanation of that action. But it was also during this period that Socialism, both as a political theory and as a political movement, threatened (with some success) to replace Liberalism, and insofar as Socialism as a theory has been taken to depend upon conceptions about the way in which the unequal distribution of wealth and control of the means of production in an industrial society entails, at the very least, unequal opportunities for the exercise of notionally equal rights, its critique of Liberalism can be seen to involve a similar appeal to a level of social explanation (presumed to be more fundamental than explanation in terms of political arrangements or beliefs) as that which characterizes sociology. Thus understood, an alliance at the theoretical level between sociology and Socialism in their common antagonism to Liberalism has been assumed to follow.[3]

Examples of an alliance of this kind can certainly be found in European intellectual history of this period, yet even here the scheme runs into trouble. Durkheim and Weber are invariably singled out to represent sociology in its Golden Age, although this is in itself a procedure of doubtful historical propriety, which encourages a tendency to pasteurize and homogenize sociology's past.[4] In fact, the differences between them were in most respects more striking than the similarities, and the possible political implications of their disparate metaphysical and methodological doctrines were correspondingly diverse. Certainly their own avowed political allegiances did not fit this simple pattern. Weber, it is true, was critical of the delusions of 'the Liberalism of 1848', but he was hardly less critical of the programmes of organized Socialism, and the major tension in his political thought has recently been identified as that between certain traditional Liberal values and a nationalist, elitist, even caesarist quest for political effectiveness.[5] Similarly, though Durkheim's fame rests above all

[3] For a recent endorsement of 'the historically accurate observation that liberalism is a doctrine based on individualist theories of man and society and thus in fundamental conflict not only with socialist but with most strictly social theories', see Raymond Williams, *Keywords: A Vocabulary of Culture and Society* (London, 1976), p. 150.

[4] This is argued more fully in Stefan Collini, 'Sociology and Idealism in Britain 1880–1920', *Archives Européennes de Sociologie*, XIX (1978), 3–50.

[5] David Beetham, *Max Weber and the Theory of Modern Politics* (London, 1974).

on his sociological criticism of individualism and though he was sympathetic to the Jaurèsian Socialists, he was far from believing that the key either to social analysis or to political improvement lay in class conflict; the mixture of republicanism, anti-clericalism, corporatism and moralism which made up his political outlook can equally adequately (or, rather, equally inadequately) be characterized as 'Liberal' or 'Socialist'.[6]

By this point, one may well begin to wonder whether such labels are not more of a hindrance than a help; all too soon, only a respectable name seems to distinguish an ideal-type from a stereotype. Their limitations seem particularly evident when we turn to the intellectual situation of late-nineteenth- and early-twentieth-century Britain. Here, Liberal political theory seemed to acquire a new lease of life in the decades before 1914, and its exponents rendered new justifications available for the distinctive policy of social reform of the ruling Liberal Party. Yet it was also during these years that sociology came into fashion in Britain, leading eventually to successful, if limited, institutionalization and to the foundation of an indigenous tradition of avowedly sociological theory and research. Furthermore, there was considerable overlap in both ideas and personnel between the New Liberalism (as it became known at the time) and the new sociology; far from being antagonistic, they appear to have been mutually supportive in a way which suggests deeper affinities. Each of these developments is, of course, a complex historical phenomenon which may be studied at many different levels, but, as my account implies, a particularly intriguing set of questions arises at this theoretical level, a set of questions which come together in the interpretation of the work of L. T. Hobhouse.

His prominence in both these fields has long been recognized and his contributions are increasingly being studied, though in a manner which on the whole has been more celebratory than historical. In the history of political thought he figures as the last exponent of Liberal political philosophy in the grand manner, the heir to the tradition of Green and Mill.[7] As the author of one, and possibly two, of the constitutive works of the canon, he is usually given a major speaking part in most recitations of the Liberal past, and his *Liberalism*, in particular, has been praised as 'timeless', 'a classic', or more moderately, 'the best twentieth-century statement of Liberal ideals'.[8] More recently, the distinctive qualities of the

[6] I draw these conclusions from the authoritative study by Steven Lukes, *Emile Durkheim: His Life and Work. A Historical and Critical Study* (London, 1973), esp. Chs. 17 and 26. There is also a useful discussion by Melvin Richter, 'Durkheim's politics and political theory' in K. H. Wolff (ed.), *Emile Durkheim 1858–1917* (Ohio, 1960).

[7] See, as a still representative example, G. H. Sabine, *A History of Political Theory* (4th edn, London, 1966 [first published New York, 1937]), Ch. 32.

[8] Guido De Ruggiero, *The History of European Liberalism*, trans. R. G. Collingwood (London, 1927), p. 155; A. Bullock and M. Shock (eds.), *The Liberal Tradition from Fox to Keynes* (Oxford, 1956), pp. xlii–xliii; C. Wright Mills, *The Marxists* (Harmondsworth, 1963), p. 25n. See also, most recently,

New Liberalism of the Edwardian period have been investigated by political historians, in the course of which Hobhouse has duly been recognized as 'the leading Liberal theorist of these years' and, along with his companion-in-arms, J. A. Hobson, as one of the major exponents of the principles frequently cited in justification of the social reforms of the Asquith government.[9] This has certainly directed attention to his involvement in the political controversies of the period, and has done something to correct the ahistorical, text-bound picture provided by the political theorists. But since even these accounts have, for the most part, consisted of little more than the quotation of a few isolated passages, often taken from different periods of his work, in order to provide the appropriate intellectual sound effects to accompany the main narrative of the action, it is hardly surprising if they have not generated any substantial reassessment of his political thought.

Among sociologists, too, Hobhouse is enjoying something of a revival. Once again, he has always been sure of his place in any team of 'Founding Fathers',[10] though his parental status has been confused by the extent to which later generations have treated him as an Aunt Sally. More recently, he has won high marks as a 'master of the developmental sociology of non-industrial countries', and he has been newly confirmed in his paternity as 'the father of theoretical sociology in Britain' and in his standing as 'unquestionably the most considerable British sociologist of the twentieth century' (although asides about the relative eminence of the one-eyed in the land of the blind have not been unknown).[11] Moreover, he was the first holder of a Chair of sociology and the first editor of a

D. J. Manning, *Liberalism* (London, 1976), pp. 10, 18, 101–2. Apart from *Liberalism* (London, 1911), the other candidate for canonical status is *The Metaphysical Theory of the State: A Criticism* (London, 1918), on which see the references cited in Stefan Collini, 'Hobhouse, Bosanquet and the state: philosophical Idealism and political argument in England 1880–1918', *Past and Present*, 72 (1976), 86–111.

9 Peter Weiler, 'The New Liberalism of L. T. Hobhouse', *Victorian Studies*, xv (1972), 141–2. The literature on the New Liberalism, and Hobhouse's place in it, has grown rapidly in the past few years. The work of P. F. Clarke has been the outstanding contribution: see his *Lancashire and the New Liberalism* (Cambridge, 1971), and 'The Progressive Movement in England', *Transactions of the Royal Historical Society*, 5th series, 24 (1974), 159–81. See also K. O. Morgan, *The Age of Lloyd George: The Liberal Party and British Politics 1890–1929* (London, 1971); H. V. Emy, *Liberals, Radicals and Social Politics 1892–1914* (Cambridge, 1973); A. J. A. Morris (ed.), *Edwardian Radicalism 1900–1914: Some Aspects of British Radicalism* (London, 1974); Michael Freeden, 'J. A. Hobson as a New Liberal theorist: some aspects of his social thought until 1914', *Journal of the History of Ideas*, xxxiv (1973), 421–43; idem, 'Biological and evolutionary roots of the New Liberalism in England', *Political Theory*, 4 (1976), 471–90. Recent editions of several of Hobhouse's and Hobson's books are listed in the Bibliography.

10 E.g. Timothy Raison (ed.), *The Founding Fathers of Social Science* (Harmondsworth, 1969), or Ronald Fletcher, *The Making of Sociology* (2 vols., London, 1971).

11 George Mariz, 'L. T. Hobhouse as theoretical sociologist', *Albion*, 6 (1974), 309; Donald G. MacRae, *Ideology and Society: Papers in Sociology and Politics* (London, 1961), p. 45; Introduction by Ronald Fletcher to John E. Owen, *L. T. Hobhouse, Sociologist* (London, 1974), p. x.

professedly sociological journal in Britain, and with the rise of interest in the history of British sociology the literature has become well stocked with pronouncements upon his 'decisive' role in its development.[12] But again, little attention has been paid to the formation of his theory, nor is there much hope for enlightenment about the odder aspects of his conception of sociology, all the while he is credited with the current concerns of the professional sociologist.[13]

Above all, the intrinsically interesting question of the relationship *between* his contributions to these two fields has received mention but not analysis. One writer has rightly remarked that 'Hobhouse saw the new sociology and the new liberalism as sides of a single coin',[14] but the nature of this numismatic rarity has never been specified. In terms of our initial contrast there is certainly something of a paradox here, though as this discussion should already have suggested, the more we consider the details of any particular example in historical terms, the less helpful this contrast comes to seem. In the present case, existing treatments of Hobhouse do not enable us to move beyond this paradox precisely because political theorists and sociologists are, understandably enough, interested in Hobhouse not in such historical terms, but only insofar as his work can be quarried to provide illustrations of points of current professional relevance. The detailed contextual account of Hobhouse's enterprise provided in this book, by contrast, is intended to be a contribution to intellectual history.

It is not, I must emphasize, a biography of Hobhouse nor even a critical analysis of his work, though it probably contains a fuller account of both than is yet available in any other source. Moreover, I do not pretend to survey the entire range of his very considerable *oeuvre*: I do not deal at all extensively with the more technical aspects of his philosophy, I only touch on his work in comparative psychology, and for the most part I make only passing reference to his post-1914 publications. Nor, in the case of those of his writings which I do discuss, do I attempt a systematic inventory of his views on either political or sociological issues. Instead, I attempt to reconstruct the relationship between his political theory and his sociology in the development of his thought by restoring his work to its original context, and to this end I draw upon his abundant journalism and occasional writings (and, where available and appropriate, manuscript sources), as well as his better-known books. But it is only fair to warn the

[12] Philip Abrams, *The Origins of British Sociology 1834–1914* (Chicago, 1968), p. 87. Cf. Edward Shils, 'Tradition, ecology, and institution in the history of sociology', *Daedalus*, 99 (1970), esp. 768–9.

[13] Owen, *L. T. Hobhouse, Sociologist*, illustrates this all too clearly. There is, however, a much more historically minded brief discussion of Hobhouse in Geoffrey Hawthorn, *Enlightenment and Despair: A History of Sociology* (Cambridge, 1976), Ch. 5.

[14] Abrams, *Origins of British Sociology*, p. 88. This seems to be offered as a paraphrase of Asa Briggs' remarks about Rowntree in *Seebohm Rowntree 1871–1954* (London, 1961), pp. 52–61.

reader that much of this book does not deal directly with Hobhouse at all. This is true in varying degrees of every chapter in Parts Two and Three, especially of Chapters 3, 5 and 6; more strikingly, Hobhouse does not even make an appearance in Chapter 1. Since this may induce in the unprepared reader some doubt as to what the book is actually *about*, it may be as well to say something about the approach which I have adopted and where it has led me.

I shall assume that there is no need to rehearse at length why the pursuit of such an enquiry must involve, among other things, the recovery in intentions, the reconstruction of conventions, and the restoration of contexts. I recognize that this approach raises some fundamental and much-debated issues in the philosophy of history, and perhaps even in epistemology generally, but I do not intend to engage with them here.[15] They are philosophical problems which need to be dealt with in their own right. I would, however, like to clarify my intentions on three rather more limited points, since they are points on which misconceptions about the nature of the book are particularly likely to arise.

The first point can best be introduced with the somewhat platitudinous remark that there is an unresolvable tension between, on the one hand, attempting to recover the past in its own terms, and, on the other, recognizing that selection on the basis of our criteria is inherent in the enterprise. Although theoretically intractable, this tension need not, if properly handled, necessarily prove to be damaging in practice. Indeed, it can sometimes be instructive to formulate a question in unashamedly anachronistic terms in order to draw attention to the differentness of the past or to highlight what needs to be explained: as long as this is recognized to be a heuristic device, a useful way of raising questions and getting an enquiry off the ground rather than of providing the terms in which it is conducted, it is harmless enough. Moreover, while we constantly need to be reminded that the past is another country where they speak what in many respects is a foreign language, the impassability of the divide can be exaggerated. To declare that the historian is inescapably the child of his time is only to announce a rather obvious truth, not to 'unmask' some sinister distorting influence. Foreign languages are among the things that historians, like other children, can learn; even our preconceptions are corrigible, and historical scholarship is in fact one of the means by which we correct them. Thus, the fact that I have introduced the theme of this book with a discussion of some current preconceptions about the

[15] There is an extensive literature on these issues: for my understanding of its implications for the practice of intellectual history I am heavily indebted to the work of Quentin Skinner; see especially his 'Meaning and understanding in the history of ideas', *History and Theory*, VIII (1969), 3–53, and 'Some problems in the analysis of political thought and action', *Political Theory*, 2 (1974), 277–303.

relationship between Liberalism and sociology does not mean that thereafter it remains within their ambit. On the contrary, a vital strand in the argument is precisely that these concepts are, in their unreconstructed form, subtly misleading guides to English intellectual life at the turn of the century, and it is only on the basis of considering the texture of that life in some detail that we can appropriately reconstruct them.

The second point is related to this since it concerns the extent of the intellectual area which such a study has to be ready to draw upon without pretending to cover at all systematically. For it has to be recognized that even when the meaning and scope of concepts such as 'Liberalism' and 'sociology' have been duly revised and expanded, the theoretical activities which they denote cannot be treated in isolation from a more general intellectual history. Which particular connections will be explored and which settings emphasized is obviously only to be discovered empirically. For example, our understanding of some of the most distinctive features of late-nineteenth-century political argument will be badly crippled unless we recognize the extent to which they were bound up with conflicting interpretations of biological theories of evolution. Or again, we shall deprive ourselves of a unique source of insight into the late-nineteenth-century understanding of sociology if we ignore the fact that the most telling criticisms of the proposed science were made from the standpoint of moral philosophy.[16] Although the particular examples might provoke disagreement, it may seem doubtful that anyone would ever wish to deny the truth of this as a general proposition. But the baleful influence of modern academic classifications is plainly evident in the kinds of histories which are written. Historians of sociology, in particular, have all too often allowed a preoccupation with the current controversies of their profession to issue in whiggish or triumphalist accounts of its past. I ought, perhaps, to take it as some small confirmation of the need for the type of historical study which I have attempted here if sociologists are puzzled that so little of it seems to be about their discipline.

The third point concerns the question of evaluation and assessment. This, as I have said, is not a critical study, but if one is to do more than merely repeat Hobhouse's own words – if, that is, one attempts to interpret, to characterize, or, still more, to explain – then some element of criticism, if only in terms of universal and hence minimal criteria of validity and rationality, is bound to enter the account. In trying to demonstrate how the theory works, one cannot, without being disingenuous, ignore the fact that some of its moving parts emit an awful grinding noise. Simply to identify this as a fault, let alone to diagnose it in terms, say, of how some rather ill-assorted parts have been spatchcocked together, is to engage in criticism. Of course, we must not rule out the possibility that what seems

[16] For these two examples see below, Chs. 5 and 6.

to us to be an awful grinding noise may have passed unnoticed by contemporaries, or may merely have struck them as the reassuring hum that they were used to; but even then the focus of explanation is simply shifted from an individual to a social level, though that in turn would require a more ambitious apparatus than could be deployed in a book of this sort. The point, however, is that in the following pages there is only such criticism as is necessary for the purposes of intelligible exposition and explanation; it is not the prime aim of the book. Equally, it has not been my intention to celebrate Hobhouse, to revive his reputation, or to call attention to the neglected merits and unnoticed relevance of his work. I do think that his historical importance has not been adequately reflected in serious scholarship, but this certainly does not entail the belief that practising political theorists and sociologists would be well advised to seek enlightenment from his putative contributions to their disciplines. Parts of his political theory will no doubt continue to retain more than an historical interest, and sociologists may come to find inspiration in his morphological and evolutionary approach, but I am not particularly concerned to encourage either of these developments. I do not mean to imply that Hobhouse's theories constitute a peculiarly unmarketable property: my conviction rather is that studies of other figures in the history of political and social thought, including some of the most fashionable, would benefit from maintaining a firmer distinction between writing history and talking-up the value of antiques.

The reason, therefore, why much of this book is not directly about Hobhouse is that it attempts to reconstruct a certain level of discourse, the medium, as it were, in which his thought moved and had its being. Unfortunately, the fashionable demand that ideas must be treated 'in context' is too often satisfied by the rehearsal of a few tired generalizations about economic development or social structure whose connection with the ideas in question is elusive at best, and more often simply reductive. By contrast, I wish to emphasize that this book provides an *intellectual* context for the major themes of Hobhouse's work. In part, this involves supplying what might be called 'the context of refutation' – that is, an account of the theories which he was attacking, the arguments he was rebutting, the assessments he was challenging. But it also involves trying to identify the forensic resources at his disposal – the overriding force of certain arguments, the emotional resonances of key terms, the exploitable tensions within accepted beliefs. As my title indicates, it is to the political argument of the three decades before 1914 that I think we must, in the first instance, look for this context, and Chapter 1 in particular is devoted to trying to sketch its main outlines. As far as my actual practice of this approach is concerned, I should like to offer a caution, a concession, and a confession.

My caution merely consists in emphasizing that the raw materials for such a study will be drawn from works written at different levels of abstraction and performing a variety of linguistic functions. For the danger is that such studies may easily degenerate into a familiar kind of intellectual needlework: patches of quotation are sewn together to form a huge patterned quilt which is then said to constitute what the individual, group or culture in question 'believed'. Apart from respecting the differences between, say, a philosophical treatise and a political pamphlet, and allowing for the place of inconsistency in human thought, the chief prophylactic against 'quilt-maker's disease' is to discriminate the various speech-acts which may be being performed in the sources from which quotation is taken. In dealing with polemical literature, in particular, there is a disabling kind of naiveté involved in regarding all utterances simply as statements of belief. It is after all not only in lapidary inscriptions that a man is not upon oath; many linguistic actions do not primarily consist in asserting propositions at all.

My concession is to grant that this approach concentrates attention on a limited and distinctively public world. A man would not necessarily argue his case in the pages of the great reviews in quite the same way as he would in the privacy of his home or his club, and he would no doubt argue it even more differently if he belonged to the great majority which never read the reviews nor saw the inside of a club. This makes the evidence conveniently accessible to the historian, but it does mean that its explanatory range is correspondingly limited. It is conceivable that a different kind of evidence might shed more light on individual psychology and motivation; and a different kind of enquiry altogether would be needed to tackle the much larger questions about the relation of the educated classes' controversies to wider social developments. I am unmoved, however, by the cynic's suggestion that this approach merely deals with rhetoric. It is one mark of the cynic that he sees other people's expression of their principles as a kind of smokescreen for their putative 'real interests', but even were he always correct it would not follow that the study of such statements was devoid of explanatory power. Even the most disingenuous legitimation involves an appeal to existing characterizations, and these bring with them constraints of their own, especially where any kind of consistent theoretical construction is involved.

My confession relates to the fact that in many places I make general assertions the truth of which requires demonstration but in fact only receives illustration. This is not, I like to think, merely due to idleness on my part, though no doubt I have left undone many of those things which I ought to have done. The difficulty is rather that in the case of such general assertions the only way to mitigate the dangers of selective quotation (other than by the intuitive judgement of the historian) would be by means of systematic quantification of the sources and rigorous sampling procedures. There is often little more than a curious kind of snobbery involved in denying that such methods could be used appropriately in intellectual history, though of course they could, like any quantitative methods, only serve strictly ancillary functions. At all events, though I would acknowledge that there are places in the present study where such methods could and perhaps should have been used, this did not, for a variety of reasons, present itself to me as a practicable option, and so, as I stress in Chapter 1, my judgement in these cases is more than usually vulnerable to correction in the light of further research.

Briefly resumed, the book is organized as follows. Chapter 1, as I have already indicated, surveys the most prominent features of the political argument which provided the setting for Hobhouse's work, concentrating on the way in which the opposition between Individualism and Collectivism was perceived to be the fundamental structuring principle of that argument. Chapters 2 and 3 then trace the development of Hobhouse's political thought in some detail, showing how, far from being undeviatingly Liberal, it grew out of an early commitment to Collectivism via the exploitation of the tension within traditional Liberalism between its exacting moral premises and its Individualistic political conclusions. In Chapter 4 I analyse his mature political theory, showing how these moral assumptions, expressed in Idealist concepts, were fundamental to its character. The argument of Chapters 5 and 6 is that Hobhouse's investment in these moral and political values led him to undertake an intellectually ambitious reformulation of the theoretical and historical case for Progress, and that this involved him in an enterprise which was then coming to be seen as 'sociology'. In Chapter 7 I demonstrate how several otherwise puzzling features of Hobhouse's sociology become intelligible when seen as emerging out of his response to these essentially political debates. Chapter 8 briefly examines the philosophical foundations of his thought, and brings out in particular the extent to which a quasi-Idealist metaphysics underwrote his social and political theory with an optimistic teleology. The Epilogue notes the fate of Hobhouse's theories after 1914. Throughout, the historically specific nature of the whole enterprise is insisted upon, and if the relationship between Liberalism and sociology in Hobhouse's work does not turn out to be what was expected, this should alert us to the possibility that neither his Liberalism nor his sociology corresponds at all readily with what is currently understood by those terms.

Part One: Political Argument

1: INDIVIDUALISM AND COLLECTIVISM

This chapter provides a brief account of certain features of political argument in Britain in the three decades before 1914, in order to establish the appropriate intellectual context for understanding the nature and development of Hobhouse's political and social theory. It concentrates upon the debate over the grounds and limits of 'state-intervention', particularly upon the way in which the contemporary understanding of the issues involved was organized around the conflict between 'Individualism' and 'Collectivism',[1] and it attempts to provide a sketch-map of the main contours of the conceptual geography of that debate. But it would be disingenuous to pretend that this was virgin territory, or to refuse to recognize the extent to which our expectations of this question have been shaped by the voluminous historiography of more than half a century. In particular, the currently prevailing view on the issue of 'laissez-faire and state-intervention in nineteenth-century Britain',[2] which maintains that there never was 'an age of Individualism', might seem to constitute a decisive objection to this approach from the outset. To concentrate on the terms 'Individualism' and 'Collectivism' might seem to be following in the footsteps of those luckless 'historians of political theory [who] have stumbled into the trap set by Dicey so long ago'.[3] If the mid-nineteenth century was a period of widespread state-intervention, then this dichotomy is simply 'misleading', a legacy of 'the muddled thinking of Dicey'.[4] If the origins of the 'welfare state' are to be found in early-Victorian

[1] These terms, in their political-theoretical senses distinguished below, were normally capitalized by contemporaries, and I have followed this practice.

[2] The title of the classic article by J. B. Brebner, first published in 1948, which launched the most recent phase of this controversy, and of the book by A. J. Taylor (London, 1972) which surveys it. Full references can be found in Taylor's excellent annotated Bibliography.

[3] Melvin Richter, *The Politics of Conscience: T. H. Green and His Age* (London, 1964), pp. 341–2.

[4] See the references cited in Taylor's Bibliography, esp. H. Parris, 'The nineteenth-century revolution in government: a re-appraisal re-appraised', *Historical Journal*, III (1960), 18.

legislation and if it grew steadily throughout the century, then it must be a mistake to take seriously a pair of terms which emphasizes a fundamental conflict of principle over such issues during this period.[5]

However, without wishing to become embroiled in the larger historiographical controversy, I would suggest that this objection is misconceived in the present case. To begin with, it can be argued that the continuous increase in the *volume* of government activity alleged by administrative historians is not necessarily incompatible with a perceived conflict between the principles of Individualism and Collectivism, and this for several reasons: first, because Individualism was considered by those who used the term to be above all a theory of the grounds rather than the frequency of legislation; secondly, and consequently, because not all government action was seen, even by Individualists themselves as 'intervention', and so many of the changes brought to light by this historiography were developments of administrative practice which, though no doubt important in the story of 'government growth', were not generally taken to be instances of Collectivism; and thirdly, because the demonstration of divergences from Individualism in practice in the mid century is not incompatible with the late-Victorian belief that it had been the dominant principle inspiring legislation up until the 1880s. Moreover, in reconstructing political argument in the last two decades of the century, it is essential to recapture what contemporaries *thought* that they were arguing about. This does not entail accepting their categories as objective and accurate descriptions of the political practice of the two previous generations, but rather it means treating these categories as evidence of what their users perceived as the nature of political disagreement in their own time. The presumption in favour of this approach is greatly strengthened by the recognition that the relevant senses of the terms Individualism and Collectivism only acquired any currency in the course of the 1880s, and only enjoyed their ascendancy in the political vocabulary for two or three decades.[6] Considered as a history of nineteenth-century legislation, Dicey's *Law and Opinion* has been subjected to almost unremitting criticism, and no doubt with some justice; but for my purposes, his book is merely the best-known example of how the terms which structured the perception of political polemic at the end of the century also embodied a tendentious account of earlier developments.

I propose, therefore, to consider the way in which disagreement over the role of the state was conceptualized in terms of the opposition between

[5] David Roberts, *Victorian Origins of the British Welfare State* (New Haven, Conn., 1960) provided a seminal statement of this view; a general survey is provided in Derek Fraser, *The Evolution of the British Welfare State* (London, 1973).

[6] I present the evidence for this claim below. If true, it helps to explain why historians of the mid century have complained, in rather unfairly attacking Dicey, that they were 'terms which contemporaries did not widely use' (Fraser, *Evolution of the Welfare State*, p. 107).

Individualism and Collectivism. I should make clear at the start that I do not thereby take these terms for static political theories, readily identifiable in terms of a few fundamental propositions or of a particular set of policy recommendations. They were, rather, part of a loose-textured political vocabulary, and, like many such terms, were 'essentially contestable',[7] that is, any definition of them necessarily embodied a particular theoretical commitment and evaluative standpoint. They referred to arguments and ideals which were certainly distinguishable tendencies in current debate, but what any given writer was doing in using them can only be determined by a fuller contextual enquiry. However, the undeniable fact that the terms were used in a variety of ways and were by their nature subject to polemical manipulation does not mean that they were inessential decorations draped around more concrete statements. The variation was neither infinite nor arbitrary. Indeed, it was precisely because the range of their use was not infinite that they possessed any polemical value: a term with no accepted criteria of application nor any recognizable evaluative force loses its utility in controversy altogether.

There are, of course, considerable practical problems in trying to chart such usage, as there are in attempting to reconstitute a level of political discourse or argument at all. Here, I should insist that I am only concerned with a particular level of discourse – the arguments which would be encountered in the pages of the great reviews, the 'respectable' press, the academic treatise, and similar published statements of the educated classes.[8] But mine is not an exercise in historical lexicography: as I suggested, I aim merely to provide a sketch-map of the terrain, not an exhaustive inventory of topographical detail. Obviously my use of quotation can only be illustrative and not demonstrative, and the representativeness of my sources is necessarily open to question. My argument is particularly vulnerable to the findings of any more systematic sampling procedure which could give more than impressionistic support to claims about the incidence, extent and importance of terms and arguments. But, fortified by Baconian maxims about the differing relations to truth of error and confusion, one should perhaps welcome the prospect of such correction, and accept that, for the present, the persuasiveness of the case must rest upon its ability to make sense of an otherwise unmanageable array of evidence.

[7] For an explanation of this term, see W. B. Gallie, 'Essentially contested concepts', *Proceedings of the Aristotelian Society*, LVI (1955–6), 167–98, and Alasdair Macintyre, 'The essential contestability of some social concepts', *Ethics*, 84 (1973), 1–9.

[8] My criteria of selection are, therefore, circular in the sense that I employ no independent social or economic indicators: the writers I am dealing with select themselves by contributing to this debate. Beyond the rather obvious point that these arguments flourished among and may have been largely restricted to the circles dominated by the university-educated elite, I would make no larger claims about the extent or representativeness of the discourse I describe.

The origin of terms is certainly not an adequate guide to their use, but the fact that the relevant senses of these antithetical terms both acquired general political currency in the 1880s suggests an intimate relationship to the experience of those years. (This does not mean that the practices denoted by these terms had not existed earlier, only that the proliferation of self-conscious statements of principle resulting from the conflicts of the period left this deposit in the language for the first time.[9]) I suggest that the relevant sense of Individualism – 'the social theory which advocates the free and independent action of the individual as opposed to communistic methods of organization and state interference; opposed to Collectivism and Socialism'[10] – was not generally used before the 1880s, had a mainly historical reference after 1918,[11] and is rarely used in its pure form today, although, of course, related senses continue to have a vigorous existence. Indeed, the truth of my claim depends upon the sense of 'Individualism' as a theory of the limits of state action in antithesis to Collectivism or Socialism being carefully distinguished from that much more general sense, common throughout the nineteenth century, of 'self-centred feeling or conduct as a principle; a mode of life in which the individual pursues his own ends or follows out his own ideas; free and independent individual action or thought; egoism'.[12] The moral and methodological assumptions of this sense may be thought to underlie the political sense, but the two must nonetheless be distinguished.[13]

[9] More systematic historical lexicography would be needed to establish more precise dates, and it is unfortunate that the entries in the recent supplements to the *O.E.D.* are flawed in that the earliest examples given for both terms are in fact examples of another sense (as I argue below). But the first editors of the *O.E.D.*, like other contemporary lexicographers, recognized that new senses of the terms had gained currency in the 1880s, as their definitions and other examples reveal.

[10] *O.E.D.*, sense 2. Other dictionaries of the period give similar definitions. *Chambers Encyclopaedia* (1889) includes a separate entry, but simply says 'see under Socialism'.

[11] As, for example, in such references as that of the Next Five Years Group in 1935 to 'the historic controversy between Individualism and Socialism'; quoted in Arthur Marwick, *Britain in the Century of Total War: War, Peace and Social Change 1900–1967* (pbk Harmondsworth, 1970 [first published London, 1968]), p. 249.

[12] *O.E.D.*, sense 1. *The Century Dictionary* (1889) distinguished this sense similarly as 'the principle of acting according to one's own will or for one's own ends; individual as opposed to associate action or common interests'.

[13] The first editors of the *O.E.D.*, for whom, after all, the political sense was a contemporary innovation, did so distinguish them, but they have been confused in the recent *Supplement H–N* (1976), where an earlier example is claimed for sense 2 in Mill's statement that 'Socialism, so long as it attacks the existing individualism, is easily triumphant' (*Westminster Review*, LVI (1851), 87). But it is clear in context that Mill is using the term in sense 1. K. W. Swart, '"Individualism" in the mid nineteenth century (1826–1860)', *Journal of the History of Ideas*, XXIII (1962), 77–90 is a helpful survey of the comparative uses of the term, but at the crucial point he falls into a similar confusion. Thus, though he rightly points out that the term was not used to describe their own political theory by writers subsequently classified as Individualists – such as Bentham or the classical economists – nor in any of J. S. Mill's writings published during his lifetime, he suggests that Mill did so use it in his posthumously published *Chapters on Socialism* (started in 1869, and published in *The Fortnightly Review* in 1879). However, the two passages cited seem to refer to,

The political sense probably derived initially from the propaganda of the extreme anti-statist organizations run by some of Spencer's more eccentric self-proclaimed disciples, such as Auberon Herbert, Wordsworth Donisthorpe and W. C. Crofts.[14] It was at first largely restricted to those who supported the views of the Liberty and Property Defence League (whose motto was 'Individualism versus Socialism'), views which were recognized at the time to be extreme. The term initially, therefore, referred to an opposition to the extension of state-intervention which regarded even the current level as excessive; the very title of the L.P.D.L., after all, implied that Liberty and Property were under attack. They celebrated a past where this had not been the case, but it was to some extent an idealized past of their own creation. Reflecting on the claims of the L.P.D.L., Henry Sidgwick observed at the beginning of 1885, 'Individualism of the extreme kind has clearly had its day'.[15]

However, as this remark also suggests, not all Individualism was of the 'extreme' kind, for the term quickly came into general usage to denote a whole range of anti-Socialist political thought. In fact, in its loosest usage, as John Rae reported in 1888, 'Socialism is identified with any enlargement, and Individualism with any contraction, of the functions of government'.[16] This being the case, it was often necessary to qualify the term when a more precise referent was intended – McKechnie, for example, spoke of the 'pitfalls' of Socialism 'dreaded by even the more moderate Individualists', and Grant Allen described his ultra-Spencerian views as those of 'an old-style Individualist'.[17] Scores of writers complained of the looseness with which the term, like its opposite, was used, and each proposed a

in one case, sense 1, and in the other a sense, possibly drawn from the Cooperative Movement (see the entry for 'Individualistic' in the *O.E.D.*), which referred to the autonomy of local economic units under certain forms of Utopian Socialism (*Collected Works*, v (Toronto, 1967), pp. 715, 744). Lukes' English chapter is acknowledgedly dependent upon these two sources, and therefore repeats these confusions. He adds a further misleading reference by suggesting that T. H. Green used both Individualism and Collectivism, but his reference (to Richter, *Politics of Conscience*, p. 343) turns out to be a statement by Green's uncle, David Vaughan, made several years after Green's death, by which time, as I am arguing, the term was well established. Steven Lukes, *Individualism* (Oxford, 1973), p. 38.

14 Edward Bristow, 'The Liberty and Property Defence League and Individualism', *Historical Journal*, XVIII (1975), 761–89, discusses these organizations. He cites Crofts' claim to have put this sense of the term into circulation in 1883 (761), but it may well have figured in the literature of some of their earlier organizations such as The State Resistance Union. See also K. D. Brown (ed.), *Essays in Anti-Labour History: Responses to the Rise of Labour in History* (London, 1974).

15 Quoted in A. and E. M. S[idgwick], *Henry Sidgwick, A Memoir* (London, 1906), p. 399.

16 John Rae, 'State Socialism', *Contemporary Review*, LIV (1888), 380. For a similar observation, see Bruce Smith, *Liberty and Liberalism: A Protest Against the Growing Tendency Toward Undue Interference by the State with Individual Liberty, Private Enterprise and the Rights of Property* (London, 1887), p. 433.

17 W. S. McKechnie, *The State and the Individual: An Introduction to Political Science with Special Reference to Socialistic and Individualistic Theories* (Glasgow, 1896), p. vi; Grant Allen, 'Individualism and Socialism', *Contemporary Review*, LV (1889), 761.

narrower definition on the basis of his own political preferences, but by 1890 its general anti-Collectivist sense was well established.[18]

Its evaluative force was less clear. The moral sense of the term certainly had carried some favourable resonances, but the connotations of selfishness and a disregard for common interests became increasingly dominant, and this pejorative force was readily transferred to the political sense, at least by its opponents. It is true that those who applied the term to their own beliefs usually tried thereby to mobilize the resonances of 'self-reliance' and 'independence' and other individualistic virtues. Such writers, however, were continually having to insist that, as Spencer explained in 1893, 'the tacit assumption that Individualism means the solitary life of the individual is an entire misapprehension. It may and does go along with an elaborate form of mutual dependence.'[19] And in 1911, the entry in *The Encyclopaedia Britannica* still had to explain that 'Individualism is, however, by no means always identical with egoism.' It is possible that those who adopted it to describe their own position did so in deliberate defiance of its dominant connotations, an attempt to take what was probably initially used as a term of contempt and convert it into a proud affirmation of the merits of a political system founded on the free action of the individual (a not uncommon history for political labels).

Much of the force of the term, as of its opposite, lay in the suggestion that all those to whom it was applied stood for views associated with the extreme end of the spectrum. Although the polemical intentions behind this ploy were transparent, there was just enough community of principle among those who accepted the description to lend plausibility to its extension. The fundamental postulate was that, on the whole, the state was only justified in restricting an individual's liberty in order to prevent his actions causing specifiable harm to others. Needless to say, in practice this principle was susceptible of varying interpretations, but it was allegiance to it as much the most important criterion which distinguished its proponents from those who urged a recognition of wider obligations on the part of the state. Thus the general understanding of what an Individualist took the aim of legislation to be was summarized by Sidgwick as follows:

> (1) to secure to every sane adult freedom to provide for his own happiness, by adapting the material world to the satisfaction of his own needs and desires, and establishing such relations with other human beings as may in his opinion conduce to the same end; (2) to secure him from pain or loss, caused directly or indirectly by the actions of other human beings – including in this loss any damage due to the non-performance of engagements made without coercion or deception.[20]

[18] Cf. McKechnie, *State and Individual*, pp. 214–15.

[19] Herbert Spencer to H. Seal, 11 July 1893, quoted in David Duncan, *The Life and Letters of Herbert Spencer* (London, 1908), pp. 353–4.

[20] Henry Sidgwick, *The Elements of Politics* (London, 1891), p. 53. He added as a subsidiary aim 'throwing on parents the duties of care, sustenance and education of children'. On Sidgwick, see below, pp. 20–2.

The two assumptions which were needed to buttress the Individualist claim to be able to achieve these aims were again neatly summarized by Sidgwick as 'the psychological generalization that individuals are likely to provide for their own welfare better than Government can provide for them, and the sociological generalization that the common welfare is likely to be best promoted by individuals promoting their private interest intelligently'.[21] In less sophisticated formulations there was also the assumption that an increase in the power of the state always meant a decrease in the liberty of the citizen.[22] To this should be added the pivotal role of the institution of contract, 'the main link', as Sidgwick observed, 'by which the complex system of cooperation which characterizes a modern civilized society is knit together'.[23] This was the mechanism by which the individual could provide his own security when pursuing his interests, and it is the foundation of several neglected aspects of Individualism. It involved, for example, a corresponding emphasis upon civil law in preference to criminal law, on the one hand, and a demand for the means of litigation to be made cheaply available on the other.[24] It could also, by treating marriage as a contract like any other, involve a more radical attitude to divorce than was generally entertained – a good example of how the conclusions of a consistent Individualism were overridden by the moral imperatives of the age. And, of course, the heart of what was generally represented as the Individualist objection to the Trade Union legislation of 1906 to 1914 lay in the claim that it imposed restrictions upon the individual's freedom to enter into such contracts as he chose, as well as exempting Trade Unions from the possibility of having most kinds of civil action brought against them.

There is no doubt that, despite the care which some Individualist writers gave to working out the practical implications of these assumptions, Individualism was still associated with the caricature of 'anarchy plus the constable' (who could have been, in view of the range of non-coercive industrial legislation, more plausibly promoted to inspector). There is also no doubt that the writer who, more than any other, was held responsible to this was Herbert Spencer. It is hard now to recapture the enormous prestige accorded Spencer's achievement at this time, a prestige which earned respectful attention for his 'scientifically' grounded Individualist politics and which recommended his peculiar synthesis as a fertile source

21 Sidgwick, *Elements of Politics*, p. 139.

22 McKechnie, for example, asserted that 'all Individualists agree in assuming an absolute antithesis between the powers of government and the liberty of the subject'. *State and Individual*, p. 220.

23 Sidgwick, *Elements of Politics*, p. 54.

24 See A. V. Dicey, *Lectures on the Relation between Law and Public Opinion during the Nineteenth Century* (London, 1905), p. xlvii for the former (and p. 150 for the reiteration of the claim that 'freedom of contract is an extension of an individual's power to do what he likes, i.e. of his freedom'), and Roland K. Wilson, *The Province of the State* (London, 1911), Ch. 1, for a particularly strong affirmation of the latter.

of anti-interventionist arguments. This is surely why, despite the fact that his actual suggestions for the proper limits of state-intervention were recognized as extreme even by other Individualists, so much effort was lavished upon the reputation of his *theory* by Collectivist writers.[25] His *The Man Versus the State*, published in 1884, was the form in which his views gained their greatest prominence in this debate – a book which D. G. Ritchie referred to as 'the most conspicuous work of recent years in defence of Individualism and in opposition to the growing tendency of state intervention'.[26]

For many moderate Individualists, however, Spencer appeared more as an embarrassment than as an ally. It was largely his standing which many of them blamed for the identification of an anti-Collectivist political position with extreme laissez-faire, an identification which some were at great pains to contest. Much the most intellectually distinguished defence of such moderate Individualism was provided by Sidgwick, whose *Elements of Politics* is surely one of the neglected masterpieces of nineteenth-century political thought. It has no doubt suffered from swimming against the tide in both method and conclusions – his was perhaps the last major treatise to employ deductive reasoning from Utilitarian premises.[27] Also, its dry style, academic precision and sheer length do not make for popularity, and it is a formidable handicap to any writer to be chiefly committed to restating Mill in duller and more cautious prose.

Nonetheless, the book is a valuable source for this debate in that it demonstrated what an extensive range of government activities could be justified on the principle of Individualism, at the same time showing how far short this fell of that conception of the state urged by Collectivists like Hobhouse. For it is a defence of a qualified Individualism against such attacks, though its text-book form may disguise its polemical intent. Sidgwick proceeded by demonstrating how a much wider range of state activity could be justified on Individualist grounds than was often assumed. He had no difficulty in showing that, on this basis,[28] it was legitimate for

[25] I discuss these efforts more fully below, Ch. 5.

[26] D. G. Ritchie, *The Principles of State Interference* (London, 1891), p. 3. Since his own book largely consisted of a series of articles originally published in 1885–6 as a direct attack on *The Man Versus the State*, Ritchie knew whereof he spoke.

[27] Even when it appeared, its 'rather old-fashioned utilitarianism' was remarked (as was the fact that 'to most students of politics and ethics at the present day, a discussion which takes no account whatsoever of the theory of natural selection as applied to society must seem a little out of date'). Ritchie also observed that although Sidgwick was arguing deductively from universal psychological premises, 'he nowhere arrives at any conclusion which would differ very widely from that of the average man of the professional and commercial middle-class at the present day'. D. G. Ritchie, Review of *The Elements of Politics*, *International Journal of Ethics*, II (1891), 254–7.

[28] He restated the 'principle for determining the nature and limits of governmental interferences...currently known as "Individualism"' as 'that what one sane adult is legally compelled to render to others should be merely the negative service of non-interference, except

the state to legislate to protect children, to enforce professional standards, to prevent deception in trade, to restrict dangerous processes of manufacture, to control disease, to make certain sorts of information available, and so on. This demonstration is also helpful from our present perspective in suggesting how it was that any plausibility attached to the presentation of the mid-Victorian period as one of Individualism. There was, as I have already argued, an element of idealization in this – that invention of an appropriate past which is a constituent of so much political writing – but it was also the case that a great deal of the legislation of the previous three or four decades could be seen as an increasingly detailed and comprehensive working out of principles generally accepted as Individualist. In practice, the distinction may seem insignificant between, say, the provision of the means of sanitation by the state and the provision of pensions by the state, or between regulation of the 'truck' system of payment and the fixing of a minimum wage, but to those contemporaries who cared about such things the difference in principle could seem momentous.

With characteristic care, Sidgwick acknowledged that there were certain activities which, while they could not be justified on Individualist grounds, were nonetheless generally recognized as properly the task of the state. These mainly consisted of that class of functions now identified as 'public goods', which ranged from defence to such things as the minting of currency and the provision of lighthouses.[29] There were also some institutions which, though taken for granted, Sidgwick found it hard to justify on any but the widest Utilitarian premises, such as absolute property rights in natural resources, certain rights of inheritance, and that lynch-pin of the Victorian social order, the Poor Law. Sidgwick was not suggesting that the state should not provide or support these institutions, but simply that a justification was not available for them in purely Individualist terms. This admission was, however, to prove an important foothold for Collectivist criticisms. But for the present, Sidgwick objected to such proposed measures as progressive taxation, state-financed pensions and a legal maximum working day, and concluded that 'I do not doubt that what I have before distinguished as the "Individualistic minimum" of governmental interference ought to constitute the main part of such interference,

so far as he has voluntarily undertaken to render positive services; provided that we include in the notion of non-interference the obligation of remedying or compensating for mischief intentionally or carelessly caused by his acts'. *Elements of Politics*, pp. 38–9.

[29] This class of activities had, of course, been recognized by all the classical economists, from Smith to J. S. Mill. See the discussions of the former in R. L. Crouch, 'Laissez-faire in nineteenth-century Britain: myth or reality?', *Manchester School of Economic and Social Studies*, XXXV (1967), 199–215, and in A. S. Skinner, *Adam Smith and the Role of the State* (Glasgow, 1974); for the latter, see Pedro Schwartz, *The New Political Economy of J. S. Mill* (London, 1972); and on this question generally, see A. W. Coats (ed.), *The Classical Economists and Economic Policy* (London, 1971); and L. C. Robbins, *The Theory of Economic Policy in English Political Economy* (London, 1952).

until the nature of an average civilized human being becomes very different from what it is at present.'[30]

It was this shared opposition to the principles of Collectivism which led Sidgwick and Spencer, profoundly different though they were in almost every other way, to be identified as occupying different ends of the same spectrum.[31] However, my focus is not upon the works of leading writers as such, but rather upon the way in which the issues were conceptualized and the arguments structured such that this could be presented as one spectrum, especially by its opponents. Accordingly, we need to consider the *types* of argument which were characteristically identified as Individualist arguments against state-intervention. For this purpose, I have isolated four main types of argument, which I have labelled the political, the economic, the scientific and the moral.[32] Obviously, these are just analytical categories or ideal-types: the concrete instance would always tend to be something of a hybrid. Moreover, though presented rather starkly here, each argument in practice drew upon a range of connotations, telling allusions, and persuasive historical examples, and in considering them as parts of the Individualist polemic of the 1880s and 1890s, we should not lose sight of the way in which they were the beneficiaries of a complex intellectual and emotional inheritance. Sometimes they bore the marks of their descent – the moral earnestness of Evangelicalism, the anxious amazement at the achievements of industrialism, the faith in science, the hostility to aristocratic privilege, the pride in English liberties and local traditions, and so on. Each element had a special resonance which was played upon in different ways. Overall, it is noticeable how each argument had, in the course of the century, become infused with that strong moral flavouring which produces the distinctive bouquet of late-nineteenth-century political thought. But such a discourse cannot be reduced to the traditions which shaped it, and the way in which these arguments were used in the late nineteenth century was peculiar to the circumstances of that debate.

[30] *Elements of Politics*, p. 139. He distinguished himself from that 'important school of political thinkers [who] are of [*sic*] opinion that the coercive interference of government should be strictly limited to the application of this principle' (p. 39).

[31] Dicey, who had read Sidgwick's book in proof, and who was well able to appreciate its Individualism, did not think it particularly contentious to place Sidgwick and Spencer on the same side of this particular fence (*Law and Opinion*, pp. 17–18), although neither Sidgwick nor Dicey had much time for Spencer's eclectic theories.

[32] These four types were not identified in these terms by any single participant in the debate, but the classification would have been immediately recognizable, and under different headings and in different combinations something similar can be found in, for example, G. J. Goschen, 'Laissez-faire and Government Interference' (1883), repr. in *Essays and Addresses on Economic Questions 1865–1893* (London, 1905); McKechnie, *State and Individual*, esp. Ch. 13; W. P. D. Bliss (ed.), *The Encyclopaedia of Social Reform* (New York and London, 1897), entry under 'Individualism'; Herbert Samuel, *Liberalism: An Attempt to State the Principles and Proposals of Contemporary Liberalism in England* (London, 1902), esp. Ch. 3.

Both the political and the economic arguments can be dealt with very briefly, partly because they have, in some form or other, received the most historiographical attention, and partly because they appeared, to the Collectivists of the end of the century, to call less insistently for refutation. In its classic form, as an objection to any increase in the powers of government, the political argument had enjoyed its heyday during the anti-aristocratic crusades of, first, the Philosophic Radicals, and, later, Cobden and Bright and their allies. It was essentially a protest against corruption, privilege and mismanagement, a suspicion that what was done by the state would be done badly, and would simply result in sinecures to be filled by relations of the governing classes and higher costs to be met by the tax-payers. This essentially middle-class and self-interested objection was often mixed with a more traditional fear that the greater the power concentrated in the hands of the government, the greater the threat which this posed to the liberties of the citizens. (This could also appear in the strong preference for relying upon established local institutions rather than creating or enlarging agencies of central government.[33]) Increasingly in the Victorian age, it was the opposite anxiety which inspired a version of this argument – that is, that it was precisely the efficiency of government action which posed the greatest danger by tending to remove projects from the spontaneous efforts of individuals or voluntary groups and to increase the size and complexity of national enterprises beyond the comprehension or effective regulation of the citizens. Obviously, in this form the objection depended upon a strong injection of the moral argument.

As a separate argument, it was not much in evidence in the last two decades of the century. Sidgwick noted that among the 'weighty objections commonly urged... against the extension of government interference' were the claims 'that the efficiency of government is likely to be impaired by any considerable increase in its functions', and 'that the consequent increase of its power and patronage constitutes a political danger'.[34] But Sidgwick himself did not make much of these arguments, and in this he was representative. The form in which this argument did appear with some frequency was in the suggestion that all forms of Socialism involved an increase in what Carlyle had referred to as 'the Continental nuisance called "Bureaucracy"'.[35] F. C. Montague, in urging an acceptance of a wider role for the state, recognized that there was 'a very general belief that such

[33] There is much evidence of these arguments in W. C. Lubenow, *The Politics of Government Growth: Early Victorian Attitudes Toward State Intervention 1833–1848* (Newton Abbot, 1971). And, of course, at a different level there is the tradition of political thought, variously characterized as Tocquevillian, Rousseauvian or even Machiavellian, which rested upon anxiety about the decline in the virtue, spirit and energy of the citizen body with the growth in the size and prosperity of modern states.

[34] *Elements of Politics*, p. 132.

[35] *Latter-Day Pamphlets*, IV (London, 1872), p. 121.

action conducts us through bureaucracy to communism', and explained that 'we may term that a bureaucratic administration which undertakes tasks capable of being as well or better performed by private individuals'.[36] Alfred Marshall treated it as self-evident that 'those tendencies of Socialism that are towards increased bureaucracy' demanded resistance, and McKechnie insisted that 'democratic forms in no degree obviate that necessity for a host of government officials which is inherent in Socialism'.[37] This last quotation refers to the fact that reformers were quick to argue that the political objection did not apply now that the government was no longer a preserve of a landed oligarchy. However, not only did this not ward off the charge of bureaucracy, it also did not meet the other common form of this argument – that the larger the range of the state's functions the less was left to individual enterprise – which was in fact heavily dependent on the economic and moral arguments.

The economic argument had obviously been the greatest single source of the presumption against state-intervention throughout the century. Indeed, even to speak of an 'age of laissez-faire' is to acknowledge the primacy of arguments supposedly drawn from classical political economy. In fact, as has since been emphasized,[38] the classical economists had all, in varying degrees, recognized a wide range of necessary state functions, and 'laissez-faire' is a misleading label if it is understood to mean complete abstinence from action by the state. They had, however, encouraged the general presumption that the economy was a system which regulated itself better than could be done by any form of direct management or control. Moreover, the fact that, in their formal analysis of the mechanics of an economic system, the economists had treated it *as if* it were one of perfect competition (including freedom from government control) was easily construed as showing that *only* in such a situation would the process function efficiently.[39] Also, the diffusion of arguments quarried from classical economics was obviously a process of vulgarization, and long after many of the so-called 'economic laws' had been discredited in theoretical

[36] F. C. Montague, *The Limits of Individual Liberty: An Essay* (London, 1885), p. 219.

[37] From Marshall's evidence to the Royal Commission on the Aged Poor, 1893, repr. in *The Official Papers of Alfred Marshall*, ed. J. M. Keynes (London, 1926), p. 253; McKechnie, *State and Individual*, p. 194. Cf. Goschen, *Essays and Addresses*, pp. 303–5.

[38] See the sources cited in n29 above.

[39] There is even a suggestion of the ambiguity in McKechnie's assertion that 'the universally accepted axioms of economics are all built on the principle that government (except in certain abnormal circumstances) does more harm than good by meddling'. *State and Individual*, p. 188. As one might expect, Sidgwick was alive to this confusion: 'The absence of governmental interference, being assumed for simplicity's sake in the hypothetical reasonings by which the values of products and services are deductively determined, is at the same time vaguely regarded as a conclusion established by such reasonings.' *The Principles of Political Economy* (2nd edn, London, 1887 [first published 1883]), p. 399.

terms, there remained a sediment of anti-interventionist prejudice which would always be shaken up by political controversy.

Bagehot rightly remarked in the late 1870s that political economy 'lies rather dead in the public mind. Not only...does it not excite the same interest as formerly but there is not exactly the same confidence in it'[40], and this lack of confidence was evident in its uses as a political argument. Ritchie could announce, with more assurance than, say, his Christian Socialist predecessors of the mid century, that the appeal to economic 'laws' was the resort of 'the doctrinaire politician who preaches laissez-faire in the name of a misunderstood science with the convenient aid of an ambiguity in language'.[41] Marshall emphasized at the beginning of his authoritative exposition of the new economics that 'the laws of Economics are statements of tendencies expressed in the indicative mood and not ethical precepts in the imperative'[42], but it was largely in combination with such moralizing that economic arguments enjoyed their most vigorous political existence.[43] Correspondingly, they tended to be overriden by moral considerations more than they were answered in their own terms. In 1883 Goschen had remarked that laissez-faire seemed 'to have lost favour chiefly owing to moral considerations', and in 1896 McKechnie was voicing what was still probably the dominant opinion when he said of the Individualist arguments that 'those drawn from political economy, in particular, if not unanswerable, have at least not yet been answered'.[44]

Of course, the form and strength of the economic arguments for Individualism varied with the subject under discussion. They retained almost knock-down status when confronted by proposals to nationalize major producing industries, and were hardly less powerful in opposition to most schemes for direct state management of commercial enterprises. Proposals for what could broadly be termed welfare legislation were less often confronted by purely economic objection, although the cost and the alleged disincentive to thrift were always put forward as insurmountable obstacles. The area of debate where the economic arguments were most

[40] Quoted in T. W. Hutchison, *A Review of Economic Doctrines 1870–1929* (Oxford, 1953), p. 6.

[41] Ritchie, *State Interference*, p. 123.

[42] *Principles of Economics* (London, 1890), pp. v–vi.

[43] Talcott Parsons long ago demonstrated how Marshall's theory rested upon the smuggling of certain normative elements into his central concept of 'activities' – see especially his 'Wants and activities in Marshall', *Quarterly Journal of Economics*, XLVI (1931–2), 101–40. Something similar could be done for much of the invocation of 'industry and thrift' in this literature. Even the normally precise language of Sidgwick is infected by this: in discussing the idea of redressing economic inequalities, he resorts to repeating the phrase 'industry and thrift' – and the harm which would be done to these virtues by such schemes – four times in the course of little more than a page. *Elements of Politics*, pp. 156–7.

[44] Goschen, *Essays and Addresses*, pp. 247–8 (he, of course, did not like this development, and thought that it was due to a lamentable tendency to let 'conscientious feeling' outweigh 'intellectual conviction'); McKechnie, *State and Individual*, p. 195.

disputed was that of taxation and even here they were underwritten by large deposits of moral capital. Proposals for progressive taxation of any sort were always met by the classic standby of financial conservatives – the claim that savings and investment would be discouraged and capital driven abroad. But, more fundamentally, they encountered an implicit theory of social justice which denied that there were any grounds for depriving the successful individual of a portion of his wealth in order to provide benefits for the less successful. Properly Socialist theories set against this a radically different vision of community, but one which was possibly too much of an outright assault on prevailing assumptions to be generally persuasive in educated circles. It was, I would suggest, the peculiar achievement of New Liberal theory to undermine this intricate blend of moral and economic arguments from within.[45]

The two types of argument which I have labelled the 'scientific' and the 'moral' enjoyed a particular vogue in the 1880s and 1890s; indeed, the former could hardly be said to have had any general political currency before then. The essence of the scientific argument consisted in presenting an account of Progress such that Individualism figured as both the mechanism of advance and a constitutive part of the goal. I shall explore the structure of this argument, and especially the crucial role in it of beliefs about Progress, more fully in Chapter 5, so I shall simply indicate its main varieties here. The most important was undoubtedly the way in which the supposed findings of evolutionary biology were pressed into service, as evidence, metaphor or law, to demonstrate that competition was the motor of advance in the natural and social world alike. *The Encyclopaedia of Social Reform* concluded its survey of Individualist arguments with the judgement that 'probably the chief arguments raised today to show the impracticability of Socialism are...biologic'.[46] This argument was overwhelmingly identified, by both advocates and opponents, with the name of Spencer.[47] Yet, in retrospect, its relationship to the complex reasoning of the 'Synthetic Philosophy' seems tenuous. In particular, the way in which Spencer's theory was widely assumed to rest upon the eternal primacy of conflict in social life would repay further study, since in fact the supercession of conflict by cooperation was the central theme of that theory.[48] At another

[45] For an account of this, and a more detailed consideration of the Individualist position, see below, Ch. 3, pp. 115–20.

[46] *Encyclopaedia of Social Reform*, p. 723.

[47] 'The leadership in the application of the doctrine of evolution to social science belongs undoubtedly to Herbert Spencer...[who] makes biology teach the folly of state intervention and the necessity of industrial competition.' *Encyclopaedia of Social Reform*, pp. 567–8. Or Samuel, *Liberalism*, pp. 12, 17: Spencer is 'the chief exponent' of the doctrine that 'mankind can only advance in obedience to the universal laws of evolution...There can be little doubt that this argument applied to politics, furnishes an intellectual basis for much of the opposition to social reform.'

[48] This is now well brought out in Peel, *Herbert Spencer*, and, following him, Hawthorn, *Enlightenment and Despair*, Ch. 5.

level, there is the oddity of the fact that the analogy between a society and a biological organism, the working out of which was the hallmark of Spencer's contribution, was susceptible of a Collectivist interpretation at least as plausibly as an Individualist one, as writers like Ritchie readily pointed out.[49] Nonetheless, the prevailing understanding of Spencer's work assimilated it to that more general tendency to misuse metaphors derived from the most prestigious science of the day, a tendency to which it remains convenient to apply the misnomer of 'Social Darwinism'.

There was also the older tradition of social evolutionary theory which could provide ammunition for the Individualist interpretation of history. The most frequently cited authority in this tradition was Sir Henry Maine, whose dictum that 'the movement of the progressive societies has hitherto been a movement from Status to Contract'[50] was eagerly deployed against the proposals of Collectivism. In fact, Maine's work was subject to much criticism in the prolonged controversy among historians and lawyers over the origin and development of private property and its associated legal forms, but insofar as this controversy had yet deposited a residue in political argument, it was the assumption that the emergence and extension of the institutions of private property and contract constituted the path of Progress. The tendency of Maine's later work was summed up in his deliberately polemical contention that 'no-one is at liberty to attack several property and to say at the same time that he values civilization. The history of the two cannot be disentangled'.[51] On this basis, his authority was invoked to support the claim that since Socialism involved the collective ownership of property, or that since factory and Trade Union legislation treated those whom it affected in terms of status rather than of contract, then in social evolutionary terms these measures constituted 'regressions'. To appreciate the force of this argument, it must be remembered that the legitimacy of historicist inferences from such accounts of the direction of evolution was barely challenged in this period.[52]

A variant of this historical argument, often combined with a properly

[49] Ritchie suggested four ways in which Spencer's construal of this analogy was tendentious. *State Interference*, pp. 14–22.

[50] H. S. Maine, *Ancient Law* (London, 1861), p. 170.

[51] H. S. Maine, *Village Communities in the East and West* (London, 1876 [first published 1871]), p. 230; cited in C. J. Dewey, 'Images of the village community: a study in Anglo-Indian ideology', *Modern Asian Studies*, 6 (1972), 310. On this literature and its political implications see also J. W. Burrow, '"The Village Community" and the uses of history in late-nineteenth-century England' in McKendrick (ed.), *Historical Perspectives*; on Maine's increasing conservatism, see John Roach, 'Liberalism and the Victorian intelligentsia', *Cambridge Historical Journal*, XIII (1957), 58–81.

[52] For an excellent account of how this kind of 'historicism' pervaded nineteenth-century thought, see Maurice Mandelbaum, *History, Man, and Reason: A Study in Nineteenth-Century Thought* (Baltimore, 1971). He defines historicism as 'the belief that an adequate understanding of the nature of any phenomenon and an adequate assessment of its value are to be gained through considering it in terms of the place which it occupied and the role which it played within a process of development' (p. 42).

Spencerian account of evolution, was the claim that with the demonstrable advance of altruism and cooperation the need for the use of force, especially by means of the law, was correspondingly diminishing.[53] An assumption of this sort was widely entertained in this period, and not merely by Individualists: it was a premise in theories as disparate as those of Marshall and Kropotkin.[54] As ever, the Individualist conclusion depended upon making rigid distinction between cooperative action by voluntary organizations and that carried out by the state; given a plausible modification of this premise, the argument could be restructured to show that the collective regulation of its own affairs by the community was the natural outcome of the acknowledged trend of social evolution. The abundance of tendentious accounts of social and biological evolution during this period testifies to both the importance and the flexibility of these arguments.

Any excavation of the role of Progress in this debate soon reveals the pervasive sediment of a certain sort of moralizing, and in suggesting that there was a distinct 'moral' argument, I certainly do not mean to imply that the other arguments were devoid of moral content. Conversely, one must recognize that a concern for the moral well-being of the citizen body could in turn be largely instrumental in the sense that such moral health might be regarded as a necessary prophylactic against essentially economic or political disasters.[55] But one of the most distinctive features of the political argument of this period seems to me to be the independent and overriding value assigned to the fostering of 'character' as a primary aim of politics. No amount of quotation could adequately convey the extent and intensity of this concern, and I shall only deal briefly with three points: first, that the development of the virtues represented by the ideal of 'character' was recognized as a positive function of the state; secondly, that with the increasing moralization of debate, this became the chief argument of moderate Individualism; and thirdly, that as 'self-reliance' was meta-

[53] See, for example, Wordsworth Donisthorpe's essay in T. Mackay (ed.), *A Plea for Liberty: An Argument against Socialism and Socialistic Legislation* (London, 1891): 'On the whole, State interference shows signs of becoming weaker as civilization progresses', and with the continued advance of altruism such 'coercion will no longer be needed' (pp. 78, 106). The belief in the advance of altruism, may have been a peculiarly English form of smug self-deception – as is hinted in Hawthorn, *Enlightenment and Despair*, Ch. 5 – but in looking forward to 'the end of politics' or a 'withering away of the state', Spencer and his followers were expressing a view which was very common in early- and mid-nineteenth-century social thought, its best-known appearances being in the work of St Simon or of Marx.

[54] For Marshall, see the discussion in Talcott Parsons, 'Economics and sociology: Marshall in relation to the thought of his time', *Quarterly Journal of Economics*, XLVI (1931–2), 316–47; for Kropotkin, see his *Mutual Aid: A Factor of Evolution* (repr., ed. Paul Avrich, London, 1972 [first published 1902]), esp. Ch. 8. The book was made up of articles first published in *The Nineteenth Century* between 1890 and 1896.

[55] Something of the sort can be seen in Goschen's fear that Socialism would destroy 'that self-reliance and independence and natural liberty which, if history has taught us anything, are the main conditions on which depend the strength of the state, the prosperity of the community, and the greatness of nations'. *Essays and Addresses*, p. 325.

morphosed into 'self-development' or 'self-realization', the argument's potential for exploitation in a Collectivist direction became greater.

The Trojan horse of 'character' was introduced into Victorian political theory at an early stage. It is doubtful whether a strictly want-regarding Utilitarianism was ever the dominant style in political debate, but in the writings of Mill and Spencer, no less than in the speeches of Gladstone and Bright, it is already clear that there is an analytically separable normative premise, represented by Spencer's declaration that 'the end which the statesman should keep in view as higher than all other ends is the formation of character'.[56] In Mill's mature work this is, notoriously, a major test of all political arrangements, and even Sidgwick's more rigorous statement of the aims of politics for the Utilitarian included the argument that men 'are likely to gain more in vigour of intellect and character by being left to manage their own affairs'.[57] It was given classic form by Green's attack on 'prohibitions and restraints, unnecessary, or which have ceased to be necessary, for maintaining the social conditions of the moral life, and which interfere with the growth of self-reliance, with the formation of a manly conscience and sense of moral dignity – in short, with the moral autonomy which is the condition of the highest goodness'.[58] And more generally, the dominant pattern of imperatives was made up of that clutch of characteristically Victorian evaluative-descriptive terms which clustered around this ideal – terms like 'self-reliance', 'independence', 'sobriety', 'self-restraint', 'respectability', 'self-improvement'.[59] The dependent man was regarded as a moral cripple; public assistance could weaken resistance to such infirmities, whereas, as Mill put it, 'the mental and the moral, like the muscular, powers are improved only by being used'.[60] Such a formulation of the ideal made for a strong presumption against state action, though it had long been used to license certain forms of it: temperance legislation, for example, could be represented as removing obstacles to the exercise of individual self-restraint and sobriety.[61]

[56] Herbert Spencer, *The Principles of Ethics*, II (London, 1893), p. 251. Of course, Spencer drew his usual conclusion from this – 'if there is entertained a right conception of the character which should be formed, the exclusion of multiplied State-agencies is necessarily implied' – but the premise is often overlooked.

[57] *Elements of Politics*, p. 12.

[58] T. H. Green, *Lectures on the Principles of Political Obligation* (London, 1895), para. 17.

[59] Cf. the suggestion of a social historian that 'independent' and 'respectable' were the crucial terms for assessing an individual's social standing; Geoffrey Best, *Mid-Victorian Britain 1851–75* (London, 1971), p. 257.

[60] *On Liberty* (pbk, ed. Gertrude Himmelfarb, Harmondsworth, 1974 [first published London, 1859]), p. 122.

[61] This is well argued in Brian Harrison, *Drink and the Victorians: The Temperance Question in England 1815–1872* (London, 1971), esp. Ch. 13. See also the same author's conclusion to his excellent essay on 'state-intervention and moral reform': '"Social" reforms were often directed at moral purposes: improved housing aimed at sexual modesty, public education at sobriety, Poor Law relief at respectability, and so on.' 'State-intervention and moral reform in nineteenth-century England' in P. Hollis (ed.), *Pressure From Without in Early Victorian England* (London, 1974), pp. 316–17.

When presented as an objection to state-intervention, 'the ethical argument probably affects the common consciousness far more than any other'.[62] The claim was that the short-run material benefit from such measures would be achieved at the cost of the removal of the stimulus to industry and thrift, and the sapping of that exercise of will which was the source of moral as well as of economic independence. Clearly, underlying this argument there was a certain anxiety about the consequences for the working classes, individually and collectively, should they fail to practise, or at least aspire to, these essentially middle-class virtues. As Goschen revealingly put it: 'We might sap for ever the self-reliance *of a class* in order to remove some present abuse which other methods might even more effectually remedy.'[63] No doubt this argument served purposes which may properly be called ideological, but even then it was no simple case of serving established interests. It carried great persuasive force, and drew upon moral and psychological assumptions which were also shared by the advocates of reform. It involved the projection on to the material condition of the working classes of that pervasive Victorian sense of the dependence of life upon the unremitting and strictly channelled exercise of will. It corresponded with the perceived facts of the economic improvement of the previous four decades, in which the working-class institutions of thrift and self-help were taken to have played a vital role; it accorded with and structured the narrow social experience of the small and relatively isolated professional classes. This understanding of a fragile achievement depending on a delicately balanced habit of will is very evident in, for example, Sidgwick's reflection on his experience in the local 'Mendicity Society':

> The positive work, the helping of people who ought to be helped, presents great difficulties: for the people we have to deal with are so often just trembling morally on the verge of helpless pauperism, and it is very hard to say in any case whether the help we give will cheer and stimulate a man to help himself, or whether it will not just push him gently into the passive condition of letting society take him in hand and do what it will with him.[64]

Given this perception of the problem, it is understandable that the moral dangers of large-scale state welfare schemes should seem the most important.[65]

[62] *Encyclopaedia of Social Reform*, p. 719: 'It is on the conviction that simple character, self-rule, self-reliance, self-poise is the one thing of worth in the universe that most men base their argument for Individualism.' Samuel cites the fear that state-intervention would be injurious to 'self-reliance and enterprise' and 'relaxing to character' as one of the most frequent objections. Samuel, *Liberalism*, pp. 21–5. (The implications of 'relaxing' are suggestive of the psychological underpinning of this argument.) Blease says much the same of what he calls 'the philosophical argument against social reform'. Walter Lyon Blease, *A Short History of English Liberalism* (London, 1913), p. 337.

[63] *Essays and Addresses*, p. 325 (my emphasis).

[64] Henry Sidgwick to his sister, 29 Nov. 1879, quoted in *Henry Sidgwick*, pp. 341–2.

[65] John Burns, for example, attacked 'Popularism' above all for its 'reckless destruction of morals in an individual district'. Quoted in José Harris, *Unemployment and Politics: A Study in English Social Policy 1886–1914* (Oxford, 1972), p. 266.

Finally, it is important to see that the case for Collectivism was not mounted by a simple rejection of the moral argument. Many reformers wished to argue that there were economic or structural causes of poverty which were more powerful than the efforts of the individual will, but the development of the individual's moral capacity remained the overriding goal. They were helped in this by the fact that the formulation of the ideal was subtly modified during this period, as the idea of self-reliance or self-improvement was subsumed under that of self-realization. Here is one of the places at which the contribution of philosophical Idealism is evident, for it was capable of offering a more coherent conceptualization of these aspirations than was readily available in the prevailing philosophical vocabulary.[66] It soon became commonplace to speak of 'self-realization' as 'the general formula of Progress and the goal of all social and political aims'.[67] But the emphasis upon the opportunity to develop one's faculties did not presume the same tight relationship with the struggle to maintain economic independence as did the ideal of self-reliance. It made it easier to claim that the removal of certain material obstacles would facilitate such development. Such claims could draw upon the long-standing anxiety about the effect of extreme poverty upon the religious and moral habits of the working classes; much of the alarm expressed at the poverty revelations of the 1880s was of this type – above all, the fear of 'the moral destruction of the next generation'.[68] Reformers increasingly insisted that their goal was 'the freest and fullest development of human quality and power', and that this entailed 'immediate State action to secure the health and the intelligence of the community and a fair chance for its moral progress'.[69] More radically, some Socialists argued that a society built less exclusively on competition would produce 'a higher type of character'.[70] It later became a standard defence of New Liberal proposals that they exhibited 'a fuller appreciation and realization of individual liberty contained in the provision of equal opportunities for self-development'.[71] The language of Idealism certainly lent itself to such purposes: as McKechnie shrewdly remarked: 'If the purpose for which the state exists is no less than the perfecting of the whole community, it follows that nothing can be excluded from its proper sphere which advances it towards that goal.'[72] But even leaving aside

[66] Green himself seems to have recognized this as part of the task of Idealism; see Richter, *Politics of Conscience*, pp. 170–1.

[67] McKechnie, *State and Individual*, p. 90.

[68] Quoted from an 1883 series of 'exposé' articles, in A. S. Wohl, '*The Bitter Cry of Outcast London*', *International Review of Social History*, XIII (1968), 203.

[69] Sidney Ball, 'The Moral Aspects of Socialism', *International Journal of Ethics*, VI (1896), 302; D. G. Ritchie, *The Moral Function of the State* (London, 1887), p. 16.

[70] *Encyclopaedia of Social Reform*, p. 1271.

[71] J. A. Hobson, *The Crisis of Liberalism: New Issues of Democracy* (repr., ed. P. F. Clarke, Brighton, 1974 [first published London, 1909]), p. xii.

[72] McKechnie, *State and Individual*, p. 92.

the possibly idiosyncratic usage of 'state', this argument as a whole provides a good example of the ways in which the moral resources massed in support of Individualism could be mobilized in the interests of legitimating Collectivism.

In turning to consider the contemporary understanding of Collectivism, it is immediately apparent that it cannot be disentangled from that of Socialism, and so it is with the usage of the older term that I shall begin. From the 1830s onwards, there are frequent references in English to Socialism, and a considerable body of literature accumulated in which its merits as a theory of economic and social organization were debated. But it was treated as a, in the strict sense, Utopian theory, not figuring seriously in the mainstream of political controversy until the 1880s. Its standard referents during this period were the ideal of the cooperatively organized society found in the works of Owen, St Simon and Fourier (it was in this form that it was discussed by Mill in his *Political Economy* and his *Chapters on Socialism*), and, less frequently, the programmes of the communistic or revolutionary groups which were thought to flourish on the Continent, and which occasionally, as in 1848 or 1871, came to the notice of the British press. The fact that its standard evaluative force was strongly unfavourable obviously gave it a marked polemical value. By suggesting that a particular measure tended in the direction of the collective control of all departments of life, it could be used by opponents to discredit legislative proposals, as, for example, in Cobden's sneer at 'the Socialist doctrines' of those who proposed the Factory Acts in the 1840s.[73] This use probably increased in subsequent decades.[74] But on the whole, Socialism in any pure form was, like many other disagreeable practices, considered a Continental phenomenon, and up to the beginning of the 1880s Englishmen were wont to compliment themselves on its comparative absence from British politics.[75]

[73] Quoted in John Morley, *The Life of Richard Cobden* (9th edn London, 1903 [first published 1879]), p. 302. Morley himself claimed that, given the extent of 'Socialistic' factory legislation since 1844, Cobden's denunciation was prescient. It is interesting to see that the biography, in effect a defence of Cobden's doctrines, had an immense sale during the early 1880s and again during the Tariff Reform controversy in the early 1900s.

[74] By the 1870s, Cairnes could argue, to such an extent was Socialism identified with 'the employment of the powers of the state for the instant accomplishment of ideal schemes', that 'it is common to hear any proposal which is thought to involve an undue extension of the powers of the state branded as Socialistic, whatever be the object it may seek to accomplish'. But since he was objecting to Mill's more Utopian use of the term, it was very much in his interest to attribute such a usage, whether standard or not. J. E. Cairnes, *Leading Principles of Political Economy* (London, 1873), p. 316.

[75] 'In England there is nothing like militant Socialism and we are often thus happily cut off from any personal acquaintance with what is to the Continent a source of permanent and sometimes vivid apprehension.' *Saturday Review*, 8 May 1880. In 1879, William Cunningham remarked upon 'the apparent immunity from this dreaded influence on which we congratulate ourselves' ('The Progress of Socialism in England', *Contemporary Review*, XXXIV (1879), 245), and thirty years later recalled

In the early 1880s this situation was thought to have changed very rapidly. Three quite separate developments were taken to be related elements of this change. The first, and most important from the present perspective, was the establishment of avowedly Socialist organizations which issued aggressive statements of aims and policy. The second was the immense popularity of the ideas of Henry George, widely perceived at the time as Socialist, though in fact based upon an extreme kind of radical Individualism.[76] The third development was the increasing radicalism of Liberal legislation (and even more of Liberal proposals), beginning with the Irish Land Acts of 1881, which were represented by opponents as the first step in a popular attack on property.[77] In the immense literature which was thus generated, the older Utopian tradition was largely eclipsed by the newly important state-Socialism (although one has to be careful with this term since it was also used to describe the anti-Socialist welfare policies of Bismarck). A new sense of urgency characterized discussions of the extent to which current legislation was, albeit in a covert and piecemeal way, embracing such Socialism and abandoning the older principles of limited state-intervention. In the course of the controversy, Collectivism came into fashion as a general description of this tendency.

Like many a pejorative political label, it was borrowed from France, and among French Socialist groups it had referred to two, ultimately conflicting, tendencies. On the one hand, it was used to describe the ideas of those, generally Marxists, who criticized the voluntarism and localism of the Utopian tradition; and, on the other hand, it could also be used to refer to the near-anarchist scheme for the organization of economic activity by local collectives.[78] With the disputes over whether Socialism should be used to describe the moral ideal shared by all putative Socialists, or simply

that 'the ordinary newspaper reader regarded it as a craze which took possession of hysterical foreigners, but which had no attraction for the common-sense of Englishmen' ('Christianity and Socialism', *Journal of the Transactions of the Victoria Institute*, XLI (1909), 70).

76 George was already advocating an attack upon landed property, though not, as yet, via the 'single tax'. On his British tours of the early eighties see E. P. Lawrence, *Henry George in the British Isles* (East Lansing, Michigan, 1957); the best exploration of his relation to the Socialist Revival is now Willard Wolfe, *From Radicalism to Socialism: Men and Ideas in the Formation of Fabian Socialist Doctrines 1881–1889* (New Haven, Conn., 1975), esp. Ch. 3.

77 Beatrice Webb, among others, remarked that 'the reaction against the theory and practice of empirical Socialism came to a head under Mr Gladstone's administration of 1880–85'. *My Apprenticeship* (pbk Harmondsworth, 1971 [first published London, 1926]), p. 196.

78 The earliest English example cited in the *O.E.D.* is, in fact, a reference to this latter usage, as the full context makes clear, and thus not an example of the same sense as the others quoted. The article from which it is taken is describing the development of Anarchist ideas within the International, and how 'the doctrine of Collectivism forced its way to the front...By Collectivism is meant that everything is to be done and managed by a society. Railways, mines, forests, and even the soil, are to be worked by associations...What is remarkable in this impracticable conception is that it gets rid of the idea of the State. The associations include everyone, but there is nothing above the associations.' 'The International', *Saturday Review*, 8 May 1880.

some more particular set of means for its achievement, Collectivism in its Anglicized form, as *The Encyclopaedia Britannica* explained in 1887, 'has recently come into vogue to express the economic basis of Socialism as above explained'.[79] At its most extreme, therefore, it stood for 'the collective ownership or control of all the means of production, and especially of the land, by the whole community or State, i.e. the people collectively, for the benefit of the people as a whole', as the *O.E.D.* defined it; or in Milner's blunter phrase, for 'the abolition of individual property'.[80] Thus understood, it was regarded, according to Sidgwick, as 'Socialism in its extremest form', that is, as the principle of political action which was most directly opposed to Individualism.[81] But this narrower sense licensed the more general use where it was applied to any attempt to implement social reform 'through the legislative and executive powers of the state'.[82] In this general sense it easily embraced legislation which was not obviously inspired by any recognizable Socialist theory, and this is the sense which was immortalized by, but certainly not invented by, Dicey when he defined it as 'a convenient antithesis to Individualism in the field of legislation'.[83]

Dicey also recognized its merits as an organizing category: 'The very indefiniteness of the expression Collectivism is for my purposes a recommendation. A person may in some respects be a Collectivist – that is to say, entertain views which are not in harmony with the ideas of Individualism – and yet not uphold or entertain any general belief which could fairly be called Socialism.'[84] This neatly encapsulates the situation facing many of the theorists of social reform: in attempting to legitimate more extensive state-intervention, they were frequently not expressing allegiance to 'any general belief which could fairly be called Socialism', but they were nonetheless bound to have the force of the general hostility to Socialism mobilized against them. The anti-Individualist had to deal with the arguments against Socialism even if he did not describe himself as a Socialist.

There is no need to dwell upon the variety of ways in which the terms 'Socialism' and 'Collectivism' were used during this period, especially by the unsympathetic, though it may be worth indicating the range involved. Socialism, for example, could refer to any or several of the following: (1) a radically different conception of society, involving the abolition of

[79] Thomas Kirkup, the author of the entry under 'Socialism', had already given a strongly ethical definition of the term; *Encyclopaedia Britannica* (9th edn Edinburgh, 1887), XXII, pp. 205–21.

[80] Alfred Milner, *Arnold Toynbee: A Reminiscence* (London, 1895), p. 52.

[81] Sidgwick, *Elements of Politics*, p. 151.

[82] McKechnie, *State and Individual*, p. 175. Compare Hobson writing in 1896 of 'that expansion of Municipal and State activity, which is termed Collectivism'. Hobson, *Crisis of Liberalism*, p. 114.

[83] Dicey, *Law and Opinion*, p. 64.

[84] Dicey, *Law and Opinion*, p. 64.

property, the family, marriage, religion, and so on; (2) the ideal of the cooperative, altruistic society where the common good was pursued by collective effort; (3) class warfare and proletarian revolution; (4) the nationalization of the means of production, distribution and exchange (and, by extension, other forms of state regulation of economic life); (5) the redistribution of wealth in favour of the poorer classes, particularly by means of welfare measures financed out of taxation (and, again, any policies of social reform which could be presented as extensions of this). On this basis, there were two ways in which the otherwise overlapping terms of Socialism and Collectivism could be distinguished: where Socialism was used in the first two senses, Collectivism could be restricted to the mechanism, political or economic, by which these ideals were to be attained; where Socialism was used in the last three senses, Collectivism could be used more broadly to refer to the general tendency to increase the powers of the state (which, as I suggested above, was the more common use by 1900). Put briefly, it would not be entirely misleading to say that Collectivism indicated a wider range of state action than strict Socialism, whereas Socialism generally connoted a level of moral aspiration beyond mere Collectivism.

I realize that this might seem like a laborious exercise in clarifying what was never particularly unclear, but a fairly precise guide to the local conventions is the best protection against the danger of incorrectly labelling some of the theorists of this period upon the basis of what is in effect a mistranslation. For this purpose, it is also worth emphasizing a further point which is that the evaluative force of Socialism in the circles whose usage I am considering was strongly condemnatory. It always retained associations with 'the crude materialism, the definitely hostile attitude towards religion, the family and other bonds of moral union' which, even a sympathizer like Hobson had to concede, 'have marked certain sections of continental Socialism'.[85] The impracticability of Socialism of any kind was continually being insinuated by citing as evidence the failure of certain well-known Utopian communities.[86] These connotations were easily extended to Collectivism: 'Look at it as we may,' wrote McKechnie, with that spurious air of judiciousness which characterized his survey, 'Collectivism always means the triumph of coercion over freedom, of authority over rights of private men, of the condition of status over that of contract.'[87] Hobhouse

[85] J. A. Hobson, *The Social Problem* (London, 1901), p. 132. Cf. below, Ch. 2, text to n118.

[86] See, for example, Smith, *Liberty and Liberalism*, Ch. 10.

[87] McKechnie, *State and Individual*, p. 176. He prefaced this judgement by quoting Flint's no less tendentious definition of Collectivism: 'Society organized as the state intervening in all the industrial and economic arrangements of life, possessing almost everything, and so controlling and directing its members that private and personal enterprises and interests are absorbed in those which are public and collective'. Robert Flint, *Socialism* (London, 1894), p. 63.

knew whereof he spoke when in 1897 he referred to the 'obloquy' incurred in calling oneself a Socialist.[88]

Those who did wish to champion the cause of Socialism or of increased Collectivism could resort to three main strategies for countering its *prima facie* undesirability. Although there was a wide range of motives and convictions in the writers involved, the three responses could be roughly characterized as those of the 'economic Socialist', the 'moral Socialist', and the 'progressive radical'. These are overlapping categories – and in the next two chapters I suggest that Hobhouse's work reveals something of a move from the first two responses to the third – but to distinguish them analytically is a useful first step in approaching the extensive controversial literature.

The first, and most obvious, response was to accept the implied criteria for the application of the term (increased use of power of the state, redistribution of property, and so on), and to accept that the measure or position under consideration was correctly identified as an instance of it, but to deny that it thereby stood condemned. This was the 'Socialist-and-proud-of-it' response, an attempt to reverse the prevailing evaluative force of the term. Needless to say, this was usually acompanied by some further claim that the implied disadvantages would be outweighed by achievements which could be so described in terms of existing values as to make their desirability recognizable. In effect, therefore, this response frequently did involve challenging *some* of the accepted criteria, although in its purest form it simply attempted to override the unfavourable connotations by claiming that the values which Socialism stood for should rightfully be considered more important. In the literature which I am dealing with, this response – at least in anything like its pure form – was the least popular.

The second response was to accept that the measure (or, more frequently here, the theory or ideal) was correctly described as an instance of Socialism, but to take issue with the criteria for the application of the term. The essence of this move was to deny that Socialism should be equated with Collectivism or with practically any kind of political or economic 'machinery', and to assert, instead, that its distinguishing mark was its moral ideal. In extreme cases this could easily lapse into high-sounding vacuity: Socialism, as J. S. Mackenzie noted, could be presented as 'simply the practical assertion that we are "members one of another", that we are parts of an organic whole', though he was quick to acknowledge that 'the

[88] L. T. Hobhouse, 'The Ethical Basis of Collectivism', *International Journal of Ethics*, VIII (1897–8), 139. In 1907, the Tories could still find it worth while to start a 'Socialist scare' against the Liberals, for to do so was to attempt, as Hobson observed at the time, 'to blacken an enemy with a vituperative epithet'. Hobson, *Crisis of Liberalism*, p. 133.

assertion must always appeal to our moral consciousness'.[89] It was a response of this sort which united figures as different as Keir Hardie and Sidney Ball – 'Socialism is so much more than either a political creed or an economic dogma', as Hardie put it.[90] Here is the ever-familiar attempt to divert criticism by distinguishing rather freely between means and ends. And, no less familiarly, the ideal was specified in such a way as to suffocate Individualist objections about the destruction of liberty and individuality: Socialism's 'animating ideal' could easily be said to embrace 'the freest and fullest development of human quality and power'.[91] But in addition, it was argued, rather more polemically, the claims of Socialism rested upon the alleged moral superiority of a society based upon cooperation rather than competition, a society in which a noble conception of service to the common good would replace the current devotion to the selfish pursuit of individual interests.[92] This line of argument made possible a subtler attempt to enlist the growing current of moralism in an attack upon that very conception of the state with which it was generally taken to be associated.

The tendency of this sort of Socialism, if divorced from any actual proposals for the achievement of its ideal, was to degenerate into a kind of pious arm-waving. It could also encourage a 'loftier-than-thou' attitude towards those Socialists who did actually recommend specific political reforms. Hobhouse himself, for example, was reproved by two older friends in just this tone. Reviewing *The Labour Movement* (favourably, for the most part), Ball lamented that the emphasis upon 'machinery' seemed to be at the expense of a sufficient concern with the more fundamental need for the creation of 'moral community'. And J. H. Bridges similarly objected that the proposed measures were superficial and would prove unworkable without a prior 'moral change'.[93] This attitude was reinforced by some of the dominant intellectual fashions of the period, such as Idealism,

[89] J. S. Mackenzie, *An Introduction to Social Philosophy* (2nd edn Glasgow, 1895 [first published 1890]), p. 326.

[90] Quoted in K. O. Morgan, *Keir Hardie, Radical and Socialist* (London, 1975), p. 206. For similar statements by Ball see any of his articles in the 1890s, particularly 'Moral Aspects of Socialism', 291–322, and 'The Socialist Ideal', *Economic Review*, IX (1899), 425–49. For an example of the way in which this account of Socialism suggested a rather cavalier denial of the importance of particular means, consider Hardie's statement in 1896: 'I am a Socialist because Socialism means fraternity founded on justice, and the fact that in order to secure this it is necessary to transfer land and capital from private to public ownership is a mere accident in the crusade.' (Quoted in Morgan, *Keir Hardie*, p. 207.)

[91] Ball, 'Moral Aspects of Socialism', 302.

[92] As, for example, in Sidney Webb's declaration that Socialism meant 'the general recognition of fraternity, the universal obligation of personal service, and the subordination of personal ambition to the common good'. *Socialism in England* (repr. London, 1893 [first published Baltimore, 1889]), p. 12.

[93] *International Journal of Ethics*, IV (1893–4), 524–6; *Positivist Review*, I (1893), 163–70. On Ball, see below, Ch. 2, pp. 59–60, 74 and n; on Bridges, Ch. 5, p. 152 and n.

Positivism, Ethicism and so on, their common emphasis being summed up in the declaration of the Idealist philosopher Henry Jones that 'we must moralize our social relations as they stand, and every other reform will come as a thing of course'.[94] The strength of this current is attested by the fact that even some of those who shared its general inspiration were alarmed at the way in which it could be obstructive of actual reform. Hobson, for example, frequently protested that 'the endeavour to solve economic problems by direct appeal to the moral conduct of individual members is foredoomed to failure'.[95] This appeal was by no means exclusively a Socialist one, but it was a constitutive part of a certain sort of Socialism.

Many of those who had begun by pursuing this strategy in the 1880s and early 1890s had come, by the 1900s, increasingly to adopt the third response, which was to accept the implied criteria for the application of the term Socialism, but to deny that the measures they were advocating were correctly described as instances of it. Many of the 'moral Socialists', of course, had wanted to claim that 'Socialism is, in fact, properly considered, only the development of Liberalism under new conditions', but they had still insisted that it was in this transcendence of Liberalism that the superiority of Socialism lay.[96] What distinguished the third response was the attempt to dissociate the favoured proposals from the charge of Socialism by suggesting that they merely involved an extension of the principles underlying Liberalism. This is the characteristic response of those who came to be called 'New Liberals'. Hobson, for example, had in the 1890s been eager to establish his Socialist credentials, and those of his current hero, too, urging recognition of the hitherto unrecognized fact that 'Ruskin was a Socialist'.[97] But by 1909, he is more concerned to argue that the conception of the state he is urging 'is not Socialism in any accredited meaning of the term', emphasizing instead 'its continuity with earlier Liberalism'.[98] It would be hard to disentangle tactics and conviction in accounting for such a change, and, as I shall argue in Chapter 3, changed

[94] Henry Jones, *The Working Faith of the Social Reformer, and Other Essays* (London, 1910), p. 114 (from an article first published in the *Hibbert Journal*, IV (1905), quotation at p. 781).

[95] Hobson, *Social Problem*, pp. 134–5. Ritchie, politically the most radical of the leading Idealists, similarly insisted, against the view fashionable amongst his philosophical allies, that 'moral and religious influences will only raise a few above the pressure of circumstances, therefore circumstances must be altered... The economic change must come before the moral before we can know certainly what the moral change will be.' Quoted in the Memoir of Ritchie prefixed to his *Philosophical Studies*, ed. Robert Latta (London, 1905), p. 48.

[96] Sidney Ball, 'Individualism and Socialism', *Economic Review*, VII (1897), 493; cf. Ramsay MacDonald: 'Socialism, the stage which follows Liberalism, retains everything that was of permanent value in Liberalism, by virtue of its being the hereditary heir of Liberalism.' *Socialism and Society* (London, 1905), p. 164.

[97] Quoted in Alan J. Lee, 'A Study of the Social and Economic Thought of J. A. Hobson' (unpublished Ph.D. dissertation, London, 1970), p. 166.

[98] Hobson, *Crisis of Liberalism*, p. xii; cf. p. 134 for the assertion, in an article first published in 1907, that his proposals involved 'no violent breach of continuity with Liberal traditions'.

political circumstances explain much. Nonetheless, this response entailed a different strategy of legitimation, since it obviously became of prime importance to demonstrate the plausibility of a form of Liberal Collectivism. At this point, therefore, the contemporary understanding of Liberalism became the focus of the wider debate.

To say that the nature of Liberalism was itself the subject of fierce controversy during this period is hardly a novel historiographical discovery, but one feature of this controversy which needs to be brought out more fully is its intimate relation to rival interpretations of the Liberal tradition. The resonances of 'Liberalism' for many intellectuals in the last quarter of the century were profound, suggesting associations with achievements and principles which deserved to be venerated, commemorated and perpetuated.[99] Even those who were urging a more progressive policy upon the party dwelt in their rhetoric as much upon the deeds of the past as the hopes for the future; in this there was a curious traditionalism about the party of Progress, a striking resort to authority by those who preached criticism and independence. Rival interpretations revealed much in common. It is by no means the case that they should therefore be thought to provide an accurate account of the doings of the Liberal Party and Liberal ministries, but the common element of tendentiousness tells us much about the prevailing perception of that past. Both traditional and progressive Liberals represented Liberalism as pre-eminently the creed of the party of *principle*, not only by way of contrast with the implied unprincipled opportunism of its traditional opponents, but also in the supposed greater moral purity of its political practices.[100] Both saw the commitment to liberty as an animating principle, such that the freeing of trade from tariffs, the freeing of Dissenters from disabilities, the freeing of nations from foreign domination, the freeing of the tax-payer from taxes, and the freeing of the individual from legal restraints upon his pursuit of his interests could all be construed as exemplifying a coherent political theory. Both celebrated Liberalism's hostility to privilege and monopoly, whether in land, public offices, ecclesiastical prerogatives or political influence, and a corresponding commitment to the impartial defence of the public good against class or sectional interests (antipathy to class-based politics was a hallmark of the Liberal intellectual, and for more than merely

[99] Within the ranks of the party there was a proliferation of commemorative clubs and publications during this perod; several are mentioned in passing in D. A. Hamer, *Liberal Politics in the Age of Gladstone and Rosebery. A Study in Leadership and Policy* (Oxford, 1972).

[100] The roots of this view are perceptively explored in John Vincent, *The Formation of the British Liberal Party 1857–1868* (London, 1966). The Liberals' image of purity in their electoral practices is touched on in Harrison, *Drink and the Victorians*, pp. 285ff. The rise of this image of Liberalism among an earlier generation of intellectuals is perceptively dealt with in the recent excellent study by Christopher Harvie, *The Lights of Liberalism: University Liberals and the Challenge of Democracy 1860–86* (London, 1976).

tactical reasons). Both, finally, spoke of 'reform' as the achievement, the task and the rationale of Liberalism, though without further criteria for identifying 'abuses', 'reform', like 'liberty', was an empty box to be filled in differently by different groups.[101]

In view of the extent of this agreement, it is striking how both groups found quite opposed reasons for being dissatisfied with the actual practice of Gladstonian Liberalism. On the one hand, the charge was of demagoguery, violation of property rights, and excessive public expenditure; on the other, it was remoteness, indifference to the claims of labour, and a refusal to engage in social reform that was complained of. In these exchanges, 'true Liberalism' was often little more than a rhetorical device for attacking the excessive Individualism or Collectivism of one's opponents – though, as I have suggested, there were limits to its flexibility.

Spencer's *The Man Versus the State* was the best-known protest of the first sort. Basing himself on a brisk history of Liberalism from the reign of Charles II, Spencer sought to show the 'confusion' by which the party had recently been led astray:

> The gaining of a popular good, being the external conspicuous trait common to Liberal measures in earlier days (then in each case gained by a relaxation of restraints), it has happened that popular good has come to be sought by Liberals, not as an end to be indirectly gained by relaxations of restraints, but as the end to be directly gained.[102]

One did not have to be a Spencerian to endorse this view. One could quote that perennial source of reactionary jeremiads, *The Times*, on how 'our actual party names have become useless and even ridiculous', and, like Bruce Smith, deplore the tendency to interpret 'Liberal' 'as meaning one who is given to liberality with the public revenue'.[103] Smith complained of the way in which 'sound Liberals' such as Goschen and Hartington had been driven into the Conservative Party by the 'Socialism' of proposals such as Chamberlain's allotment scheme. If Liberalism could not be recalled to its true historical role – and by 1887 it was beginning to seem a bit late in the day for this – then he advocated 'resisting over-legislation and maintaining Individualism as opposed to Socialism – entirely irrespective of party politics'.[104] This was a view with which many old Liberals were sympathetic, and if in practice this involved migrating to the Conservative Party, albeit on the ferry of Liberal-Unionism, then this was a journey which Liberals as diverse as Dicey and Goschen were prepared

[101] This is well brought out in Hamer, *Liberal Politics*.

[102] Herbert Spencer, *The Man Versus the State* (repr., with Introduction by D. G. Macrae, London, 1969 [first published 1884]), p. 70.

[103] Smith, *Liberty and Liberalism*, p. 8, quoting *Times*, 4 March 1886.

[104] *Liberty and Liberalism*, pp. 52, iv. Smith outdid Spencer in historical zeal, surveying the development of Liberalism from 1066 in order to show that 'true Liberalism' demanded 'greater freedom from restraint'. *The Radical Programme* was his particular bogey.

to make.[105] Clearly, any approach which identifies Liberalism with Individualism will be unable to account for these reactions.

However, those who were urging a progressive policy on the Liberal Party in the late 1880s and 1890s were scarcely more confident of success. Editors like H. W. Massingham and C. P. Scott, in their different styles, berated 'the older, stagnant, hopeless form of the Liberal creed', especially its attachment to 'Manchesterism'. Their ideal was rather to move 'towards that blending of the older Liberalism with the new aspirations of the labouring masses out of which the party of progress of the future must spring'.[106] For some of these progressives it was an open question whether this development would result in an entirely new party. Reporting on the trend of British politics, William Clarke wrote in 1897:

It may be expected that the closing years of the century will witness an attempt at the completion of the evolution of modern Liberalism by shedding altogether the 'moderate' or Individualist wing, which is visibly declining and must start to disappear. The new party of progress in England can scarcely avoid being largely Collectivist, since it will probably be the outcome of a union of radicalism with the labour movement, nearly all the rich and socially influential classes gravitating steadily to the Conservative party.[107]

In the form of exhortation rather than prediction, Clarke and his associates on *The Progressive Review* harped on the same theme: 'the disintegration and enfeeblement of the great political party whose watchword has been Progress' was the polemical premise which supported the conclusion that what was needed was 'the re-formation and re-statement of the principles of Progress in terms which shall include and give due emphasis to the new ideas and sentiments of social justice, and of a clear rational application of those principles in a progressive policy and a progressive party'.[108] By no means all, or perhaps even a majority of, radical intellectuals in the 1890s accepted this analysis or endorsed this proposal – there were many 'Liberals [who] still cling to their honourable name' – but it is clear that their party allegiance was more than usually volatile during this period.

Whether attached to the Liberal Party or not, what increasingly came

105 For Dicey, see *Memorials of A. V. Dicey, Being Chiefly Letters and Diaries*, ed. R. S. Rait (London, 1925), pp. 110–17; for Goschen, see Thomas J. Spinner Jnr, *George Joachim Goschen: The Transformation of a Victorian Liberal* (Cambridge, 1973), Chs. 6–8; Sidgwick, too, aligned himself with the Conservatives after 1886; see W. C. Havard, *Henry Sidgwick and Later Utilitarian Political Philosophy* (Gainesville, Florida, 1959), p. 26. On the impact of the Home Rule crisis upon this group as a whole, Harvie, *Lights of Liberalism*, Ch. 9, is now the best account.

106 *Daily Chronicle*, 16 July 1895, quoted in A. F. Havighurst, *Radical Journalist: H. W. Massingham (1860–1924)* (Cambridge, 1974), pp. 78–9); *Manchester Guardian*, 1 May 1894.

107 Article on 'Liberalism and Social Reform', in *Encyclopaedia of Social Reform*, p. 812.

108 *Progressive Review*, 1 (1896), 1, 3. As an alternative they allowed that 'if Liberals still cling to their honourable name they must be willing and desirous to assign a new meaning to liberty: it must no longer signify the absence of restraint, but the presence of opportunity'. It is an interesting indication of a changing rhetoric that whereas in the 1830s, say, such exhortations were addressed to 'the party of reform', by the 1890s it was more commonly 'the party of Progress'.

to distinguish the radical intellectual was opposition to Individualism. The term 'radical' itself came to denote not so much attachment to 'peace, retrenchment and reform' (or opposition to 'the peerage, the beerage and war'), as support for a policy of social reform which was to a greater or lesser extent Collectivist.[109] 'Reform' came increasingly to mean 'social reform'. Whatever the realities of party politics during these years, Henry Jones was surely right to reflect on the development of political argument at this level that 'the difference between Socialist and Individualist has become more immediately important, as well as more passionate, than perhaps any other'.[110]

This, I suggest, sketches the appropriate framework in which to situate the dominant political concerns of Hobhouse and his generation. Nonetheless, there are three other contenders with well-established historiographical claims to be considered the central antinomies around which to organize an account of the political-theoretical debates of this period, and which point to conflicts which are in some ways similar to that which I have been discussing. Each, however, is of a different type and operates at a different level of abstraction, and it is important, therefore, to indicate briefly why the opposition between Individualism and Collectivism is not reducible to one of these further antitheses.

The first and most obvious candidate is the opposition between Liberalism and Socialism. This clearly corresponds to a real issue in the history of this period generally, and has figured prominently in many accounts of its political argument.[111] In essence, the claim here is that the 'Socialist Revival' of the 1880s brought a new range of distinctively Socialist arguments into prominence, that in the ensuing decades these arguments became increasingly influential, and that the New Liberal political theory of the 1900s represents a compromise between the traditions of Liberalism and the insights of Socialism. For obvious reasons, this view is frequently associated with studies which concentrate upon the rise of separate working-class political organizations, and which tend to portray the New Liberalism as intellectually and electorally an unstable compound with a low life-expectancy.[112]

From the discussion in the earlier part of this chapter, however, it should be clear that the central difficulty, from the present point of view, in

109 A transition of this kind from 'old' to 'new' radicalism is argued for in Emy, *Liberals, Radicals and Social Politics* (quotation at p. 48).

110 Jones, *Working Faith*, p. 234 (from an article first published in 1905).

111 Helen Merrel Lynd, *England in the Eighteen-Eighties: Toward a Social Basis for Freedom* (2nd edn London, 1969 [first published New York, 1945]) was an important early statement of this view, and it is now, understandably, a widespread one.

112 For example, Paul Thompson, *Socialists, Liberals and Labour: The Struggle for London 1885–1914* (London, 1967).

adopting this framework lies in the definition of Socialism. Defined strictly, it can easily be shown to be peripheral to the mainstream of educated political discussion during this period, whatever its standing in other circles, and hence is an implausible category in terms of which to represent the dominant tensions of that discussion. But any looser definition does not enable a strictly Socialist contribution to be isolated from the general ferment of radical politics and as a historical category it will be parasitic upon a reconstruction of the contemporary use of the term. Moreover, once Socialism is regarded in this way, Liberalism can no longer be treated as an entirely distinct, let alone antithetical, category since it was *within* Liberalism that much of this kind of 'Socialism' would be found. This is not to dismiss the impact of properly Socialist theory during this period, but to suggest that it needs to be seen as a stimulant of a broader debate rather than as commanding the allegiance of one side in that debate. As I have implied above, the so-called 'Socialist Revival' was less a matter of the widespread dissemination of Socialist ideas, and more a dramatic rise in the discussion of the merits and prospects of something referred to as Socialism. Certainly the founding of avowedly Socialist organizations and the importation of the rhetoric of revolutionary Socialism were instrumental in stirring up and giving a sense of urgency to the early stages of this discussion, but even during the early 1880s a larger proportion of the substance of controversy related to the ideas of Henry George or to the 'practical Socialism' of some of the measures undertaken by central and local government. The role of 'doctrinaire Socialism', as it was often called, was to provide a reference-point, one extreme of an alleged spectrum (or, more polemically, the thick end of the wedge), although of course this view, like any other, embodied a particular, and in this case hostile, evaluation of it. Laski was surely right to conclude that 'the trend to collectivism in the last third of the century did not mean an acceptance of socialism... There was, of course, a socialist collectivism, but its influence was less profound than its advocates made it appear.'[113] It remains important to insist, therefore, that in the most general sense of the term the antithesis of 'Socialism' was not 'capitalism', as it largely is today, but 'Individualism'.

The second dichotomy is also well established, but deals with a rather different level of analysis, for it looks at the development in political theory during this period in terms of a change from Utilitarianism to Idealism. It was during this period that Idealism enjoyed its brief reign as the dominant philosophical school in Britain (at least in the universities), and in terms of social and political theory Idealism is traditionally characterized

[113] H. J. Laski, 'The Leaders of Collectivist Thought' in H. Grisewood (ed.), *Ideas and Beliefs of the Victorians* (London, 1949), p. 419.

by its 'organicism', that is, its emphasis upon society as a unity rather than an aggregate, upon the social specification of individual morality, and upon the supreme role of the state as the expression of the general will of the community. It is thus argued that the political and moral individualism of Utilitarianism gives way to the more naturally Collectivist theories of Green and his pupils in the last two decades of the century, and it is this 'change in the philosophical assumptions of Liberalism' which is central to the development of the New Liberalism in particular.[114]

It is certainly the case that Idealism did make available a vocabulary which was capable of providing a more satisfactory conceptualization of some dominant issues in moral and political thought, and that elements of Idealist philosophy are discernible in the writings of several political theorists of this period, including those of some of the New Liberals. But this is too partial an account to offer a satisfactory framework, and is distinctly misleading as a general explanation.

To begin with, the correspondence of either philosophy with convictions about the proper role of the state was not as direct or as simple as this suggests. Although in the late nineteenth century Benthamism was frequently equated with, or at least assumed to be more than contingently related to, Individualism, there is in fact nothing in the structure of the theory to restrict it to such an association. On the contrary, since its primary goal is the maximization of want-satisfaction, without attaching any value to the efforts or putative rights of the individuals concerned, it can rather more readily be seen as providing the rationale of a managerial – or bureaucratic – Collectivist approach to politics. There were historical reasons why, in its heyday, it was generally deployed in attacks upon state action as then practised, which had more to do with the alliance with classical economics and the assault on privilege than with theoretical requirements, internal to Utilitarianism itself. It was inherently pragmatic in its view of the role of the state, and, indeed, one of the few examples of a genuinely Utilitarian contribution to the late-nineteenth-century debate – Jevons' *The State in Relation to Labour*[115] – made a virtue of just this.

Equally, Idealist metaphysics and philosophy could be, and were, used to justify a variety of political preferences. The relationship here is more complex, since any properly Hegelian understanding of the connection

114 Bullock and Shock (eds.), *Liberal Tradition*, p. xliv. This is a pervasive view in the older text-books – Ensor, for example, saw Idealism as 'providing a theory of the state which, in opposition to the individualism of Mill and Spencer, justified the new trend towards collectivism in public affairs' (R. C. K. Ensor, *England 1870–1914* (Oxford, 1936), pp. 162–3) – and is endorsed by several more recent ones, for example, R. K. Webb, *Modern England: From the Eighteenth Century to the Present* (London, 1969), p. 455.

115 W. S. Jevons, *The State in Relation to Labour* (London, 1882).

between 'civil society' and 'the state' was not compatible, without evasive inconsistency, with the traditional Individualist account of the role of the state, and to that extent Idealism could be said to have encouraged a more 'organic' view. But even then, this could still be coupled with opposition to many actual proposals of social reform, and the more Kantian theory of Green, though it spoke of the state as a community whose end is moral, emphasized that the worth of an action lay in the purity of its motivation, which hardly tended to draw attention to what could be achieved by the coercive power of the state. Melvin Richter has persuasively argued that Green's political affinities were rather with the mid-Victorian moralizing of someone like John Bright than with the Collectivists who invoked his name after his death, and certainly many of the next generation of Idealists – such as Bosanquet, Jones or Muirhead – were critics rather than advocates of the Collectivism of the New Liberals.[116] Idealism provided the tools for criticism, at a high level of abstraction, of many of the assumptions and arguments associated with Individualism, but its contribution to less elevated political discussions was ambiguous.

Moreover, this perspective exaggerates the role of both of these philosophies. Even in its diluted forms (and Hegelianism-and-water was more common among its British enthusiasts, lacking the traditional German head for spirits), Idealism was only ever a minority taste, though an ingredient in many of the intellectual cocktails of this period. Similarly, though Utilitarianism had undoubtedly reached a wider audience earlier in the century, it could not really be said to be the prevailing outlook at the beginning of the last quarter of the century. It is quite true that many radical intellectuals in the 1880s and 1890s thought of Utilitarianism as the last coherent theory to hold the field, and as the example of the kind of body of principles now needed as a basis for political action.[117] But this does not mean that political argument of the 1860s and 1870s was dominated by an unalloyed Utilitarianism, and the most cursory glance at

116 Richter, *Politics of Conscience*, esp. pp. 269–73; Collini, 'Hobhouse, Bosanquet and the state', 91–111.

117 For example, in 1894 the prospectus of the Rainbow Circle declared that it would deal with '(1) the reasons why the old Philosophic Radicalism and the Manchester School of Economics can no longer furnish a ground of action in the political sphere; (2) the transition from this school of thought to the so-called "New Radicalism" or Collectivist politics of today; (3) the bases, ethical, economic and political of the newer politics, together with the practical applications and inferences arising therefrom in the actual problems before us at the present time'. A copy of this prospectus is in the Samuel Papers, box A10, and much of it is paraphrased in the opening Editorial of the *Progressive Review* (1 (1896), 1–9), which grew out of the ensuing discussions. On the Rainbow Circle, a radical discussion group whose moving spirits were J. A. Hobson, William Clarke and Ramsay MacDonald, see Bernard Porter, *Critics of Empire: British Radical Attitudes to Colonialism in Africa 1895–1914* (London, 1968), Ch. 6; and L. A. Clark, 'The Liberal Party and Collectivism 1886–1906' (unpublished M.Litt. dissertation, Cambridge, 1957). The identification of Benthamism with pre-Collectivist politics is another issue upon which Dicey has been berated for his eccentric views when he was in fact repeating one of the commonplaces of the day.

the polemical literature reveals that the idiom of the day was far from Benthamite. The moralism which pervades the very different contributions of, say, Mill and Gladstone was far more representative. Certainly, in the generation which included Stephen, Morley and, above all, Sidgwick, Utilitarianism of some kind did not lack advocates, though even in their contributions there is discernible a certain tenderness for the virtues of character and altruism, the non-Utilitarian moral imperatives of the age. Nor is this surprising, for classical Utilitarianism involves an emphasis upon hedonism, a hostility to categorical obligations and an indifference to motives which would have restricted its persuasive appeal in a society whose moral vocabulary was increasingly dominated by the residues of Evangelicalism and humanitarianism. The procession of great names in nineteenth-century thought easily creates the impression of a more general transition from Utilitarianism to Idealism, though even here Hobhouse, at once the foremost New Liberal and most famous critic of Idealism, does not fit in easily. But trawling with these two nets would not catch most of the smaller fish, for they do not well describe the more fundamental process of change in the dominant categories and evaluations at a less abstract level of political argument.

The third possible organizing dichotomy is of a different kind from the previous two, and is to some extent present in both of them. This is the view which sees late-nineteenth-century political argument in terms of the clash between two rival views of freedom, usually characterized as negative and positive freedom.[118] By concentrating on freedom from restraint to pursue expressed wants, the concept of negative liberty, it is argued, encouraged a minimalist view of the role of the state, whereas positive liberty, in its attention to the presence of opportunities for the realization of 'real' wants, is taken to support a more interventionist standpoint. Obviously, these are not arbitrary associations, and they point to a feature of the debate widely noted by contemporaries themselves, itself a recommendation as far as recovering their sense of what was at issue is concerned. But it focuses on too narrow an area to serve the present purpose, and is unsatisfactory in two more concrete ways also.

To begin with, even if the terms of the distinction are accepted, a closer inspection suggests that it fits the facts rather poorly, and, in particular,

[118] This distinction, of course, had some currency at the time, particularly in the work of Green and his followers; see especially his 1881 lecture on 'Liberal Legislation and Freedom of Contract'. Isaiah Berlin's 'Two Concepts of Liberty' (repr. in his *Four Essays on Liberty* (Oxford, 1969)) is the source of the modern discussion, and the distinction has generally been taken for granted by historians; though for an attempt to use it as an explicit organizing principle, see David Nicholls, 'Positive liberty 1880–1914', *American Political Science Review*, LVI (1962), 114–28. As the basis for an analysis of late-nineteenth-century political thought, the distinction is rejected (though on different grounds from those advanced here) in W. L. Weinstein, 'The concept of "liberty" in nineteenth-century English political thought', *Political Studies*, XIII (1965), 145–62.

exaggerates the extent to which 'negative liberty' was dominant in political argument before 1880. It is so in the works of the great Utilitarians, no doubt, and even in that far from Utilitarian tract, *On Liberty*, which was so frequently taken by later critics as the prime example of how a negative conception of liberty sustained a negative conception of the state.[119] But this obscures the extent to which Mill's essay was attacked at the time of its publication for its inadequate and negative conception of liberty,[120] the extent to which, as Brian Harrison notes, 'T. H. Green's "positive" Liberalism was commonplace among his prohibitionist connections',[121] and generally the extent to which there was a 'positive' conception of liberty implicit in the dominant hostility to licence and appetite, the emphasis upon abstinence and self-control, and the imperative to develop 'character' (surely an endorsement *avant la lettre* of Green's dictum that by freedom 'we do not mean merely freedom to do as we like irrespective of what it is that we like...We mean a positive power or capacity of doing or enjoying something worth doing or enjoying, and that, too, something that we do or enjoy in common with others').[122] Providing an individual with the freedom to pursue his 'self-development' is not an acceptance of the negative conception of liberty unless that individual is also recognized as the sole judge of what is to count as his self-development, a degree of subjectivism not countenanced by these dominant imperatives. The point is that both ways of talking about liberty were widespread in England before 1880, and that both could, with the aid of further assumptions and arguments, be made the basis for opposition to state-interference.

The more serious objection to making this distinction the focus of enquiry, however, is the unsoundness of the distinction itself. It has been persuasively argued that freedom-citations always refer, often only implicitly, to the relation between three variables – the freedom *of* agent A *from* obstacle B *to* do action C – and so their force in any particular claim is dependent upon the content given to these three variables.[123] Now this is not to deny that freedom has very often been understood simply as a substantive value in itself and a powerful emotive cry. As we have seen,

119 For examples, see Stefan Collini, 'Liberalism and the legacy of Mill', *Historical Journal*, XX (1977), 237–54, which also suggests that this conscription of *On Liberty* into the late-nineteenth-century debate somewhat misrepresented the point of that famous essay.

120 Well documented in J. C. Rees, *Mill and his Early Critics* (Leicester, 1956).

121 B. Harrison, 'State-intervention and moral reform', 316–17.

122 T. H. Green, *Liberal Legislation and Freedom of Contract* (Oxford, 1881), p. 9.

123 See G. C. MacCallum, 'Negative and positive freedom', *Philosophical Review*, 76 (1967), 312–34. This analysis has since been extended and modified in various ways, and I am indebted to two discussions in particular: Joel Feinberg, *Social Philosophy* (Englewood Cliffs, N.J., 1973) esp. Chs. 1 and 2, and S. I. Benn and W. L. Weinstein, 'Being free to act, and being a free man', *Mind*, LXXX (1971), 194–211. Although parts of the following analysis were suggested by these works, it cannot, in this form, be attributed to any of them.

it was the sacred word in nineteenth-century Liberalism, at once a description of health in the body politic and a cure-all for its ailments. But even in these cases where the variables of the relationship were suppressed or taken for granted, there were conditions which gave such claims their intelligibility, which are in principle recoverable by the historian. Since much of the argument about the role of the state revolved around such claims, it may be worth setting out the analysis of these conditions here. The claim that freedom is being restricted is only plausible where (1) there is a desirability-characterization available for the activity concerned – it must, roughly stated, be capable of being described as an activity which it is understandable to want to engage in; (2) there is something which can be identified as an obstacle to this activity which is removable, or, at least, is the result of human action rather than natural causes; (3) the disagreeable consequences of engaging in the activity without removing the obstacle must be thought to be unreasonably great; (4) the justification available for the obstacle can be shown to be inadequate, that is, it can be overridden or undermined. This is, of course, a purely formal analysis, and tells us nothing about the actual content of any specific claim. But the value of such a scheme is that it directs our attentions to the *kinds* of argument involved in these debates about liberty in a way in which merely assigning the participants to 'positive' and 'negative' teams cannot do. Contributions to these debates characteristically involved suggesting reasons for considering an activity desirable, an obstacle removable, a consequence unacceptable, a justification inadequate and so on, and, as the adjectives indicate, such debate is essentially contentious and is conducted in an inherently evaluative vocabulary.

When reformulated in this way, therefore, this approach can usefully be employed in the service of a more detailed examination of arguments about state-intervention, directing our attention to the questions of whose freedom was involved, of what kinds of desirable activity were being cramped, of what sorts of social arrangements could be identified as obstacles, and so on. It was engagement with questions of this sort which led some contemporary writers to suggest that the conception of freedom most prominent in struggles against aristocratic or clerical authority – 'that a man is free to the extent that he is not interfered with or coerced by other human beings' – was inadequate to describe the goal of social reform, where the conception needed was more like that 'which identifies liberty with, roughly, the individual's power to live according to the best in himself'.[124] This has since been seen as a transition from negative to positive liberty, whereas it can more plausibly be represented as a changing

[124] These are Berlin's canonical definitions of negative and positive liberty.

evaluation of the variable terms involved. Thus the prominence of the so-called positive concept in the late-nineteenth century is better seen as parasitic upon changes in the content of moral and political debate rather than as a cause of them, and hence the presumed dichotomy between negative and positive liberty does not provide an adequate basis upon which to organize an account of such debate.

Finally, this brief consideration of these three further theoretical conflicts also highlights the wide area of common agreement underlying this debate. This was particularly important in the case of those ubiquitous invocations of overriding moral values which give the literature its distinctive tone. Melvin Richter has indicated the way in which intellectuals who share the dominant assumptions and values of their society, but who deplore the extent to which the practices and institutions of that society fail to embody them, will characteristically formulate their criticisms in moral terms.[125] In the present case this response was reinforced by the widespread sense of the 'growing earnestness' of the age, of the 'tendency to carry morality into every sphere of life'.[126] That robust reactionary Fitzjames Stephen grumbled in 1885 that 'England seems to have become a huge Gladstone with a conscience like the liver of a Strasbourg goose', but in the succeeding generation only a few unorthodox characters complained of the fact that it was 'an age in which many moralists desire to force morals into every part of life and art'.[127]

The political form of this moralism is evident in the phrases which are intoned like hallelujahs in the litany of every reforming group of the period: the ideal of service, the duty to contribute to the common good, the need to make the best of oneself, the duty of self-development, and so on. Far from being the exclusive property of Collectivist reformers, these ideals

[125] Melvin Richter, 'Intellectual and class alienation: Oxford Idealist diagnoses and prescriptions', *Archives Européennes de Sociologie*, VII (1966), 1–26. Richter distinguished this response from, on the one hand, that which, accepting both values and practices, makes mainly technical criticism, and, on the other, that which accepts neither and so resorts to sociological or ideological criticism.

[126] A. Marshall, *Principles of Economics*, p. 750; Hubert Bland, quoted in David S. Thatcher, *Nietzsche in England 1890–1914: The Growth of a Reputation* (Toronto, 1970), p. 223 (Bland's remark dates from 1898). One contributor to *The Encyclopaedia of Social Reform* summarized the conventional wisdom: 'Perhaps no characteristic of the present efforts for social reform are [*sic*] more hopeful and more important than the deepening emphasis now placed – however far we may yet be from placing all the emphasis we ought – on the moral element in social reform. A hundred years ago the key-word in social reform was "natural rights", and in economics "laissez-faire". Today the key-word in reform is "cooperation" and in economics "character". If this may seem to some too optimistic a view, we remind them that individualist, socialist, and even anarchist reformers all seek cooperation, while in economics the reason why individualist economists fear socialism is that they believe that it will deteriorate character, and the reason why socialist economists seek socialism is their belief that under individualism character is deteriorating' (p. 895).

[127] Stephen quoted in Roach, 'Liberalism and the Victorian intelligentsia', 71; Havelock Ellis, writing in 1896, quoted in Thatcher, *Nietzsche in England*, p. 122. Given his sexual habits, Bland perhaps had more cause than most to feel vulnerable to 'the danger of being done to death by Ethical Societies' (quoted in Thatcher, p. 223).

were the very heart of the hegemonic assumptions of the age. For example, both Bosanquet and Sidgwick took for granted, in contesting the claims of Collectivism, that 'moral socialism' – defined negatively as the antithesis of 'egoism' and 'the materialist or Epicurean view of life', or positively as that 'genuine regard to the interests of others' – was 'the only thing for which any healthy human being at the bottom of his heart cares a single straw'.[128] But the beliefs which gave content to these clichés – about what activities constituted the 'development' of the 'self', for example – were not made explicit because, presumably, they were not the subject of dispute. The rational, earnest, self-improving, altruistic individual was the ghost at the feast in late-Victorian political debate. It is to the significantly named 'immoralists' – such as the advocates of Ibsenism in the 1890s or of Nietzscheanism in the 1900s, outside the mainstream of political discussion – that we must turn for an explicit attack upon the prevailing hierarchy of values or for a rejection of what Wilde called 'the sickly cant about duty'.[129]

In addressing the arguments against greater state-intervention, therefore, writers like Hobhouse were to a large extent working new patterns out of a common cloth. This set limits both to their theoretical ambitions and to the forensic material available for their execution. In tracing the development of Hobhouse's thought in the following chapters, I shall continually draw attention to the context of argument sketched here, in the belief, to misquote only slightly, that men make their own theory but they do not do so in circumstances of their own choosing.

[128] Bernard Bosanquet, 'The Antithesis between Individualism and Socialism Philosophically Considered' (1890), repr. in *The Civilization of Christendom and Other Studies* (London, 1893), pp. 356–7; Sidgwick, *Elements of Politics*, p. 38.

[129] Oscar Wilde, *The Soul of Man under Socialism*, first published 1891; republished in *The Collected Works of Oscar Wilde* (repr. London, 1969 [first published 1908]), VIII, p. 326. Shaw and others looked to Ibsen to unseat 'duty, unselfishness, idealism, sacrifice' from their primacy; quoted in Thatcher, *Neitzsche in England*, p. 177. Thatcher's book provides a more general and more useful guide to turn-of-the-century 'immoralism' than his title suggests.

Part Two: Liberalism

2: OXFORD COLLECTIVIST

This chapter will examine Hobhouse's early life and the evolution of his political views up to 1897, when, at the age of thirty-three, he left Oxford to become a leader-writer for the *Manchester Guardian*. But 'personal' and 'social' are merely convenient abstractions, and this concentration on Hobhouse's development is also a slice cut from the social and intellectual history of the New Liberalism. One has come to expect a certain sort of background for the radical and social-reforming intellectuals of this period. Sons of the genteel but not rich middle and professional classes, from religious homes (Anglican clergymen predominate among the fathers) set in the country or smaller provincial towns, they most commonly went to public schools and then read Greats at Oxford, losing their faith and gaining a sense of guilt about their social advantages in the process, and then came to London to do social or journalistic work of some kind. Hobhouse's background meets one's expectations splendidly.

Leonard Trelawny Hobhouse was born in 1864 in the village of St Ive, near Liskeard in Cornwall.[1] His father, the Venerable Reginald Hobhouse, was an undistinguished member of a distinguished family: after a mediocre career at Eton and Balliol, he took Orders, and in 1844, as a result of his father's political connections with Sir Robert Peel, was appointed to the Crown living of St Ive. Being an unambitious man, he remained Rector of this small rural parish until his death fifty-one years later. He was diligent but not unduly energetic in the performance of his duties; neither visiting his parishioners nor proselytizing in the (largely Methodist) neighbourhood formed any part of his conception of his vocation, and he regularly preached

[1] Information on Hobhouse's family background is contained in J. A. Hobson and Morris Ginsberg, *L. T. Hobhouse, His Life and Work* (London, 1931); L. T. Hobhouse and J. L. Hammond, *Lord Hobhouse: A Memoir* (London, 1905); Anna Ruth Fry, *Emily Hobhouse* (London, 1929); John Fisher, *That Miss Hobhouse* (London, 1971) – though this last is unreliable and often inaccurate and must be checked against the other sources. I have also drawn on the collection of Hobhouse's papers, which mainly contains material of family interest.

to congregations of seven or eight people. His political and religious opinions were unbendingly orthodox and, as one of his children wrote later, 'he was rather inflexible and narrow in his views'. Far from seeking to widen his outlook, 'he strictly ruled out all that was modern in thought and science from his reading'.[2] In 1851 he had married a daughter of the West Country gentry family of Trelawny, and although in the following thirteen years she bore him eight children, the death of the two eldest in infancy seems to have dried up the well of his never very abundant emotions. The gloom which his presence cast over the rectory was not lessened by his being a semi-invalid for the later part of his life.

'With a father whose sternness with himself showed itself in sternness to his children,' Emily later remarked, 'a little over-indulgence in the mother was needed, and until her death in 1880 she was the medium between us and our reserved and silent father.'[3] This was especially the case with Leonard, who was very close to his mother, being, as he later recognized, 'the spoilt youngest'.[4] Relations with his father were strained during Leonard's youth, and he wrote of him many years later: 'He was remorseless in exacting duty and the repair of neglect, and a few mild words of disapproval fell from him with tons' weight...He was for us all an incarnation of justice and iron rectitude...perhaps not so entirely to the good, singularly immovable in his resolutions when once deliberately formed. His sole guide was duty, and of the psychological effects of this regime he seems to have had no glimpse.' The greatest oppression of all 'came from the doctrine of eternal punishment with which the air of a Cornish parish of that period was over-charged and which certainly affected my mind at times'.[5]

The relation between this upbringing and Hobhouse's later personality and opinions is a speculative matter,[6] but it is clear that at the time his intellectual identity was largely shaped by this oedipal antagonism. While at Marlborough, Hobhouse abandoned his inherited religious beliefs, and Hobson later wrote of 'the strong emotional strains set up in adolescence

[2] Emily Hobhouse, quoted in Fry, *Emily Hobhouse*, p. 20.

[3] Fry, *Emily Hobhouse*, pp. 21–2.

[4] Quoted in Fry, *Emily Hobhouse*, p. 36.

[5] Quoted in Fry, *Emily Hobhouse*, pp. 37–8.

[6] In general terms, connections have been suggested between the psychological effect of a strict moral upbringing and a later tendency to project the resulting doubts about one's own moral worth as strenuous moral judgements on the world (see, for a restrained version of this account of the relation between personality and political opinion, Robert E. Lane, *Political Thinking and Consciousness: the Private Life of the Political Mind* (Chicago, 1969), esp. pp. 211–15). This is an approach which might prove fruitful in looking at that generation of late-Victorian reformers who rejected the religious faith in which they were brought up but who continued, with not a little anguish, to judge themselves and the political world by exacting moral standards. It is certainly an approach, concentrating as it does on the changing cultural determinants of character, which would be preferable to the endless repetition of the claim that they were seeking a 'substitute faith' for their lost Evangelical beliefs.

by the intellectual break away from the stern religious orthodoxy of his home', while his undergraduate contemporary, Hubert Llewellyn Smith, recalled that 'Hobhouse, on first entering college life, seemed irritable in mind and often moody, due partly, no doubt, to the recent unsettlement of accepted religious opinions.'[7]

His inherited political attitude suffered a similar fate. He had grown up in the status-conscious surroundings of the genteel Toryism of a decaying branch of the landed classes, remarking once early in his school career 'how unpleasant it must be to have a surname like Butcher or Chandler which showed the low origins of one's family'. But as a school-friend testified, 'some time before he left Marlborough he became a keen radical'.[8] In this process, an important part can often be played not only by the cultural style of a generation, but by identification with an older figure more congenial than the father. In Leonard Hobhouse's case, this latter role was filled by his uncle, Arthur, Lord Hobhouse. Unlike his elder brother, Reginald, Arthur had had a brilliant career at Eton and Oxford, where he took a First in Greats. Leonard remarked in writing a life of his uncle – itself an act of almost filial piety both in conception and execution – that it had been a constant challenge to his own remarkable precocity to be told by his family that his uncle 'could read when he was two, learnt latin when he was four, and went to school when he was six'.[9] Owing to his father's illness and to the Victorian habit of taking holidays as an extended family, Leonard saw a good deal of his uncle as he grew up. Emily, Leonard's closest companion at home, recalled their enjoyment of being with their uncle and aunt, 'feeling the great happiness of their delightful company, due to their wide interests and sympathies, and their charm of character'. In a phrase revealing the significance of the relationship, she added, 'Since I was six years old I had been closely linked to my uncle, and I always looked upon him and my aunt as my mental parents.'[10]

It was while Leonard was at Marlborough that Arthur Hobhouse, whose sympathies were strongly Gladstonian, began to take an active part in politics, contesting Westminster in 1880 in harness with John Morley. Leonard's letters of the early eighties reveal his intense interest in current politics and his fervent support for the Radical cause. Morley, Bradlaugh and Bright are his heroes,[11] Radicals, like his uncle, whose distinguishing

[7] Hobson and Ginsberg, *L. T. Hobhouse*, pp. 21, 23.

[8] Maurice Llewellyn Davies, quoted in Hobson and Ginsberg, *L. T. Hobhouse*, p. 20. Hobhouse's father seems to have disapproved of his children having any close contact with members of the lower orders; see Fisher, *That Miss Hobhouse*, pp. 22–3.

[9] Hobhouse and Hammond, *Lord Hobhouse*, p. 3. Cf. Fisher, *That Miss Hobhouse*, pp. 14–15. Emily recalled a similar precociousness in Leonard's 'intellectual powers'; Fry, *Emily Hobhouse*, pp. 22–3.

[10] Quoted in Fry, *Emily Hobhouse*, pp. 33, 232.

[11] See, for example, his letters to Emily of Juny 1881, and Feb. and March 1882 in the Hobhouse Papers.

characteristic was the relentlessly exalted moral tone of their political pronouncements, particularly on foreign affairs.[12] In March 1882 he hopes that in visiting their uncle Emily will meet 'some other glorious Radicals' such as Morley, Bradlaugh and Dilke, and was later 'surprised and sorry' to hear 'that Uncle Arthur condescended to go to the house of a man who has recently introduced perhaps the most disgracefully intolerant bill of modern times. I refer, of course, to the measure recently proposed by Lord Rosebery in the House of Lords to prevent Atheists from sitting in parliament.'[13] But his greatest esteem was reserved for 'the greatest and best man of this century – I allude of course to John Stuart Mill'.[14] He praised *Liberty* and *Representative Government*, and since in his first term at Oxford he reported, 'I have read through Mill's *Subjection of Women* which is very good though I think in some parts inferior to his other works',[15] it seems that he was already well acquainted with Mill's major writings. He also admiringly read Spencer and Mazzini, and moved democratic and republican motions in the school debating society.[16] The fact that he was rebuked by his father for his 'extreme' opinions can only have confirmed him in them at this stage.[17] Certainly when he went up to Corpus Christi College, Oxford in 1883, he was 'in politics...a firm radical. In religion...an (if possible yet firmer) agnostic.'[18]

Both politically and philosophically, Oxford was the formative experience for Hobhouse. He arrived in October 1883, the month which more than any other marked the beginning of that great stirring of the national conscience over 'the social question' which dominated the rest of the decade. In that month appeared *The Bitter Cry of Outcast London*, a pamphlet revealing the abysmal living conditions in the London slums. Thanks to a campaign based upon it in *The Pall Mall Gazette* by W. T. Stead, it produced 'a spasm of public emotion'.[19] *The Bitter Cry* was

[12] Lord Hobhouse was a vigorous advocate of the application of the standards of personal morality to international relations: 'Precisely the same moral laws and sanctions apply to nations as to the individuals who compose them.' (Quoted in Fry, *Emily Hobhouse*, pp. 65–6.) His own personal standards were high: Beatrice Webb, herself no abandoned hedonist, found him 'thoughtful and conscientious to an almost painful degree'. Diary entry for 21 Oct. 1888, in Beatrice Webb, *My Apprenticeship*, pp. 308–9.

[13] To Emily, 5 and 26 March 1882, Hobhouse Papers. Rosebery always remained a particular object of Hobhouse's political hatred: see for example 'The Foreign Policy of Collectivism', *Economic Review*, IX (1899), 202.

[14] To Emily, 4 June 1882, Hobhouse Papers.

[15] To Emily, 4 June 1882, n.d. (in bag marked 'Letters from Marlborough'), and 25 Oct. 1883, Hobhouse Papers.

[16] Hobson and Ginsberg, *L. T. Hobhouse*, pp. 18–21. See also an article in the school magazine, *The Marlburian*, for June 1883 comparing Mill and Mazzini 'as types of the two different classes of Radicalism which have had most effect on the course of 19th century politics' (XVIII, 81).

[17] To Emily, n.d. (the reference to John Bright's resignation over the bombardment of Alexandria suggests July 1882).

[18] Oliver Elton, Hobhouse's senior at both Marlborough and Corpus, as quoted in Hobson and Ginsberg, *L. T. Hobhouse*, p. 23.

[19] *The Spectator*, quoted in Wohl, '*Bitter Cry of Outcast London*'.

concerned with the moral and religious as much as the physical degradation of the poor, and a large part of the controversy which it created centred on what 'the educated classes' could do to remedy this. This was the theme of an address given by Canon Samuel Barnett, Rector of St Jude's, Whitechapel, when in November 1883 he made the most significant of his many trips to Oxford. In a characteristic speech, he lamented that the combination of social and geographical distance made 'friendship between classes almost impossible', and so the poor were deprived of 'contact with those who possess the means of higher life'. For that reason he urged that 'residence among the poor is...a simple way in which Oxford men may serve their generation...and do something to weld classes into society'.[20] His call was answered enthusiastically, and in 1884 Toynbee Hall opened in Whitechapel with its first batch of Oxford residents.

It was named in commemoration of Arnold Toynbee, Balliol Tutor and economic historian, who had died in April 1883 at the age of thirty-one. His reputation in Oxford as a leader of the new movement of social reform was immense, and his personal example of involvement and self-sacrifice on behalf of the poor was widely quoted.[21] In the war of words discussed in the previous chapter, he was called a 'Socialist', but the nature of his 'Socialism' emerges from remarks such as that of his pupil F. C. Montague, who wrote: 'The redistribution of wealth and the diffusion of political power he valued less as ends in themselves than as means to the attainment by all of a better, purer and more spiritual life.'[22] As his close friend, Alfred Milner remarked: 'In this spiritual ideal lay the profound difference between his point of view and [that of] materialistic Socialism'; 'in his view, nothing that tended to discourage self-reliance or to weaken character could possibly lead even to material well-being'.[23] In these terms, a new 'Oxford Movement' was under way. As *The Oxford Magazine* observed in November 1883: 'The question has been asked "Is the new Oxford Movement to be a Socialistic one?", and if this is interpreted to mean "Is the most living interest in Oxford now that in social questions?", the answer must be distinctly, Yes!...A new faith, with Professor Green for its founder, Arnold Toynbee as its martyr, and various societies for its

20 Quoted in Henrietta Barnett, *Canon Barnett: His Life, Work and Friends* (London, 1918), pp. 307–8. See also J. A. R. Pimlott, *Toynbee Hall* (London, 1935), Ch. 1.

21 See Milner, *Arnold Toynbee*; Gertrude Toynbee (ed.), *Reminiscences and Letters of Joseph and Arnold Toynbee* (London, n.d. [?1910]); Richter, *Politics of Conscience*.

22 F. C. M., 'Arnold Toynbee', *Oxford Magazine*, I, 151 (18 April 1883).

23 Milner, *Arnold Toynbee*, pp. 54–5. The best statements of Toynbee's views are in '*Progress and Poverty*': *A Criticism of Mr Henry George* (London, 1883), and his lecture 'Are Radicals Socialists?' in *Lectures on the Industrial Revolution in England* (repr., with Introduction by T. S. Ashton, Newton Abbot, 1969 [first published London, 1884]). Toynbee's most famous statement about the 'sins' of the rich against the poor is in '*Progress and Poverty*', p. 53, but it is worth pointing out that this confession of middle-class guilt ends with a typically moralizing demand that in return the working class should 'lead a better life'.

propaganda, is alive among us.'[24] As Arthur Acland, an intimate of both Green and Toynbee, and a leading exponent of this new faith, wrote in his diary in March 1885: 'I think Oxford is more influenced by the idea "whatever our future is we must try to do some *good*" than it ever was before.'[25]

Hobhouse had left school as a Gladstonian Liberal of his uncle's type, but through his involvement with this 'Oxford Movement' in the mid eighties he was led to a more radical position on domestic politics. In his first term, he reported that 'the housing of the poor' was 'the burning question of the hour, or perhaps rather of the minute', adding rather loftily, 'it will, I think, soon be settled'.[26] He soon began to speak at debates, both in college and at the Union, in favour of advanced radical causes: he defended democracy and called for the abolition of university seats; he advocated Home Rule, local option, the abolition of the House of Lords, and support for *The Radical Programme*.[27] He was elected President of the Russell Club, the University Radical Society, where he gave papers on such favourite topics as Mazzini, and 'Radicalism Past and Future'. Of the latter he reported: 'I took a great deal of trouble about it. I was a long time writing it and read the whole of Wallace's *Land Nationalization* and Mill's *Political Economy*, besides essays of Herbert Spencer and others.'[28]

Such radical causes were greatly in the minority at Oxford at this time among both dons and undergraduates. In December 1885, *The Oxford Magazine* observed that as a result of Gladstone's and Chamberlain's extremism 'seldom has there been such strength of conservative opinion in Oxford', and in June 1885 it noted the great unpopularity of Home Rule in the University, suggesting that it was supported by 'only seventeen senior members and not many more undergraduates'.[29] Hobhouse was almost invariably on the losing side in debates, and his extreme opinions were remarked upon. For example, in one letter to his sister he proudly announced: 'Yesterday week I abolished the monarchy at the C.C.C debate but found only one supporter, the common opinion being that it was a disgrace to the college. Whereat I laughed.' With equal satisfaction he

[24] *Oxford Magazine*, I, 384 (21 Nov. 1883).

[25] Quoted in Roger Davidson, 'Sir Hubert Llewellyn Smith and Labour Policy 1886–1916' (unpublished Ph.D. dissertation, Cambridge, 1971), p. 5. Llewellyn Smith was Hobhouse's exact contemporary and close friend at Corpus. Note also Davidson's judgement that 'in the years 1883–7...Oxford experienced an unprecedented emotional outburst of concern over "the social problem"'.

[26] To Emily, 2 Dec. 1883, Hobhouse Papers.

[27] *Oxford Magazine*, IV, 26–7 (3 Feb. 1886), 41 (10 Feb. 1886), 313 (27 Oct. 1886); V, 42 (2 Feb. 1887), 65 (9 Feb. 1887), 81 (16 Feb. 1887).

[28] To Emily, n.d., Hobhouse Papers; *Oxford Magazine*, IV, 60 (17 Feb. 1886).

[29] *Oxford Magazine*, III, 427 (9 Dec. 1885); IV, 253 (16 June 1886). This figure was challenged by an anonymous correspondent in the next issue, IV, 270.

informed another correspondent that 'the Tories in the College are very wrath' about his most recent Debating Society performance.[30] During these years Hobhouse derived evident pleasure from this defiance of the prevailing social and political opinions. In this connection it must be remembered that Oxford was still dominated by the sons of the noble and the wealthy, who were generally conservative in politics, and athletic rather than intellectual by inclination. For clever Scholars from genteel but relatively impoverished backgrounds such as Hobhouse's, their Oxford identity partly derived from opposition to this association of wealth, snobbery and sport. Personal circumstances and political opinions are obviously intertwined here. For example, Hobhouse's earliest letters from Oxford are filled with his financial anxieties. 'One spends an awful lot of money here. They rook you on every conceivable pretext.'[31] His particular anxieties were compounded by the difficulty of extracting the necessary sums from his never over-generous father. It is a telling indication of his concern about money at this time that he often went to the Oxford Union to write his letters home 'as I can write here without paying for paper or stamps'.[32]

Hobhouse's political commitment was further increased by his being included among that group of undergraduates 'carefully picked out for sound radical principles, including temperance and women's suffrage, or else for cricket'[33] who were invited to vacation parties at the baronial house of the 'Radical Countess', the redoubtable Lady Howard.[34] She encouraged 'above all an interest in causes, causes to work for, fight for, or at any rate argue for', and as Hobhouse reported from his first visit in August 1884, 'the atmosphere of the house is very political, the changes being rung on Lords, Franchise, and Egypt'.[35] Through such radical connections, Hobhouse became a member of Acland's 'Inner Ring' and of Alfred Marshall's discussion group on social and economic questions at Balliol,

30 To Emily, n.d., Hobhouse Papers; to Mary Howard, Dec. 1886, quoted in Hobson and Ginsberg, *L. T. Hobhouse*, p. 22.

31 To Emily, 25 Oct. 1883, Hobhouse Papers. Corpus in the eighties evidently had more than its share of the traditional English antagonism between the 'hearties' and the 'swots'; see Henry Newbolt, *My World as in My Time* (London, 1932), pp. 95–6.

32 To Maud (an older sister), 19 Oct. 1883, Hobhouse Papers.

33 Gilbert Murray, *An Unfinished Autobiography* (London, 1960), p. 87.

34 On Lady Howard, see Dorothy Henley, *Rosalind Howard, Countess of Carlisle* (London, 1958), and Charles Roberts, *The Radical Countess: The History of the Life of Rosalind Countess of Carlisle* (Carlisle, 1962). Lady Howard's distinguishing characteristics were her dogmatic radicalism and her seven unmarried daughters. The chosen young men were supposed to evince a suitable interest in both. While two of Hobhouse's close friends, Gilbert Murray and Charles Roberts, came up to expectations on both counts, Hobhouse's political zeal was perhaps too single-minded on these occasions, though by 1891 he had controlled it sufficiently to concentrate on the successful wooing of Nora Hadwen, the daughter of a Yorkshire manufacturer.

35 Murray, *Unfinished Autobiography*, p. 101; to Emily, 2 Aug. 1884, Hobhouse Papers.

both of which were increasingly preoccupied with the question of what could be done to improve the welfare of the working classes. He was also an early member of Sidney Ball's Social Science Club, the purpose of which was quite definitely 'to find a way to the solution of social difficulties by practical investigation'.[36] Hobhouse had the conventional doubts about his capacity to do any good in this direction. In December 1884 he confided to Mary Howard: 'You know I am a little speculative by nature, and am always in danger of caring more for knowing truth than for doing good, e.g. for finding out what is the best reform to be carried than for the real effect on the happiness of the people that it will have when carried.'[37] Nonetheless, as an undergraduate he compaigned for temperance in the neighbouring villages, became interested in the cause of the agricultural labourers, and appears to have contemplated a period of residence at Toynbee Hall, by then established as Oxford's post-graduate school of social work.[38] In 1889 he was still hoping to spend a term in London doing 'some social and political work in a very small way'.[39]

By that date, however, Hobhouse's philosophical inclinations and the class of his degree had determined his career. A First in Greats in June 1887 had been followed by a summer of intensive work in preparation for Fellowship exams in September, in which he was triumphantly successful, being elected to a Prize Fellowship at Merton.[40] But the strain brought on the first of those nervous breakdowns which were to plague him for the rest of his life, and which surely contributed to that volatility of humour and those frequent fits of depression which characterized his personality. The doctors ordered him to take 'a complete rest'.[41] He went on a long recuperative holiday with the Howards to Egypt, where he was later joined

[36] Hobson and Ginsberg, *L. T. Hobhouse*, p. 23; Harold Spender, *The Fire of Life: A Book of Memories* (London, n.d. [?1926]), pp. 12–13, 105; Davidson, 'Llewellyn Smith', p. 9; W. A. S. Hewins, *The Apologia of an Imperialist* (2 vols., London, 1929), I, p. 16.

[37] Quoted in Hobson and Ginsberg, *L. T. Hobhouse*, p. 27.

[38] Hobson and Ginsberg, *L. T. Hobhouse*, p. 22; *Oxford Magazine*, IV, 78 (24 Feb. 1886); H. Barnett, *Canon Barnett*, p. 413. The visit of John Burnett to Oxford, recalled Llewellyn Smith, 'gave a great impetus to the intelligent interest of young Oxford in organized labour'. (Quoted in Davidson, 'Llewellyn Smith', p. 9.). On Burnett, see Joyce M. Bellamy and John Saville (eds.), *Dictionary of Labour Biography*, II (London, 1974), pp. 71–6.

[39] Hobson and Ginsberg, *L. T. Hobhouse*, p. 26. By then, many of Hobhouse's close friends among his generation had taken this step; for example, residents at Toynbee Hall between Aug. 1886 and Dec. 1889 included J. A. Spender, C. R. Ashbee, Harold Spender, Vaughan Nash, John Sinclair, Hubert Llewellyn Smith, F. S. Marvin, and Charles Roberts. (See the list at the beginning of Pimlott, *Toynbee Hall*, p. 1.)

[40] Llewellyn Smith to his mother, 12 Sept. 1887 and n.d.; Hobhouse to Mrs Llewellyn Smith, 25 Oct. 1887, where he hopes that the Fellowship 'will enable me to follow out the lines of work for which I feel myself most fitted. For some months my chief anxiety has been how I should be able to gain my bread and butter and yet work at the things which I wished. I hope the problem is on the way to solution now.' Llewellyn Smith Papers.

[41] Hobhouse to Maud, 19 Feb. 1888, Hobhouse Papers.

by Sidney Ball.[42] He had recovered sufficiently to be pursuing his own research again in the Michaelmas Term in 1888, and in 1890 he was appointed to an assistant tutorship at his old college, being elected to a Fellowship there in 1894. So during these years his time was largely taken up by those ageless pursuits of the Oxford Greats Tutor–lecturing on Aristotle, teaching the rudiments of philosophy to undergraduates and writing on the problems of epistemology.[43]

His political activities, however, increased rather than lessened after his graduation. In particular, he became more closely involved with the labour movement which was gathering pace in the late 1880s. He took a leading part in the campaign to unionize the local agricultural labourers, and organized meetings to agitate for higher wages.[44] Together with Arthur Sidgwick, he became a trustee of the Oxfordshire Agricultural Labourers' Union, and was well acquainted with the leaders of the New Unionism such as Tom Mann and Ben Tillett. At the time of the Great Dock Strike he was visiting Toynbee Hall, from where he wrote enthusiastically: 'I think the mere fact that the men have won is so good. It seems to one like a turning point in the history of labour.'[45] This involvement with the labour movement met personal needs too: after one enthusiastic meeting he wrote to his future wife, 'I like talking to the village people. I understand them and feel *en rapport* with them. I feel friends with them, and it always makes me feel happy.'[46] He continued to work for various other good causes, complaining in 1889 about 'the Toynbee Hall work [which] consumes a good deal of energy', and in January 1891 his future wife wrote to Emily that 'he is doing a good deal of social work this term as well as lecturing, and sounds busier than ever'.[47]

His closest companion-in-arms in these activities was Sidney Ball, Greats Tutor at St John's and, as G. D. H. Cole later discovered, 'the recognized head of university socialism'.[48] For, as Hobson observed of Hobhouse during this period, 'his economic views are visibly ripening towards

[42] See the letters to his family between Dec. 1887 and April 1888. On Sidney Ball, see below, pp. 59–60; 74 and n.

[43] There is an account of Hobhouse's Oxford life in Hobson and Ginsberg, *L. T. Hobhouse*, pp. 24–36. For further discussion of the nature of his own research during this period see below, Ch. 5.

[44] P. L. R. Horn, 'The farm workers, the dockers and Oxford University', *Oxoniensia*, 32 (1967), 60–70; Hobson and Ginsberg, *L. T. Hobhouse*, pp. 28–30; Herbert Samuel, *Memoirs* (London, 1945), pp. 13–17; Arthur Sidgwick to Hobhouse, 1 Oct. 1892, Hobhouse Papers.

[45] Hobson and Ginsberg, *L. T. Hobhouse*, p. 27.

[46] Quoted in Hobson and Ginsberg, *L. T. Hobhouse*, p. 29. There was perhaps something of the educated Englishman's ambivalent distaste for his own reserve here: compare his earlier reflection after observing the uninhibited social behaviour of a group of young Spaniards: 'I thought this behaviour was so much more agreeable than the reserve of an English public-school varsity fellow like self.' To Emily, 2 Aug. 1884, Hobhouse Papers.

[47] To Emily, 13 Oct. 1889; Nora Hadwen to Emily, 29 Jan. 1891, Hobhouse Papers.

[48] Oona Howard Ball, *Sidney Ball: Memories and Impressions of 'An Ideal Don'* (Oxford, 1923), p. 228.

Socialism', and here Ball was, as Hobhouse's pupil and friend Barbara Bradby (who later married J. L. Hammond) recalled, 'his chief ally, and alone, I think, among the dons shared his socialist views'.[49] They organized meetings together, and attracted several of the leading spokesmen for Socialism and the labour movement to speak. Ball was a member of the Fabian Society, and although Hobhouse never seems to have joined, he was very close to the Fabians at this time.[50] He met Wallas, Shaw and Bland, as well as Beatrice Potter, and in February 1889 had a long conversation with Sidney Webb who 'is one of the most interesting men I have met. We simply sat and talked and talked and settled the affairs of the universe one after another.' But he added cautiously: 'I don't see my way with the same clearness, but we may come to anything. Think of the change of opinions in the last five years.'[51] Although, as we shall see, Hobhouse later became fiercely critical of the Fabians, their early desire 'to preach socialism as a faith, as a scientific theory, as a judgement of morality on the facts of life' accorded closely with Hobhouse's own attitude.[52] Several years later, in the course of a bitter denunciation of the Fabians, Hobhouse admitted that

> in its opening years, the Fabian leaders did good service as missionaries and educators. They saw clearly, and exposed with impassioned reasoning, some of the causes of social misery, urging, with eloquence and logic, a large policy of practical reform, based upon a firm recognition that the State is not a thing apart from and above the people, but simply the people organized for all purposes of self-help to which such collective action can be made adaptable.[53]

He recalled how in 'the enthusiasm of the 80s' and early 1890s such a transformation seemed imminent, an expectation widely shared among 'progressives' at this time.[54] As he wrote elsewhere, it seemed 'to many of us' as if 'the watchwords of the old Liberalism' were 'worn out phrases'. 'We began to hear them with a certain impatience. The old Liberalism, we thought, had done its work...What was needed was to build a social

[49] Hobson and Ginsberg, *L. T. Hobhouse*, pp. 30, 35. The anonymous author of 'Modern Oxford from a Progressive Point of View', *Progressive Review*, I (1896), 212–24, bracketed them together as the only exponents of Socialism in the University.

[50] Ball joined the Society in the 1880s, though an Oxford branch was not formed until 1895. Beatrice Webb's remark in her diary at the end of 1895 that 'Leonard Hobhouse is recruiting for us at Oxford' is as ambiguous, teasing, and possibly unreliable as much else in that all too quotable document. (*Our Partnership* (London, 1948), p. 92.) Beatrice's elder sister, Margaret, was married to Hobhouse's cousin, Henry Hobhouse.

[51] Hobson and Ginsberg, *L. T. Hobhouse*, p. 30; Horn, 'The farm workers'; Hobhouse to Emily, n.d. (obviously late 1880s), Hobhouse Papers.

[52] Sidney Webb in an 1886 Fabian lecture, quoted in A. M. McBriar, *Fabian Socialism and English Politics 1884–1918* (Cambridge, 1962), p. 14. The best treatment of the early Fabians which brings out the transition from Radical-Liberal attitudes to a strongly moral Socialism – a development not unlike Hobhouse's – is now Wolfe, *Radicalism to Socialism*.

[53] [L. T. Hobhouse,] 'The Career of Fabianism', *Nation*, 30 March 1907.

[54] 'Career of Fabianism.'

democracy on the basis so prepared and for that we needed new formulas, new inspirations. The old individualism was standing in our way, and we were for cutting it down.'[55] This is the context in which to see Hobhouse's political writings of his Oxford period, when he was an enthusiastic advocate of, as he put it, 'those forms of Socialistic aspiration which may be included under the wider name of Collectivism'.[56]

The Labour Movement (1893) is a vigorous exposition of such Socialistic aspirations, written when Hobhouse's anti-Individualist sentiment was at its most belligerent and most sanguine. Its central thesis is that the Cooperative Movement, Trade Unionism, municipal and state Socialism are complementary attempts to achieve a common end, 'the collective control of industry and its products by the community'.[57] It is a plea for each of these groups to overcome their long-standing suspicion of and even hostility towards each other, and to recognize not only that they were working towards a common end but that each had an indispensable part to play in its successful fulfilment.

> The remuneration of the workers (of every kind) being fixed by the Trade Unions in agreement with the public at large, the surplus remaining would pass to the community for common purposes; the profits of enterprise going to communities of consumers, whether in the form of Cooperative Societies, Municipal Bodies, or the State; while Rent and Interest would go directly to the Municipality or the nation. Thus each part of the Labour Movement has its appropriate part of the general problem to work out, and united they give hope of a complete solution.[58]

What is not apparent from the text alone if read in isolation from the literature of contemporary political debate is what a very Fabian book it is. Hobhouse's later hostility to the Fabians, and Fabianism's own development into a far more opportunistic and elitist doctrine, have between them obscured this relationship.[59] But not only does the main argument

[55] *Democracy and Reaction* (repr., ed. P. F. Clarke, Brighton, 1972 [first published London, 1904]), pp. 213–14. Hobhouse frequently recalled the contrast between the optimism of this period and the reaction which set in in the middle 1890s: e.g. 'Foreign Policy', 8; 'Career of Fabianism'; 'The Prospects of Liberalism', *Contemporary Review*, XCIII (1908), 349.

[56] 'Foreign Policy', 198.

[57] L. T. Hobhouse, *The Labour Movement*, with a Preface by R. B. Haldane, M.P. (London, 1893), p. 76. 2nd edn, with minor changes, 1897, repr. 1905, 1906; 3rd edn, completely revised (and without Haldane's Preface), 1912. (This edn has been reissued with an Introduction by Philip P. Poirier, Brighton, 1974.) All quotations are from the 1st edn unless otherwise specified.

[58] *Labour Movement*, p. 79.

[59] Philip P. Poirier does note Hobhouse's indebtedness to Beatrice Potter, but, like most commentators, seems to assume that his economic views derive from Hobson (Introduction to 1974 edn, pp. x, xix–xx). See Weiler, 'New Liberalism of L. T. Hobhouse', 154, who also gives Hobson as Hobhouse's source. While this is certainly true of his later economic views (see below, Ch. 4), Hobhouse could hardly have drawn from Hobson in 1893 since Hobson had not fully worked out his doctrine of the 'surplus' at that point (see below, n70) whereas it was well developed in Fabian literature (see Wolfe, *Radicalism to Socialism*, pp. 179–80, 198–211, 278–9, 289–90; McBriar,

reproduce in many respects official Fabian doctrine of the early 1890s, but its economic analysis in particular relies heavily on the theory of rent developed by the Fabians. As has often been remarked, the Fabian theory of rent is an adaptation of a particular aspect of classical and early neo-classical economics. It is worth discussing this derivation very briefly, since Hobhouse claims to be following Marshall in his economic analysis, but in fact it is Marshall with a Fabian twist.

Following Ricardo, the classical economists argued that, as J. S. Mill put it, 'the rent of land consists of the excess of its return above the return to the worst land in cultivation'.[60] Rent was thus treated as being different from any other form of income, since 'it constantly tends to increase, without any exertion or sacrifice on the part of the owners'. Landlords, therefore, 'grow richer, as it were in their sleep, without working, risking or economizing', and so, argued Mill, it would be 'no violation of the principles on which private property is grounded, if the state should appropriate this increase of wealth, or part of it, as it were' in the form of a land tax.[61] Mill's particular political predilection for a land tax was not generally shared by orthodox economists, but towards the end of the century, the notion that the return to other factors of production might be in some way analogous to rent began to be explored. Marshall, in an early work, spoke of a 'rent of rare natural abilities', an insight which was developed by the American economist F. A. Walker as an explanation for high business profits.[62] It was in reply to Walker in particular that Sidney Webb wrote his article on 'the laws of distribution', which was to be the foundation of Fabian economics.[63] He argued that there was not only a rent of ability as well as a rent of land, but also a rent of capital employed in any situation more favourable than that at the margin of production, and luck, timing and local variations could all contribute to such a situation. The question of whether the law of rent could be extended in this way was a subject of considerable controversy among economists in the next three or four years. With characteristic caution, Marshall declared: 'I regard it

Fabian Socialism, pp. 29–47). Furthermore, when Hobhouse revised the book for the 3rd edn in 1912, he changed the economic arguments considerably and acknowledged in the Preface that 'in its new form [it] owes much to the work of this most original and independent of our economists [Hobson]' (p. 7), which surely indicates that it did not do so in its old form.

60 J. S. Mill, *Principles of Political Economy*, I, Ch. 16, as quoted by Bernard Shaw in *Fabian Essays in Socialism* (6th edn, with Introduction by Asa Briggs, London, 1962 [first published London, 1889]), p. 38.

61 *Principles of Political Economy*, Book V, Ch. 2 (Books IV and V, pbk, with Introduction by Donald Winch (Harmondsworth, 1970), pp. 169–70).

62 A. and M. P. Marshall, *The Economics of Industry* (London, 1879), p. 144; F. A. Walker, 'The Source of Business Profits', *Quarterly Journal of Economics*, I (1887), both quoted in Wolfe, *Radicalism to Socialism*, pp. 200–2.

63 Sidney Webb, 'The Rate of Interest and the Laws of Distribution', *Quarterly Journal of Economics*, II (1888), 188–208.

only as an analogy, and, moreover, as one which, if pressed too far, is likely to be misleading',[64] and in his *Principles* (1890) he carefully distinguished such 'quasi-rents' (as he now called them) from rent proper.[65] One reviewer of Hobhouse's book (in the austerely orthodox *Economic Journal*) remarked in 1894 that although 'it is possible to distinguish a producer's surplus...yet few conceptions have of recent years given birth to a larger progeny of crude illusions than that of an unearned increment'.[66]

Nonetheless, it was soon incorporated into Fabian doctrine. Using a marginalist analysis of the determination of price, they argued that an 'economic wage' is the wage of the least skilled worker, labouring on the poorest land with the least capital assistance and the worst natural conditions. 'Any income above this economic wage must be the result of productive power unshared at the moment by others – a productive power that is thus differential and, therefore, rental.'[67] Such income could be the result of effort and skill, but also of position, status, opportunity and luck. In these cases it is a return over and above that which is necessary to bring that factor of production into play, and is therefore economically functionless. It is also socially created, arising merely from the unforeseen consequences of human association. The rise in site values as a result of the increase in the size of great towns was a favourite Fabian example, well calculated to appeal to the radical land-reforming tradition.[68] And since in the nature of the case such inequalities could not be removed, rent could never be abolished but could be appropriated by the community in the form of a graduated income tax, large death duties and some form of site value taxation.[69] Following the Fabian lead, this theory enjoyed some popularity in radical circles in the 1890s.[70]

64 A. Marshall, 'Wages and Profits', *Quarterly Journal of Economics*, II (1888), 223. Webb repeated his argument, II (1888), 469–70.

65 Marshall, *Principles of Economics*, pp. 492–502, 608–10; see also the 9th (Variorum) edn, ed. C. W. Guillebaud (2 vols., London, 1961), II, pp. 442, 495.

66 Review of *The Labour Movement* by L. L. Price, *Economic Journal*, IV (1894), 84.

67 David M. Ricci, 'Fabian Socialism: a theory of rent as exploitation', *Journal of British Studies*, IX (1969), 108.

68 It is repeated by Hobhouse, *Labour Movement*, p. 73.

69 See Shaw in *Fabian Essays* (1962 edn), pp. 413–14; and Webb, *Fabian Essays*, p. 86; Webb, *Socialism in England*, p. 126. Of course the Fabians were not alone in advocating such fiscal measures, but they were the first to present such taxation as a corollary of the developed theory of rent.

70 Hutchison, *Review of Economic Doctrines*, pp. 258–9 and n. McBriar is surely right when he suggests (p. 46n) that Hobson 'was obviously influenced by Fabian theory, although for personal reasons he failed to acknowledge his indebtedness fully' (a judgement endorsed by Clarke, 'Progressive Movement in England', 164). In his autobiography, Hobson merely says that he was working on this theory of distribution in 'the late 90s' (*Confessions of an Economic Heretic* (London, 1938), p. 44), and Clarke follows him in seeing *The Economics of Distribution* (New York, 1900) as the first statement of his theory of the surplus, 'extending the Ricardian theory of rent from land to capital and labour too' (Introduction to Hobson, *Crisis of Liberalism* (repr. Brighton, 1974), p. xv). Now it is certainly true (as I suggest above, n59) that this is the first time Hobson *fully* sets out his theory of the surplus, but it is worth adding that he had taken part in the debate in *The Quarterly Journal*

It certainly forms the basis of Hobhouse's chapter on 'The Distribution of Wealth', even though Marshall is his most frequently acknowledged authority.[71] Arguing that 'rent is the price paid for differential advantages in production to those who own such advantages', Hobhouse, like Webb, insisted that Marshall had neglected 'good fortune' as an important source of such rent.[72] Furthermore, he, too, insisted that the main forms of 'the producer's surplus' are 'rewards determined by price and not determining it', which was an important radical move in showing their economically functionless, and hence taxable, character; and this despite the fact that Marshall seems to have argued precisely the opposite.[73] Again, Hobhouse considers the objection that rent and interest are not strictly comparable, only, like the Fabians, to dismiss it on both ethical and practical grounds, without mentioning that it was Marshall who was most insistent on this distinction being maintained.[74] Hobhouse also argues that 'some goods are bound to be produced under more favourable conditions than others', and so 'no legislation can abolish rent'.[75] Accordingly, the surplus must be 'communized' by means of taxation, and Hobhouse proposes a steeply graduated income tax, higher death duties, and ('if we do not deal more drastically with the Unearned Increment') taxation of ground rent.[76] There

of Economics around 1890 referred to above, and had published an article then ('The Law of the Three Rents', v (1891), 263–88) which implicitly followed Webb in moving beyond Walker's analysis to argue that there were rents of capital and labour as well as land. It is upon the basis of this 'law' that he went on to develop his 'unified theory of distribution' upon which he lectured at the L.S.E. in 1897, and which he incorporated in *The Economics of Distribution* (see the Preface). It would seem as though both Hobhouse and Hobson independently derived their early economic views from a theory similar to that developed by the Fabians; that Hobson then went on to develop his own characteristic position from this basis (see, particularly, *The Industrial System: An Enquiry into Earned and Unearned Income* (London, 1909); and that in his later works Hobhouse, as he acknowledged, drew upon Hobson's works (especially in *Liberalism* (London, 1911) and the 1912 edn of *The Labour Movement*). The fact that both men became hostile to the Fabians after their association with them in the 1890s, may have meant that they later became rather reticent about acknowledging these early intellectual debts.

71 Of course, Socialists who were, by definition, proclaiming a heterodox economic doctrine were always prone to attempt to confer legitimacy on their theories by associating them with the authority of orthodoxy. To take but one example, consider Sidney Ball's use of quotations from Marshall – 'the highest economic orthodoxy', 'the leading representative of the economic tradition' – in his 'The Socialist Ideal', *Economic Review*, IX (1899), 440, 443–4. (Cf. Hobhouse, *Labour Movement*, p. 56n, citing Marshall's treatment as 'the most comprehensive'.)

72 *Labour Movement*, pp. 73, 68–9. In what follows, I do not mean to suggest that Hobhouse necessarily *directly* derived his views from Fabian sources, only that they would have been recognized in the early 1890s as Fabian in character.

73 *Labour Movement*, p. 61. Marshall, *Principles of Economics*, p. 609; 9th edn, II, p. 629. Marshall became increasingly aware that his authority could be cited to support theories with which he did not agree, and later specifically protested against misquotation on this point (9th edn, II, p. 439).

74 *Labour Movement*, p. 74. Marshall, *Principles of Economics*, p. 421 on 'the fundamental difference' between rent and interest.

75 *Labour Movement*, p. 73. Cf. the references cited in n69 above.

76 *Labour Movement*, pp. 76, 77, 78. It is a sign of his political optimism at this date that he asserts that it is along these lines that the question 'probably soon will be dealt with by the state' (p. 76).

was a very Fabian ring to his confident assertion: 'In time the community will become the chief, perhaps the sole, owner of Capital and Land. But it will be by gradual steps. The progress of public enterprise admits of indefinite extension, and at each step some fragment of Land or Capital passes to the community.'[77]

The central argument of *The Labour Movement* was based on this economic analysis. For neither 'raising wages to a trade-union level' nor 'the utmost extension of cooperative and municipal enterprise' could deal with 'the problem of rent and interest'.[78] For this, some degree of state Socialism was necessary, and here again Hobhouse was repeating a favourite Fabian point. Sidney Webb had insisted in *Socialism in England* (1891) that although the Cooperative Movement, like the Trade Unions, 'afford a valuable moral training', 'it does not so much as attempt to deal with economic rent, or with such public services as railways, gasworks or schools', for which Socialism was needed.[79] And, of course, in viewing the Cooperative Movement not primarily as a profit-sharing organization, but as a way of determining production to meet ascertained demand, Hobhouse was, as he acknowledged and as reviewers widely commented, following Beatrice Potter's *The Cooperative Movement in Great Britain.*[80] She, too, had argued that the Trade Union and Cooperative Movement, though bringing valuable 'moral reform', needed to be supplemented by Socialist legislation.[81] Finally, the Fabian recognition of the role of local government, as being associations of consumers where membership was obligatory not voluntary, was a point which Hobhouse emphasized repeatedly (and a point which Webb later acclaimed as 'an important addition to Socialist theory').[82] In fact, it was in the early 1890s that the Fabians were incorporating these three 'subsidiary' movements, whose significance they had underestimated in 1889,[83] into their doctrine, a revision of their theory to which Hobhouse was obviously highly sympathetic. His own starting-

77 *Labour Movement*, p. 77. Consider also his declaration: 'True administrative reform consists simply in such mechanical changes as will put power into the hands of those who will use it best' (p. 5). This was one of the (many) sentences which he omitted from the 1912 edn, possibly being aware of its uncomfortable similarity to the elitist remarks of the Fabians for which he had by then been berating them for over a decade.

78 *Labour Movement*, pp. 75–6. And compare Hobhouse's remark that 'we should still be paying toll...for the privilege of living in England' (p. 75), with Webb's on what is paid 'to the landlords for permission to live in England' (*Fabian Essays*, p. 84n).

79 *Socialism in England*, pp. 91–5. On the beneficial moral effect of the Cooperative and Trade Union Movements on the 'character' of the workman, see *Labour Movement*, p. 48.

80 London, 1891; *Labour Movement*, pp. vi, 38; Hobhouse's fidelity to the argument of 'Mrs Webb's remarkable book' was noted by L. L. Price, *Economic Journal*, IV (1894), 82–4, and by W. G. Smith, *Economic Review*, III (1893), 598–600.

81 *The Cooperative Movement*, pp. 235, 237–9.

82 *Fabian Essays*, p. 273 (repr. from the Introduction to the 1920 edn); cf. *Labour Movement*, p. 50.

83 Webb in the Introduction to the 1920 edn singles out the omission of adequate discussion of these three elements as a major weakness of the *Essays* (1962 edn, pp. 272–4).

point had been the political tradition of Radicalism and 'a genuine sympathy with the toiling and suffering mass of men who in wealthy England struggle painfully for a bare subsistence'.[84] By 1893 he was publishing a book which showed him to be very close to Fabian Socialism. He was perhaps an example of Webb's dictum that: 'It is a matter of common experience that a course of lessons in the "law of rent" will usually convert a mere Radical into something very like a Socialist.'[85]

However, it is important to realize once again what an umbrella term 'Socialism' was at this date. One reviewer of *The Labour Movement* remarked: 'Since Oxford lost Professor T. H. Green, in whose school Mr Hobhouse has himself been reared, and whose influence is patent in almost every line of the present volume, no more serious and philosophic treatment of social questions has been committed to print by an Oxford Lecturer.'[86] This is a salutary reminder that there was no necessary incongruity at this date in a reformer seeming to be both Fabian and a disciple of Green. Both groups were commonly identified as 'Collectivists', since they were, in their various ways, critics of Individualism, and there was considerable overlap in membership as well as in rhetoric. In these terms there seemed around 1890 little to choose between, say, Graham Wallas, Sydney Olivier and William Clarke on the one hand, and F. C. Montague, J. H. Muirhead and D. G. Ritchie on the other. Pushed too far, this becomes a dangerous simplification: both within and between these groups, there were many important differences,[87] but since these have been emphasized by posterity, it is worth recalling the contemporary perspective in which their similarities seemed more important. They shared an emotional as well as an intellectual aversion to Individualism, an insistence on the need for – at times, it seemed, a craving for – a new ethical spirit in social relations, a stronger sense of community and of the duties of its members to each other. In the most general terms, they went on to argue that the state as the political

[84] These are the terms in which Hobhouse himself commended the author of *The Redemption of Labour* in a review, *Economic Review*, III (1892), 123.

[85] *Socialism in England*, pp. 87–8.

[86] *Economic Review*, IV (1893), 598.

[87] Thus, for example, Ritchie (a Fabian for a while) was a more pronounced Collectivist than Muirhead (who shared lodgings with Wallas); Clarke's Fabian Essay was a good deal more hard-headed than Olivier's, though he left the Society much sooner, and so on. The six names I mention represent the greatest points of contact: the picture looks slightly different if George Bernard Shaw and Bernard Bosanquet are taken to represent the two groups. The overlap is exaggerated if, like Wolfe, one describes Bosanquet as a member of the Fabian Society (Wolfe, *Radicalism to Socialism*, pp. 274, 282). Bosanquet gave a lecture *by invitation* to the Fabian Society but never joined it, and surely was unlikely to, given their mutual antipathies (see, e.g. J. H. Muirhead (ed.), *Bernard Bosanquet and his Friends* (London, 1935), pp. 73–4; Bosanquet, *Civilization of Christendom*, pp. 304–57; Sidney Webb, 'The Moral Aspects of Socialism', *International Journal of Ethics*, VII (1896), 80–4). J. H. Muirhead, *Reflections by a Journeyman in Philosophy*, ed. John W. Harvey (London, 1942) gives an informal picture of the overlapping worlds of Fabian and Ethical Societies among London Radical circles at this time.

expression of the community should embody this 'new moral world' in its legislation. On the substance of such legislation, of course, they differed widely: it was easier, for example, to state piously that private property should not be used to destroy the moral welfare of one's fellow citizens than to agree upon what legislative action followed from this. Such disagreement sent it back to the drawing-room rather than the drawing-board, for it was distinctively Socialism for the middle classes – no mention of necessary antagonism between employers and employees, no celebration of the class solidarity so prized by the labour movement, little reference to the need for organization, agitation or expropriation. Socialism was presented as a moral ideal which bound men together, not as a political programme which set them apart. But these declarations of moral intent were not merely decorative; like the insignia worn by mediaeval soldiers, they served to make one's allegiance easily identifiable. Those who wanted to reform the abuses of Individualism and particularly to see a new altruistic ethos replace the competitive spirit upon which the present system was alleged to rest, but who wanted at the same time to dissociate themselves from the merely 'mechanical' or even confiscatory schemes popularly associated with economic Socialism, frequently felt obliged to display their moral colours in this way.

Hobhouse wore the livery of this Socialism proudly in *The Labour Movement*. He condemned, at length and with passion, the aggressive selfishness fostered by competitive commercialism, and he proclaimed that under Socialism social and economic arrangements would be determined by, and would in turn create, an altruistic ethic. Thus 'born and bred in the most outspoken individualist selfishness, the spirit of competitive commercialism has never belied its origin...The love of profit-making corrupts all industry...the signs of wealth are held the proofs of merit and ability...This taint...corrupts the life [of all social classes]...It fills the world with ugliness and discomfort.' The phrases vary, but the message is the same: the Individualist system 'produces a competitive spirit concentrated on personal gain instead of public good'.[88] He then goes on to argue that no deep or lasting improvement can come without a change in the spirit of an industrial system: 'Mere reform of machinery is worthless unless it is the expression of a change of spirit and feeling. If the change from individualism to socialism meant nothing but an alteration in the methods of organizing industry, it would leave the nation no happier or better than before.' So any movement of 'far-reaching, economic reform must, so far as its effects extend, be introducing a new spirit into industry – a feeling for the common good, a readiness to forgo personal advantage

[88] *Labour Movement*, pp. 4, 69–70, 71.

for the general gain, a recognition of mutual dependence'.[89] It was just this strenuous morality which for Hobhouse was the most valuable of the changes which it was hoped that Socialism would produce. It was an ideal to which he always paid homage, but he came in time to doubt whether those organizations which had become identified with 'Socialism' were those most likely or best fitted to bring it about.

Like any writer who wished to advocate Socialism at this time, Hobhouse had to deal with the major anti-Collectivist arguments, and he does in fact touch on all four of the arguments outlined in the last chapter. He says relatively little in reply to the political argument. Repeating the familiar progressive equation – 'if we municipalize tramways we may with equal reason nationalize railways' – he notes that 'it is commonly argued that a State department is a bad manager'. In reply he simply offers the counter-assertion that this need not be so, and suggests 'our "socialistic" postal system' as an example of the benefits of state management.[90] And in general, he relies upon the growth of the social spirit. 'Laissez-faire economists' may argue that the profit motive is essential to the performance of any function in the economic system, but, Hobhouse rather glibly asserts, 'there is no reason why Mill's ideal should not yet be realized and men learn to dig and weave for their country as well as fight for it. And if men can dig and weave for a fixed wage and exert themselves to earn it, well, men can also follow earnestly and strenuously the higher calling of guiding those who dig and weave.'[91] As with his breezy treatment of the means of 'communizing' the surplus, Hobhouse pays little attention to the political difficulties which the Collectivist cause would have to face. The book was written at the high peak of his confidence and optimism about the success of Socialism. Only a few years later he would be gloomily reflecting on 'the wrecked Ideal of the Socialism of the "eighties"'.[92]

In the concluding chapter of *The Labour Movement*, Hobhouse dealt with 'one or two theoretical objections which are almost certain to arise'.[93] He first disposes of the economic objections, which range from the belief that economic laws render Collectivism impossible in the same way as physical laws do the defiance of gravity, to the neo-Malthusian claim that the Law of Diminishing Returns ensures that a rise in population must be accompanied by a decline in prosperity. The first of these, he claims, rests on a misconception as to the nature of economic 'laws', and notes in passing that the science of economics, having arisen during a period of free competition, is widely taken to endorse that situation which it analyses. He

[89] *Labour Movement*, pp. 4–5. See also p. 45 for the claim that it was generally agreed that 'a higher tone in business enterprise is desirable'.

[90] *Labour Movement*, pp. 40–1.

[91] *Labour Movement*, pp. 71–2.

[92] Journal of C. R. Ashbee, Jan. 1900, Ashbee Papers.

[93] *Labour Movement*, p. 83.

easily demonstrates that the second is a misuse of the Law of Diminishing Returns, and he is able tellingly to quote Marshall on 'the constant and nearly steady increase in the amount of accumulated wealth per head of the population'.[94] By invoking the existence of the surplus, he is also able to dispose of what was in effect a variant of the discredited 'wages fund' theory – that the country possesses insufficient wealth to meet the vastly increased wage bill which would be the result of such Collectivism – and so concludes, unsurprisingly, 'that the economic objections to the control of industry are not sound'.[95]

Although he disclaims any intention of attempting 'an exhaustive discussion of the arguments for individualism', he does in fact consider the other two at greater length. As always, it is the moral and scientific rather than the political and economic arguments which he engages with most fully. His treatment of 'the scientific arguments for individualism' I consider below in Chapter 5. Here I shall look in some detail at his extended reply to the objection: 'Does not the growth of the central authority militate fatally against the liberty of individual citizens which is essential to progress?'[96] It is here that his reliance on Green is most obvious. He pours scorn on any lingering notion of 'natural rights', asserting dogmatically that 'a right is nothing but what the good of society makes it'.[97] Then, in a section which amounts to a preview of his mature political philosophy, he attempts to reconcile the teachings of Green and of Mill on the question of freedom. But, as with his later work, although he pays due homage to Mill's defence of individuality for its own sake and of 'a man's right to make his own mistakes', his own statement of the case for liberty leans much more heavily towards Green than Mill.[98]

He begins with the ritual denial that 'the regulation of industrial life' would 'run everybody into one mould'. Collectivism will not regulate religion, thought, taste, leisure and so on: it will rather enable these to flourish, for 'the best social life consists precisely in the working out to their fullest possible development of the best capacities of all members of the community'.[99] True liberty, therefore, 'is found when each man has the

[94] *Labour Movement*, p. 87, quoting Marshall's *Principles of Economics* (2nd edn), p. 729.

[95] *Labour Movement*, p. 88.

[96] *Labour Movement*, pp. 88–91.

[97] *Labour Movement*, p. 90. The beginnings of an illiberal tendency in the treatment of rights (or of an excessive briskness of phrasing, at least) are to be seen here, for he goes on: 'If it were well for society as a whole to destroy every right of private property tomorrow, it would be just to do so...If...any right to any form of property or freedom no longer serves a good social purpose, it must go.' (p. 90)

[98] In a later work, he notes the superiority of Mill's formulation to Green's on this (*Democracy and Reaction*, pp. 223–4 and n), but, as Clarke points out (Introduction to 1972 repr., p. xxi), he seems to lose sight of this point in his treatment of liberty in his other works.

[99] *Labour Movement*, p. 93. This is, of course, a hidden quotation from Green, as is the next quotation, which Hobhouse acknowledges.

greatest possible opportunity for making the best of himself'. Here it is instructive to see how he evades the standard difficulty alleged against this conception of freedom, the difficulty of whether, as he later put it, 'a man is to judge for himself what is best for himself'.[100] He begins with the indisputable assertion that some restraint is necessary for the existence of society: 'The curtailment of the liberties of some, then, may mean the maximum of liberty upon the whole.' From this quantitative, almost Utilitarian starting-point, Hobhouse slides into the characteristically Idealist distinction between higher and lower freedom. He cites the Factory Acts and compulsory education as cases of the enlargement of freedom (the examples were, of course, the staples of the anti-Individualist argument, the more telling for being drawn from legislation which was now widely accepted). But the terms of his justification are not entirely quantitative: these acts give the individual, he argues, 'a better chance of developing his nature in the long run', they 'augment...the power of satisfying higher needs'. The potentially restrictive conclusions which such a view can support are also manifest in the following passage:

> The actual control itself is, in fact, a small obstacle to liberty in its higher aspects. Just as it matters little to control the body if you leave the spirit free, so it is a small thing to order man's doings in the way of providing material needs if you leave him to roam unfettered in the large field of mental and spiritual development. And as our object is to enable men to realize such development, and find in it their greatest happiness, we insist at one and the same time on perfect freedom in this direction, and perfect organization of all the material basis of society which forms the foundation of the wider life.[101]

Later in his career, Hobhouse would be wary of using such a phrase as 'the *perfect* organization of *all* the material basis of society', and would not so hastily assert that ordering a man's physical life is 'a small thing'. This early sermonizing, however, is revealing of an ideal of the organized, ascetic, closely integrated community pursuing the noblest aims – a kind of moral keep-fit camp – which, even in muted form, underlay his later political theory. Admittedly, he does recognize that the question may arise: 'Who is the judge of higher and lower, and who decides what is essential to the interests of the higher?' But his unblinking reply is that 'only one answer can be given – the majority of the citizens'. Once again, he tries to accommodate Mill's more libertarian views by saying that we must recognize 'the fallibility of any human authority', and must, therefore,

100 *Democracy and Reaction*, p. 224n. It is perhaps only in the light of twentieth-century relativism that this has become the 'standard' difficulty: it is raised less often in the late nineteenth century than this term suggests.

101 *Labour Movement*, p. 94. Note also his stern disapproval of indulgence and his fear that wealth is a threat to its owner, likely to prevent him from leading a rational, self-controlling life (pp. 13, 69). Compare Sidney Ball's moral indignation at 'this present world of Rudyard Kipling and Golf'. (Oona Howard Ball, *Sidney Ball*, p. 43.)

always safeguard 'free thought and free discussion'.[102] Restating the theory of the General Will in biological language, he goes on to conclude that the decisions of a democratic community present 'the nearest approach to a collective judgement of the social organism upon its collective interests', and having thus ascertained 'what is necessary as the fundamental condition of social health, it is our right and duty to enforce that by any and every form of collective authority, legally or voluntarily constituted'. Against the use of the state, he balances the mandatory acknowledgement of the role of 'individual effort and voluntary association', but his account of rights only goes so far as to allow that 'it is equally right and good to leave a fair field of discussion open to all who consider themselves aggrieved, or who think we are in the wrong path'. It is a sign of the strength of Hobhouse's organicist assumptions that dissenting individuals are accorded nothing more than 'a fair field of discussion'. On the crucial question of whether, when free discussion has resulted in disagreement, the individual may be legitimately coerced by the community, Hobhouse is silent. If it could be said that some notion of the rights of the individual *against* the community is essential to a properly Liberal political theory, then Hobhouse's early zeal to legitimate Collectivism seems to have been at the expense of his Liberalism.[103]

In his other political writings of the 1890s, Hobhouse repeats the arguments of *The Labour Movement*, but there are two changes to be noted. The first, and less significant, is that he becomes less involved with the Trade Union Movement and less optimistic about what it will achieve. Again, he reflects an opinion widespread among social reformers of this period: in the early nineties, the successes of the New Unionism were still recent enough to sustain hope and enthusiasm, but by the mid nineties this momentum was clearly spent. Several Unions organized in the wake of the Great Dock Strike collapsed, and, in the face of a fresh counter-attack from the employers, the weakness of isolated Union action was revealed.[104] When *The Labour Movement* was reissued in 1897, the few changes which

[102] *Labour Movement*, p. 95.

[103] *Labour Movement*, pp. 96–8. Plainly, it is his desire to refute those arch-Individualists 'the Apostles of Liberty in the abstract, of the right divine of all men to do wrong' which spurs him on (p. 50). There is self-awareness in his later comment that many Collectivists of this period heard the old phrases about liberty – 'not seldom used for obstructive purposes' – 'with a certain impatience'. (*Democracy and Reaction*, p. 209.)

[104] For a general account of Trade Unions in this period see H. A. Clegg, A. Fox and A. F. Thompson, *A History of British Trade Unions since 1889*, I: *1889–1910* (Oxford, 1964); the difficulties encountered by the Unions in the 1890s are well analysed in John Saville, 'Trade unionism and Free Labour: the background to the Taff Vale decision' in Asa Briggs and John Saville (eds.), *Essays in Labour History*, I (London, 1960); the particular case of the Oxfordshire Unions is discussed in Horn, 'The farm workers'; Hobhouse recognized the general change in opinion in the 1890s in the 3rd (1912) edn of *The Labour Movement*, p. 11.

Hobhouse made were nearly all in the direction of moderating his earlier optimism about the Unions. Although he had spent much time trying to unionize the agricultural labourers around Oxford, he was now forced to admit that, owing to the difficulty of keeping such Unions in being for any length of time, 'it is doubtful whether they have much part to play in the permanent improvement of village life'. He also noted that the federation of Unions had failed to progress as quickly as he had hoped.[105] Hobhouse remained an ardent supporter of the Unions and maintained many contacts with them, but they never again figure so prominently among the agencies of social reform.

The second and more important change in Hobhouse's views is that he becomes more concerned to distinguish the ideal of Socialism from its not entirely satisfactory manifestation in current Socialist organizations. In particular, one can see here the beginning of his alienation from the Fabians. This is first noticeable in an article written at the very end of his period in Oxford, called, characteristically, 'The Ethical Basis of Collectivism'.[106] For example, he cautions that 'Marxist teaching', although unsound economically in resting upon the theory of surplus value rather than of rent, contained 'elements of truth' which it was 'easy to overlook' in criticizing it.[107] Above all its 'ideal of abstract justice' was its great strength, and this, claims Hobhouse, is as valuable as ever. Faith in the inevitability of Socialism is a poor substitute: 'If Socialism is coming of itself, why should anyone incur the obloquy of calling himself a Socialist, or put himself to any trouble in securing the advent of the inevitable?' Or again, the claim that 'the good of society' is the overriding standard for Collectivists can be invoked too readily: 'It is not enough to say that the right of equality, the right to live and work, the prescriptive right of property are to be judged and measured by what is good for society as a whole. We want to know what place these rights would have in a sound conception of social welfare as attainable in Western Europe in the 20th century.' And in formulating this conception, Socialists must beware of exaggerating the importance of equality: 'Equality is not the sole aim and object of society.' To treat it as such 'is hopelessly one-sided', and accounts for 'the dreariness of the mechanical schemes of Socialism which appear

105 *Labour Movement* (2nd edn 1897), pp. 15n, 47–8; he omitted the example on p. 16n of the success of the Oxfordshire Union in raising wages. In 1900, his friend C. R. Ashbee noted Hobhouse's disillusionment with the labour leaders who had been his heroes in the late 1880s such as Mann, Tillett and Burns. (Journal, Jan. 1900, Ashbee Papers.)

106 *International Journal of Ethics*, VIII (1898), 137–56.

107 From the early days of their *Capital* reading circle, the Fabians had constantly repeated this criticism. (See Wolfe, *Radicalism to Socialism*, pp. 178–80, 206–11; McBriar, *Fabian Socialism*, Chs. 2 and 3, and Webb, *Socialism in England*, pp. 84–5 for his proud declaration that 'English Socialists are by no means blind worshippers of Karl Marx'; they 'reject his special contribution to pure economics...His theory of value meets with little support.')

from time to time'.[108] He is clearly afraid that such Socialists will give Socialism a bad name.

This sort of distortion of Socialism 'is pushed to its furthest and most repulsive point when the economic mechanism of the Socialist theory is made into the ultimate end and object of the whole movement. This is done not only by critics but by supporters of Socialism.' He admits that 'in view of the Individualist theories which still linger on, Socialists are often forced to contend for the abstract right to extend them [the functions of the state] to fields which they do not at present cover'. (As we have seen, he had been engaged in precisely this exercise in the last chapter of *The Labour Movement*.) But the danger is 'to hail any and every extension of state authority, whatever its principle or its object, as a triumph for Socialism', and in two topical references he indicates that the Fabians are the chief culprits here.[109] In the heat of their opposition to Individualism such Socialists were too ready to 'applaud the running of the machine merely because it is a machine and is being run'. The point, as he was frequently to repeat in the next few years, was that 'some Socialists...have yet to learn that their synthesis must include all the elements of value represented by the older Liberalism'.[110] The beginnings of the New Liberalism are visible here.

At this date, Hobhouse's main concern is still to show that 'the true end of Socialism...is...ethical', and he rehearses the by now standard arguments.[111] His tone is that of the elevated moral appeal: the teaching of the Sermon on the Mount and the relations within the family are both

108 'Ethical Basis', 138–41.

109 'Even the Agricultural Rating Act is hailed by the incautious or the paradoxically inclined as marking a step onward in the march of Collectivist ideas, and a measure designed to assist the clergy in maintaining an undivided authority over the administration of public funds is hailed as at least a blow to laissez-faire Liberalism.' 'Ethical Basis', 142. The first reference is to the 1896 Agricultural Rating Act which, according to Halévy, 'had reduced by half the rates payable on agricultural land; the relief amounted to an annual gift to the farmers of £1,500,000'; the second is to the 1897 act which provided a grant in aid to 'voluntary' schools, on which Halévy comments: 'The voluntary schools were not even obliged to purchase this grant by accepting the control of the county councils. Its distribution was entrusted by the Act to associations of the voluntary schools, which, of course, would be purely denominational.' (Elie Halévy, *A History of the English People in the Nineteenth Century*, v: *Imperialism and the Rise of Labour* (*1895–1905*) (2nd English edn London, 1951 [first published in French 1926]), pp. 299, 192–3). In the following year Hobhouse again berated those Socialists who, with the help of their '"positive conception of the state", have even seen an excuse for doles to distressed landlords'. 'Foreign Policy', 199.

110 'Ethical Basis', 142–3.

111 Including the citation of the 'Factory Acts, sanitary regulations, and even perhaps poor laws' all of which 'have long been admitted as the most important application of the Collectivist principle in modern legislation' ('Ethical Basis', 155). On the use he makes of the arguments drawn from evolution, see below, Ch. 5. Of course, all these arguments were the common coin of the 'moral' defence of Socialism at this time. Hobhouse is presenting the same case to an educated audience which Blatchford's *Merrie England*, for example, made familiar to a much wider public. (For some comments on the persistence of this sort of Socialist message in the Labour Party, see Samuel H. Beer, *Modern British Politics* (London, 1965), pp. 126–37.)

invoked as models of Collectivist ethics, as he presents Collectivism in terms of 'the development of that rational organization of life in which men freely recognize their interdependence, and the best life for each is understood to be that which is best for those around him'.[112] Throughout, it is the image of Socialism as materialistic which he wants to correct,[113] and its moral character as the antithesis of competition which he stresses. Despite his emerging criticisms of official Fabianism, then, Hobhouse was still recognizably an advocate of that 'Socialism of good intentions' which had drawn many earnest young reformers to early Fabianism. A curious testimony to the purity of Hobhouse's moral brand of Socialism at this date is provided by the fact that when two years later Sidney Ball published his credo – 'The Socialist Ideal' – he incorporated almost verbatim several lengthy passages from Hobhouse's earlier article.[114]

By the time that Ball's article appeared, Hobhouse was already moving closer to traditional Liberalism, a change which we shall consider in the next chapter. But since his relations with the Fabians are so crucial to this story, and since the New Liberalism was to be marked by its persistent anti-Fabianism, it may help to situate Hobhouse's development if we briefly note the parallel history of attraction and disaffection experienced by certain other radical intellectuals of this period. There was a more general pattern here than historians have allowed, and the following figures are merely representative examples.

As editor of *The Nation* from 1907, H. W. Massingham was the focus of the New Liberalism's impressive array of journalistic support, and he led frequent verbal assaults on the Fabians. But as a young radical journalist

[112] 'Ethical Basis', 150–5. He acknowledges that 'this process has been described by Green, in a well-known chapter, as the extension of the area of the common good' (153). The casual reference to 'a well-known chapter' is some indication of the audience which Hobhouse thought he was addressing. Hobhouse was always willing to have his work regarded as the continuation of Green's: this constituted both a recommendation of his own work and a claim about Green's real political preferences. (On Hobhouse's relation to Green see Clarke's Introduction to 1972 repr. of *Democracy and Reaction*, pp. xix–xxi; Collini, 'Hobhouse, Bosanquet and the state', 107–9, and Ch. 4 below.)

[113] 'The Collectivist has been supposed, absurdly enough, to put material comfort above character' ('Ethical Basis', 155). This may well have been a reference to the controversy between Bosanquet and Ball in the previous year when Bosanquet had made precisely this charge. See Bernard Bosanquet (ed.), *Aspects of the Social Problem* (London, 1895); Sidney Ball denied the charge in 'The Moral Aspects of Socialism', *International Journal of Ethics*, VI (1896), 291–322; Bosanquet replied in the same volume, 503–6; Sidney Webb chimed in, VII, 80–4; Ball replied to Bosanquet, VII, 85–91; Bosanquet fired his last shot, VII, 226, and Ball ended the exchange, VII, 229–30. Ball and Hobhouse had often discussed together 'the best formula for the moral ideal' (Oona Howard Ball, *Sidney Ball*, pp. 85–6).

[114] Compare the following pages of Ball's article with those of Hobhouse's in brackets after them: 427 (139), 428 (140), 431 (150–1), 436 (156), 445 (141); furthermore, on 449 there seems to be a hidden quotation from *The Labour Movement*, p. 53, and on 447 Ball quotes and summarizes Hobhouse's 'Foreign Policy' article.

in London in the early 1890s he had been very close to Webb and Shaw, and as assistant editor of the *Star* he solicited Fabian contributions and advertised Fabian views. In 1891 he resigned, since his 'socialistic bias' married poorly with the proprietors' desire to 'Gladstonize' the paper's politics, but he joined the Fabian Society in the same year and was almost immediately elected to its executive. For a short period he was prominent in the Fabian efforts to dominate the Progressive party in London politics. However, in November 1893 the Fabians published their manifesto 'To your tents, O Israel!' which bitterly criticized the failure of the Liberals to implement an advanced social policy, repudiated the previous Fabian policy of permeation, and declared support for independent labour representation. Massingham immediately resigned from the Society. 'I disagree with everything in this unhappy and ridiculous document', he wrote to Webb, and to Shaw he declared: 'I have been a permeator all my days, a Collectivist Radical working on journalistic lines, and that I remain. It is Fabianism which has changed and I who remain the Fabian.'[115] As with so many Radicals, the early 1890s had been the peak of Massingham's attraction to the Fabians; thereafter, he reverted to his advanced Liberalism and even Pease had to acknowledge that he was 'bitterly hostile to the Fabians'.[116]

Like Massingham, William Clarke was a radical journalist first and only secondarily and temporarily a Fabian. He always yearned for an ethico-religious faith which would endow his far from easy existence as a free-lance journalist and reformer with some meaning; without such a 'higher purpose', he admitted, one would 'agree with Schopenhauer that social reform was a weak delusion, and would logically take to quietism as every true pessimist does'.[117] In the early 1880s he saw Socialism as merely a threat to all that he valued: 'Socialism (by this I mean of course collectivism, the only thing which is now preached) would destroy property, family, state, religion, as all its Continental advocates admit. This seems to me to be damnable; fatal to progress, to freedom, to love.'[118] In the mid 1880s he experienced a conversion, and was, briefly, an ardent exponent of Marx. Having been a member of its predecessor, the Fellowship of the New Life, he joined the Fabian Society in 1886, and was,

115 Both quoted in Havighurst, *Radical Journalist*, pp. 49–50. A very slightly different version of the second quotation is given in Thompson, *Socialists, Liberals and Labour*, p. 147, which also discusses Massingham's involvement in London politics.

116 E. R. Pease, *The History of the Fabian Society* (London, 1916), p. 117. The most complete account of Massingham's Fabian period is now in Havighurst, *Radical Journalist*, pp. 41–53. D. G. Ritchie also resigned from the Society on this issue: McBriar, *Fabian Socialism*, p. 250.

117 William Clarke, *Walt Whitman* (London, 1892), p. 108, quoted in Peter Weiler, 'William Clarke: the making and unmaking of a Fabian Socialist', *Journal of British Studies*, XIV (1974), 86n. In this paragraph I am heavily indebted to Weiler's excellent article.

118 Clarke to Thomas Davidson, 12 Dec. 1884 (quoted in Weiler, 'William Clarke', 83).

of course, an Essayist. But as early as 1890 he expressed criticism of the Fabians, particularly Shaw, for their want of concern with 'ultimate aims', and he withdrew from active participation in the Society in the early 1890s.[119] According to Pease he had always been 'just a little of an outsider' in the Society, although this was as much a matter of temperament as doctrine. His articles of the mid 1890s certainly reveal a very unFabian emphasis on 'the Limits of Collectivism'.[120] What finally damned the Fabian leaders in his eyes was their temporizing over imperialism, and in 1897, the year in which he finally resigned from the Society, he published a fiercely worded attack on imperialist sentiments (which was later praised by both Hobhouse and Hobson).[121] On the outbreak of the Boer War, to which he was strongly opposed, he wrote rather bluntly to Webb: 'I fear we are separated widely in our ideas...I detest bureaucratic imperialism so much I can scarcely trust myself to speak on it.'[122] In the following year *Fabianism and the Empire* was published, the tract which officially announced the Society's endorsement of 'bureaucratic imperialism'.

The story of Wallas' relationship with the Fabians is, of course, longer and more complex. But although he long remained sympathetic to the Society, and could never have been easily classed as a New Liberal, the curve of his Fabian involvement plots a similar course. His background matches Hobhouse's – clergyman father, Greats at Corpus, Oxford, loss of faith and conversion to Collectivism (they were in fact friends, with similar careers – they were both the first incumbents of their respective Chairs at the L.S.E.). Wallas, six years Hobhouse's senior, joined the Society in 1886 after drifting into London Radical circles. He soon became one of the leaders of the Society, and was an Essayist.[123] Among its leaders, Beatrice Webb noted, he 'represents morality and scrupulousness' and with his 'moral fervour' he 'appeals to those of the upper and educated class who have good intentions'.[124] But, as he recalled much later, 'I always, after the first few years, felt rather restless in the Society.'[125] He, too, had objected to the 'To your tents' manifesto; indeed, by 1904 he could write

[119] Weiler, 'William Clarke', 97n; McBriar, *Fabian Socialism*, pp. 6, 120.

[120] Pease, *Fabian Society*, p. 64; William Clarke, 'The Limits of Collectivism', first published *Comtemporary Review*, 1893, and republished in Herbert Burrows and J. A. Hobson (eds.), *William Clarke: A Collection of His Writings with a Biographical Sketch* (London, 1908), pp. 24–43; H. W. Nevinson called him 'that model Liberal' (*Changes and Chances* (London, 1923), p. 184).

[121] 'The Genesis of Jingoism', *Progressive Review*, II (1897), repr. in Burrows and Hobson (eds.), *William Clarke*, pp. 108–17; McBriar, *Fabian Socialism*, p. 120.

[122] Quoted in Weiler, 'William Clarke', 107.

[123] Wallas' Fabian career is now fairly well documented: see McBriar, *Fabian Socialism;* Wolfe, *Radicalism to Socialism*; Martin J. Wiener, *Between Two Worlds: The Political Thought of Graham Wallas* (Oxford, 1971).

[124] Beatrice Webb, *Our Partnership*, pp. 137–8.

[125] In a review of Pease's *History*, first published 1916 and repr. in Graham Wallas, *Men and Ideas*, ed. May Wallas (London, 1940), p. 105.

to Pease, 'I am still a "permeator" and not a follower of I.L.P. tactics', and 'on the questions which divide the Liberal and Conservative parties, I am a Liberal'.[126] Ever an opponent of the clerical domination of education, he had reservations about official Fabian support of the Conservatives' legislation on this issue, just as he had been uneasy about Fabian support for the Boer War. Finally, in 1904, he resigned over the Society's tract on Tariff Reform. But, as his later reflections make clear, this was as much the occasion as the cause of his departure, and specific policies apart, he had long felt himself out of sympathy with the 'specialist' attitude advocated by Webb and Shaw. As Martin Wiener concludes, 'Wallas' alienation from the Fabian Society was a mutual process: as he developed away from the Society, it was developing away from him.'[127]

The direction in which the Society was developing, so it seemed to many of its erstwhile adherents, was away from the moral and humanitarian impulses which had initially inspired its 'Socialism', and towards 'Efficiency'.[128] Increasingly dominated by the Webbs and Shaw, the Society came more and more to be identified with the ideal of bureaucratic rule by the specially trained expert. They were prone to treat liberal values as one of the many forms of outdated sentimentality which obstructed the realization of this ideal. J. H. Muirhead was, as so often, speaking as the representative of *l'homme moyen Idéaliste* when he said: 'What we distrusted in Fabianism was its tendency to emphasize social efficiency and to fail to take sufficient account of the reactions of Collectivist reforms on the minds and wills of individuals on whose response to them their ultimate success must depend.'[129] Above all, it was the Fabians' pragmatic support of imperialism and, eventually, the Boer War which finally damned them in the eyes of Hobhouse and his friends. Elie Halévy, contemporary witness (and close friend of Wallas) as well as distinguished historian, summed up this view when he later wrote of the Webbs: 'Convinced imperialists and looking to a national and militarist state to realize their programme of moderate collectivism, they had never felt anything but contempt for every formula of Liberalism and Free Trade.'[130] In the years around the turn of the century, the 'formulas of Liberalism and Free Trade' came to have a new significance in political debate, and this established a lasting division between the Fabians and the emerging New Liberalism.

[126] Quoted in Wiener, *Between Two Worlds*, p. 57; cf. Beatrice Webb, *Our Partnership*, p. 110.

[127] Wiener, *Between Two Worlds*, p. 60.

[128] For the cult of Efficiency in Edwardian politics, and the prominent involvement of the Fabians in it, see G. R. Searle, *The Quest for National Efficiency: A Study in British Politics and Political Thought 1899–1914* (Oxford, 1971).

[129] Muirhead, *Reflections*, p. 95.

[130] Halévy, *Imperialism and the Rise of Labour*, p. 365. The judgement is, of course, exaggerated, and the use of 'never' obscures the earlier idealism of both Sidney and Beatrice; but it is indicative of the reputation which they were coming to have.

However, when Hobhouse left Oxford to join the staff of the *Manchester Guardian* in the summer of 1897, this development had hardly begun. There was a widespread assumption among 'Progressives' in the mid 1890s that Liberalism, at least as represented by the Liberal party, was tottering to its end. As William Clarke wrote to the American reformer H. D. Lloyd in 1896: 'The Liberal party here is almost knocked to pieces, and the time is certainly ripe for a new movement of some kind if the very idea of progress is not to die of inanition.'[131] The opening Editorial of the short-lived *Progressive Review* (run by Clarke, J. A. Hobson and Ramsay MacDonald) noted 'the disintegration and enfeeblement of the great party whose watchword has been progress', and called for the formation of a new 'Progressive Party' composed of the 'advocates of experimental collectivism or of social radicalism'.[132] This was a recurring theme in political speculation in the mid 1890s. As Pease ruefully admitted many years later: 'In one respect it must be confessed we shared an almost universal delusion. When the Liberal party was crushed at the election of 1895 we thought that its end had come in England as it has in other countries.'[133] The main reason why this expectation was falsified was that in the next few years, as Clarke wrote to Ramsay Macdonald, 'the real crux of politics is not going to be Socialism and anti-Socialism, but Jingoism and anti-Jingoism.'[134]

[131] Quoted in Weiler, 'William Clarke', 102.

[132] *Progressive Review*, I (1896), 5. See above, Ch. 1, pp. 41, 45n.

[133] Pease, *Fabian Society*, p. 117.

[134] Quoted in Porter, *Critics of Empire*, p. 165.

3: RADICAL JOURNALIST

In the mid 1890s, Hobhouse was recognized as offering 'an interpretation of Socialism'.[1] When in 1910 the first editors of the Home University Library commissioned authoritative statements on the political philosophy of the three parties, it seemed appropriate to ask Hobhouse to write the volume on Liberalism.[2] He had by then become recognized as one of the leading theorists of the New Liberalism, often spoken of as the successor to Mill and Green, and the volume which he contributed has ever since been considered a classic statement of Liberal political philosophy. There are both personal and social dimensions to the explanation of this development. It is by no means simply the familiar story of the abandonment of a youthful Socialism for the more pessimistic Liberalism of middle age. Hobhouse's political allegiances were somewhat modified during their years, but so were the terms of political debate, and much which was condemned as 'Socialism' in the 1890s was in the vanguard of Liberalism in 1910. Moreover, as I shall argue in the next chapter, certain fundamental features of Hobhouse's Liberal political theory continued to reflect the Collectivist aspirations out of which it had developed. In this chapter I shall examine the progress of Hobhouse's career and political thinking in relation to these developments, and in particular the way in which he came to legitimate the policy of progressivism by extending more traditional Liberal arguments.

By the autumn of 1896 Hobhouse was ready to leave Oxford. The trial of its climate to his always precarious health was the reason he publicly avowed, but there were more fundamental sources of his discontent. He felt that *The Theory of Knowledge* – his lengthy defence of a modified Realist epistemology with its explicit attack on the prevailing Idealism – had been neglected by the dominant orthodoxy, and he despaired of affecting a philosophical climate which he always took to have a conservative political influence.[3] He had long been scornful of the privileges and

1 'Modern Oxford from a Progressive Point of View', *Progressive Review*, I (1896), 213.

2 Admittedly, the editors, Hobhouse's friends and Oxford contemporaries Gilbert Murray and H. A. L. Fisher, may have been predisposed at that date to choose an 'advanced' Liberal. Hugh Cecil wrote the volume on Conservatism and Ramsay MacDonald that on the Socialist Movement.

3 This is dealt with in more detail in Ch. 8 below.

parochialism endemic to Oxford life, and given that 'Oxford was in a very reactionary phase at that time', Hobhouse became increasingly restive there and 'he longed to use his powers in the world of action'.[4] At all events, when C. P. Scott, the editor of the *Manchester Guardian*, wrote to Arthur Sidgwick, Hobhouse's senior colleague, in an attempt to recruit yet another Greats-educated leader-writer, Sidgwick had no hesitation in recommending Hobhouse, 'quite the ablest of our younger Greats men, and a strong Liberal and progressive of the best type'.[5] Hobhouse had been attracted to the *Guardian* by its strong pro-labour line, particularly its defence of the miners in the strike of 1893, but in responding to Scott's invitation he made clear that he did not wish to become a regular journalist, his own studies still being his primary commitment.[6] However, after a short trial period Hobhouse began to write leading articles on a regular basis in the summer of 1897, when he revealed for the first time the prolific and not inconsiderable talent as a political journalist which he was to exercise for the rest of his life.

This was the beginning of his close, durable and fruitful relationship with Scott and the *Guardian*. Hobhouse admired Scott's resolute commitment to moral principle as the guide to political life, while there was no doubt that Scott trusted Hobhouse as he never trusted any other member of his staff: they liked each other and they approached problems in the same way'.[7] The relationship was decisive not only in directing Hobhouse's energies into the higher journalism, but also in helping to draw him into a closer identification with Liberalism. In this combination, Hobhouse found his voice. In his vigorous, occasionally ironic and tirelessly hortatory articles he called upon Liberalism to attend to the promptings of its better nature, to beware the devious influence of the all too numerous forces of reaction, and to take strength from the ultimately inevitable triumph of righteousness. The radical press was the Edwardian Liberal Party's super-ego, demanding, rigid and merciless in its moral judgements, and this was a role which suited Hobhouse splendidly. As he himself later said

[4] This is the opinion of Barbara Hammond, one of Hobhouse's pupils in the 1890s, as quoted in Hobson and Ginsberg, *L. T. Hobhouse*, pp. 35–6.

[5] Arthur Sidgwick to C. P. Scott, 20 Nov. 1896, Scott Papers.

[6] On his early attraction to the *Guardian* see his much later essay on 'Scott as Liberal and Humanist' in A. P. Wadsworth (ed.), *C. P. Scott, 1846–1932: The Making of the 'Manchester Guardian'* (London, 1946), p. 85. What Hobhouse initially had in mind was 'to contribute the occasional article of a somewhat solid and useful character which the Guardian often prints. Any political, social or economic subject interests me and I would be ready to try my hand at any such topic that wanted treatment. If e.g. the contents of a Blue Book had to be presented in readable form I would like to undertake it. Such a thing, for instance, as the movement of wages shown in the Labour Dept.'s report seems to want summarizing in some place accessible to the vulgar. As long as the thing may be treated thoughtfully and without journalistic omniscience I should not much mind what it was.' Hobhouse to Arthur Sidgwick, 18 Nov. 1896, Scott Papers.

[7] David Ayerst, '*Guardian*'. *Biography of a Newspaper* (London, 1971), p. 373.

of his years at the *Guardian*: 'I was in my right milieu there as I have never been before or since.'[8]

The beginning of Hobhouse's career as a journalist coincided with the rise of imperial issues to a dominant place in British politics. Chamberlain's aggressive colonial policy, the campaign in the Sudan, the treatment of native races, and the sequence of events in South Africa culminating in the Boer War were the most frequent targets of Hobhouse's leaders in the later 1890s. Many years later he recalled that he had 'always been a Gladstonian in foreign politics', and at Oxford he had agitated on behalf of various humanitarian causes, being particularly outraged at the Turkish massacre of Armenian Christians in 1894 and 1896.[9] During his *Guardian* period, he was keen to distinguish 'the Gladstonian principle of internationalism' from the 'Cobdenite doctrine of non-intervention', since the former prescribed interference based upon 'the moral law' and imposed upon nations and individuals alike the obligation to obey 'the sovereign duty to a common humanity'.[10] Accordingly, the issues of foreign affairs were assessed in these relentlessly moral terms. He arraigned 'the lust for empire...the dream of conquest, the vanity of racial domination, and the greed of commercial gain'; he condemned 'the slaughter of Omdurman' and the 'enslavement of the Bechuana'; he urged intervention against 'Turkish barbarity' and called for 'the execution of justice upon a scoundrel like Abdul Hamid'.[11] The 'bag-and-baggage' rhetoric suggests that for Hobhouse a crusade like Gladstone's Bulgarian agitation remained the paradigm for the national expression of political righteousness.

At the end of the century, Hohouse came to feel, like Scott, that 'more and more...foreign policy is the touchstone of all policy'.[12] Indeed, it remained for Hobhouse a surer touchstone of fundamental political morality even than attitudes to domestic politics and it is crucial to the explanation of many of his otherwise puzzling political allegiances and antipathies. The convinced Individualist might be dogmatic or blind, but at least his position did not rest upon a negation of morality; by contrast, the ardent imperialist was not to be trusted no matter what his views on domestic politics, and some of the more Collectivist-minded political leaders of the day, such as Rosebery or Chamberlain, were candidates for the ninth circle of Hobhouse's hell on account of unscrupulous policies

8 Hobhouse to Scott, 19 April 1907, Scott Papers.

9 Hobhouse to Emily Hobhouse, 14 Sept. 1915, Hobhouse Papers. F. W. Hirst recalled that 'Arthur Sidgwick and Hobhouse, in their enthusiasm for small persecuted minorities, once gave a garden party to four Armenian refugees from Turkish tyranny', who later turned out to be Turkish spies. F. W. Hirst, *In the Golden Days* (London, 1947), p. 143.

10 *Democracy and Reaction*, pp. 207, 192, 207–8.

11 *Democracy and Reaction*, p. 56; 'Foreign Policy', 203, 215, 220.

12 Scott to Leonard Courtney, Sept. 1899; quoted in Clarke, *Lancashire and the New Liberalism*, p. 177.

overseas. Hobhouse and Scott later opposed Asquith as Campbell-Bannerman's successor in 1908 because of his untrustworthy leanings towards imperialism, and they never forgot that thereafter it was 'a Liberal League Government'.[13] In fact, although I shall not deal in any detail with his views on foreign affairs, it is important to remember that from his earliest activities on behalf of 'The Friends of Russian Freedom' to his anxieties in the 1920s about how a Labour government would deal with Egypt and India, questions of international politics absorbed much of Hobhouse's political energy and were frequently decisive in shaping his political sympathies.

The classic example of this was the Boer War, 'the test issue of this generation' as Hobhouse called it.[14] In its consistent opposition to the government's South Africa policy and then to the prosecution of the war itself, the *Guardian* attracted great attention as the voice of the 'pro-Boer' minority (as they were somewhat inaccurately labelled by their opponents).[15] Hobhouse, in particular, made a name for himself through his closely argued critical articles. This position was, of course, an extremely unpopular one in the country at large, and this general hostility certainly helped to give the 'pro-Boers' a great sense of solidarity which endured for decades.[16] Hobhouse would have endorsed Scott's reflection in 1930, in writing to Lloyd George, that 'the best thing the *Manchester Guardian* has done in my time was to oppose the Boer War...We were together there.'[17]

Above all, the experience of the Boer War and of related controversies over imperial matters suggested to Hobhouse a fresh examination of current political alignments, and led to his rediscovery of the importance of certain fundamental features of the Liberal tradition. The first lesson which he drew from it was that two groups which had been in the vanguard of progressive politics on domestic issues were basically unsound in their

[13] See Hobhouse's letters to Scott on the issue in Feb. and March 1908, Scott Papers. And by 1911 Scott was sympathizing with Lord Loreburn's lament over 'the great weakening of the real Liberal element in the cabinet since Campbell-Bannerman's death' leading to the current 'almost purely Liberal League Cabinet'. Diary entry for 6 Sept. 1911 in Trevor Wilson (ed.), *The Political Diaries of C. P. Scott 1911–1928* (London, 1970), p. 53. The Liberal League had been founded in 1902 by Rosebery, Asquith, Grey, Haldane and others to propagate the creed of Liberal-Imperialism abroad and 'Efficiency' at home in opposition to the supposed Gladstonianism of the bulk of the party. The most detailed study of this group is H. C. G. Matthew, *The Liberal Imperialists: The Ideas and Politics of a Post-Gladstonian Elite* (Oxford, 1973).

[14] 'Career of Fabianism'.

[15] On the 'pro-Boers', see in particular Stephen Koss (ed.), *The 'Pro-Boers': The Anatomy of an Anti-War Movement* (Chicago, 1973), and John W. Auld, 'The Liberal pro-Boers', *Journal of British Studies*, XIV (1975), 78–99.

[16] The memory 'of all the old South African days when we all put up a good fight together' was one to which they constantly returned in subsequent years (this example is from Hobhouse to Barbara Hammond, 25 March 1927, Hammond Papers).

[17] Quoted in Wilson (ed.), *Political Diaries of C. P. Scott*, p. 29.

political principles. As we have seen, by the late 1890s Hobhouse already felt the need to protest that the Collectivists' 'positive conception of the State' by no means entailed support for imperialism.[18] This was the beginning of his suspicion of the Fabians, a suspicion which was amply confirmed by their conduct over the Boer War. Their flirtation with imperialism issued in the tract on *Fabianism and the Empire* (largely drafted by Shaw), which agreed that any state, such as the Boer republics, which 'obstructs international civilisation will have to go', and that the prospects of the nationalization of mineral deposits would be much better under an imperial government.[19] It was this characteristically Shavian combination of Socialism and realpolitik which particularly infuriated Hobhouse. 'Here was a professedly Socialist society so sophisticated in its politics and economics that its only official pronouncement was a screed of smart chatter about the folly of nationalism and the advantages of public ownership of the mines.'[20] Thereafter, although Hobhouse could cooperate with the Fabians on a limited domestic issue such as the campaign for the break-up of the Poor Law, he was an unforgiving critic of Fabian opportunism and elitism, with an implacable hatred for Shaw above all. Years later J. L. Hammond recalled, in an anecdote which hints at the source of this hatred: 'I was with L.T.H. when the news that Shaw had been lost on the Welsh mountains was followed by the news that he had been found. L.T.H. took it as hardly as if it had been a Boer defeat.'[21]

The other group with 'advanced' views on social reform whose essential unsoundness was revealed in these years was that coterie of Liberal leaders known thereafter as 'the Liberal Imperialists'. Rosebery, their leader, had long ago damned himself in Hobhouse's eyes,[22] and now Asquith, Haldane and the others also stood revealed in their true moral nakedness. They supported the war, denounced the 'little Englanders' within their own party who opposed it, condemned Campbell-Bannerman's 'methods of barbarism' speech, and espoused the fashionable elitism of 'national efficiency'.[23] Rosebery called for government by 'scientific methods' and looked favourably upon the idea of 'a dictator, a tyrant, a man of large mind

18 'Foreign Policy', 189. See above, pp. 73–4.

19 For a full discussion of the tract see McBriar, *Fabian Socialism*, Ch. 5 (quotation at p. 126).

20 'Career of Fabianism'.

21 J. L. Hammond to Gilbert Murray, 16 Aug. 1947, Murray Papers. Hobhouse singled out Shaw as the 'evil genius' of the Society in his 1907 attack, but by then his animosity was already of long standing. In 1905, Ada Wallas (Graham Wallas' wife) noted in her diary Hobhouse's 'great bitterness against Shaw', and that Hobhouse's 'private hell has Balfour, Shaw and Milner in it'. Ada Wallas' diary, 9 July and 8 Oct. 1905, Wallas Papers (copies courtesy of the late May Wallas). And in 1928 he was still lamenting 'the unmitigated selfishness with which Shaw has indoctrinated his generation'. Quoted in Hobson and Ginsberg, *L. T. Hobhouse*, p. 69.

22 See above, Ch. 2, n13.

23 As Beatrice Webb noted, 'the cleavage about the war runs right across the cleavage about economic affairs'. Diary, 20 Feb. 1900, quoted in Matthew, *Liberal Imperialists*, p. 149.

and iron will who would see what had to be done and do it'.[24] Even Asquith, much the most moderate of the group, announced in 1901 that he wanted the Liberal Party to be 'a national party to which you can safely entrust the fortunes of the empire' and which would carry out social reform 'not as a moral question...but as a question of social and imperial efficiency'.[25] The attack upon Gladstonian morality in both international and domestic politics, the anti-democratic rhetoric of 'efficiency', and the opportunism of the 'social-imperialist' programme revealed to Hobhouse the essential illiberalism of the group, and explains why, despite their continuing commitment to social reform, he thereafter remained hostile to them. As he saw it, they were throwing the baby of Liberal principle out with the bath water of Individualist prejudice. In the previous decade he had been less sensitive to such nuances, and the Haldane who had provided the Preface to *The Labour Movement* was the Haldane who had declared a few years earlier: 'The Liberal party has accomplished the main part of what it has to do in the way of establishing more freedom from interference for the individual. It now has to win for him the conditions of freedom in a more subtle and far-reaching sense.'[26] Haldane's Preface was retained in the second edition of 1897 (and thus in subsequent impressions of that edition), but it must soon have become an embarrassment to Hobhouse; it did not appear in the third edition. The alliance which sprang up between the Fabians and the 'Lib-Imps' towards the end of the Boer War only served to vindicate Hobhouse's assessment of their common unsoundness.[27]

By contrast, imperialism, and again the Boer War above all, revealed the essential soundness of two other groups. The first was organized labour. As we have seen, Hobhouse added to the traditional Gladstonian faith in the natural virtues of the 'masses' against the self-seeking of the 'classes', a close sympathy with the Trade Union Movement itself. Thus, although he, like other Liberal intellectuals, was depressed by the popular excesses of jingoism and 'Mafficking', his confidence in *organized* labour was confirmed by the way in which the I.L.P. and Trade Union representatives were for the most part strongly opposed to the war, as much on the grounds of morality and sympathy with the Boers as of any perception of the

[24] Quoted in Matthew, *Liberal Imperialists*, p. 146.

[25] Quoted in Matthew, *Liberal Imperialists*, pp. 71–2.

[26] R. B. Haldane, 'The Liberal Party and its Prospects', *Contemporary Review*, LIII (1888), 155.

[27] This alliance and its intellectual foundations have been extensively documented in recent scholarship. See Bernard Semmel, *Imperialism and Social Reform: English Social-Imperial Thought 1895–1914* (London, 1960), esp. Ch. 2; McBriar, *Fabian Socialism*, esp. pp. 253–6; Searle, *Quest for National Efficiency*, *passim*; Matthew, *Liberal Imperialists*, esp. Chs. 3, 5, 7; Auld, 'Liberal pro-Boers', 95–7.

interests of the working class.[28] The contrast between 'organized labour' as the natural allies of Liberalism, and 'the public house and unorganized labour' which could always be manipulated in the interests of the propertied classes became a staple theme of New Liberal political analysis.[29]

But what was more crucial for the development of Hobhouse's political allegiances during this period was the fact that a significant section of the old guard within the Liberal Party also opposed the war, while a further group criticized both the policy which led to it and, subsequently, the methods by which it was prosecuted. Again, Hobhouse's preconceptions were confirmed in that it was largely the 'men of principle', the exponents of Liberalism as a moral imperative, who composed this group.[30] It vindicated his long-standing admiration for Leonard Courtney who, although a Liberal-Unionist, assumed heroic stature in Hobhouse's eyes as a result of his principled anti-imperialism. He agreed with Scott's assessment that 'he is about the finest – I think *the* finest – and strongest figure in our politics'.[31]

The best example of how Hobhouse's political judgement could be lastingly affected by the glory of a stand of principle in foreign affairs is provided by his admiration for the other outstanding opponent of the war, John Morley. Morley, the fragile rock of the Gladstonian church, was a staunch Individualist in domestic politics, but following his outspoken attacks upon the imperialism of the late 1890s, he was pressed by Scott and Hobhouse to come forward as the leader of anti-jingoism and, if need be, of the 'true' Liberal Party. The most tangible fruit of their labours was to make Hobhouse 'vexed and depressed by Morley's vacillations'.[32] Still, personal acquaintance failed to dim the lustre of Morley's reputation, and the peak of Hobhouse's enthusiasm for him was reached when he and Scott persuaded Morley to speak on behalf of the 'pro-Boer' Transvaal Committee in September 1899. Morley's righteous enunciation of the moral laws which were being infringed by the government's foreign policy moved

[28] Details of this opposition can now be found in R. Price, *An Imperial War and the British Working Class* (London, 1972), which should be supplemented by Porter, *Critics of Empire*, Ch. 4.

[29] See particularly J. A. Hobson, 'The General Election: A Sociological Interpretation', *Sociological Review*, III (1910); this point is also made in Clarke, 'Progressive Movement in England', 173–4.

[30] Porter, *Critics of Empire*, Ch. 3 summarizes the divisions within the Liberal Party over imperialism.

[31] Scott to Hobhouse, 3 Nov. 1901, Scott Papers. Hobhouse's cousin, Henry Hobhouse, was married to Kate Courtney's sister, yet another of the maritally enterprising Potter sisters. The Courtneys came to play something of the role for Hobhouse which had been occupied by Lord Hobhouse before his death – see letters in the Courtney Collection. When Courtney died in 1918 Hobhouse wrote that he was 'one of the very few I have known whom I could call great'. Hobhouse to Lady Courtney, 13 May 1918, Courtney Collection.

[32] F. W. Hirst's report in his diary for 11 Sept. 1899, quoted in Hirst, *Golden Days*, p. 180.

Hobhouse to declare that 'Morley's one hour speech was worth months of ordinary life.'[33] The admiration was to some extent reciprocated, which surely enhanced it. Morley praised 'the acuteness, industry, grasp and power with which Hobhouse had carried on this fight. It is one of the finest pieces of journalistic ability (in the highest sense) which I can remember', and such praise evoked from Hobhouse the characteristic response that it 'is the kind of thing that makes one feel that journalism is worth while'.[34] Thereafter, his regard for Morley was not to be easily shaken. Needless to say, Morley was never as politically effective as Hobhouse and Scott would have liked,[35] but it is an indication of their devotion to the ethic of pure intention that they were prone to regard his very presence in a Cabinet as a guarantee of its political rectitude. For example, the task of guiding India towards some form of self-government was referred to by Hobhouse in 1909 as 'the supreme test of statesmanship and the touchstone of Liberal principle'. This was a test which, in the judgement of later historians, the Liberal government never seemed likely to pass, but Hobhouse rejoiced that 'Fortune has dealt fairly by us in entrusting it to the greatest living disciple of Mill and Gladstone.'[36] He struck a more telling note in August 1914 when, once it was clear that Asquith's Cabinet had committed Britain to war, his plea was 'Could not Morley be persuaded to resign for his name's sake?'[37]

Finally, the experience of attempting to combat imperialism led Hobhouse to a fresh awareness of two points of more theoretical significance – the continuity of the principles underlying the old and the new radicalism, and the interconnectedness of the forces of reaction. In commenting on this experience, Hobhouse wrote:

[33] Quoted in Hirst, *Golden Days*, p. 184. The episode is described in full in Clarke, *Lancashire and the New Liberalism*, pp. 177–80.

[34] Morley's praise is quoted in Hobson and Ginsberg, *L. T. Hobhouse*, pp. 39–40; see also Hirst, *Golden Days*, pp. 180–1, where Morley is again praising Hobhouse's 'fine brain and great courage'. Hobhouse's remark is from his letter to Scott, undated but probably May 1898, Scott Papers.

[35] Their feeling was always, as Scott wrote to Hobhouse in 1899, that 'Morley, as you know, is terribly disappointing, though on occasions he can do wonders.' Scott to Hobhouse, 2 March 1899, Scott Papers. When yet another foreign policy crisis developed in 1911, Scott had to recognize the truth of Loreburn's view: 'Morley very little use – weak and very captious.' Diary entry, 6 Sept. 1911, Wilson (ed.), *Political Diaries of C. P. Scott*, pp. 52–3.

[36] *Democracy and Reaction* (2nd edn London, 1909), p. xxiii (pp. 260–1 of 1972 repr.). Morley was Secretary of State for India, 1906–10.

[37] Hobhouse to Lord Courtney, 4 Aug. 1914, Courtney Collection. A similar commitment to the primacy of moral principle underlay the political allegiances of many of the New Liberal publicists to an extent which historians have for the most part failed to appreciate. For example, Stephen Koss finds it 'curious' that the *Daily News* under A. G. Gardiner should support Morley, or that Gardiner should so often have found his allies among Individualists. But the evidence which he cites should make clear that it was these 'certain moral issues' which bound them together. Stephen Koss, *Fleet Street Radical: A. G. Gardiner and the 'Daily News'* (London, 1973), pp. 90, 178.

> The fight made by the Labour party and the Socialists generally against the South African War will not readily be forgotten, and here as in the defence of Free Trade, the Socialist leaders and the most notable spiritual descendants of Cobden and Mill stood on the same platform. Was this alliance an accident, or did it rise out of the nature of things, the logical working out of principles in political practice?[38]

What gave particular plausibility to an affirmative answer to this question was the fact that the old and the new radicals both relied upon a broadly similar analysis of the roots of imperialism. For the old radical tradition which was opposed to 'the peerage, beerage, and war' tended to identify the sinister interests behind both corruption at home and wrong-doing abroad in terms of monopoly and privilege, and this tradition did not lack spokesmen at the turn of the century. Morley himself attacked imperial policy as the work of 'the money interest': 'the whole thing is tainted with the spirit of the lust for gold'.[39] In 1899, *The Speaker* – under new management as the voice of an old-fashioned kind of Liberal Radicalism – inveighed against 'that spirit which has led through the stock-exchange to foreign adventure and through the power of vested interests to internal atrophy. The fight against the influence of speculative finance in imperial affairs must run parallel with the attack upon class privilege in the ownership of land, the liquor interest and other great monopolies at home.'[40] Meanwhile a similar line of attack was being mounted in the 1890s by Collectivist radicals such as William Clarke or J. A. Hobson. For example, Clarke, writing in 1897 in *The Progressive Review*, presented an analysis of imperialism as 'a force directed by a vast international money-power' which 'cannot live except by fresh conquests'.[41] It is the hint in this last phrase that the disorders of an unregulated economy drove capital overseas which distinguished the critique of this group from that of the older Radicals. Hobson, above all, pursued this line in a series of articles written before and during the Boer War, culminating in his classic analysis in *Imperialism* in 1902.[42]

Hobhouse himself had argued this case in his 'Foreign Policy of Collectivism' article of 1899. Although 'it is obvious that expansion of trade

[38] *Democracy and Reaction*, p. 211.

[39] Quoted in R. Koebner, 'The concept of economic imperialism', *Economic History Review*, II (1949), 19.

[40] Editorial, *Speaker*, 7 Oct. 1899. The review's conception of its task was 'to apply the permanent principles of Liberalism to actual conditions'.

[41] *Progressive Review*, II (1897), 216–17.

[42] Of the earlier articles, see in particular 'Free Trade and Foreign Policy', *Contemporary Review*, LXXIV (1898), and 'Capitalism and Imperialism in South Africa', LXXVII (1900). The fullest analysis of *Imperialism* is in Porter, *Critics of Empire*, Ch. 7, which emphasizes the place of Hobson's underconsumptionism in his theory of imperialism. But for a persuasive account of how Hobson's 'economic interpretation...arose out of and depended upon a political analysis' see Clarke's Introduction to *The Crisis of Liberalism*, pp. xix–xxii.

is a very nice thing, especially for traders', Hobhouse drew upon Hobson's findings to argue that no benefit accrued to the community as a whole as a result of colonial annexations. The needs of investors threatened by 'the pressure of competition upon the margin of profits and, through them, on the return of capital' was the real motive behind the policy, which was engineered through the influence of this class upon government and, through the press, upon public opinion. Pursuing, therefore, a more purely economic analysis than Hobson (paradoxically in the light of their later reputations), Hobhouse concluded: 'In short, commercial jingoism is a necessary consequence of competitive industry.'[43] Hobhouse, in turn, found that his analysis was applauded not only by fellow-Progressives like Hobson, but by the Cobdenite authors of *Liberalism and the Empire*. Given the title and strongly Collectivist drift of Hobhouse's article, it is significant that what they particularly praised him for was showing that 'the enemies of Liberalism are the same everywhere'.[44]

This realization of the unity of reaction was the other legacy in Hobhouse's thought left by the experience of the Boer War. It equipped him with a rudimentary political sociology which enabled him to explain – and often to explain away – the all too frequent but theoretically puzzling failures of Progress to realize itself in contemporary political developments.[45] The essence of his explanation was expressed in January 1898 when, in reflecting on the failure of the recent Engineers' Strike, he wrote: 'The power of organized capital is the standing danger of democracy.'[46] The Boer War provided striking illustrations of the forces which this power had at its disposal, and in the following years Hobhouse devoted some of his most eloquent writing to elaborating on this theme. Naturally, he included among these forces the institutions of 'all that we call "Society"': the clubs, the church, the public schools and ancient universities.[47] He particularly singled out the 'obstructiveness' of the permanent officials of the civil service and 'the permanent determined opposition of the Bench to democratic measures'.[48] Reflecting this constituency was the House of Lords, a brake upon Progress which was

[43] 'Foreign Policy', esp. 206–9.

[44] 'Colonial and Foreign Policy' (by Hammond) in J. L. Hammond, F. W. Hirst and Gilbert Murray, *Liberalism and the Empire* (London, 1900), p. 211.

[45] On his failure to integrate this analysis into the optimistic teleology of his political philosophy, see below, pp. 145–6.

[46] Leader, *Manchester Guardian*, 29 Jan. 1898.

[47] E.g. *Democracy and Reaction*, pp. 72–4; *Liberalism*, p. 123. 'Properly speaking, we have no educated classes; we have numerous men and women who in spite of the schools have educated themselves.' *Democracy and Reaction*, p. 73.

[48] *Liberalism*, p. 123. Reflecting on the judges' anti-Trade Union decisions at the turn of the century, he warned: 'In this country we have to realize that within wide limits judges are in effect legislators with a certain persistent bent which can be held in check only by the constant vigilance and repeated efforts of the recognized organ for the making and repeal of law.' *Liberalism*, p. 114.

actually built into the constitution.[49] Above all, he attributed great importance to the role of the press in shaping opinion, and he increasingly came to feel that 'the great material interests' of reaction 'have now almost the whole press which is definitely ceasing to be a representative organ of public opinion'. Instead, 'the dissemination of news becomes more and more the exclusive property of a few men of colossal wealth'.[50] In its malign influence, the press was only rivalled by the liquor interest, 'which is, after all, the really potent instrument of government from above'.[51]

To this fairly standard account of the bogeys of Radicalism he added a more original historical analysis. He argued that the very 'prosperity and the political tranquillity achieved by the efforts of reformers of an earlier generation had led to the easy materialism of our own time which wanted to hear no more of principles in politics'; 'whole classes have become satisfied with the existing order – that is to say, have become, by natural inclination and in the strictest sense of the term, conservative'.[52] He was scathing about the boom of interest in sport, so marked in this period, which he saw as 'a bar to the maintenance of any widespread interest in public affairs'. He hinted ironically at the dangers of the 'lionizing' of working-class leaders by Society – 'In old days they hanged the leaders of popular movements. Now they ask them to dinner – a method of painless extinction which has proved far more effective.' And he devoted several incisive pages to 'suburban villadom' as 'a political and social portent the meaning of which has never yet been fully analyzed', and to the equally recent phenomenon of 'the-man-in-the-street' as 'the faithful reflex of the popular news-sheet and the shouting newsboy'.[53] Moreover, the political expression of these forces represented 'no mere inertia of tradition. It is a distinct reactionary policy with a definite and not incoherent creed of its own.' For in contemporary thought 'it has found more than one theory ready to serve it,' he argued, thus rounding out his analysis by revealing the politically reactionary contribution of his old intellectual opponents,

[49] He frequently returned to this issue whenever the Lords were being more than usually obstructionist – e.g. 'The Question of the Lords' and 'The Constitutional Issue', *Contemporary Review*, XCI (1907), 1–11 and 312–18; 'The Contending Forces', *English Review*, IV (1910), 359–71; *Government by the People*, People's Suffrage Federation pamphlet (London, 1910). In *Liberalism*, pp. 125–6, he proposes an ingenious scheme for converting the Lords into a more democratic assembly, by continually restocking it with an elected proportion of the members of the outgoing House of Commons.

[50] *Democracy and Reaction*, p. 265 (cf. pp. 70–6 for a further attack upon the 'sensationalism' of the Yellow Press); *Government by the People*, p. 11.

[51] *Liberalism*, p. 111.

[52] *Democracy and Reaction*, p. 63; *Manchester Guardian*, 17 Oct. 1900.

[53] *Democracy and Reaction*, pp. 75–6 ('No social revolution will come from a people so absorbed in cricket and football' (p. 76)); pp. 68–73. The puritan streak in Hobhouse's personality surfaces in some of these strictures. He was, as C. E. Montague put it, 'a man whom you couldn't imagine going to a football match'. Quoted in Ayerst, '*Guardian*', p. 456.

Absolute Idealists and Social Darwinists.[54] This analysis remained a staple ingredient in his political outlook. Given the perpetual oscillation of his thought between the poles of pessimism and optimism, this analysis should be seen as the outcome of his frequent moods of despondency, to be balanced by his evolutionary teleology which was the programmatic expression of his optimism. But although the conclusions of the latter could be used to override the insights of the former, they could not, I would argue, satisfactorily take account of them.

However, this analysis did provide the basis for Hobhouse's claim that the assumption that 'the work of the old Liberalism was done once and for all' was 'too hasty'.[55] Since the forces of reaction posed an ever-present threat to the cause of Progress, the task of combatting them was a permanent one. It was in the interest of Liberals and Socialists to cooperate with each other in this task. As he put it later, the ardent Collectivist had to recognize that the traditional Liberal political issues were not simply 'difficulties interposed by half-hearted Liberals to distract attention from the Social problem'.[56] Certainly, 'in domestic politics the problem of social progress has in some respects changed its character', and traditional Liberals would have to recognize this. 'Still, at bottom it is the same general sense of justice at home and abroad to which Liberalism appealed in the past, and to which it must appeal in the future.'[57] He became fond of citing Green's dictum that it was 'the same old cause of the social good against class interests, for which, under altered names, Liberals are fighting now as they were fifty years ago'.[58] Demonstrating the essential continuity of Progressivism with the older Liberalism thus acquired a fresh importance. As he put it in commenting on the defeat of a 'Tory Socialist' candidate in a by-election: 'There is no more important truth than that social reform as conceived by the best reformers of our time is a legitimate outgrowth and development of the older Liberal principles. To throw over these principles in the name of Socialism is to turn towards reaction in the search for Progress.'[59]

As we have seen, in the 1890s Hobhouse did not look to the Liberal *Party*

[54] *Liberalism*, p. 111; *Democracy and Reaction*, p. 77. See also his attack on these theories in 'The Nineteenth Century: A Retrospect. Some Aspects of Thought', *Manchester Guardian*, 1 Jan. 1901.

[55] *Democracy and Reaction*, p. 211.

[56] *Liberalism*, p. 115.

[57] Leader, *Manchester Guardian*, 17 Oct. 1900.

[58] E.g. *Democracy and Reaction*, p. 11. The quotation is from Green's lecture on 'Liberal Legislation and Freedom of Contract', repr. in his *Works*, ed. R. L. Nettleship (3 vols., London, 1885–8), III, p. 367.

[59] Leader, *Manchester Guardian*, 7 July 1899. Thus in 1911 Hobhouse could claim: 'It is now sufficiently clear to all parties that the ideas of Liberalism have a distinctive permanent function.' *Liberalism*, p. 114.

for the realization of social progress, but in the decade after leaving Oxford, national and personal developments combined to bring him into closer contact with organized Liberalism. He was certainly never to have that unshakeable loyalty of the true party follower,[60] and in the downswing of his moods the Liberal Party was always likely to be spoken of in terms which combined contempt and despair. 'Unless some great and unforeseen change occurs the Liberal party seems to me to be destined for futility' was a characteristic sentiment at such moments.[61] In more sanguine moods the historic role of the Liberal Party as the vehicle of Progress seized his imagination strongly. But principles were always more important than party, and during the last decade of his political life, as during the first, his hopes (such as they were) really rested upon the formation of a new progressive party which would combine the essentials of Liberalism with the best elements from the labour and Socialist movements. His natural inclination was always 'to maintain principles, define aims, advocate causes, and let party organization adapt itself to these'.[62]

In the early years of the century, however, the Liberal Party was the beneficiary of a sequence of events which restored its political fortunes, culminating in the landslide victory of 1906. Hobhouse was encouraged by these developments, and in one case was brought closer to the Liberal Party as a direct consequence. This was in 1903 when Chamberlain attacked Free Trade with his Tariff Reform campaign, thus raising an issue of sufficient theoretical, historical and emotional resonance to unite Liberals in its defence. Hobhouse had recently left his post at the *Guardian*, largely in order to devote more time to his own studies, but unexpected financial problems meant that he needed a fresh source of income.[63] In July 1903

[60] He was several times asked to stand for Parliament, safe Liberal seats being offered to him, but, as his son recalled 'he would not undertake the necessary subservience to party principles'. Quoted in Hobson and Ginsberg, *L. T. Hobhouse*, p. 89. For example, Northampton was offered to him as 'a man of outstanding ability and reputation, deep convictions, and independence of character and action'. Northampton Liberal Party to Hobhouse, 23 July and 1 Aug. 1909, Hobhouse Papers.

[61] Hobhouse to Scott, 14 Feb. 1901, Scott Papers. At the turn of the century he shared Scott's despair of Campbell-Bannerman as party leader: they found him 'so feeble' and with 'no backbone' (Scott to Hobhouse, 23 April 1902, Scott Papers). But his famous protest against the government's use of 'methods of barbarism' in South Africa was an appealing piece of political righteousness, and his subsequent granting of independence to South Africa was seen as an act in the best tradition of Liberal statesmanship. Soon they were recalling that he had 'stood fast by Liberalism in its darkest days' and 'championed the cause of freedom when it was most unpopular'. (Leader, *Manchester Guardian*, 6 April 1908. On Hobhouse's collaboration with Scott on this issue see his letters of 15 and 28 Feb. 1908 and especially 3 March 1908.) Later, when Hobhouse, with characteristic excess, was magnifying the virtue of the past to emphasize the corruption of the present, he reflected that the party had not really represented essential Liberalism 'since C-B's death'. Hobhouse to Scott, 7 Nov. 1924, Scott Papers.

[62] This was the policy which he urged upon Scott in 1924. (Hobhouse to Scott, 9 Nov. 1924, Scott Papers.) Cf. pp. 247–8 below.

[63] In his last two years at the *Guardian* Hobhouse had intermittently been dissatisfied with his situation there – see, for example, his exchange of letters with Scott in Feb. and March 1901, Scott Papers.

he therefore accepted, rather reluctantly, the appointment of Secretary to the Free Trade Union, an official Liberal organization newly formed to counter Chamberlain's propaganda. For nearly two years he polemicized on behalf of 'the good old cause', firmly establishing his reputation as one of Liberalism's leading controversialists.[64]

He was able to resign this post in the spring of 1905, but always remained a distinguished practitioner of the kind of 'higher journalism' which was such a feature of the radical press during this period. Scott, of course, continually tried to tempt him back to the *Guardian*, and although he never resumed a full-time appointment there, he did an immense amount of writing for it over the years.[65] He was also a frequent contributor to weeklies, such as *The Speaker* and its more famous successor *The Nation*,[66] and overall his casual output of articles, reviews and letters was enormous. On any question touching Liberal principles his mind seemed naturally to deliver itself in the required three paragraphs. 'His facility in writing was truly amazing', one of his colleagues recalled, but anyone who has read extensively in his journalism will be more likely to concur with the obituary judgement that 'he wrote "as it came", and it came too easily'.[67]

In Hobhouse's conception of politics, the forming of opinion was central, and could only be done with lasting benefit by expounding views which rested on a coherent theory. In this sense, his journalism was continuous with his political theory; both were directed towards remedying 'the present decadance of Liberalism', the roots of which he traced 'to the weakening of the intellectual basis upon which the reformers of an older generation founded themselves'.[68] Moreover, such an intellectual basis had also to yield a moral imperative, for 'an ideal is as necessary to the

[64] See, for example, the correspondence with Herbert Gladstone, the Liberal Chief Whip, especially Gladstone to Hobhouse, 5 April 1904, Gladstone Papers. Most of Hobhouse's work went into the production of pamphlets issued by the F.T.U. but for an example of a contribution in his own name see 'Five per cent All Round', *Independent Review*, 5 (1905), 37–52. His efforts won warm praise from his uncle: see Hobhouse and Hammond, *Lord Hobhouse*, p. 238.

[65] On his role at the *Guardian*, see Ayerst, '*Guardian*', esp. pp. 355, 373–8, 455–6. In 1911 he became 'the first non-family member of the board of directors' of the paper (Scott to Hobhouse, 23 May 1911, Scott Papers; Ayerst gives the date as 1912 (p. 355)); and thereafter he wrote more frequently for it, contributing 47 leaders in 1913, while 'Scott and Hobhouse between them wrote nearly half the long leaders in 1916, and over half in 1918. In 1915 and 1917 they wrote well over a third' (pp. 373, 377–8). Moreover, 'Scott was always happy to leave the control of the paper to Hobhouse during holiday periods' (p. 373).

[66] For an account of his part in the famous *Nation* lunches – in effect weekly policy discussion meetings – see Havighurst, *Radical Journalist*, pp. 143–53; and for a livelier account see H. W. Nevinson's autobiographical volume, *More Changes, More Chances* (London, 1925). This draws on the vivid first-hand reports to be found in Nevinson's diary (Nevinson Papers); 'Hobhouse comes no more for rage against Asquith' is a standard entry (24 March 1908).

[67] David Mitrany, quoted in Hobson and Ginsberg, *L. T. Hobhouse*, p. 83; Ernest Barker, 'Leonard Trelawny Hobhouse, 1864–1929', *Proceedings of the British Academy*, xv (1931), 546.

[68] Leader, *Manchester Guardian*, 4 Feb. 1902. Note also his characteristic exaggeration of the intellectual achievements of mid-Victorian Liberalism.

reformer as the established fact is to the conservative'.[69] The optimistic assumption underlying his efforts was that 'the people are prepared to move if intelligible and inspiring ideals are set before them', and it was always his charge against opportunists like the Fabians that they attempted 'to force progress by packing and managing committees instead of by winning the popular assent'.[70] There is a glimpse here of Hobhouse's view, to be examined in later chapters, that as Progress depends upon the growth of rational control, so the growth of rational control is impossible without a coherent account of Progress.[71] Furthermore, in the context of Hobhouse's evolutionary teleology, it would be hard to separate his conviction about how politics should work from his intellectualistic assumptions about how it does work, or at least would work but for temporary local difficulties. At all events, it was undoubtedly in these terms that he defined the role of the journalist:

> In so far as there is a real advance in public life, in so far as politics are a serious study designed towards the betterment of humanity, there must be principles guiding the actions of statesmen standing above mere self-interest and rooted in something deeper than party... The truth is forced upon us that it is precisely the absence of clearly thought-out principles such as these men [Cobden, Bright, Bentham, Mill] understood and applied, that has destroyed the nerve and paralyzed the efforts of Liberalism in our own day. The hope for the future of the party of Progress must largely depend upon the efforts of thinkers – not thinkers of the study, but thinkers in close contact with the concrete necessities of national life – to restate the fundamental principles of Liberalism in the form which modern circumstances require.[72]

Given this affirmation of faith in the journalist's role, it is worth looking in some detail at one episode in which it was put to the test. Hobhouse and Scott had often mooted the idea of a London edition of the *Guardian*, and Hobhouse once declared 'to create a new *Guardian* in London, I would give up my books'.[73] Such an opportunity offered itself in the summer of 1905 when Franklin Thomasson, a successful Lancashire businessman of decidedly old-fashioned Liberal views, announced the launching of a new London daily to be called the *Tribune*.[74] Grumbling that, apart from the

[69] 'Ethical Basis', 139.

[70] 'Career of Fabianism'.

[71] In one of his earliest contributions to the *Guardian*, Hobhouse remarked that 'though Conservatism will always fail through its inherent weakness, there will be no steady and continuous social progress until an adequate progressive theory is reconstituted to suit the needs of our own time'. 'The Early Essays of J. S. Mill', *Manchester Guardian*, 9 Feb. 1897.

[72] Leader, *Manchester Guardian*, 17 Dec. 1904. In practice, Hobhouse oscillated, as ever, between the view that 'public spirit and good sense are not, even under modern conditions, necessarily destructive of a newspaper', and the view that given 'popular imbecility [and] vulgarity', they were. 'A feeling for truth is, of course, against a man in journalism as in all professions.' 'A Great Journalist' [W. T. Arnold, Hobhouse's predecessor on the *Guardian*], *Nation*, 8 June 1907.

[73] Hobhouse to Scott, 19 April 1907, Scott Papers.

[74] On the commercial aspects of the *Tribune* enterprise, see Alan J. Lee, 'Franklin Thomasson and the *Tribune*; a case-study in the history of the Liberal Press', *Historical Journal*, XVI (1973), 341–60;

Guardian, 'the other Liberal papers are so futile', Hobhouse reflected: 'I could have wished to have had a hand in the early days of such a paper as Thomasson's is intended to be, but I suppose I am too Socialistic for him.'[75] In fact Hobhouse was offered and accepted the post of political editor. 'Knowing the Lancashire type I fancy I can understand and get on with him' was the reassurance which he offered to Scott.[76] As Hobson later speculated: 'It is possible that [Hobhouse] was able to persuade himself that the immediate problems in the political field, largely concerned with the aftermath of the Boer War, and domestic issues such as the new Education Bill and reform of the House of Lords, need not bring into serious conflict the two schools of Liberalism to which he and the proprietor of the proposed paper respectively adhered.'[77] At all events, some agreement was reached, since the first issue appeared on 15 January 1906, with a characteristic leader by Hobhouse on Liberalism and its task.[78]

The actual arrangement agreed upon was a delicate one, for although as political editor Hobhouse was 'to be responsible for the leaders only, but for them answerable only to Thomasson himself', the precise jurisdiction of responsibilities between him and the managing editor was difficult.[79] Moreover, by temperament Hobhouse was not the ideal candidate for the position. His health was unreliable and he had already suffered several collapses due to nervous strain; he was all too familiar with 'the trials of journalism to a nervous temperament'.[80] As a colleague, some found him 'inconsiderate and not easy to work with'; there was a hint of paranoia in his readiness to perceive slights, and this may have led to his 'unfortunate way of treating his fellow-workers'.[81] And as Barbara Hammond shrewdly noted, 'I think he would be unhappy without some sort of crisis on.'[82]

for a rather limited account of its place in the radical press of the period, see Alan J. Lee, 'The Radical Press' in Morris (ed.), *Edwardian Radicalism*.

75 Hobhouse to Scott, 18 June 1905, Scott Papers.

76 Hobhouse to Scott, 24 Aug. 1905, Scott Papers.

77 Hobson and Ginsberg, *L. T. Hobhouse*, p. 44.

78 The Liberals had just won the election by a massive majority, and Hobhouse issued his usual philippic against the snares of reaction: 'The belief too easily held that Liberalism had done its work was, in fact, itself partly responsible for the reaction which we have described. The work of Liberalism is never done because its essence is the permanent protest of Right against Force, of the common good against class interest, of an ideal element in political life against a merely mechanical efficiency.'

79 Hobhouse to Scott, 24 and 26 Aug. 1905, Scott Papers.

80 Hobhouse to Barbara Hammond, 4 Sept. 1907, Hammond Papers. While at the *Guardian*, Hobhouse had frequently been ordered by doctors to rest when suffering from 'nervous strain' and 'nerve exhaustion' – e.g. Hobhouse to Scott, 17 April 1899 and 2 June 1900, Scott Papers.

81 Hobson and Ginsberg, *L. T. Hobhouse*, p. 95; Barbara Hammond to Mary Murray, 2 Aug. 1906, Murray Papers. I owe the reference to this and to Barbara Hammond's subsequent letters on the *Tribune* to Peter Clarke.

82 Barbara Hammond to Mary Murray, 30 Nov. 1906, Murray Papers.

Crises soon became *de rigueur* at the *Tribune*. Hobhouse had been left free to recruit his own staff for his section of the paper, and he drew upon the services of the by now standard crew of radical contributors – Hobson, J. L. Hammond, Harold Spender, Vaughan Nash, H. N. Brailsford. They were all men of high moral principle with an equally lofty conception of the journalist's role, but the compromises demanded when writing for a new daily paper attempting to establish a circulation, especially under such awkward editorial arrangements, strained their cooperation. What Barbara Hammond called 'epidemics of Tribunitis' were endemic and references to 'the great comedy on the *Tribune*' became a staple of her correspondence. It became a regular event for her husband to arrive home at 1.00 a.m. with the news 'I left L.T.H. writing his resignation', followed with 'by 1.30 Mr Brailsford has prevailed upon him not to send it'. She regularly reported that 'wounded feelings are the fashion at the *Tribune*', where much time was spent 'drawing up letters to vindicate their injured dignities' (at one point 'they carried them about in their pockets and read and altered them every 10 minutes').[83] Finally, after many false alarms, they all resigned at the beginning of 1907 when it became clear that an infusion of American money, the commitment to a 'popular' policy, and the extension of the managing editor's control meant that they could no longer write for the paper in good conscience.[84] What was particularly offensive was that the newly empowered managing editor, Pryor, had been a 'jingo' editor during the Boer War. 'He is the *Daily Mail* incarnate' was Hammond's ultimate condemnation. Thomasson countered that Pryor 'is a journalist before he is a politician' but Hammond proudly declared: 'I am a politician first and a journalist afterwards.'[85] In Hammond's intended sense of the term – a man of consistent political principle – this was true of all of them, and they sacrificed their jobs accordingly. Hobhouse was fortunate that later in the same year he was offered the Chair of sociology in London University, and never again had to rely upon journalism for a living. But, as usual, he had already generalized the gloom with which the experience had filled him. 'Journalism is a profession,' he wrote, 'which may be carried on (a) by people of independent means or (b) by people without convictions. Otherwise it has become impossible.'[86]

These developments in the decade after Hobhouse left Oxford shifted the focus of his political writing. He was now less prone to insist on the moral

[83] Barbara Hammond to Mary Murray, 2 Aug., 12 Aug., 30 Nov. 1906, Murray Papers.

[84] Since he had to justify his resignation to the equally fastidious conscience of Gilbert Murray, Hammond presented a full analysis of his reasons, Hammond to Murray, 30 Jan. 1907, Murray Papers.

[85] Hammond to Hobhouse, 29 Jan. 1907, Hammond Papers.

[86] Hobhouse to Barbara Hammond, 4 Sept. 1907, Hammond Papers.

superiority of Socialism, or to emphasize the new spirit of altruism and cooperation which Collectivism both required and fostered. Instead, he concentrated on the capacity of traditional Liberal arguments to yield legitimation to a more progressive social policy; he now drew attention to the way in which the contradictions within Individualism arose out of an implicit recognition of the role of the state in furthering the welfare of its citizens; and he constantly exploited the prestige of those figures in the Liberal pantheon who could be represented as having had intimations of the Progressive's case (not only were Mill and Green put to work in this way, but so, even less plausibly, were Cobden and Gladstone). He increasingly favoured the 'New Liberalism' as the appropriate label for the cause he was advocating. This was obviously more a response to a changed situation and the consequent need for new tactics than an alteration of fundamental political convictions. It is worth emphasizing that his goal was still Collectivism of a kind and to an extent quite beyond what was generally accepted within the Liberal Party. His vision of an organic community occasionally peers out from behind the restrained language of traditional Liberalism, and we should be reminded that the achievements of the New Liberalism constituted only an interim instalment of social progress as far as Hobhouse was concerned. Moreover, as the parameters of political argument shifted in a more Collectivist direction in the last five or so years of this period, and as the Progressives' optimism about the likely extent of legislative interference with the rights of property increased, Hobhouse was able to reveal the full extent of his Collectivist aspirations. Indeed, as I shall argue in the next chapter, the logic of his theory even in its New Liberal phase presupposed a conception of society and of the role of the state which would certainly be recognized as Social Democratic and even, on many definitions, as Socialist. In fact, given the degree and extent of the moral agreement which it assumed, it cannot easily be categorized as Liberal. This strain of his thought became more obvious after the First World War when Hobhouse was no longer primarily addressing actual or potential Liberals.[87]

However, in the 1900s he *was* addressing such an audience, and the change which this signified from the early 1890s was remarked by F. W. Hirst, a young Liberal of distinctly old-fashioned Individualist views. He noted in his diary in August 1899 that he and Hobhouse had

> a good talk, and found ourselves in agreement on most questions of foreign and home politics, including rating reform and anti-bureaucracy, and the right methods of dealing with natural monopolies and municipalization. His views have changed a good deal since he left Corpus. Three years ago...I felt that we were rather far apart in politics. Both of

[87] See in particular his major statement of his later political thought, *The Elements of Social Justice* (London, 1922).

us have moved, but he, I think, the most. He speaks and thinks now very differently of Cobden and Bright.[88]

The extent and depth of this agreement should not be exaggerated: the issues they discussed were, as we shall see, precisely those on which old Liberal arguments were most capable of being taken in a New Liberal direction. (Moreover, it was short-lived; as the dogmatic editor of the financially orthodox *Economist*, Hirst disapproved of the extravagance of the New Liberal measures which Hobhouse applauded.) But Hirst's remark does indicate Hobhouse's conception of his task during this period, and particularly suggests how it revolved around a reinterpretation of the Liberal past.

That task was to show that 'the difference between a true, consistent, public-spirited Liberalism and a rational Collectivism ought, with a genuine effort at mutual understanding, to disappear'.[89] This involved, on the one hand, attacking what he called 'the confusion of liberty with competition', dissolving the long-standing tie between Liberalism and Individualism, and arguing that there were contingent historical reasons for this union which were no longer operative. On the other hand, it meant arguing that there was a kind of Collectivism which did not represent the thin end of a wedge marked 'expropriation', and which did not fall foul of the knock-down arguments against the confiscation of the property of one class by another. He saw himself as defending a true Liberalism against its recent Individualist distortions, a true Collectivism against threatened Socialist distortions, and both against their ever-present imperialist distortions.

In rewriting the history of Liberalism in order to support these claims, Hobhouse made great play with his idea that the end of the century was dominated by a period of reaction. This was particularly valuable in helping to explain why, if the germ of progressive social reform had been present in the Liberal principles of the mid century, it had borne so little legislative fruit in the last twenty or thirty years. The actual time-span of the alleged period of reaction oscillated with Hobhouse's moods and the needs of his case. In 1899, he suggested that Liberalism had been confused by the rise of labour issues between 1889 and 1891, and then both had been swept aside by the imperialist tide after 1895.[90] By 1904, the idea had been expanded to become the theme of a book. 'During some twenty, or it may

[88] Diary, 21 Aug. 1899, quoted in Hirst, *Golden Days*, p. 174. Hirst had been one of the authors of the anti-Collectivist *Essays in Liberalism* by 'Six Oxford Men' (London, 1897), and was currently secretary to John Morley.

[89] *Democracy and Reaction*, p. 237.

[90] 'Foreign Policy', 197–8. But earlier he had already remarked 'a return to earlier ways of thinking which are at bottom incompatible with Progress and are naturally associated with a theological and political reaction'. 'The Early Essays of J. S. Mill'.

be thirty years, a wave of reaction has spread over the civilized world and invaded one department after another of thought and action' was how he began *Democracy and Reaction*, and this became something of a trope in his writings.[91] It is a particularly vital ingredient in the organization of *Liberalism*. The survey of Liberalism's history (in which the kernel of proto-New Liberal truth present in each stage is extracted from the husk of historical circumstance[92]) breaks off after dealing with Mill and Gladstone, whereupon occur the three chapters which in effect expound Hobhouse's redefinition of Liberalism. Then in the last chapter, entitled 'The Future of Liberalism', he obliquely shows why the Liberal Party of the last thirty years has not exactly embraced its heritage thus conceived. The Home Rule crisis of 1886 was a crucial watershed, for 'the party fissure took place on false lines' ('false', that is, according to Hobhouse's conception of politics as the struggle between Radicals and Reactionaries). He is then able to excuse the lack of achievement of the 1892 Liberal government by suggesting, in effect, that it had reversed the happy prerogative of the harlot, having responsibility without power. Then 'the rise of Imperialism swept the whole current of public interest in a new direction'. The resistance to the Boer War and the Tariff Reform campaign marked the turning of the tide, which continued to rise at the elections of 1906 and 1910. Thus, by 1911 he can argue that 'Liberalism has passed through its Slough of Despond', and is now 'a broader and deeper movement' with 'a genuine unity of purpose' beneath 'the differences of party names'.[93] Like a war of independence which, in separating true patriots from collaborators, becomes the founding myth of the new republic, the 'period of reaction' was the historical foundation for the legitimacy of the New Liberalism.[94]

It also accorded respectability to what Hobhouse urged as a disregard for 'the differences of party names' – that is, to the so-called 'Progressive

[91] E.g. the beginning of his article on 'The Prospects of Liberalism' (much of which is reproduced in the Introduction to the 1909 edn of *Democracy and Reaction*). This explanation was also used to show how 'the expectations founded on the enthusiasm of the eighties' ('Career of Fabianism') became 'the wrecked Ideal of Socialism of the eighties' (Journals, Jan. 1900, Ashbee Papers).

[92] Along the way, the ideals of an earlier age are subtly re-expressed in the language of late-Victorian Progressivism: Cobden's ideal, for example, had been described as 'the unimpeded development of human faculty'.

[93] *Liberalism*, pp. 112, 113, 115–16. But note that in *Social Evolution and Political Theory* (New York, 1911), where he is taking a broad survey of the recent past in order to substantiate the case for Progress, he finds that 'the period which we have reviewed has witnessed a progressive deepening of humanitarian feeling and of the sense of collective responsibility' (p. 183).

[94] This account of the recent past is also relevant to Clarke's observation that 'the New Liberalism was not proto-socialist but revisionist' ('Progressive Movement in England', 170) in that, but for the 'period of reaction' and the 'rediscovery of Liberalism', many of the New Liberal intellectuals could have expected to be 'Socialist' in at least some of the senses in which that word was understood in the 1880s.

Alliance' of Liberalism with Labour.[95] Throughout his life, Hobhouse was a passionate advocate of the claims of labour. He always considered that as a class it had a legitimate grievance on the grounds of social justice. His preference was for the use of means other than the strike where possible, but he recognized the need for the workers to organize to withstand the ever-present threat to their livelihood posed by the employers' economic power, and in actual disputes his emotional sympathies were nearly always with the men against the masters.[96] But his ideal was class harmony rather than class warfare, and whilst recognizing the achievements of the Trade Unions he was increasingly critical of their political solipsism. As he was to put it in the twenties, 'the trade union organization...is essentially sectional in its structure and has all the blindness and collective selfishness characteristic of sectionalism'.[97] Succinctly expressed, his view was: 'Labour is presumably suffering from the wrong of unequal distribution, and in all its efforts commands, therefore, a certain sympathy. It does not follow that every particular effort it makes to right that wrong is wise or even fair.' He was particularly concerned that as a result of ill-considered strikes 'unorganized labour and the very poor will suffer', and society would become increasingly polarized along class lines. In reply to the recommendation of such consequences on the grounds that 'it all brings us nearer to the great class war, nothing is to be got except by fighting', his revealing and impassioned response was:

> The moment you convince me of this I shall shut up shop as a radical or socialist or anything reforming, because I shall be convinced that human nature is hopeless and that the attempt to improve society had better be left alone. Moreover, all that I see or read goes to convince me that if it comes to a class war, the class in possession will win hands down. Numbers are nothing. When it comes to force, organization, drill and tradition are everything.[98]

95 In the wake of the controversy about whether the Liberal Party was doomed to be replaced by Labour in the early twentieth century, there is a growing literature on the Progressive Alliance. Its electoral difficulties are emphasized in Henry Pelling, 'Liberalism and Labour' in *Popular Politics and Society in Late-Victorian Britain* (London, 1968); Thompson, *Socialists, Liberals and Labour*; Martin Petter, 'The Progressive Alliance', *History*, 58 (1973), 45–59; and R. I. McKibbin, *The Evolution of the Labour Party 1910–24* (Oxford, 1974). A more encouraging account of its performance emerges from Clarke, *Lancashire and the New Liberalism*; *idem*, 'The electoral position of the Liberal and Labour Parties 1910–14', *English Historical Review*, XC (1975), 828–36; Neal Blewett, *The Peers, the Parties, and the People. The General Elections of 1910* (London, 1972).

96 This was true from the Great Dock Strike of 1889 – 'I think the mere fact that the men have won is so good' – through the protracted struggle of the Engineers in 1897 – it was in pleading their case that he first distinguished himself on the *Guardian* – to the Railway Strike of 1911 and the Miners' Strike of 1912 – see his leader on the former in *Manchester Guardian*, 19 Aug. 1911 and his remarks on the latter in the Preface to the 1912 edn of *The Labour Movement*.

97 From an unpublished article written in 1928–9, printed in Hobson and Ginsberg, *L. T. Hobhouse* as 'The Problem', quotation at p. 265. It is also repr. in *Sociology and Philosophy: A Centenary Collection of Essays and Articles*, ed. Morris Ginsberg (London, 1966) under the title 'Industry and the State'.

98 From a letter to Margaret Llewellyn Davies of Feb. 1914, quoted in Hobson and Ginsberg, *L. T. Hobhouse*, pp. 64–5.

This qualified support for the labour movement was the basis for his advocacy of the Progressive Alliance. Given his conviction that the Trade Unions could not establish social justice in the community by their own unaided efforts, and given his opposition to the use of force for merely selfish ends, his commitment was always to urging the community as a whole to regulate its affairs for the common good. His faith was always in political solutions, especially since in his view these were determined ultimately by the movement of moral opinion; but he was opposed to a party which was explicitly and narrowly sectional in its aims. Rather, he wanted to see the Liberal Party, at least when in alliance with Labour and kept up to the mark by its radical intellectuals, as representing 'the same old cause of social good against class interests', and he thought that it offered a better hope of true social progress than a Labour Party divided between narrow Trade Unionists and dogmatic Socialists. Indeed, one could say that as Hobhouse understood the terms, the best chance for the realization of true Socialism lay with true Liberalism. In time, as noted above, the actual course of party politics brought him to doubt whether the Liberal Party 'any longer stands for anything distinctive', and to reflect that 'moderate Labour – Labour in office – has on the whole represented essential Liberalism, not without mistakes and defects, but *better* than the organized party since C-B's death'.[99] Although he did not actually join the Labour Party in the 1920s, he gave it his qualified support, and just before his death he exulted that the Labour victory of 1929 'is like the sunrise'.[100] But by then it was Labour *faute de mieux*. Several years earlier he had still retained a lingering hope in what was always his ideal: 'It seems to me that there is possible a distinctive kind of Socialism viz. one based not on the Trade Unions but on the community and social service...I have once or twice written in the M.G. that the Liberal party might teach Labour true Socialism in the point of view of the community as a whole.' In the twenties, he could conclude gloomily 'but I don't think hitherto they have shown much enthusiasm for this role'.[101] In the heydey of Edwardian Progressivism, however, it was to the Liberal Party as the dominant partner in such an alliance that he looked for the first instalments of that ideal.

He was therefore committed to legitimating the necessary measures of 'state-intervention' in Liberal terms. As he later put it, 'the problem was to find the lines on which Liberals could be brought to see that the old

[99] Hobhouse to Scott, 7 Nov. 1924, Scott Papers. Cf. n62, above.

[100] From a letter to Margaret Llewellyn Davies of June 1929, quoted in Hobson and Ginsberg *L. T. Hobhouse*, p. 67.

[101] Hobhouse to Scott, 16 Nov. 1924, Scott Papers. For a brief discussion of the fate of such Progressive ideals in the twenties, see Clarke, 'Progressive Movement in England', 177–81. In retrospect, Hobhouse seemed to think 'the tactical mistake of 1918' had irreparably damaged the electoral alliance. 'Scott as Liberal and Humanist', p. 86.

tradition must be expanded to yield a fuller measure of social justice, a more real equality, an industrial as well as a political liberty. In particular they had to understand that this development must involve a good deal of what was still being decried as Socialism.'[102] What made the task all the more pressing for Hobhouse was that the lack of such understanding was particularly prevalent amongst those old Liberals with whose principled stand in foreign affairs he most closely identified. Hobhouse would have felt this very keenly, for example, when John Morley, the most eminent member of that group, reviewed *Democracy and Reaction*. He strongly commended Hobhouse's attack on 'spurious imperialism' and 'bureaucratic Socialism', his 'warm faith in social progress' which is 'the mainspring of Liberalism', and paid him the highest compliment (which Hobhouse duly returned in the second edition) of finding the book worthy of the tradition of Mill. But he baulked at the last chapter with its attempted demonstration of the essential compatibility of Liberalism and Collectivism. This he found 'dubious' and he rehearsed what were by now the tritest of arguments against Socialism – for example, that it would involve 'subordination of individual energy and freedom not merely to social ends but to more or less rigorous social direction'. This, he concluded unbendingly, 'marks a vast difference and is the dividing line' from Liberalism.[103]

In examining Hobhouse's attempt to turn the edge of such criticism by showing that certain forms of Collectivism were merely the logical extension of time-honoured Liberal principles, it will be convenient to consider the measures involved under four headings: (1) the control of monopolies, (2) the extension of welfare services, (3) the provision of public goods and, (4) finance. These categories overlap to some extent, and obviously some measures could be considered under more than one of them; but they seem to me to provide an illuminating way of looking at the relationship between the arguments characteristic of the old Liberalism and those developed on behalf of the New.

In the case of natural monopolies, especially those where restriction of supply threatened the public interest, Individualist Liberalism had long recognized a *prima facie* case for state control, 'supposing the business to be such as may efficiently be carried on by or under the control of Government'. Indeed, Sidgwick had declared the problem of monopolies to be 'the most deep-seated weakness and the most formidable danger of

102 'Scott as Liberal and Humanist', pp. 85–6.
103 John Morley, 'Democracy and Reaction', *Nineteenth Century*, LVII (1905), 361–72 and 529–47, quotations from 540–2.

Individualism'.[104] Hobhouse could thus gleefully point out how, simply 'on the lines of a strictly consistent Individualism', traditional Liberals had attacked various forms of monopoly, and on the question of public ownership or control, he could point to the much-cited precedents of the municipalization of utilities such as gas and water or urban tramway services.[105] A slightly different class of monopolies were those which were created by government activity in the first place. In this class an example with particular resonance in the Liberal tradition was the liquor trade. Here was the paradigm case of how the moral resources of Liberalism could be mobilized against its Individualist tendencies.[106] But liquor licences were also, as Hobhouse argued, a source of wealth 'in a special sense created by society' which therefore 'should be retained as far as possible in the hands of society'; thus 'the taxation of licensed premises ought to be so arranged that the monopoly value returns to the community'. And, by extension, it was argued that it was legitimate to tax incomes derived from 'ownership of some monopoly or restricted supply to which the public needs give an ever-enhancing value'.[107]

But much the most important issue in this category was the land. This was a central and much-underestimated part of New Liberal theory. It has usually been dismissed by historians as an atavism, an indication of how the party was tied to the outworn shibboleths of the past.[108] But seen in the context sketched here, it appears as an issue rich in political potential.

The irony of the extreme Individualist position had always been that the demand for 'a fair field and no favour' could be turned into a radical attack upon the existing distribution of property, and throughout the nineteenth century there had been those who, though often strong Individualists in their defence of competitive commercialism, held that private property in land was incompatible with this premise, and so called for its extinction through taxation or even nationalization. Herbert Spencer was the best-

[104] Sidgwick, *Elements of Politics*, pp. 555–6.

[105] *Liberalism*, pp. 52–4. He noted that the problems of monopoly arising from combinations of producers had not yet attracted much attention in Britain, and it was never to be as important an issue as it was in the United States in the corresponding period, owing in part, of course, to very different industrial patterns.

[106] It had, of course, been the example around which T. H. Green had constructed his elaborate redefinition of liberty – see particularly the 'Liberal Legislation and Freedom of Contract' lecture; and cf. above, Ch. 1, at n121.

[107] *Democracy and Reaction*, pp. 230–1; *Liberalism*, pp. 53–4; C. R. Buxton *et al.*, *Towards a Social Policy* (London, 1905), pp. 122–3. Its hostility to self-indulgence was evident in the *Speaker* committee's recommendations here: on orthodox Free Trade grounds they were in favour of removing all duties, but 'other considerations of public welfare, as well as of finance, demand the retention of the custom and excise duties upon alcohol and perhaps upon a few other luxuries' (p. 122).

[108] Two recent exceptions are Emy, *Liberals, Radicals and Social Politics*, Ch. 6, and Clarke, 'Progressive Movement in England', 175–7.

known example of this type, and he also illustrates its difficulties. As a radical in the 1840s and 1850s he had advocated land nationalization, but when in the 1880s and 1890s he found his arguments being used to give authority to a variety of Collectivist measures which he abhorred, he had to recant.[109] On the other hand, Henry George, the other best-known example of this type, was instrumental in prompting the so-called 'Socialist revival' of the 1880s in Britain, even though the premises of his single tax proposals were very similar to Spencer's.[110] (Thus, in denouncing Spencer's recantation of his land nationalization arguments, George compared him to 'one who might insist that each should swim for himself in crossing a river, ignoring the fact that some had been artificially provided with corks, and others artificially loaded with lead'.[111]) This strain of Individualism which looked to land reform or taxation as a panacea for residual social evils continued to thrive into the twentieth century.[112]

Even among the most respectable Liberal political theorists and economists the land was singled out for special treatment. The authority of John Stuart Mill's *Political Economy*, the last word in economic orthodoxy for several decades, could be invoked against large landholders (although in later life he moved towards a more radical position on the land than most Liberals were willing to countenance).[113] 'Whenever, in any country, the proprietor, generally speaking, ceases to be the improver, political economy has nothing to say in defence of landed property as there established' was the principle which enabled him to conclude 'landed property in England is thus very far from completely fulfilling the conditions which render its existence economically justifiable'. As a practical step, he vigorously recommended the taxation of increases in site values: this, he argued, 'would not properly be taking anything from anybody; it would merely be applying an accession of wealth, created by circumstances, to the benefit

109 He had proposed land nationalization, most famously, in Ch. 9 of his *Social Statics* (London, 1851) – 'equity does not permit property in land' was his stern conclusion (p. 114); this chapter was omitted when the book was reprinted in 1892, and a qualified defence of existing property rights took its place, though Spencer himself claimed that this was consistent in that his earlier condemnation of them had been on the grounds of 'absolute ethics'.

110 The best discussion of George's arguments in the setting of the 'Socialist Revival' is now in Wolfe, *Radicalism to Socialism*, Ch. 3.

111 Henry George, *A Perplexed Philosopher: Being an Examination of Mr Herbert Spencer's Various Utterances on the Land Question with some Incidental Reference to his Synthetic Philosophy* (London, 1893), p. 87.

112 For example, the declaration of principles made by Franklin Thomasson as proprietor of the *Tribune* was 'in effect a statement of rigid adherence to the laissez-faire individualism of the old Manchester school, qualified by taxation of land values'. Hobson and Ginsberg, *L. T. Hobhouse*, p. 44. The Single-Taxers remained a significant pressure group in the pre-1914 parliaments; see Emy, *Liberals, Radicals and Social Politics*, Ch. 6.

113 For an original and persuasive account of Mill's increasingly radical attitude to the land, see Wolfe, *Radicalism to Socialism*, pp. 52–65.

of society, instead of allowing it to become an unearned appendage to the riches of a particular class'.[114] Even the more conservative Sidgwick could find no legitimate justification for private property in land which was not balanced by the right to compensation on the part of those members of the community who were thereby deprived of the rightful expectation that, on the Lockean principle, as much and as good should be left to give all an equal opportunity to its cultivation.[115] And on a more popular level, the land was readily identified with the aristocracy, and was thus the focus for a variety of less reasoned class and status emotions. That strain of resentful independence and envious schadenfreude which had always beeen a powerful part of the motivation of Liberal voters found a peculiarly satisfying object in attacking the great landlords.[116]

The coup achieved by Hobhouse and the New Liberals was to show, first, how the land question underlay a range of problems which had appeared to be peculiarly urban and industrial in character, and, secondly, how some of these arguments were extensible to other forms of property. The first move was particularly evident in the *Towards a Social Policy* volume, as its structure immediately reveals. It began with six chapters on the rural land question, including remedies for depopulation and the provisions of smallholdings and labourers' cottages, followed by four chapters on urban land, showing its relation to the housing problem. Almost as appendages of these sections, the whole gamut of issues concerning unemployment, poverty, finance and the regulation of industry was covered in the remaining eight chapters. The security of the tenant farmer and hitherto landless labourer, for example, was presented as a step towards restoring the prosperity of the countryside, and hence halting the migrations to towns which intensified problems of housing and unemployment. And given the opposition of the great landowners to such improvements, central and local government would need to be equipped with the powers necessary 'to encourage the social use of the land'.[117] In particular, site value taxation is proposed as an essential step, and the authors quickly point out that the proposal was supported by Morley who showed that 'it had the authoritative sanction of J. S. Mill'. Moreover, it was a key measure linking old and New Liberals: 'Upon this question the disciples of Henry George make common

[114] *Principles of Political Economy*, Book II, Ch. 2, sect. 6; Book V, Ch. 2, sects. 5–6.

[115] *Elements of Politics*, pp. 67–9.

[116] The classic delineation of this mentality is Vincent, *Formation of the British Liberal Party*; see also his *Pollbooks: How Victorians Voted* (Cambridge, 1967).

[117] *Towards a Social Policy*, p. 28. The hostility to the landowners' dedication of their property to sport and other 'pleasures of the rich' is very evident throughout – e.g. p. 37. (Hobhouse's son later reported how his father 'hated all forms of sport which involved taking life'. Quoted in Hobson and Ginsberg, *L. T. Hobhouse*, p. 90.)

cause with the disciples of Richard Cobden; at this point the Liberal tradition and the Socialist movement converge.'[118]

The issue of increments in land values was also central to the second move – the extending of arguments about the land to other forms of property. For example, in 1899, when the chief obstacle to any state-financed pension scheme seemed to be the cost, Hobhouse wrote a series of articles showing how, as part of a reform of the outdated system of local rating, pensions could be financed by taxation of site values, and he specifically insisted that this was only one example of 'economic rent' which could thus be appropriated by the community. (He also pointed out that although this combination of measures was a natural outgrowth of Liberalism, 'the principle on which we have based them would also be accepted by many Socialists as a fragment of their belief'.)[119] In *Democracy and Reaction*, he repeated that the income from site values was only one of the 'ways of accumulating wealth which depend merely on the growth of society', and argued that starting from this point, the Collectivist 'would carry his analysis of property a step further' to encompass 'certain great sources of private wealth'.[120]

The reconstitution of rural life also involved important principles concerning the communal ownership of property. For example, Hobhouse always opposed the much-touted remedy of the creation of a class of peasant proprietors. Apart from the fact that Conservative support for this measure suggested that it was designed 'to reinforce the voting strength of property', Hobhouse opposed the idea that 'the State, having once regained the fee simple, should part with it again': 'communal ownership' with 'small tenants' was the correct approach. The state 'would give to this class access to the land, and would reward them with the fruits of their own work – and no more. The surplus it would take to itself in the form of rent'.[121] Furthermore, as the New Liberals were keen to point out, this maxim could be generalized. Hobson summed up the general significance of the land question in this respect when he wrote:

The effective liberation of the land, as we now perceive, involves large permanent measures of public control, and brings in its wake a long series of further enlargements of State activity

[118] *Towards a Social Policy*, p. 44. Hobhouse repeated this point in *Liberalism*. Cobden's 'attack on the land monopoly could be carried much further, and might lead the individualist who was in earnest about his principles to march a certain distance on parallel lines with the Socialist enemy. This has in fact occurred in the school of Henry George' (p. 52).

[119] Leader, *Manchester Guardian*, 23 March 1899. In a letter to Scott at the same time, he outlined the scheme in great detail, concluding 'this union of measures is what I beg to propound to you as the social programme of the party'. Hobhouse to Scott, 25 Feb. 1899, Scott Papers.

[120] *Democracy and Reaction*, pp. 230–1. He was forever returning to this theme – e.g. 'Prospects of Liberalism', 357–8 – until Lloyd George's budgets of 1909 and 1914 promised to put such a scheme into effect.

[121] *Liberalism*, pp. 91–2.

in transport, credit, housing and other matters. The slow education which the land question has conducted upon the nature of monopoly and socially-created values, was bound in time to bear fruit in a growing recognition of similar elements of monopoly and social values inherent not only in liquor licences and other legalised monopolies but everywhere throughout the industrial system where competition is impeded or estopped.[122]

These strands were drawn together in the land campaign of 1913.[123] Hobhouse and the *Guardian* were very much in league with Lloyd George here, and Hobhouse contributed a series of articles specifically designed to be a favourable preview of the first volume of the Land Enquiry Committee's report.[124] These made clear both that land reform was a necessary pre-condition for the solution of a variety of other social problems, and that the arguments relating to it were in fact extensible to other sorts of property. The proposal for a rural minimum wage was the upshot of the analysis and the lynch-pin of the remedies. The tactic used to justify such an alarming interference with freedom of contract was to redescribe agriculture as a 'sweated industry', and hence to make it eligible for minimum wage regulation under the Wages Boards system recently established for certain designated trades.[125] In fact, on the general principles involved, Hobhouse is willing by this date to give fuller expression to his Collectivist leanings. For example, he commends the proposals to tax site values and to endow a land court with powers of compulsory purchase, on the grounds that 'a considerable part of that element of value in land which depends upon social considerations and political power would disappear, but that is a form of property which does not conduce to the public good, and which the public are not bound to

[122] Hobson, *Crisis of Liberalism*, p. 4. Hobhouse, too, reflected 'we are, in fact, witnessing in regard to the land one of those slow changes of mental attitude which are more potent than any mere revolution. From looking upon it as the property of a small number of individuals who were once politically and still remained socially the leaders of the nation, people have come to look on it rather as the great national asset, of which the owner is a steward who may be called to account, which must be used for national purposes...In this sense, the Progressive "trend" is setting strongly towards making England the property of the English nation, not by any wholesale expropriation of individuals, still less by any high-handed disregard of prescriptive right, but rather by the moderate and cautious but resolute and many-sided application of the principle of public overlordship.' 'Contending Forces', 369.

[123] For details, see H. V. Emy, 'Lloyd George as social reformer: the land campaign' in A. J. P. Taylor (ed.), *Lloyd George: Twelve Essays* (London, 1971).

[124] See, for example, Lloyd George to Hobhouse, 3 Oct. 1913, Hobhouse Papers. Hobhouse had been priming Scott on this issue for some time – e.g. Scott to Hobhouse, 18 Jan. 1913, Scott Papers. The eight articles appeared in the *Guardian* from 2 to 10 Oct.; Lloyd George opened the campaign with his speech at Bedford on 12 Oct.

[125] 'The Rural Labourer and the Minimum wage'; *Manchester Guardian*, 6 Oct. 1913. Throughout his argument, Hobhouse drew heavily upon Seebohm Rowntree's empirical researches into the insufficiency of present wages. Rowntree was, of course, the driving force on the Land Enquiry. Reviewing Rowntree and Kendall's *How the Labourer Lives*, *The Nation* had already claimed that the book showed 'the necessity of treating agriculture in most districts as a sweated industry, and of bringing the power of organized society to bear upon it so as to enforce the policy of a minimum wage'; *Nation*, 28 June 1913.

maintain'.[126] And he makes quite clear that the purified Individualism of the Single-Taxers is not enough: 'We shall not in fact, solve the land or any other problem by trusting to the play of self-interest with the elements of monopoly removed. We need ultimate public control of the land, the intelligent direction of its use by the collective will for the common good.'[127] For the full justification for such claims we need to turn to Hobhouse's more theoretical works, though it is a reflection of the close relationship between his writings of various kinds that his long essay on the sociological and philosophical development of the idea of property appeared in a volume on the rights and duties of property published shortly before the land campaign.[128] But in such writing, and indeed in his contributions to the land campaign generally, it is clear that the issue of the land can no longer be treated in isolation from a more comprehensive programme of social reform.

This brings us to the second large category of measures for which Hobhouse argued by developing Individualist premises in a Collectivist direction – measures which involved the provision of assistance or protection to those unable to provide it for themselves (including legislative control of contractual relations or conditions of employment for whole classes of the population). The heritage of Individualism was ripe for exploitation here, for the bulk of cases of so-called 'state-interference' in the middle of the century were measures of this sort, ranging from Factory Acts to Irish Land.[129] This principle could be easily extended by redescribing existing situations as in fact fresh cases of it. But the example which was in some ways the most telling was that measure which formed the very cornerstone of the most extreme Individualist schemes of social order – the New Poor Law of 1834. For on a strict Individualist interpretation, an individual had no positive claim on any other individual except for what that other individual had contracted to provide (or for compensation for the failure

[126] 'The Protection of the Tenant', *Manchester Guardian*, 9 Oct. 1913. F. M. L. Thompson suggests that these features of large landholding were already declining during this period, *English Landed Society in the Nineteenth Century* (London, 1963), Ch. 12 and pp. 325–6. Thompson's book also shows how substantial were the *urban* holdings of the great landowners.

[127] 'Social and Imperial Taxation', *Manchester Guardian*, 10 Oct. 1913.

[128] 'The Historical Evolution of Property in Fact and Idea' in Charles Gore (ed.), *Property, Its Duties and Rights Historically, Philosophically and Religiously Regarded* (London, 1913) (I discuss this essay more fully below in Ch. 4). Clarke remarks a similar conjunction with the rural and urban land reports in the case of the Hammonds' historical studies of *The Village Labourer* and *The Town Labourer*, 'Progressive Movement in England', 175–6.

[129] Examples of such measures can be found in Taylor, *Laissez-Faire and State Intervention in Nineteenth-Century Britain*, and Fraser, *Evolution of the Welfare State*. Neither author, however, recognizes how much of this legislation was entirely consistent with the principles of the 'Individualist minimum'; Sidgwick's *Elements of Politics* still remains the best and most careful demonstration of this point.

to fulfil such a contract), such claims exhausting the positive rights which it was the duty of the state to enforce. Now the provision of relief was a tacit recognition of the duty upon all members of the community to make provision out of public funds for those utterly unable to provide for themselves. The meagreness of this relief and the harshness of the conditions under which it was administered, together with the emphasis upon 'less eligibility' as its limiting principle, should not obscure the fact that it was an acknowledgement of this residual duty upon the state, the justification of which on Individualist grounds caused earlier Liberal theorists some embarrassment. Mill dismissed – and dodged – the issue by saying: 'Apart from any metaphysical considerations respecting the foundations of morals or of the social union, it will be admitted to be right that human beings should help one another.'[130] Sidgwick could see no way round the theoretical difficulty, and classed it as a case of 'Socialistic Interference', though a defensible one.[131] It was an integral part of the justification that those who were given such relief correspondingly forfeited certain rights of citizenship such as the vote. But the tensions of the theory revealed themselves in practice, and an increasingly large class of exceptions had to be admitted.[132] By the end of the century, therefore, the state was in fact providing certain minimal benefits out of public funds for classes of the population, without demanding services or loss of rights in return.

This was a precedent the principle of which Hobhouse and the New Liberals were very willing to generalize. He could thus preface his justifications of a variety of welfare measures by writing:

> Whatever the legal theory, in practice the existing English Poor Law recognizes the right of every person to the bare necessaries of life. The destitute man or woman can come to a public authority and the public authority is bound to give him food and shelter. He has to that extent a lien on the public resources in virtue of his needs as a human being and on no other ground.[133]

While willing to exploit the Poor Law for forensic purposes, Hobhouse never wished to defend it, and always worked for its supersession by a more extensive and humane set of welfare measures. Moreover, he recognized that the fact that relief carried the stigma of pauperism vitiated its character

[130] *Principles of Political Economy*, Book v, Ch. 11, sect. 13.

[131] *Elements of Politics*, pp. 156–9. In another context, Sidgwick remarked that 'the Government risks some of the evils of communism in order to secure the present citizens from want of the necessaries of life' (p. 174). Both Mill and Sidgwick recognized the practical problem that all the while a minimum of subsistence was secured to those in prison, some system of poor relief was necessary if this was not to be a stimulus to crime.

[132] For example, by the Medical Relief (Disqualification Removal) Act of 1885 those who resorted to the Poor Law for medical treatment only were not deprived of the franchise. In part, of course, the very extension of the franchise put pressure on the 'pauperization clauses: before 1884 a very small proportion of those who went on the parish would have been enfranchised.

[133] *Liberalism*, p. 96.

as a true civic right, whereas the essential characteristic of the measures he advocated was that they gave benefits as of right.

It was in these terms that he persistently pleaded the case for old age pensions. Thus in his 1899 articles he argued that it was the 'duty' of the state to support those whom the industrial system did not enable to support themselves (note the subtle modifications of the Individualist premise here, whereby the responsibility is in fact shifted from the individual to the economy). 'From this point of view – which is, after all, admitted implicitly in the bare existence of the Poor Law – provision for the old age of the workman is not so much a matter of benevolence as of justice.'[134] Accordingly, Hobhouse always insisted, in the face of a variety of conflicting proposals, that pensions must be given on a universal and non-contributory basis. The full justification of this relied upon his 'organic' theory of society which will be considered in the next chapter. But an important supplementary premise was the empirical claim that the average workman simply could not provide for his old age out of his present earnings, and he was able to invoke the prestige of Booth's findings in support of the point that 'insufficiency and irregularity of incomes' meant that pensions were the only alternative to the workhouse for whole sections of society. Hobhouse restated the point that pensions were therefore 'a method of assigning to [the workman] a small fraction of the enormously increased wealth which he helps to create, and which the play of demand and supply in competitive industry will not give him'. For this reason, the pension was not a dole and would not 'sap independence of character or weaken the incentives to industry', an objection which always had to be undermined in such cases.[135] Once pensions became law in 1908, it is interesting to see that Hobhouse was less concerned to demonstrate their derivations from accepted principles, emphasizing rather that they constituted 'the most startling departure from old traditions'.[136] Once established, they in turn became a precedent to be exploited in justification of further measures.

In the years after 1908, Hobhouse was indeed optimistic about what else

[134] Leader, *Manchester Guardian*, 23 Feb. 1899.

[135] 'Old Age Pensions: The Principle', *Manchester Guardian*, 29 Feb. 1908. Here he again argued that the pension should be seen 'as a right which membership of the community should carry with it, just as it now carries with it the right to personal protection and the right to be saved from actual starvation'.

[136] *Social Evolution*, p. 173. Cf. *Liberalism*, p. 93: 'It is very important to realize what the new departure involved in the Old Age Pensions Act amounted to in point of principle.' When first drawn up, the Old Age Pensions Bill had excluded various groups who, by their immoral or 'habitually improvident' behaviour, were deemed to be unworthy of the pension. Hobhouse was glad to see that many of these restrictions were ultimately removed, but it is notable that even he is content that it should be available 'for all persons of respectable standing' (*Social Evolution*, p. 174). I take up the implications of this in Ch. 4.

could now be achieved in this field. 'Few things are more remarkable,' he reflected in 1910, 'than the way in which a practicable social policy commanding wide agreement has crystallized itself in the last two or three years.'[137] He applauded the achievements of the Asquith government, with some reservations, always exaggerating the extent to which each piece of legislation – often in practice an ad hoc measure designed to meet various immediate pressures – exemplified a new understanding of the rights and duties of the state. 'The newer view', as he now called it, 'recognizes a joint obligation – an obligation on the individual to make such provision as he can afford for the contingencies of life, and on the state to afford the basis of financial support and supervision by which alone can such provision be made effective in the case of the poorer classes.'[138] And he supported, again with reservations, the Webbs' campaign for the break-up of the Poor Law on the grounds that society 'instead of redeeming the destitute... should seek to render generally available the means of avoiding destitution'.[139]

In respect of one measure, the National Insurance Bill of 1911, Hobhouse differed interestingly from the proposal put forward by the government.[140] He welcomed the recognition that the state has some duty to provide here, but objected in particular to the idea that the employer should have to make a fixed contribution for each of his employees. He objected that such a requirement did not discriminate between those conditions for which the employer could be held responsible and those for which he could not, and so provided him with no incentive to improve the former. The latter, such as sickness and invalidity, 'are, in the main, common incidents of life, and so far there is no reason why the employer, more than anyone else, should be charged for them'. The cost, he argued, should be borne by a partnership between the individual and the community as a whole.[141] But where there are 'industrial processes which directly or indirectly cause sickness, and... which bring on premature old age', then the aim should be 'to give the employer a direct financial interest in the removal of such causes'. This could be done 'if the form of the employer's contribution were not so much per week for each person employed, but were of the nature of a tax based on the calculation of the amount which

137 'Contending Forces', 369.

138 'Workmen's Insurance and Employers' Liability', *Nation*, 4 Feb. 1911.

139 *Liberalism*, p. 93. He particularly objected to the lack of democratic control over the administrative officials in the Webbs' scheme. See his series of articles on the Reports of the Poor Law Commission, 'The State in Relation to Poverty', *Manchester Guardian*, 22 and 24 Feb., 1, 4, 8 and 15 March 1909.

140 Hobhouse's arguments are given in detail in the 'Workmen's Insurance' article, and substantially repeated in the 1912 edn of *The Labour Movement*, pp. 134–40.

141 Cf. *Labour Movement*, p. 135: 'The provision against sickness is a joint responsibility of the individual and the State.'

his industry costs the state under these heads'. He advocated a similar distribution of responsibility with regard to unemployment contributions.[142] He wanted to see this combined with a redivision of the existing employer's liability under the Workman's Compensation Act, so that again the employer was only liable for those accidents for which he could, in the normal way, be held responsible (rather than for all those incurred by workers in his employment). Again, the aim was to stimulate the employer to reduce the dangers which were reducible, and to make compensation for unavoidable accidents a charge on the community as a whole. The eventual form of the act still did not meet Hobhouse's objections. He argued that the employee's contribution hit the lowest-paid too hard; that it was not a charge on the 'surplus' and, therefore, not redistributionary; and that it was a tax upon production which would eventually be reflected in prices.[143] Once again, the more comprehensive principle which he insisted on was that 'a man needs provision against sickness not because he is employed but because he is a man. The state owes it to him not because he is employed by somebody but because he is a citizen.' 'The true cure of poverty', he insisted, 'is in the establishment of a defined right of income in times of helplessness, charged on the "surplus" fund of industry.'[144] Much of Hobhouse's political philosophy was devoted to justifying this notion of a right.

In the case of the numerically larger though theoretically less significant measures relating to the regulation of conditions of employment, Hobhouse again found many footholds in the Liberal tradition. For here, in the very heartland of contractual relations, the state had recognized that some classes of individuals – children and, more often than not, women – were not always capable of protecting their own interests, and that, moreover, even some freely entered contracts were not devoid of undesirable consequences for others than those who were party to them, so that even on the

142 'That in bad times the employer should pay a weekly tax as long as he keeps a man employed, and cease paying it as soon as he discharges him, will not, so far as it goes, tend to shorten periods of unemployment. Its tendency is just the reverse. But if the employer paid a tax based (a) on the average number of his employees, and (b) on a five, or still better, a ten years' average of the percentage of unemployed in his trade and his locality, employers generally would have a wholesome financial incentive to attempt as far as they can the regularization of employment.' 'Workmen's Insurance'.

143 J. R. Hay, who consistently neglects the views of anti-Efficiency, social-reforming Liberal theorists like Hobhouse, seems to suggest that only Socialists criticized the act on this ground. J. R. Hay, *The origins of the Liberal Welfare Reforms 1906–14* (London, 1975), p. 59. Cf. *Labour Movement*, p. 136: 'All such taxes are bad unless the aim is to diminish production as in the case of taxes on liquor. Otherwise all taxation should fall on surplus. This is the simple principle of democratic finance.'

144 *Labour Movement*, pp. 139–40. This, he declared with reference to the Webbs' rather different proposals, 'is the true break-up of the Poor Law, the true line of emancipation for the great majority...To assure them a certain definite provision, small as it may be, as their own is to treat them as independent citizens' (p. 139).

Individualist minimum they became legitimate targets of control. Again it is clear that by putting pressure on the criteria for the application of the key terms – 'capable of protecting their own interests' and 'undesirable consequences' – and by including fresh examples as cases of them, this category could easily be extended. Thus, by a skilfully selective reading of Cobden's views on child labour, Hobhouse suggests that even such a staunch Individualist recognized the two principles upon which 'the advocates of much of what is called "socialistic" legislation habitually rely'.[145] Equally Gladstone could be shown, by concentrating on his Irish Land Act of 1881, to have endorsed the principle of the state's duty to redress inequality of bargaining.[146] Hobhouse then squeezes the principle hard: 'If we look at the matter a little more closely, the actual freedom of choice is in all contracts a variable quantity', and so 'where a whole class of men is permanently at a disadvantage in its bargains with another, for example, where one class is economically weaker, by the strict Gladstonian principle the State has a right to intervene as arbitrator'.[147]

On these grounds, Progressives advocated a considerable extension of the complicated regulations which had grown up in the nineteenth century, particularly to cover 'sweated' and 'domestic' industries.[148] Their support for the restoration to the Trade Unions of the legal rights which they had lost as a result of the Osborne and related judgements could be seen under this heading also. But the measure with which Hobhouse was most closely identified was the Trade Boards system. These Boards, composed of representatives of the employers and of the employees with an impartial Chairman nominated by the Labour Department of the Board of Trade, were set up in 1909 to regulate wages and conditions in certain carefully specified 'sweated' trades.[149] Hobhouse soon became committed to them as the most desirable way of drawing upon the machinery of the state to establish a minimum measure of economic justice in negotiations between masters and men without resorting to force.[150] He also recognized their

145 *Democracy and Reaction*, p. 214. The two principles were: 'On the one hand it was admitted that apparent freedom of contract was not necessarily real freedom; on the other hand it was insisted that the state has an interest in and a responsibility for conditions, which, operating upon a large scale, determine the health and welfare of its own members.'

146 *Democracy and Reaction*, p. 215. Recognizing 'that it is a mere pretense to talk of a fair and open bargain between the Irish landlord and the cottier tenant... the principle adopted by Mr Gladstone was that where the necessities of one party deprived the apparent freedom of choice of all reality, it is legitimate for the community as a whole to step in and regulate the bargain'.

147 *Democracy and Reaction*, p. 216.

148 See, for example, the suggestions in Ch. 15 of *Towards a Social Policy*. Its authors note that by the act of 1891 many of the regulations previously applicable only to women and children were extended to cover the working conditions of the adult male 'by prescribing a minimum of sanitation and decency' (p. 93).

149 On the establishment of the Boards, see Davidson, 'Llewellyn Smith', Ch. 5.

150 Hobson and Ginsberg, *L. T. Hobhouse*, p. 55. Under the auspices of the Ratan Tata Foundation, of which Hobhouse was Honorary Director, R. H. Tawney conducted an enquiry into the working

potential for expansion, believing that 'the actual method by which we shall achieve the living wage will be by the extension of Wage Boards'.[151]

Owing in part to his authority and good standing in the world of labour (and perhaps in part to the friendship of his Oxford contemporary Hubert Llewelleyn Smith, who was responsible for the administration of the system at the Labour Department), Hobhouse eventually became the Chairman of several of these Boards (ten by 1922), and was widely praised for his success in the role.[152] When the Cave Committee was set up in 1922 to review the working of the system, 'his evidence constituted the main defence of the work of the Boards'.[153] The Boards were, after all, very much an expression of Hobhouse's political ideal: matters were to be settled not by force, but by the appeal to the rationality and good-will of those concerned, directed towards an outcome (always assumed to be available) which was in the interests of the community as a whole. 'He strove, and induced his colleagues to strive, often successfully, for settlements which were founded on principles; he helped the Boards to feel that their decisions were moral acts'.[154] They were thus a characteristic product of the Progressive ethos: as class conflict intensified in the years after the war, the government, under pressure from the employers, effectively killed them.[155]

Our third category, the provision of public goods, can be treated more briefly, if only because it was the heading which embraced the bulk of those measures already recognized, even on strict Individualist grounds, as among the basic functions of government.[156] The principle underlying this category is, very roughly, that there are goods which it is in the public interest to have but which it may not necessarily be in the interest of any individual or groups of individuals to attempt to provide, such as those cases where the benefit could not be restricted to those willing to pay for it, or, at least, where the expense and inconvenience of trying to collect such payment would be too great. Defence and the maintenance of law and order have always been the two most obvious examples, but most Individualist theorists recognized that it licensed a wide variety of measures ranging from the provision of lighthouses and the maintenance of street lighting to the

of Trade Boards in the chain-making and tailoring industries, publishing his findings as the first two volumes in the 'Studies in the Minimum Wage' series in 1914 and 1915.

151 'The Right to a Living Wage', p. 73, in the cooperative volume *The Industrial Unrest and The Living Wage* (with Introduction by William Temple (London, n.d. [?1913]).

152 For further details, see F. J. Bayliss, 'The Independent members of the British Wages Councils and Boards', *British Journal of Sociology*, VIII (1957), 1–25.

153 Hobson and Ginsberg, *L. T. Hobhouse*, p. 56.

154 The testimony of J. J. Mallon, quoted in Hobson and Ginsberg, *L. T. Hobhouse*, p. 57.

155 C. L. Mowat, *Britain Between the Wars 1918–1940* (repr. 1972 [first published London, 1955]), pp. 124–5.

156 For an interesting discussion of the extent to which this category was recognized in classical political economy see Crouch, 'Laissez-faire in nineteenth-century Britain'.

collection and publication of information and the establishment of museums, research laboratories and libraries (though not necessarily lending libraries – unless considered as a supplement to a necessary minimum of education – since these could be operated for a profit at the expense of those who wished to use them).[157] Of course, in public debate the distinction between the justifiable provision of public goods and the allegedly Collectivist extension of state or municipal responsibility was not always clearly maintained, and given the general acceptance of the government's right to provide the chief instances of the former category, this confusion could often be exploited to the Collectivist's benefit.[158]

The Progressives were mostly concerned, therefore, to extend the range of this category in a fairly straightforward way. The authors of *Towards a Social Policy*, for example, in urging the restoration of rural prosperity, claimed that the state was uniquely competent to undertake schemes of afforestation and agricultural research.[159] A more important range of measures in this category was suggested to deal with the evils of unemployment. The establishment of Labour Exchanges in 1909 was easily justifiable in these terms, but proposals for the creation of counter-cyclical public works programmes, though justifiable in similar terms, were usually overridden by purely economic arguments.[160] On the other hand, the setting up of the Development Commission in 1909, though Hobhouse pointed out its 'Socialistic' tendencies, aroused much less opposition.[161] A sub-class of legislation on related principles which Hobhouse supported was provided by those 'cases in which cooperation, if not universal, is altogether ineffective', and he instanced the early closing of shops.[162] Here was a case where the benefits accruing to the tradesman who did not comply

157 Sidgwick suggests a considerable list of such measures (which, though defensible on Individualist grounds, he classes under the more peculiar of his two senses of 'Socialistic' – which on inspection looks quite like a synonym for 'public goods'), *Elements of Politics*, Ch. 10. The best-known modern discussion of the category is in Brian Barry, *Political Argument* (London, 1965), Chs. 11–13.

158 Something like this is surely what is going on in Sidney Webb's famous passage about the Individualist who denounces 'Socialism' as he walks along the municipal pavement past the municipal park. . . and so on. The extent of the acceptance of some measures undertaken on these grounds should not be exaggerated: J. S. Mill, to go no further, was not entirely happy that the Post Office should be a government-run monopoly.

159 *Towards a Social Policy*, Chs. 4 and 5.

160 Hobhouse was only moderately enthusiastic about this scheme, anyway, and in his more confident moods hoped that 'a much more radical form of the collective organization of industry' might in time come to strike at the roots of cyclical fluctuations themselves. *Labour Movement*, p. 139 and n.

161 The 1909 act enabled the Treasury 'to make free grants and lands [*sic*] to a Development Commission for the purpose of developing forestry, agriculture, rural industry, rural transport, harbours, canals, and fisheries'. Emy, *Liberals, Radicals and Social Politics*, pp. 187–8. Hobhouse remarked that it was 'far more "Socialistic"' than most of the measures which the Lords so violently opposed; Leader, *Manchester Guardian*, 13 Dec. 1909.

162 Since the Shop Act of 1911 was primarily intended to benefit the shop-assistants, this measure could also be considered under the previous category.

would soon induce others to follow his example, and so destroy the whole scheme. 'In such cases it would seem that an end, which the community holds valuable and which the majority of those affected by it desire, is a fair subject for enforcement by the common law with its compulsory powers.'[163] On the whole, however, measures justified in these terms were less contentious than most, in part because of the long-standing acceptance of some prominent examples, and in part because, apart from the taxation necessary to sustain them, these measures often did not involve coercion: 'The State may provide for certain objects which it deems good without compelling anyone to make use of them.'[164] The question of taxation, however, raised much more controversial issues.

With financial policy, our fourth and final category, we reach the theoretically most significant feature of the New Liberalism, and the one which was least susceptible of being justified by the simple extension of old Liberal arguments. It is important to insist upon this because, in the historiography of the period, descriptions of the 'growth of Collectivism' or the 'rise of the welfare state' have concentrated upon social-reforming measures of 'state-intervention', several of which did not represent a significant departure from the premises of Individualism.[165] But the measures needed to be financed, and in political-theoretical terms taxation is a crucial instance of coercion, in which the state directly interferes with the liberty of its citizens. A fiscal system embodies an implicit political philosophy, and the justification of New Liberal financial policy required a more extensive statement of principle than had been the case with most welfare measures.[166] Differential taxation on 'earned' and 'unearned' incomes and a graduated tax upon high incomes, for example, rested upon implicit conceptions of the operation of social forces in the creation of wealth, and of the rights and duties involved in belonging to such an interdependent community, the justification of which led theorists like Hobhouse and Hobson to their most fundamental revisions of Liberal theory.

To appreciate the significance of this innovation we need to recall the

[163] *Social Evolution*, p. 194. Mill had recognized this argument but thought it unwise to enact any such measure; *Principles of Political Economy*, Book v, Ch. 2, sect. 12.

[164] *Liberalism*, p. 75. This point had been insisted upon by Mill and Sidgwick; see particularly *Elements of Politics*, p. 335.

[165] For example, Derek Fraser's text-book, *The Evolution of the British Welfare State*, pays no attention to finance. But as Sidgwick noted, many of the measures which he classed as 'Socialistic' 'are usually not coercive, except in the indirect way of requiring funds that have to be raised by taxation'. *Elements of Politics*, p. 335.

[166] H. V. Emy should be credited with drawing attention to the importance of financial policy during this period, though he has concentrated upon its political rather than its theoretical significance. H. V. Emy, 'The impact of financial policy on English party politics before 1914', *Historical Journal*, xv (1972), 103–31, most of which is reproduced in Ch. 6 of *Liberals, Radicals and Social Politics*.

orthodox nineteenth-century arguments on the principles which ought to govern taxation. Stated briefly, the dominant view was that, insofar as society was made up of contracting individuals who recognized the authority of the state for their mutual convenience and defence, the aim of taxation should be to raise sufficient revenue to defray the necessary costs of government. The idea that taxation could be an instrument of distributive justice was precluded by this view. In fixing the incidence of this irreducible minimum of taxation,[167] it was argued that 'equality of sacrifice', the agreed maxim, did not entail progressive or differential taxation (though 'degressive' abatements or exemptions were allowed). Progressive taxation was held to be unjust because it would 'impose a penalty on people for having worked harder and saved more than their neighbours', and inexpedient because of 'its danger of economic loss to the whole community caused by checking accumulation or driving capital from the country'. Of course, any measure which threatened 'the springs of industry' or the practice of thrift fell foul of a batch of less purely economic arguments. The question of differentiation was more complicated and more bound up with practical difficulties. The basis of opposition to it in theory was that 'a peculiar tax on the income of any class not balanced by taxes on other classes is a violation of justice and amounts to a partial confiscation', but, of course, Mill and others treated income from land as qualitatively different, and there was always a strong body of opinion in favour of distinguishing in some way between inherited and other wealth. Nevertheless, beyond exempting a certain minimum income, a small, uniformly applied, proportionate tax was the most that was considered legitimate, and the lower the tax the better it realized the Gladstonian ideal of leaving money 'to fructify in the pockets of the people'.[168]

Towards the end of the century radical opinion was certainly moving beyond this orthodoxy, without, however, formulating an equally coherent set of alternative principles.[169] The foundation of one rather simple kind

[167] In fact, revenue from indirect taxation and other sources could, in times of commercial prosperity make it plausible to dispense with the income tax altogether, as Gladstone proposed to do in 1874.

[168] The two authorities upon the general principles of taxation, from whom the quotations are taken, were Mill, *Principles of Political Economy*, Book v, Ch. 2, esp. sect. 2; and Sidgwick, *Elements of Politics*, Ch. 11, esp. pp. 170–7. Apart from exempting from taxation 'needful expenditure on the instruments of a man's handicraft, trade, or profession', Sidgwick justified exemption at the bottom of the income scale on the slightly peculiar ground that 'in a community where indigence is relieved from public funds...consistency requires that [the Government] should not endeavour to *take* by taxation from the poor who remain independent a part of what it would have to *give* them if they sought its aid'. This is perhaps a further indication of the theoretical embarrassment which the Poor Law caused Sidgwick.

[169] For example, *The Radical Programme* proposed a progressive income tax in 1885, but the National Liberal Federation did not (though from 1889 the latter did propose taxation of land values, ground rents and mineral royalties). In the budget of 1894, Harcourt introduced graduated death duties (and he seems at one point to have contemplated a 'super-tax' – see Emy, 'Impact of financial

of justification was available in later Utilitarian economic thought, since if the criterion of maximizing satisfaction is combined with the application of the theory of diminishing marginal utility this produces a *prima facie* case for redistributing large incomes (F. Y. Edgeworth, for example, argued for graduation of the income tax on some such grounds).[170] But, as I suggested in Chapter 1, such unadorned Utilitarianism was not the dominant idiom of political debate in this period, and a case mounted in these terms alone could not gain sufficient purchase upon the prevailing mode of political argument to forestall objections grounded in deep-seated notions of the individual's entitlement to the wealth which he had created, nor to legitimate such an unprecedented assertion of the place of the state in arranging a system of distributive justice. New Liberal theory was an attempt to meet these requirements.

The easiest place for Progressives like Hobhouse to obtain a handhold upon the recognized principles of Liberal finance was the taxation of monopolies. As we have seen, the taxation of site values and the income from the liquor trade could be approached in this way, and in hinting that there were other 'certain great sources of private wealth' which could be thus dealt with Hobhouse singled out inheritance and 'speculation'. The examples were shrewdly chosen. After Harcourt's impositions of a mildly progressive rate of duty on large legacies, Hobhouse could plausibly maintain that 'in marking out inherited property as an appropriate source of revenue, the Collectivist is again in full sympathy with the principles of the last great Liberal budget, and has no revolution to propose'. Also, of course, large accumulations of inherited wealth inspired some of the same aggressive Liberal sentiments as the land. This was true of 'speculation', too, a powerfully pejorative term in a vocabulary dominated by the values of individual effort and thrift. Moreover, in the aftermath of the Boer War, 'speculative finance' was an easy target. Nonetheless, it was difficult to distinguish the fruits of such unpopular activity from the normal returns of commercial operations, and Hobhouse tried to generalize a much more extreme principle out of these limited examples. 'Aggregations of wealth not acquired by labour service, are, I apprehend, regarded by the Collectivist as a kind of surplus from which the funds necessary to meet public responsibilities should in the first instance be drawn.'[171] Even allowing for an elastic interpretation of 'acquired by labour service', this

policy', 108 and n). Bernard Mallet, a financially conservative Treasury official, found this budget 'memorable for the first really drastic assertion of the place of direct taxation in our fiscal system, and for the introduction of the democratic principle of graduation'. Bernard Mallet, *British Budgets 1887–1913* (London, 1913), p. 298.

[170] See F. Shehab, *Progressive Taxation* (Oxford, 1953), Ch. 12.

[171] *Democracy and Reaction*, pp. 230–2.

suggested a far too 'Socialistic interference with the rights of property to serve as the basis for an appeal to traditional Liberals.

In the *Towards a Social Policy* series there was a similarly revealing abrupt transition from the established targets of radical finance to a more Collectivist conception. Initially, its authors tactfully paid homage to the Gladstonian tradition: the Tories were condemned for their wasteful expenditure on imperial adventures, retrenchment was urged, and a stand made against indirect taxation. In explaining how their programme of social reform was to be financed, they relied upon the more flexible maxim of 'ability to bear', and singled out inheritance and monopolies, especially land and liquor, as legitimate sources. But they then pressed on to suggest that 'the sheet-anchor of future Liberal finance should be a further development of the principle of graduation applied to the income-tax so as to place an increasing share of the burden upon the upper portion of the incomes of the wealthy'. And in attempting to justify this, they fell back upon an argument which in effect suggested that the individual had no right to the enjoyment of any large accumulation of wealth.[172]

It was Hobson who most fully worked out the characteristically New Liberal justification for a redistributionary financial policy.[173] Its central feature was the attempt to discriminate social and personal factors in the creation of wealth. By acknowledging that the latter were entitled to their due reward, this theory did not do violence to the basic Liberal assumptions about the individual's right to the property he can gain by his own efforts; but at the same time, it could be presented in such a way as to justify extensive interference with private property, as currently understood, in the interests of the community. Hobson based this theory upon an account of the economics of distribution which was basically a modification of the theory of rent discussed in Chapter 2. It was most fully set out in *The Industrial System*, and Hobhouse drew upon it for the main economic arguments in *Liberalism* and the revised edition of *The Labour Movement*.

Hobhouse's exposition of this theory in justification of the Liberal government's fiscal measures is another example of how he exaggerated the extent to which the legislation actually enacted was an instalment of the much more comprehensive ideal of social reorganization which he cherished.

[172] 'On the one hand, it is a matter of common knowledge that incomes which are very large usually comprise gains which are derived from privilege or special opportunity, evasion of free competition or superior power of buying or selling in one or more of the processes of industrial, commercial or professional life. On the other hand it is equally certain that these upper strata of high incomes, however got, satisfy less urgent needs than any other part of the general income; the richer a person is, the larger proportion he can spare for public purposes "without feeling it".' *Towards a Social Policy*, pp. 123–4.

[173] Much the fullest treatment of Hobson's theory is in Lee, 'J. A. Hobson'. See also Freeden, 'J. A. Hobson as a New Liberal theorist'; and Introduction by Clarke to his edition of Hobson's *Crisis of Liberalism*.

The increasing need to raise revenue, and in particular to demonstrate that there was no need to turn to Tariff Reform for fresh sources of finance, led the Liberal government to capitalize upon the movement of opinion in favour of a revised system of direct taxation. The report in 1906 of the Select Committee of Taxation reflected the growing body of authoritative support for both differentiation and graduation. In 1907 Asquith introduced differentiation between 'earned' and 'unearned' incomes; in 1909 Lloyd George brought in the 'super-tax' and made a move towards the taxation of income from site values, and in 1914 he introduced graduation upon the higher earned incomes.[174] In defending these measures,[175] Hobhouse oscillated between, on the one hand, trying to present them as legitimate developments of established Liberal values, and, on the other, emphasizing how they embodied a new conception of property. Thus, by presenting the budget of 1909 as an expression of 'Free Trade Finance' against the claims of Tariff Reform, he could argue that the choice in the first election of 1910 was to see 'whether we shall adhere to the fiscal system of sixty years or revert to the methods of an older age'.[176] Yet in defence of the same budget he urged the extremely radical principle that 'the true function of taxation is to secure to society the element in wealth that is of social origin, or, more broadly, all that does not owe its origin to the efforts of living individuals'.[177] It was difficult to show, without a much more elaborate exercise in social theorizing, how a 'super-tax' made this discrimination, as Hobhouse admitted.[178]

It was in the years between 'The People's Budget' and the outbreak of the First World War, when Hobhouse's optimism about social progress was at its peak, that he went furthest beyond this compromise with traditional Liberal arguments. The period of restraint, of having to urge an 'advanced' social policy upon a still Individualist Liberal Party seemed to be past. Progressives felt they had cause to lift their eyes to further horizons. As *The Nation* announced in reflecting on 'The Reality of Social Progress' in 1913:

> There has come about a close body of agreement on the meaning of social progress, and on the most urgent and feasible lines of immediate advance. Moreover, we have recovered

[174] For details see Shehab, *Progressive Taxation*, Chs. 13 and 14.

[175] He did not do so uncritically. For example, he thought the distinction between 'earned' and 'unearned' income not properly drawn by Asquith's budget: he was in favour of taxing 'socially created' (and so to that extent 'unearned') wealth by attacking large incomes, and since 'income derived from capital or land may represent the savings of the individual and not his inheritance', he suggested that the right basis for differentiation was 'between the inherited and the acquired'. Reflected here was his view that inherited wealth was 'the main determining factor in the social and economic structure of our time'. *Liberalism*, p. 102. Hobson had proposed precisely the same criticism and the same remedy in *The Industrial System*, pp. 231–2.

[176] 'Contending Forces', 359.

[177] *Liberalism*, p. 104.

[178] See below, text to n35 in Ch. 4.

a belief in the power and the duty of government as a powerful adjutant in the work of social progress which was conspicuously lacking a generation ago...The new land policy on which we are embarking would have seemed chimerical before this century set in. The belief in progress is such that we are now almost prepared to take it 'in one stride'. It seems quite evident to most of us that in a few years' time our railways and our mineral resources, most of the houses in our villages, and in the outlying residential sections of our towns will have passed from private into public possession.[179]

It was in such a sanguine climate of opinion that Hobhouse set out that theory upon which this interference with private property could be based, and this drove him beyond merely financial arguments. For, as he recognized, the enquiry into 'the equitable basis of taxation' went along with an enquiry into 'the appropriate ends of the state', and 'these enquiries take us to first principles'.[180]

179 'The Reality of Social Progress', *Nation*, 8 Nov. 1913. The change of opinion was widely remarked: Haldane said of the 1914 budget, 'you could not have had this budget ten years ago' (quoted in Emy, *Liberals, Radicals and Social Politics*, p. 227). Equally, Mallet, an opponent of the changes, mournfully reported that 'the principles of state Socialism have largely superseded those of free exchange' (*British Budgets*, p. vii).

180 *Liberalism*, p. 55.

4: NEW LIBERAL THEORIST

In his political writings of the period considered in the previous chapter, Hobhouse was primarily concerned with showing how the measures which he was advocating could be justified even on the premises of (selectively described) traditional Liberal principles. There are occasional glimpses of a more Collectivist theory of community, but it is kept in the background, and its fundamental postulates are never examined with any thoroughness. However, in the mood of optimism about social progress in the period immediately following the first instalments of the Liberal government's social reform programme and the vindication of the 1910 elections, Hobhouse displayed less caution about revealing the anti-Individualist premises of his political theory, and it was during these years that he produced his most extended discussion of political first principles.

The central text here must obviously be Hobhouse's classic volume on *Liberalism*, written in the winter of 1910–11.[1] It was acclaimed immediately as an authoritative statement of New Liberal political theory, and has since been accorded classic status as 'the best twentieth-century statement of Liberal ideals'.[2] Invariably included in any survey or anthology of Liberal thought, it is too easily treated as an all but timeless discussion of Liberal principles, and the extent to which it is a *pièce d'occasion* is lost sight of. For not only was it an attempt to redefine the tenets and traditions of Liberalism so that their culminating expression seemed to be the New Liberalism, but it was also addressed very directly to the highly charged political situation of 1910–11.[3] Surrounding *Liberalism*, and to be discussed with it, are several other discussions of his 'harmonic' conception of society dating from the same period.[4] In this chapter I shall analyse the principles

1 *Liberalism* (London, n.d. [1911]); repr. many times. All references are to the Oxford pbk edn, with Introduction by Alan P. Grimes (New York, 1964; repr. 1971). Hammond reported to Murray that 'Hobhouse seems to be enjoying doing his book on Liberalism.' 24 Jan. 1911, Murray Papers.

2 The opinion of Mills in *The Marxists*, p. 25n. Cf. Ruggiero, *History of European Liberalism*, p. 155 for a similar view. For an example of its contemporary reception see the not entirely impartial review by Hobson, *Manchester Guardian*, 13 June 1911.

3 A reflection of the first point is the fact that the penultimate chapter on 'economic Liberalism' is almost twice as long as any preceding it. The discussion in the last chapter of the crisis over the House of Lords veto and its relation to the 'reaction' of property against social reform amply demonstrates the second point.

4 E.g. *Social Evolution and Political Theory* (1911), the revised 3rd edn of *The Labour Movement* (1912), and the essays on 'The Right to a Living Wage' and 'The Historical Evolution of Property in Fact and in Idea' (both of 1913).

and presuppositions of his mature political theory, drawing mainly on these texts, and in particular I shall discuss the extent to which it is proper to describe it as a *Liberal* political theory.

The concept of liberty, the prime value of traditional Liberalism, was the pivotal point of debate over the nature and limits of state action during this period, and it is correspondingly the central theme of Hobhouse's political philosophy. The structure of contemporary argument about liberty has been sketched in Chapter 1: at the simplest level, the problem for anyone wishing to justify an increase in 'state-intervention' was the long-standing claim that any increase in activity by the state, particularly by means of compulsion, necessarily resulted in diminishing the liberty of its citizens. For the most part, this was not a claim which could simply be overridden: the status of liberty-citations in the hierarchy of evaluative language was such that it was nearly always necessary to adopt some strategy for undermining the objection. One of the subsequently best-known examples of this strategy was T. H. Green's attempt to provide, in the language of Idealism, an account of 'positive freedom' which demonstrated how certain very limited forms of 'state-intervention' (particularly those aimed against drunkenness) could give expression to the real will of those thereby coerced, and could thus increase their real liberty. Although this account drew upon an important range of moral resources – especially with reference to the drink question – by equating freedom with a certain kind of rational self-control, it needed modifying if it was to be used to justify direct financial assistance to the poor. Hobhouse's analysis, which was not particularly original, did incorporate elements of the Idealist view, but it did not rest upon the notion of a real will.

The first move in his argument was to emphasize, as he did repeatedly, that freedom in society must rest upon restraint: A is only free to do x insofar as B is restrained from preventing him. So 'there is no true opposition between liberty as such and control as such, for every liberty rests upon a corresponding act of control'.[5] The second equally obvious but no less important move was to remind his readers that there were many forms of coercion in social life other than that exercised by the state, and so by preventing such coercion the state was not necessarily diminishing the total quantity of liberty enjoyed. 'There are other enemies of liberty than the state, and it is in fact by the state that we have fought them.' The third and boldest move was then to redescribe certain features of current social and economic circumstances as forms of coercion against whole

[5] *Liberalism*, p. 78; or again, pp. 50–1; 'The restraint of the aggressor is the freedom of the sufferer, and only by restraint on the actions by which men injure one another do they as a whole community gain freedom in all courses of conduct that can be pursued without ultimate social disharmony.' Cf. *Social Evolution*, p. 202.

classes of individuals, which only the power of the state could combat. This, of course, was not so easily done, in part because the concepts which could present social forces in these terms were not an established element in the prevailing political language, in part because the empirical evidence could always be interpreted in terms of a failure of individual effort. Still, the two aspects of the argument could be handled separately: certain conditions could be recognized to be restraints on the individual's freedom without it necessarily being the case that it was peculiarly the task of the state to remove them. A fuller justification of the collective responsibility for the welfare of the community was necessary for that (and Hobhouse did go on to provide it). For the present, the argument about liberty allowed the conclusion that the issue was one 'not of increasing or diminishing, but of reorganizing restraints', and thus once again opened up the question of a set of criteria by which to decide which restraints are desirable.[6]

Hobhouse approaches this question by asking for what reasons liberty is valued, thereby shifting the ground of the debate. His argument here provides a good example of how the moral values of the Liberal tradition could be exploited to counter its Individualist politics. The essence of his argument was that 'liberty is necessary to the development of personality. And since personality consists in rational determination by clear-sighted purpose as against the role of impulse on the one side or external compulsion on the other, it follows that liberty of choice is the condition of its development.'[7] This extremely rationalistic account of personality – in which 'choice' is held to be exclusive of 'impulse' – means that liberty has already ceased to be defended on the want-regarding grounds often taken to be characteristic of traditional Liberalism. Instead, the value of liberty is seen explicitly in terms of the moral ideal implicit in that tradition. Liberty is presented as 'the condition of mental and moral expansion', and thus 'the fundamental importance of liberty rests on the nature of the "good" itself'. Control, therefore, must be 'aimed at securing the external and material conditions, of [the] free and unimpeded development' of 'the personal life and the spiritual order'.[8] By now, the emphasis has been

[6] *Liberalism*, p. 81. Cf. *Social Evolution*, p. 200: 'It is only by an organized system of restraints that such liberty is made available for all members of society.'

[7] *Social Evolution*, p. 199.

[8] *Social Evolution*, pp. 199–200; *Liberalism*, pp. 70, 78. This, of course, was the distinction characteristically drawn by the British Idealists such as Green and Bosanquet; see particularly the latter's *Philosophical Theory of the State* (London, 1899), Ch. 8. There could, however, be some considerable difference in practice between securing the material conditions 'of self-development' and 'securing the performance of external actions' (*Philosophical Theory*, p. 176), the latter suggesting a more negative role. Later, Hobhouse certainly objected to Bosanquet's reliance upon the Kantian formula of the state as 'hindering the hindrances' to self-development, but he did not make the grounds of his objection clear (*Metaphysical Theory of the State*, p. 78).

shifted on to a teleological justification of liberty, and with it a much more positive – and potentially extensive – role for 'control'.

The bearing of this upon the traditional issues in the 'state-intervention' debate is suggested by his remark about paternalist legislation that 'if we refrain from coercing a man for his own good it is not because his good is indifferent to us, but because it cannot be furthered by coercion'. This is a quite different basis for the limitation of interference than some version of 'the right to be left alone'; the implication is that coercion is legitimate where the individual's own good *can* be so furthered. Moreover, it makes the right to liberty dependent upon the capacity for rational self-direction, and so those deemed not to be exercising this capacity (or perhaps, more generously, only those not capable of exercising it) could legitimately be subject to control against their wishes. Consider, for example, his discussion of whether the drunkard is capable of exercising the kind of rational choice for which liberty is necessary, or whether he 'should be regarded as a fit object of tutelage'. Where he is judged not to be capable of such choice, 'it is right...to put [him] under conditions in which the normal balance of impulse is most likely to be restored'. He has no right of resistance because he lacks the capacity upon which that right is founded, and the evidence that he lacks it is his drunkenness. That this makes the right to liberty vulnerable to a particularly puritan interpretation of 'the normal balance of impulse' is suggested when Hobhouse adds that in 'all cases where overwhelming impulse is apt to master the will', it is 'a still more obvious and elementary duty to remove the sources of temptation, and to treat as anti-social in the highest degree every attempt to make profit out of human weakness, misery and wrong-doing'.[9] Not only does this seem to rest upon a distinction between 'impulse' and 'the will' in which the latter is not subject to 'temptation', but it assumes an extraordinarily stringent prohibition against selling anything which caters to uncontrolled 'human weakness'. By urging an extensive role for the state limited only by a rationalist concept of the self which was heavily coloured by this kind of moral strenuousness, Hobhouse revealed again the potentially illiberal elements in his theory.

Also, it leaves unresolved one of the perennial problems of political theory – what happens when the liberty necessary for A's self-development conflicts with the liberty necessary for B's? I shall return to this question below in discussing the notion of the common good. For the present, Hobhouse's argument for liberty can be summed up in terms of the scheme sketched in Chapter 1 by saying that he is demanding the freedom *of* all citizens capable of rational self-direction *from* removable socially created economic obstacles *to* develop certain features of their personality in a morally desirable and socially harmonious direction.

[9] *Liberalism*, pp. 76, 80–1.

Such liberties, Hobhouse argued, were rights, rights being claims to the conditions for the development of personality.[10] Since the state was recognized to be the maintainer of rights, extending the list of what counted as rights was always one way to legitimate new measures of state action. In fact, in more general terms one could say, adopting a recent distinction, that Individualists characteristically concentrated on defending 'active' and 'negative' rights – what an individual must be guaranteed against interference from others in his freedom to *do* – whereas Collectivists urged greater consideration of 'passive' and 'positive' rights – the guarantee to the individual of the *receipt* of certain benefits from others.[11] As we have seen, it was in terms of 'rights' that Hobhouse argued for welfare measures such as pensions and health insurance, and he extended the notion to cover less specific claims such as 'the right to a living wage'. It was particularly important to emphasize that such measures were rights, both because the Liberal tradition was so receptive to claims based upon rights, and because so to identify them pre-empted any description of them as benevolent 'doles' which might harm the character of the recipient.[12]

At a more abstract level, however, the theoretical grounding of the notion of rights relied upon what Hobhouse called the 'organic' or 'harmonic' conception of society, and from this perspective 'liberty then becomes not so much a right of the individual as a necessity of society'. The validity of rights in these terms rests ultimately upon their contribution to the realization of the moral aims of society as a whole; in short, rights 'are defined by the common good'.[13] In making the concept of the common good the core of his political philosophy, Hobhouse follows Green very closely. Given the historiographical dispute about the comparative strength of Hobhouse's affinities with Mill and with Green, it is worth pressing this point.[14] It is clear that Hobhouse was attracted to both of them as moral heroes: their earnest humanitarianism, commitment to social justice, and

10 In *Democracy and Reaction* he had paraphrased Green to the effect that 'the moral right of an individual is simply a condition of the full development of his personality as a moral being' (p. 125).

11 I take these terms from the useful discussion in Feinberg, *Social Philosophy*, pp. 59–61. I am grateful to Peter Nicholson for pointing out to me that the latter category contains at least one important ambiguity relevant to my argument, namely, whether they are 'rights' which an individual 'earns' by the performance of certain actions (e.g. the right to a pension as the result of a lifetime's work), or whether they accrue to him merely in virtue of his humanity (e.g. the right to medical treatment even if he has never worked or paid contributions). Hobhouse's 'functionalist' account of rights – and the pressure of Individualist imperatives – inclined him to speak as if he limited his case to the former view, though some of his examples only seem justifiable in terms of the latter.

12 See, for example, his firm insistence on talking the language of rights with reference to a minimum wage (as opposed to the invocation of 'duty' by the Chairman of the Conference of Social Service Unions) in 'Right to a Living Wage', pp. 66–7.

13 *Liberalism*, pp. 66, 68.

14 Cf. the interpretation underlying A. S. Kaufman's study: 'Hobhouse's social philosophy is primarily a development of Mill's social thought, not of Green's views as is often claimed.' 'Liberalism in Transition: The Political Philosophy of Leonard Trelawny Hobhouse' (unpublished Ph.D. dissertation, Columbia, 1955), p. 1.

courageous radicalism struck many chords within him. It is also true that he often quoted Mill's 'argument of imperishable value' in defence of liberty, and declared that 'Mill's statement of the socialistic ideal remains one of the best available'.[15] But such citations can be matched by an equal number of acts of homage to Green, and there seems to me to be no doubt that in terms of formal theory Hobhouse is much closer to Green. His account of the 'organic' conception of society, of the primacy of the common good, and of the basis of rights in the fulfilment of functions often amount to little more than a restatement of the relevant sections from *The Principles of Political Obligation*.[16] This is evident at this point as he explains how rights are related to the common good, since his discussion reveals the same problems as those associated with the concept in Green's theory.

Leaving aside the epistemological difficulties of how and by whom the common good is to be identified, the essential problem about this concept is that it is hard to see how in political terms the 'good' which it postulates is in fact 'common'. As both Green and Hobhouse use the concept,[17] it clearly does not refer simply to a good which all agree to pursue. It is proposed as a feature of a shared situation of which any one individual finds the value increased rather than diminished by the fact of its being shared by others. Insofar as it has a general currency in political argument, it is usually deployed as an appeal for cooperation in an undertaking which is not necessarily in any one individual's net interest.[18] But again, neither Green nor Hobhouse seem to allow that an individual can have an interest, at least one which is the source of a legitimate moral claim, which conflicts with the common good. Certainly Hobhouse argues that 'an individual right. . . cannot conflict with the common good',[19] and his whole discussion strongly suggests that if men properly understood the common good then the question of a conflict of interests would not arise. What seems to be at issue here is a very strong thesis to the effect that only those activities which contribute to a good which can be shared by all should be accorded

[15] *Democracy and Reaction*, pp. 223, 225. This book represents the high peak of Hobhouse's enthusiasm for Mill, as for the Liberal tradition generally (a point which is also made by Clarke in his Introduction, p. xxi).

[16] Sometimes this is evident by the many quotations from that work, but more often it is simply the case that Hobhouse is mounting much the same argument as Green only in less obviously Idealist language. For one example, compare Hobhouse's discussion of rights as functions with Green's *Principles of Political Obligation*, sect. N. This does not mean that in terms of the political debate Green should be classed as a 'Collectivist': as far as actual policy recommendations were concerned, Mill and Green had much more in common with each other than either had with Hobhouse (on this point, see Collini, 'Liberalism and the legacy of Mill', 248–50).

[17] Their use of the concept is not identical: in particular, it is part of Green's Idealist epistemology that he considers 'recognition' a necessary constituent of both rights and the common good, whereas Hobhouse takes a more objectivist line.

[18] Barry, *Political Argument*, p. 203.

[19] *Liberalism*, p. 68.

any moral standing.[20] The premise which makes this plausible is surely the Idealist notion that man's 'nature', defined teleologically in terms of its 'best' or 'highest' manifestations, is such that its fulfilment is dependent upon a shared moral world which realizes the fulfilment of others.[21] Without this premise, the claim suggests that only the goods of altruism, self-restraint and cooperation are what Green called 'true goods'. In either case, there is the implication that there is no right to perform an activity which, though harmless, does not contribute to the common good.

I doubt that Hobhouse would actually wish to endorse this implication, thus stated, though he would, I think, always give priority to a good which was shared over one which was not (and this on grounds other than quantitative, utilitarian ones). He, too, avoids having to confront this result because of his belief that liberty for self-development on the part of each individual is a constitutive element in the common good. The credibility of this belief can only be sustained by some rather restrictive stipulation of what is to *count* as self-development. After all, it is not difficult to conceive of forms of self-development which clash fatally with the expression of self-development by others, as every primary-school teacher knows. But Hobhouse does in fact implicitly restrict self-development to those activities which not only do not conflict with, but actually stimulate, the development of others.[22] The conditions in which this harmony obtains is then projected as the political goal which overrides any purely 'selfish' claims. In both Green and Hobhouse there is evident a streak of the puritanism of the active radical who combines an austere asceticism with an exclusively political moral philosophy. The upshot is, as Richter says of Green's theory, 'there are no purely personal and non-social goods'.[23] Even within the political sphere, it means that the central question of arbitrating between competing interests is evaded: the ideal of the common good is allowed to obscure the actuality of political conflict.

This is evident as Hobhouse proceeds to spell out his 'organic conception

20 Barry suggests a similar reading in an Appendix, *Political Argument*, p. 311.

21 Cf. T. H. Green, *Prolegomena to Ethics*, ed. A. C. Bradley (Oxford, 1883), sect. 177: 'The true development of man...consists in so living that the objects in which self-satisfaction is habitually sought contribute to the realisation of a true idea of what is best for man.'

22 He was more explicit about this in *Democracy and Reaction* where he acknowledged that 'it is not any and every self-development that is good', but only 'a development which harmonises with social life, and so fits in with and contributes to the development of others' (p. 125n).

23 Richter, *Politics of Conscience*, p. 257. Cf. Green's extraordinarily stern injunction: 'It is no time to enjoy the pleasures of eye or ear, of search for knowledge, of friendly intercourse, of applauded speech or writing, while the mass of men whom we call our brothers, and whom we declare to be meant with us for eternal destinies, are left without the chance, which only the help of others can gain for them, of making themselves in act what in possibility we believe them to be. Interest in the problem of social deliverance, in one or other of the innumerable forms in which it presents itself to us...forbids a surrender to enjoyments which are not incidental to that work of deliverance, whatever the value which they, or the activities to which they belong, might otherwise have.' *Prolegomena to Ethics*, sect. 270.

of the relation of the individual and society'. At first, this seems to amount to little more than a restatement of the claim that man is social, that he is in some sense formed by his social relationships and so 'the life of the individual...would be something utterly different if he could be separated from society'.[24] As in the work of Green and other Idealists, this is to be understood rather as a moral than as a sociological proposition.[25] For what it tells us, according to Hobhouse, is that rights and duties (which he recognizes as 'cardinal for Liberal theory') 'are alike defined by the common good' which such community presupposes. So 'an individual right cannot conflict with the common good nor could any right exist apart from the common good', since the individual 'finds his own good in the common good'. It is precisely in such statements that it is difficult to be sure whether the state of affairs being described is an actual or an ideal one, and this ambiguity – the central ambiguity of Idealist moral and political philosophy – bedevils Hobhouse's argument.

Thus, he acknowledges that 'the fundamental postulate of the organic view of society' is the belief that 'such a fulfilment or full development of personality is practically possible not for one man only but for all members of a community. There must be a line of development open along which each can move in harmony with others.'[26] The logical status of this 'must' is elusive. It is clearly intended to do more than simply to propose an ideal; it claims that such harmony is at least implicit in the nature of things. He certainly wishes to argue, with Green, that there must be 'some elementary trace of such harmony in every form of social life that can maintain itself' (though the extent to which some such minimal working agreement is necessarily a recognition of a common good is surely debatable).[27] But what really underwrites the 'must' is a teleological concept of Progress. Man's inherently social nature demands such a harmony, and history, the progressive realization of that nature, is therefore moving towards it. This is the 'line of development' which 'must' exist. Moreover, he is not content to accept that this line of development has no greater chance of being followed than any other. As ever, he wants to disavow any belief in automatic Progress, but still to endow this line of development with a particular significance and a more than even chance. His quasi-Idealist concept of the 'natural' meets this need:

[24] *Liberalism*, pp. 67–8.

[25] Also, Sabine's shrewd assertion about Green is to the point here, given the starting-point of Individualist arguments: 'Green's assertion that the self is a social self was indeed an important statement as long as anyone was inclined to neglect it.' Sabine, *History of Political Theory*, p. 617.

[26] *Liberalism*, p. 69.

[27] That is, it might simply be founded upon recognition of superior force or a mistaken view of one's interests or a variety of things which could not properly be described as a common good.

The progress of society, like that of the individual, depends...ultimately on choice. It is not 'natural' in the sense in which a physical law is natural, that is, in the sense of going forward automatically from stage to stage...It is natural only in this sense, that it is the expression of deep-seated forces of human nature which come to their own only by an infinitely slow and cumbersome process of mutual adjustment.[28]

In effect, this is to claim that a less harmonious development – one, for example, which was powered by other apparently 'deep-seated forces of human nature', such as aggression and domination – would be less 'natural', and *therefore* less likely to prevail. Without this reassurance, there would be no reason to think that the ideal of harmony would see active service, at least not without fairly promptly appearing on the casualty lists of political life. My preliminary conclusion (to which I return below), is, therefore, that Hobhouse's account of the common good is only sustained by his concept of Progress.

Nonetheless, the notion of the common good is the cornerstone of his political theory, and the basis for his more immediate claims about the role of the state. *Liberalism* is a polemic on behalf of the New Liberalism, or rather of the New Liberalism as Hobhouse wanted it to be, and so the notion of the common good was particularly put to work to justify the extensive interference by the state with existing rights of private property which he anticipated was to be characteristic of that movement. The outcome of this exercise is a theory of distributive justice in the economic sphere which would certainly be recognized as 'Social-Democratic', and possibly as plain 'Socialist'.

Hobhouse begins his discussion of 'Economic Liberalism' by dissociating himself from two kinds of Socialism – the vulgar, historical materialist Marxism represented in Britain by the S.D.F., and a savagely portrayed bureaucratic, elitist 'Official Socialism' which is easily identifiable as Fabianism. The 'Liberal Socialism' which he proposes in their stead must be unlike them in two important respects: it 'must be democratic...it must emerge from the efforts of society as a whole to secure a fuller measure of justice and a better organisation of mutual aid', and it 'must be founded on liberty, and must make not for the suppression but for the development of personality'.[29] This kind of flag-waving was obviously undertaken for polemical purposes, but like his announcement that his discussion will 'proceed from those principles of Liberalism which have been already indicated', it emphasizes that for Hobhouse 'Socialism' could be seen as an element of Liberalism. The sphere of 'Liberal Socialism' is the arrangement of the economic life of society, and it is simply one that is

[28] *Liberalism*, pp. 72–3.

[29] *Liberalism*, pp. 90–1.

compatible with Liberal principles. As contrasted with a confiscatory, levelling Socialism, its aim would be 'not to destroy property, but to restore the social conception of property to its right place'. It would do this 'by distinguishing the social from the individual factors in wealth, by bringing the elements of social wealth into the public coffers, and by holding it at the disposal of society to administer the prime needs of its members'.[30] (Here, in effect, is to be found that justification for an advanced fiscal policy which, it was argued in the last chapter, could not easily be provided in traditional Liberal terms.) The viability in theoretical terms of this 'Liberal Socialism' clearly hinged upon the claim to be able to discriminate the social from the individual factors in wealth.

Hobhouse begins by suggesting two arguments to demonstrate the social dimensions of property. The first is that the creation, accumulation and distribution of wealth is in fact dependent upon the maintenance of social order and the provision and enforcement of legal processes by the state. The second is that the production of wealth is itself always a cooperative process in that it rests upon the division of labour, the exploitation of natural and social resources, and the social mechanism of the market. Of course, insofar as these arguments hold, they apply to all wealth and do not yet distinguish the social from the personal. But Hobhouse next argues that different individuals make different use of the opportunities thus created, and so are entitled to correspondingly different rewards. He claims that it is in society's interest to have individuals exercise their abilities in these different ways since there are a variety of 'functions' to be performed. Therefore, 'economic justice is to render what is due not only to each individual but to each function, social or personal, that is engaged in the performance of useful service, and this due is measured by the amount necessary to stimulate and maintain the efficient exercise of that useful function'.[31] Before analysing his justification for this argument, it is worth noticing that this distribution is proposed as a matter of *justice*, but the actual reward is, it seems, to be determined by economic means. For to say that each function should receive the amount necessary to call into play the human energies needed to sustain it is in fact to rely upon a modified version of marginalist economic theory. This interweaving of ethical and economic arguments characterizes the whole of Hobhouse's discussion.

He introduces the discussion of this notion of justice with a 'thought-experiment'. (It is a strategy which latter-day theorists of justice have also found helpful: in part, of course, its appeal is that it removes the need to face up to the problems of the present distribution of property and the rights and expectations which it creates.) Suppose some omniscient central authority could perfectly determine the most appropriate function for each

[30] *Liberalism*, p. 98. [31] *Liberalism*, p. 99.

individual, and the remuneration necessary to stimulate and maintain the performance of that function, then the remainder of the total of wealth produced would be revealed as an unproductive surplus. It could be appropriated by the community through taxation without diminishing any productive capacity. But the basic ambiguity of the original argument is still in evidence here. It is not clear whether the surplus is defined as that which is left over after a minimally *just* distribution has taken place (the criteria of justice being, it seems, some mixture of need and desert), or whether it is what remains when the costs of labour, determined by some modified marginalist mechanism, have been satisfied. I wish to argue that in proposing this ideal of economic justice as the criterion by which society should determine its fiscal arrangements in the present, Hobhouse is committed to a scheme whose practical difficulties reflect the underlying theoretical ambiguity at every stage.

To begin with, the notion that 'individual' factors in the creation of wealth could be distinguished in terms of the minimum reward necessary to stimulate the performance of a particular activity is itself conceptually incoherent. Any attempt to determine the *amount* of this reward seems bound to oscillate between the poles of the original ambiguity. Thus, the amount could be arrived at by the play of market forces. But even in a hypothetical state of pure competition, some individuals – possessing certain characteristics which were in short supply and great demand – would thereby receive very large incomes even although they would, in altered circumstances, undoubtedly exercise their capacities for a lower sum (and even though the exercise of their capacities might not have any intrinsic worth judged by any other criteria). The imperfections of any actual market would further allow other social factors, such as legal privilege or monopoly power, to influence the distribution of rewards, and so there would be no reason to assume that the amount which any individual actually received represented the minimum necessary to stimulate him to produce his best efforts – at least, in any but a trivially tautologous sense.

Indeed, it was precisely in order to remedy the defects of the distribution of wealth as thus determined that Hobhouse was proposing his theory at all. However, it was equally the case that the only alternative basis for determining the appropriate levels of reward – in which society simply stipulates by collective decision what each 'function' should receive – also fails to discriminate in any economic sense 'individual' and 'social' factors in the creation of wealth. For such a figure would merely represent a judgement of social worth based upon some combination of moral and practical decisions, rather than the conclusion of an economic analysis. Moreover, unless the figure thus decided upon did to some extent reflect the play of supply and demand, the community might also have to undertake a certain degree of direction of labour in order to ensure that the less well-rewarded and less agreeable functions were adequately manned. Psychologically, too, it is hard to see how this would meet Hobhouse's requirement that the individual should receive the amount necessary 'to stimulate him to put forth his best efforts'. For here the individual's expectation of what return he should receive, or could receive for the investment of his efforts in an alternative function, becomes crucial. This, in turn, will depend upon the way in which the general scale of rewards is determined, which again resolves into the alternatives of market forces or collective decision. So neither alternative provides a way of identifying 'individual' and 'social' factors in the creation of wealth.

It is clear that Hobhouse himself envisages taxation as the principal instrument for achieving this discrimination, and it was this account of economic justice which he relied upon for the ultimate justification of the fiscal policy discussed in the last chapter. In practice, it amounted to an acceptance of the market mechanism within the limits set by society in fixing a minimum income at one end and a high rate of taxation at the other. The former (to which I return below) could be determined on the basis of need. The latter was in fact fixed by political pressures, since there was no theoretically sound way of establishing the point at which an income began to be drawn from the putative 'unproductive surplus'. The actual level of taxation was necessarily arbitrary from the point of view of theory.

Thus, he offered inheritance and 'speculation' as two examples of income derived from the 'unproductive surplus', and therefore taxable. The examples certainly have an intuitive appeal, but they hardly illuminate his theory, and the second in fact reveals its inherent problems. He suggested that both could be taxed without stunting any productive capacity, but he had to concede that this was not necessarily true of all investment (it is here that he suggests that the 1907 budget's distinction between 'earned' and 'unearned' income was inexactly drawn). For, a tax on the returns from investment 'may operate, so far as it goes, to diminish the profits, and so far to weaken the motive springs of industry', and *a fortiori* this would be true of any more active exercise of capacities. Nor is it a very satisfactory response to propose that the point at which this begins to happen will have to be determined 'by experience'. In the first place, it will be extremely difficult to decide when a productive capacity is being 'stunted' or when an individual is not being stimulated 'to put forth his best efforts' (short of the situation where a particular function is not being performed at all). Secondly, even if this could be decided in some very approximate way for any given function, there would be no reason to assume that the point would be reached at the same level of income for other functions – indeed, it would almost certainly be different in different cases, even amongst the highest incomes. But rates of taxation would precisely have to be fixed by *levels* of income rather than for separate types of activity (beyond, perhaps, one or two large category distinctions), and so there would be no way of avoiding the situation whereby either some productive capacities were stunted because the rate of taxation was too high, or else some individuals were allowed to retain more than was necessary to stimulate them to expend their energies in their particular function because the rate of taxation was too low.

In effect, therefore, Hobhouse was reduced to supporting a more pragmatic and less ambitious fiscal policy which was based upon the assumption that very large incomes could be subject to some kind of progressive taxation without thereby stunting any productive capacity. As he said in justifying Lloyd George's introduction of a 'super-tax' on incomes above £5000 a year: 'The ground principle...I take to be a respectful doubt whether any individual is worth to society by any means as much as some individuals obtain.'[32] But the criterion of social worth was not susceptible of any precise or systematic interpretation for fiscal purposes, nor could it be used to establish that the unproductive surplus actually coincided with large incomes. (Thus, those Conservatives who argued that the tax as introduced was in terms of principle the thin end of a Socialist wedge, which could be pushed as deep as the political situation and the constraints of international finance and commerce would allow, were not simply being alarmist, as subsequent tax rates confirmed.) Hobhouse claimed that 'when we come to an income of some £5000 a year we approach the limit of the industrial value of the individual', but his amplification of this remark revealed that the figure was merely conventional.[33] He recognized that

> so long as it remains possible for a certain order of ability to earn £50,000 a year, the community will not obtain its services for £5000. But if things should be so altered by taxation and economic reorganization that £5000 became in practice the highest limit attainable, and remained attainable even for the ablest only by effort, there is no reason to doubt that that effort would be forthcoming.[34]

It may well be that as a result of living in a society whose fiscal policy made it impossible to earn more than a certain sum, individuals would in the future come to regard the lower figure as a sufficient reward for their exertions, and this might arguably be a preferable state of affairs. But Hobhouse tries to legitimate the first steps towards this future state by using

32 *Liberalism*, p. 103.

33 *Liberalism*, p. 104 and n. It is worth noting that this argument justifies taxation at a rate of 100% above £5000, a rather higher rate than Lloyd George's 6d in the £.

34 Hobhouse's moralistic strain is also evident here: in his eyes, a further recommendation of the super-tax is that it may 'quench the anti-social ardour for unmeasured wealth, for social power and the vanity of display' (p. 104).

his theory of 'individual' and 'social' factors in the creation of wealth. In fact, as we have seen, the so-called 'unproductive surplus' is dependent upon a social decision about what should be the maximum reward which any individual can claim: income above that point is *thereby* declared to be unproductive.

So Hobhouse continues to dodge the central issue which his political theory raises of choosing between communal control of the distribution of income and the market mechanism. It seems that he hides behind this ambiguity because he wants both to have his cake of Socialism and to eat it in accordance with Liberal principles – that is, to introduce a basic justice into the distribution of wealth but to reward individual efforts unequally, and thus to avoid the standard charges against Socialism of stifling individual initiative and creativity. By resting the argument on the distinction between 'individual' and 'social' factors in the creation of wealth, and by claiming to leave the former undisturbed, he can seem to avoid the unacceptably Socialist enterprise of fixing income, and the distribution of wealth generally, according to the decision of a central authority. In fact, as the foregoing analysis reveals, the operation of the distinction itself depends precisely upon some prior determination (presumably by collective authority) of what the rewards for each 'function' ought to be. At the root of Hobhouse's theory, therefore, is a moral decision disguised as an economic truth.

Hobhouse had acknowledged in defending the 1909 budget, that 'the distinctions drawn are not perfectly scientific, but they are the best rough-and-ready approximations that have yet been made on this side to a form of taxation tending to relieve steady industry at the expense of good fortune'.[35] But the incoherence in his theory rendered him vulnerable to attack from the Left as well as the Right, as emerged in his lively controversy with George Bernard Shaw over the distribution of income.

Shaw attacked Hobhouse's claim that a just distribution of income could be determined so that unequal contributions to the common good could be rewarded unequally. He argued instead that the only defensible distribution was complete equality of income, and he demanded that Hobhouse, if he were to put his principle into effect, invent 'two necessary instruments: one for measuring exertion and one for measuring the gratification derived from money'.[36] Hobhouse replied that reward for exertion was not the only criterion which he proposed; and he restated his

[35] Leader, *Manchester Guardian*, 13 Dec. 1909.

[36] Letter of 'Equality of Income', *Nation*, 17 May 1913. The previous issue of *The Nation* had contained a criticism of a speech by Shaw advocating equality of income. In his letter Shaw bracketed together *The Nation*'s article and a recent exposition by Hobhouse of the economic arguments set out in *Liberalism*.

view 'that in a good social order, exertions in directions useful to society would be, except for those who are incapacitated, a condition of obtaining any income at all, and I think it should be open to men and women to increase their income by increased exertion'. He readily agreed that he could not provide a measure of the gratification derived from money (and so, presumably, his theory is, strictly speaking, about the distribution of *income* and not of *reward*); but he did suggest that there were ways of measuring exertion, including such rough-and-ready ones as time and piece-work. He was particularly anxious to discriminate idleness from effort, and objected that Shaw's proposal would 'supply a man with an income throughout life whether he works or idles'. This, he complained, was to give not equal opportunity but 'equal treatment to the man who uses his opportunities and the man who neglects them'.[37]

Much Shavian wit was directed at the inadequacies of Hobhouse's principle in the ensuing exchange. Shaw's central contention was that, having abandoned the mechanism of the market, Hobhouse could find no alternative basis for distributing income. Time and piece-work were easily ridiculed as measures of exertion, especially as between different activities ('Mr Hobhouse's notion that two hours' work means twice the exertion of one hour's work is the notion of a bricklayer; and as Mr Hobhouse is not a bricklayer, I cannot imagine how he came to entertain it'), and the actual rates would anyway tend to reflect current market rates. Other differences, such as those of sex and of colour, will also affect economic opportunity and thus reward.[38] Moreover, not everyone can engage in socially useful work, and so 'no matter how you distribute the national income, a good deal of it will have to go otherwise than under the form of remunerating services'. Even the idle man should be supported precisely because poverty and ignorance perpetuate themselves and produce even more evils (the idle man could be punished but will anyway soon 'succumb to the English horror of not doing what everybody else is doing').[39]

Hobhouse's long-standing hostility to Shaw was not diminished by the combination of flippancy and cogency in this attack, and his reply was marked by much anti-Fabian irony.[40] He naturally accepted that there were

37 Letter on 'Equality of Income', *Nation*, 24 May 1913. This anxiety recurred throughout his letter: 'It does not seem to most of us just that a man should receive the same payment for two hours' work as for one of the same kind, or for making two pairs of boots as for making one, or, for that matter, none at all.'

38 'I do not believe that any readjustment of economic conditions would enable Mr Hobhouse to bear twins or to achieve popularity as a Christy Minstrel. If Mr Hobhouse really believes that he ought, on this account, to get less than his charwoman or than the nearest negro with an ear for music, let him say so at once and be removed to a lunatic asylum.'

39 Letter on 'Equality of Income', *Nation*, 31 May 1913.

40 Letter on 'Equality of Income', *Nation*, 7 June 1913. For example, Shaw had frivolously suggested that the idle man might also be kicked, shamed and hanged but not deprived of his income.

some classes, especially children, whom society was bound to maintain at its own expense, but he still insisted that 'the adult and responsible person' needed an income 'as a basis for the guidance and direction of his own life, and if he is healthy and fit, he owes society the exertion of his powers in useful ways as a return'. He stuck to his claim that such exertion needed to be stimulated by the provision of the necessary reward, and this would naturally result in unequal incomes. But he ducked the central question of how the amount of this reward was to be determined, and left himself as open as ever to the change of simply reflecting the existing distribution of bargaining power in the market. Certainly, this was not what Hobhouse had in mind, given that the inspiration of his theory was the attempt to replace the Individualist's reliance on the anarchy of the market with some principles of just distribution. As ever, his citation of the values of individual effort and the performance of socially useful functions invoked an assumed moral order which obviated any necessity for further analysis. It was enough for Hobhouse to establish the moral superiority of the case for remuneration on these terms: the potential problems of arbitrating between conflicting claims in the distribution of scarce resources did not appear on the agenda of his political theory.

It is, of course, true that, considered in very general terms, any writer arguing for a redistribution of wealth by means of social welfare policies had in effect to propose some version of a theory of distributive justice to replace the Individualist's reliance upon 'entitlement' as the sole criterion of justice. For the characteristic strength of an entitlement theory is its appeal to the individual's sense of his right to what he has legally gained, and so of different entitlements depending upon differing histories of labour and initiative (the fluctuation of fortune being assumed to be arbitrary and therefore impartial). Correspondingly, its characteristic weakness is its inability to consider the pattern of the social distribution of benefits as a whole and its bondage to previous legally undertaken transactions: by considering always the single case, the question of the 'fairness' of certain patterns of distribution is begged. It is precisely the justice of this overall pattern which distributivist theories make the prime political value.[41] However, Hobhouse's is not a pure example of such a theory, in that it relies upon the criterion of need at the bottom of the economic scale, and a rather peculiar form of desert at the top. All are to be guaranteed a

Hobhouse expended much sarcasm in imagining how the process might be 'controlled, let us say, by three Fabians, a muscular one to do the kicking, a superior one to do the shaming, and a peculiarly expert Fabian to hang a man in the luncheon hour so that the work might go the more merrily in the afternoon'.

[41] The contrasting features of these kinds of justice are clearly brought out in the recent confrontation between John Rawls, *A Theory of Justice* (Cambridge, Mass., 1971) and Robert Nozick, *Anarchy, State and Utopia* (New York, 1974), the *Social Statics* de nos jours.

minimum, and this is the first claim upon the public purse, a claim which even overrides existing entitlements (of, for example, the wealthy man to the full enjoyment of his property). Above that, each individual may 'deserve' more if more is needed to stimulate the performance of a certain social function. (As we have seen, this notion of need is in fact parasitic upon some implicit assumption about what an individual ought to be able to earn.) By such a combination of criteria, Hobhouse hoped to be able to justify interference with property through redistributive taxation without actually denying the individual the opportunity to increase his rewards by his own exertions (so long as they are in a socially useful direction). The focus of attention, as is perhaps the case with all essentially social-democratic welfare theories, is upon the needs of the poor; the primary purpose of the redistribution of wealth is to pay for these needs to be met, not to attack the social power of property as such. The attack on poverty was certainly the motivating impulse of this generation of reformers, and Hobhouse's theory grew, albeit in a complex and indirect way, out of this urge.

From this point of view, the claim that every member of society was entitled to a guaranteed minimum standard of living was the central practical conclusion supported by the theory. It was in these terms that Hobhouse prescribed the goal for reform:

> The function of the State is to secure conditions upon which its citizens are able to win by their own efforts all that is necessary to full civic efficiency. It is not for the State to feed, house, or clothe them. It is for the State to take care that the economic conditions are such that the normal man who is not defective in mind or body or will can by useful labour feed, house, and clothe himself and his family.

He pointed out that this did not mean that 'the wages earned by the labour of an adult man ought to suffice for the maintenance of an average family, providing for all risks'. For the citizen was also entitled to his share of 'social wealth', the services and amenities financed out of the 'surplus'. 'This share should be his support in the times of misfortune, of sickness and of worklessness, whether due to economic disorganization or to invalidity and old age.' Such support would not 'infringe upon the income of other individuals', since 'if fiscal arrangements are what they should be' the surplus is not drawn from wealth earned by any individual. Furthermore, and this was a point of some polemical value, the citizen in receipt of this benefit has not compromised his independence: 'The man who, without further aid than the universally available share in the social inheritance which is to fall to him as a citizen, pays his way through life is to be justly regarded as self-supporting.'[42]

[42] *Liberalism*, pp. 83, 107.

An integral part of this ideal was the claim for a minimum wage. Although Hobhouse was committed to the support of this claim, his allegiance to the principle of 'the equation of social service and reward' – which he tendentiously referred to as 'the central point of Liberal economics' – meant that it was inseparable from a strenuous emphasis upon the performance of duties. In his topical plea in 1913 for 'the right to a living wage', for example, his starting point was that, insofar as it did not provide even 'the material means of health and efficiency' for a considerable proportion of the population, 'the competitive system has failed'. A conception of social rights and duties is needed to replace the 'higgling of the market'. Society

> requires the performance of various functions to maintain its well being, and the business of its economic system is to secure the adequate stimulation and maintenance of those functions. To each man and to each class that is justly due which serves to maintain them in the adequate exercise of the function which it is theirs to fulfil in the social life.

Clearly, there could be socially conservative implications to this, but it was intended to legitimate a measure which was considered very radical at the time. The individual has a right to be guaranteed by society the wherewithal to maintain the performance of his function; conversely, society has a right to demand that all who are guaranteed this maintenance fulfil the duty of providing the appropriate service. Indeed, the duties seem to go further than that: Hobhouse insists that the worker is also a citizen, 'and as such ought to take his part not only in the individual but in the higher interests of the society to which he belongs. As this is his *duty*, so the conditions of work and wages which enable him to perform it are his rights.'[43] It is characteristic of Hobhouse's theory to exact from the individual in return for this right the high price of compulsory participation in society's common purposes.

The dangers of basing rights on the positive performance of such duties are suggested by Hobhouse's references to the treatment appropriate for those who fail to perform them.[44] In the case of those physically incapable of fulfilling these duties, 'there is no question here of payment for a function but of ministering to human suffering'. They are simply 'a charge on the surplus'. Although Hobhouse obviously thinks that society should provide for them, it is not clear whether, by failing to perform any function, they have forfeited their *rights* to such provision. His remark that this class 'must depend, to its misfortune, on private and public charity' certainly does not suggest that they have an enforceable claim. In the case of the 'mentally defective', the question of rights of any kind does not arise for Hobhouse,

[43] 'Right to a Living Wage', pp. 66, 68, 70 (my emphasis).

[44] *Liberalism*, pp. 86, 95, 106; *Social Evolution*, p. 179; 'Right to a Living Wage', p. 74.

because the justification for the liberty which rights are supposed to provide rests upon the capacity (if only potentially) for rational self-direction, a capacity which, by definition, this class does not have. Again, society is expected to provide humane treatment and 'life-long care', although, strictly speaking, there is no warrant in the theory for ascribing them the right to such treatment. Of course, the justification of economic rights was not designed with either of these classes in mind, and Hobhouse could no doubt have grounded their claims more satisfactorily had the need arisen. But a class whose proper treatment was much discussed in Edwardian England were those referred to as 'the idle', 'the unemployable', or 'the residuum' – those whom Hobhouse revealingly called 'the morally uncontrolled'. Now, Hobhouse and his fellow-Progressives always protested against the severity and degradation which the Poor Law visited upon those who were driven by economic circumstances to ask for relief. Their objection, however, was to the fact that the deserving and undeserving poor were treated alike, not to the treatment as such. Hobhouse, for example, always presented as a virtue of the economic reorganization the fact that 'individual responsibility can be more clearly fixed and more vigorously insisted upon when its legitimate sphere is properly defined'.[45] Given such reforms in the economic system, 'it will become possible to say of any individual whether he is out of work through his own fault or not...When the sheep are thus parted from the goats, it will be possible to deal with both classes. The determined idler must not be allowed to prey upon society.' His wife and children must be provided for at public expense: 'as to the man, he is a fit subject for discipline and restraint. For him a labour colony must be provided.'[46] Hobhouse particularly insists that the discipline must be 'punitive'. It is the individual's 'right and duty to make the best use of his oportunity, and if he fails he may *fairly* suffer the penalty of being treated as a pauper or even, in an extreme case, as a *criminal*'.[47] In such passages, there can be no doubt but that the moral severity is intended, and that in these cases rights are indeed treated as being entirely dependent upon the fulfilment of social functions.

The value of such a 'functionalist' view of rights for Hobhouse was that it enabled him to justify welfare measures in terms of securing the individual a proper return for a social service. Seen in this way, cash benefits were not 'doles' which the state gave to those who had failed to obtain a sufficient reward for their activities, but a payment for a contribution to the life of society. For example, he justified allowances for widowed or

45 *Liberalism*, p. 95.

46 *Social Evolution*, p. 179.

47 *Liberalism*, p. 86 (my emphasis); cf. *Labour Movement* (1912 edn), p. 37: 'Idleness would be regarded as a social pest, to be stamped out like crime.'

deserted mothers in this way. Rather than forcing her to go to work to provide for her family by her own efforts, the state should 'recognize that the mother of young children is doing better service to the community and one more worthy of pecuniary remuneration when she stays at home and minds her children'. Accordingly, she should be given 'a payment for a civic service, and the condition that we are inclined to exact is precisely that she should not endeavour to add to it by earning wages, but rather that she should keep her home respectable and bring up her children in health and happiness'.[48] Obviously, the danger of building a certain moral preference into the very notion of a 'civic service' is not altogether absent even in cases of this kind. Yet again, the problems of this part of Hobhouse's theory seem to step from the initial commitment to justifying radical economic measures within the framework of traditional moral values.

It must be emphasized that the potential illiberalism of these arguments may have been to some extent at odds with Hobhouse's own intentions, for he was always a staunch defender of traditional personal liberties against contemporary attacks upon them in other spheres. A good example of this was his opposition to a bill for dealing with the 'mentally deficient', introduced by the government in the autumn of 1912. He complained that the looseness of the initial drafting gave certain appointed officials extravagantly wide powers to detain anyone who could be suspected of being 'feeble-minded', the specification of which was so vague as to allow mere eccentricity to count as evidence.[49] When a revised version of the bill was introduced, he was pleased to see that it now displayed more respect for the traditional legal safeguards of individual freedom, remarking ironically that this was 'quite noteworthy in these days of sublime confidence in the administrator'. He was particularly irked by the bill's abandonment of democratic principles in favour of 'the dominant "expert craze" of the hour'.[50] This was a feature of Edwardian politics for which he had no sympathy – in his hostility to the Fabians he always emphasized this – and his responses were of the most traditional kind. He reiterated the need to subject the power of the official, especially where he was not democratically elected, to careful legal circumscription and continuous control. Above all, he always suspected that the claim that a political proposal was based upon the teachings of the latest science was simply a piece of anti-democratic ideology, a further instance of 'how quasi-scientific

[48] *Liberalism*, pp. 93–4.

[49] Leader, *Manchester Guardian*, 14 Oct. 1912. Hobhouse was not alone in his opposition to the initial proposals. Josiah Wedgwood (an Individualist Single-Taxer) led the attack on it in parliament, and *The Nation* contributed its usual quota of outrage – see, e.g., *Nation*, 25 May 1912, on 'The Crime of being Inefficient'.

[50] Leader, *Manchester Guardian*, 3 Jan. 1913.

arguments against progress change with times [*sic*]'.[51] The final debate on the bill provided the occasion for Hobhouse to read a lesson on the dangers of the very impulse which was sometimes evident in his own arguments for social reform.

There is in operation a tendency, which will have to be closely watched, to use compulsion as the master-key to unlock all doors. The name of liberty was so often profaned in the last two or three generations by those who used it for the defence of oppressive labour contracts, bad housing, sweating or any other social ill, that it has in great degree lost its hold, and new obligations are put upon men and new opportunities of interference given not only without hesitation but almost as though there were something good in compulsion as such... [Liberals must] distinguish between the kind of compulsion which is necessary for liberty – the compulsion which prevents A from injuring B – and the kind which necessarily restricts liberty – which coerces A for his alleged good and orders his life for him in the name of philanthropy...We shall do well in the future to keep a sharp watch on legislation motived by philanthropy but operating through machinery which, disregarding the ordinary securities of law and tangible evidence, may end by putting some of the dearest interests of men at the mercy of the inspector and the expert.[52]

This was the kind of Liberal protest which Hobhouse was much given to, and it underlay his opposition to Eugenicists, Fabians, 'Efficiency' advocates, and all forms of bureaucratic authoritarianism. He even differed from Hobson, his great companion-in-arms throughout this period, over the right formulation of concepts like 'the social will' and 'the social organism', on the grounds that Hobson's tendency to hypostatize them could be exploited to license an undemocratic assertion of the national interest against the wishes of individuals.[53] On issues of civil liberty and democratic control, Hobhouse spoke with the authentic voice of traditional Liberalism. It was only in attempting to turn the moral imperatives of that tradition against its economic individualism that he developed a theory which, in its combination of Collectivism and moralism, demanded a very exacting level of social cooperation.

[51] *Labour Movement* (1912 edn), p. 144n.

[52] Leader, *Manchester Guardian*, 31 July 1913.

[53] Their mutually congratulatory reviews of each other's books were qualified only by their reservations over this difference: see, for example, Hobhouse's review of *Work and Wealth*, *Manchester Guardian*, 24 July 1914; and Hobson's review of *Social Evolution and Political Theory*, *Manchester Guardian*, 22 Feb. 1912. Hobhouse's criticism was that 'we think even Mr Hobson goes too far in admitting a "mind" of the nation that is not precisely the minds of the individuals composing it'; and he complained that 'as applied to the rights of the individual the "organic" view of society has had a somewhat destructive effect'. Leader (on Hobson's 'Restatement of Democracy' article), *Manchester Guardian*, 4 Feb. 1902. Partly this difference arose out of Hobhouse's tendency to be much more of a purist about the formulation of his concepts than Hobson, who minded rather less about the shape of the weapon with which he was hitting out so long as he could land a few good blows with it; but in part Hobhouse may have had a justified suspicion that Hobson was not always entirely sound on some of these issues – he had, for example, been a keen advocate of selective breeding and other measures designed to improve 'social health' (see his articles on 'The Population Question' in *Commonwealth*, 2 (1897); also *Social Problem*, pp. 213–15).

Hobhouse anticipated that a change of attitudes would indeed increase the range of such cooperation. The expectations of a growth in the sense of social responsibility and an increase in altruistic sentiments were commonplaces of the period, and recur frequently in his writing (and indeed in the works of an otherwise very diverse range of nineteenth-century social theorists). But he never accepted the conclusion frequently drawn from these premises, notably by the Idealist exponents of the philosophy of the C.O.S., that reforms of 'machinery' were therefore both otiose and doomed to failure. His reply to this was that 'if machinery without moral force is worthless, good intentions without machinery are helpless. A better spirit, if it is to survive, must be incarnated in better institutions.' Economic reform was a necessary but far from sufficient condition of social progress.[54] Still, his fundamental conviction was that 'machinery, laws, administration, organizations – are after all valuable only as the lever by which the moral forces of society can work'.[55] So the crucial task was to encourage the development of the appropriate social attitudes, and nowhere was this reformation more needed than in the case of attitudes towards property.

This was a common conviction among Progressives in this period, especially in the years immediately before 1914 which the opponents of government policy saw as marking the beginning of a democratic attack on property. The idea of the land campaign particularly stimulated these concerns, and, as I have suggested, the collective volume on *Property, Its Duties and Rights* to which Hobhouse contributed was deliberately intended to influence this debate. What was needed, as the editor of the volume, Bishop Gore, observed, was 'a principle of property, such as will tend to form a corporate conscience...We cannot act with any power as mere individuals without a coroporate mind and conscience on the subject; and we can form no corporate mind and conscience without a clear principle.'[56] In his contribution, Hobhouse attempted to provide such a principle by developing a distinction between 'property for use' and 'property for power'. Property for use was control of things essential to self-development and self-expression, 'an integral element in an ordered life

[54] *Labour Movement* (1912 edn), pp. 16–18; cf. also p. 14: 'And though no economic progress can of itself produce good family life, nor intellectual culture, nor public spirit, yet that all of these may flourish certain economic conditions must be fulfilled, and the object of industrial reform is to bring about these conditions.' (It is interesting to note that in the 1893 edn, Hobhouse had written: 'If the change from individualism to socialism meant nothing but an alteration in the methods of organizing industry, it would leave the nation no happier or better than before.' (p. 4) In 1912 he changed this to: 'If economic reform meant nothing but economic reform, it would leave the nation no happier or better than before', an indication of the continuity of his theory underlying the change from 'Socialism' to 'Liberalism'.)

[55] *Labour Movement* (1912 edn), p. 18. Cf. *Liberalism*, p. 73: 'The heart of Liberalism is the understanding that progress is not a matter of mechanical contrivance, but of the liberation of living spiritual energy.'

[56] Gore (ed.), *Property, Its Duties and Rights*, pp. viii–ix.

of purposeful activity'. Property for power was control of resources which commanded a market value sufficient to force others to act in certain ways, and so in effect was control of the labour of others.[57] Once again, in accepting that property was essential for the 'rational and harmonious development of personality', Hobhouse took particular delight in showing that a principle often deployed in defence of the existing system of private property (it was thus employed by Bosanquet, for example, one of Hobhouse's perennial targets) could in fact be made the foundation of a radical attack upon that system. For he pointed out that not only did a large proportion of the population not at present have access to property sufficient for this purpose, but also those who owned very large accumulations of wealth might in fact thereby be hampered in such development. 'Cherished as a conservative principle, it has in it the seed of radical revolution.'

The degree of collective ownership and control which he proposes upon the basis of this principle is very striking in a purportedly Liberal theory. He repudiated the ideal of a return either to a primitive communism or, by way of parcelling out the means of production, to a primitive individualism. 'The rise of large-scale industry has abolished the possibility of any form of individualism as a general solution of the economic problem.' Furthermore, he insisted that just as private property is essential to the individual, so 'common property is equally of value for the expression and development of social life'. The way to achieve this was for the community to receive 'the ultimate ownership of the natural sources of wealth and of the accumulation of past generations, together with the supreme control of the direction of industrial activity and of labour contracts'. Nor was this outright state Socialism a departure from the main lines of his mature theory. For he concluded his essay (ostensibly a philosophical and historical survey of the concept of property) with the demand: 'We have to restore to society a direct ownership of some things, but an eminent ownership of all things material to the production of wealth, securing "property for use" to the individual, and retaining "property for power" for the democratic state.'[58] This suggests that Hobhouse assumed that 'property for power' coincided with 'the surplus', and that 'property for use' coincided with the individual's earned income. In fact, it would be more accurate to say that both distinctions were expressions of the same implicit moral standard of how much an individual ought to have for self-development. Just as the distinction between individual and social factors

[57] The radical potential of this distinction (derived, as Hobhouse acknowledged, from Aristotle) was also recognized by Clarke – see his essay 'Aristotle's Politics' in Burrows and Hobson (eds), *William Clarke*, esp. p. 165.

[58] 'Historical Evolution of Property', pp. 103, 104, 98, 105, 106.

in wealth is given the trappings of a grounding in economic theory, so the distinction between 'property for power' and 'property for use' is presented as the outcome of the Liberal ideal of self-development: in both cases, the extent to which the community is being licensed to enforce this moral standard is disguised.

In reviewing this volume, *The Nation* warned that unless the prevailing 'stiff-set ideas and sentiments regarding property can be dislodged, social progress appears to involve a class war...If this dangerous and degrading warfare is to be averted, a successful endeavour must be made to resolve the stiffness of this class antagonism by bringing home to the hearts and intellects of owners the wider and juster social significance of property.' The reviewer claimed that Hobhouse's 'brilliant essay...contains in germ the whole substance of the needed reformation of idea and policy'.[59] This may be an exaggerated estimation of the fertility of the essay, but it accurately describes Hobhouse's aspiration. It is also a representative example of the immense optimism shared by this generation of reformers about the likely outcome of an appeal to the 'hearts and intellects' of the propertied classes, an optimism which is fully embodied in Hobhouse's theory. Given his own deeply felt and frequently expressed pessimism about the actual state of current politics, this optimism at the level of theory is all the more striking. On further analysis it turns out that what underwrites this programmatic optimism is the faith in a progressive trend in social development generally. The final point to be made in this chapter is thus that the coherence of Hobhouse's political theory ultimately rests upon the belief in Progress.

This point can best be approached by returning briefly to the idea of the common good, the keystone of Hobhouse's political philosophy. The reliance upon this concept is readily intelligible in terms of the attempt to stimulate the sense of personal and social responsibility to greater practical activity by means of an appeal to the shared values of cooperation, altruism, service and self-restraint. From this point of view, Hobhouse can be seen as trying to put some Collectivist economic flesh upon Green's skeletal account of the practical consequences of taking the idea of the common good seriously. However, the more concrete and extensive its consequences are made, the less plausible the central idea becomes. It was one thing for Green to argue that the common good was unrealized all the while 'the good is sought in objects which admit of being competed for', and that its realization would only come when 'the object generally sought as good comes to be a state of mind or character of which the attainment, or

[59] *Nation*, 29 Nov. 1913.

approach to attainment by each is itself a contribution to its attainment by every one else'.[60] But it is quite another for Hobhouse to claim that when the state takes a proportion of the wealth of the propertied classes to provide a certain standard of living for the propertyless it is enacting a good common to them both. Hobhouse might argue that the nature of a rational good was such that it could not be enjoyed at another's expense, or even indeed without being shared by another, but to the individual being deprived of his property or otherwise coerced such a measure was bound to seem to involve a conflict of 'goods', and he could, with some justice, object that Hobhouse's theory contained no account of how such conflicts were to be settled nor why his particular good should be overridden. In formal terms it did not need to because of its crucial contention about there being 'a line of development' which is 'natural' and 'along which each can move in harmony with others'. There cannot, therefore, be a conflict of goods because each 'finds his own good in the common good'.[61] This in turn rests upon a claim about the rational nature of man. It is because this has so far been imperfectly realized that there appears to be a conflict of goods. As the rational (social) nature of man is more fully appreciated, so, in Green's phrase, the area of the common good is extended.

The strength of this underlying teleology is observable in Hobhouse's more immediate political reflections. As we have seen, his intermittent despondency about current politics produced a rudimentary political sociology, an angry denunciation of the reactionary influence of various vested interests. There is, especially in his journalism (and its products, such as *Democracy and Reaction*), much incisive analysis of how the propertied classes benefit from certain features of the British political system and from their capacity to suppress conflict. But there is no corresponding description of the actual social groups pressing for reform, nor of the machinery for exercising pressure and bringing about political change. Something similar can be said of his view of democracy. In his journalism, he could draw a damning portrait of the failings of popular government, its intolerance, its wrongheadedness, its gullibility. And yet in his theory the extension of the suffrage is treated almost as a guarantee of political virtue, and democracy fulfils the role which 'the universal class' occupies in other political theories: 'The people as a whole have no sinister interests.'[62] The forces of reaction are described in terms of the power they

[60] *Prolegomena to Ethics*, sect. 245.

[61] *Liberalism*, p. 69. The last phrase is taken from Green.

[62] *Democracy and Reaction*, p. 139. To be quite accurate, it must be said that he uses this phrase in describing the old ideas of Liberalism which now stood in need of modification. But the main modification which he suggests is that 'in the doctrine that the people as a whole can have no sinister interests foreign and colonial relations are left out of account' (p. 141). Moreover, the point is not that he was unaware of the imperfections of actual democracies, but rather that his theory only incorporates the ideal of democracy, not its reality.

wield; the forces of Progress are described in terms of the ideal they pursue. This is a telling asymmetry. It means that political advance is primarily seen as a matter of removing obstacles to the working out of an immanent teleology.

The increasing realization of the true meaning of the common good will, therefore, be the path of such advance, a process to which the theorist is assumed to make a necessary and vital contribution. Hobhouse had always argued that 'though conservatism will fail through its inherent weakness, there will be no steady and continuous social progress until an adequate progressive theory is reconstituted to suit the needs of our own time'.[63] A progressive theory, however, had also to be a theory of Progress. 'Every constructive social doctrine rests upon the conception of human progress.'[64] The use of the singular definite article is revealing. Given the belief in an overall, directional development in human history, the maintenance of the reforming impulse depended heavily on the belief that the development was a progressive one. Moreover, given the assimilation of social and biological evolution in this belief, it was also important to show that the ideal animating such efforts 'is not in conflict with immovable laws of evolution but is continuous with *the line of advance* which educed the higher from the lower animal forms, which evolved the human out of the animal species and civilized from barbaric society'.[65] The political theory and the theory of Progress are, therefore, inextricably intertwined: the political theory postulates an ideal of the community pursuing the common good which the account of Progress shows to be the direction of actual development. Conversely, this ideal of the harmonious pursuit of the common good provides a criterion by which Progress is to be measured. Thus, the goal of Hobhouse's theoretical efforts was to show that

> the conception of social progress as a deliberate movement towards the reorganization of society in accordance with ethical ideas is not vitiated by any contradiction. It is free from any internal disharmony. Its possibility rests on the facts of evolution, of the higher tendencies of which it is indeed the outcome. It embodies a rational philosophy, it gives scope and meaning to the best impulses of human nature, and a new hope to the suffering among mankind.[66]

As I shall argue in Part Three, this account of Progress is the key to understanding the relationship between Hobhouse's Liberalism and his sociology.

[63] 'The Early Essays of J. S. Mill', *Manchester Guardian*, 9 Feb. 1897.
[64] *Liberalism*, p. 73.
[65] *Social Evolution*, p. 204 (my emphasis).
[66] *Social Evolution*, p. 205.

Part Three: Sociology

5: THE METAPHYSICS OF PROGRESS

In the last three chapters the account given of Hobhouse's political theory has been broadly chronological. But since the organizing intention of this study is to exhibit the intimate connection between his Liberalism and his sociology, a change in strategy now recommends itself. Moreover, a glance at Hobhouse's intellectual-cum-professional development suggests that there is no simple narrative of the evolution of his sociological theory: in 1890 he was an Oxford don, lecturing on Aristotle and pondering over the problems of knowledge; in 1900 he was dividing his days between writing leading articles for the *Manchester Guardian* and observing the efforts of monkeys in the local zoo to reach unreachable bananas; in 1910 he was Professor of Sociology in London University, lecturing and writing on social development. The conventional treatment of Hobhouse's place in the history of sociology is incapable of illuminating this curious odyssey. To the present-minded practitioners of this genre, it is 'clear that Hobhouse was trying, in his "synthesis", to incorporate all the most worthwhile developments in the making of sociology that had taken place from the beginnings of the subject onwards'. Indeed, to such historians it is even clear that 'he was doing this with a certain eye on the teaching of the subject in the universities'.[1] It would seem to have been the assumption of those who write in this way that some men are born to sociology; it will be the contention of this and the next two chapters that, at best, some men achieve sociology, and that sometimes, as in Hobhouse's case, they have sociology thrust upon them.

Far from assuming at the outset that Hobhouse was trying to 'contribute' to a 'subject' whose past can be separated without difficulty from the general intellectual history of the period, I shall concentrate upon reconstructing, in the context of certain features of late-nineteenth-century social

[1] Ronald Fletcher, *The Making of Sociology* (2 vols., London, 1971), II: *Developments*, pp. 136–7.

thought, his theoretical intentions in his own terms. In particular, the pivotal role of the belief in Progress needs to be recovered, for it was the working out in contemporary debate of his ambitious theoretical formulation of this belief which involved him in an enterprise then considered a constitutive part of sociology.

From this perspective, Hobhouse's own account of the genesis of his evolutionary social theory appears as a natural starting-point. He wrote no autobiography nor left any extensive collection of private papers, but his own view can be partially reconstructed from the retrospective Prefaces to three works dating from very different periods of his writing life.[2] From this composite account, three points call for immediate remark. First, Hobhouse insists that he saw all his major theoretical works up to and including *Development and Purpose*, published in 1913, as partial executions of one overall plan. The latter book, he wrote in its Introduction, 'completes a scheme which has occupied the present writer for twenty-six years'.[3] Secondly, he always identifies his final year as an undergraduate – 1887 – as the time when he first conceived his project. Given his precocity, his involvement with political and philosophical questions as an undergraduate, and his remark in a letter of that year that he hoped his Fellowship would enable him to follow out 'certain lines of work' which he had in mind, there seems no reason to doubt this.[4] Furthermore, in the first year of his Fellowship he devoted himself to an intensive course in empirical work on the physiology and anatomy of animals, a course of action which, as we shall see, makes some sense if seen as a preparation for his own work on mental evolution, but which would otherwise have been bizarre behaviour for a young Greats don.[5] Thirdly, he makes it quite clear that the initial inspiration for his scheme was political. It was his interest 'in questions of social reform' and the consequent confrontation

[2] Preface to *Mind in Evolution* (London, 1901), pp. v–vii; Introduction to *Development and Purpose: An Essay towards a Philosophy of Evolution* (London, 1913), pp. xv–xxix; Biographical Note to 'The Philosophy of Development' in J. H. Muirhead (ed.), *Contemporary British Philosophy* (1st series, London, 1924), p. 150. Such sources certainly have their limitations as historical evidence; but they are also particularly valuable for my present purpose, and only on the question of 'orthogenic evolution' (see p. 153 below) is there any suggestion of retrospective distortion.

[3] He also announced that it had 'been carried through successive stages in three previous works' (p. xv) – presumably *The Theory of Knowledge* (London, 1896), *Mind in Evolution*, and *Morals in Evolution* (2 vols., London, 1906). As it turned out, it was optimistic to think that this book 'completed' the scheme; see the Preface to the 2nd edn (1927).

[4] See above, Ch. 2, n40.

[5] Hobson and Ginsberg, *L. T. Hobhouse*, p. 28; see also his own later account of this work, Hobhouse to F. S. Marvin, 19 Aug. 1906, Marvin Papers. By most people in Oxford at that time such laboratory work was considered a very peculiar thing for anyone to do, let alone a young philosopher fresh from Greats. See, for example, H. W. Nevinson, 'The Oxford Mood' in his *Visions and Memories* (Oxford, 1944), esp. pp. 19–20. Indeed, it was only in the 1880s that objections to such work had been overridden in the interests of constructing the very laboratory in which Hobhouse worked; see the *D.N.B.* entry on J. Burdon-Sanderson, the first Professor of Physiology at Oxford, and letters in his papers, esp. the testimony of Samuel Alexander (13 Jan. 1895).

with 'the social implications of natural selection', especially when 'made the basis of an uncompromising economic individualism' by Spencer, which led him to construct his theory, and among its component parts he listed 'T. H. Green's social and ethical outlook', 'the requirements of liberty as set out by Mill', and 'the Comtist conception of Humanity (especially as interpreted by Bridges)'. Its roots were in the 'new demand for the extension of collective responsibility and the social control of industrial life', which he later recognized to have been characteristic of that decade.[6] In effect, therefore, it was his response to the perception that Collectivism needed its own Spencer.

So once again the importance of the controversies of the 1880s is emphasized. Up to 1914 (and, in many ways, beyond, as I indicate in the Epilogue) Hobhouse was engaged in working out a theory which had formed itself in his mind as a response to these controversies. Of course, he was constantly involved in the changing course of political debate for the rest of his life, and often dealt very fully with theoretical developments which had taken place since the eighties. But, as is so often the case in intellectual history, the identification of problems and of possible lines of solution which a man makes in the first decade or so of his adult life moulds and dominates his later thought. By 1924, 'the theory of natural selection as applied to society' had long ago lost its persuasive force in general political argument, but Hobhouse still felt compelled to condemn it as 'the great intellectual standby of all opponents of social justice', and his *oeuvre* is clearly shaped by this antagonism[7]

In 1913 Hobhouse began his retrospective account by immediately identifying the source of this antagonism: 'In the middle of the 'Eighties when the writer was first studying philosophy, the biological theory of evolution was already very generally accepted, and the philosophical extension of the theory by Mr Herbert Spencer was, except in academic circles, in the heyday of its influence.'[8] It is worth noting here that the fact that Spencer's popularity lay outside academic circles was, if anything, a greater stimulus to refute him, for Hobhouse was always at least as much concerned with the general level of educated discussion on social and ethical questions as he was with the more philosophically sophisticated exponents of any theory. The possibly sinister practical influence of ideas worried him far more than their academic reputation.[9] Indeed in this case it almost seems to have been the popular misunderstanding of Spencer as much as Spencer himself that was the source of his concern: 'Philosophically, Mr Spencer

[6] 'The Philosophy of Development', p. 150; *Development and Purpose*, p. xvii.

[7] L. T. Hobhouse, *Social Development: Its Nature and Conditions* (London, 1924), p. 328.

[8] *Development and Purpose*, p. xv.

[9] This was so throughout his life: see the Preface to *Theory of Knowledge* (1896), and his Chairman's Address to the Philosophical Studies Association. *Journal of Philosophical Studies*, II (1926), 595–6.

was not a materialist. But his metaphysical safeguards did not rescue the evolution theory from some of the most unfortunate consequences of a materialist system.' Two consequences of the theory 'in its bearing on human life and action' Hobhouse found particularly repugnant. The first was that 'the human mind...was to be thought of...as a sort of glorified reflex action'. It had no 'special significance', and 'the ultimate goal of its efforts' was nothing more than a merely temporary equilibrium with its environment which would soon disappear. 'The appearance of an upward process in evolution then was illusory.' The second unacceptable consequence was that if man's existence, like that of all living creatures, was determined by natural selection – which was what, in a modified Lamarckian form, Spencer was taken to assert – then 'so far as there was anything like progress it was due to the internecine struggle for existence'. But, contended Hobhouse: 'A little reflection suffices to show that if progress means anything which human beings value or desire, it depends on the suppression of the struggle for existence, and the substitution in one form or another of social co-operation. There was here a conflict between the scientific and the ethical points of view which threatened social ethics with extinction.'[10] So to the familiar moral objection that materialism of this sort gave no special status to the human species, that it made the belief in Progress a delusion, and voided human life of its spiritual significance, Hobhouse added the more political anxiety that such an account of evolution supported an excessively individualist view of social life (as ever, he makes 'social cooperation' the essence of 'social ethics'). The perceived 'conflict between the scientific and the ethical points of view' was a characteristic experience of this generation – as that between science and religion had been of the previous one; Hobhouse's only distinction, perhaps, lay in the intensity of his allegiance to both sides.

One obvious way in which to confute or at least to avoid the materialistic implications of Spencerian philosophy – and of the aggressive positivism of much contemporary science – was to follow Green and Caird back to Kant and Hegel. This was a pilgrimage which, for philosophical reasons, Hobhouse was not prepared to make, much as he was attracted by Green's 'social and ethical outlook'. In particular he could not accept Idealism's disdain for, even hostility to, the claims of natural science in general, for he was 'convinced that a philosophy that was to possess more than a speculative interest must rest on a synthesis of experience as interpreted by science, and that to such a synthesis the general conception of evolution offered a key'.[11]

Hobhouse's use of the concept of evolution was not merely instrumental;

[10] *Development and Purpose*, pp. xv–xvi.

[11] *Development and Purpose*, p. xviii. On Hobhouse's philosophical development, see below, Ch. 8.

it was one of the organizing axes of his thought, but in applying the concept 'the immediate question was whether it was possible to overcome the contradiction of that theory as applied to human progress'. This is a revealing statement. Not only does the question of Progress appear to Hobhouse as the *immediate* question – in practice it remained the immediate question throughout his life – but what he asks is not whether, in the light of the new knowledge provided by evolution, the idea of Progress should be modified or perhaps even abandoned, but how, to accommodate it to the fact of human Progress, the theory of evolution itself could be reconstructed. It is an essential part of the argument of this study that this was not a mere quirk of syntax: the problem presented itself to Hobhouse's mind in that form, and the justification of the belief in Progress became one of the central themes of his work throughout the rest of his life.

Although Hobhouse's initial concern was with the formulation of an ostensibly scientific theory of evolution, he was, as I shall argue in more detail below, essentially dressing up some familiar philosophical notions in fashionable scientific clothes. In particular, he owed more to Idealism than he was for a long time willing to acknowledge.[12] But his starting-point, as he recalled it, was rather to make Hegel give evidence in a Darwinian court. Instead of seeing mind as the 'given' or precondition of reality, that which made possible the conception of a development in time, Hobhouse proposed to treat it as 'an empirical fact within the world of time'. At the same time, however, he wished to avoid the reductionism characteristic of recent evolutionary psychology. 'I conceived', he later wrote,

> that if the mental or spiritual side of evolution were treated quite dispassionately, without any attempt to minimise differences of kind, but setting them out impartially and using them to measure the length of line which by whatever means evolution had somehow traced out, a very different interpretation of the whole process might be reached. As I followed this line of thought, it seemed to me that, details apart, the Hegelian conception of development possessed a certain rough, empirical value. There were grades or degrees of consciousness and self-consciousness, and as personal self-consciousness was distinctive of man, so there was a higher self-consciousness of the human spirit which would represent the term of the present stage in development. Further, if this conception was interpreted in terms of experience, it indicated a point of union where one would not expect to find it, between the Idealistic and the Positivistic philosophy. This higher self-consciousness would be the Humanity of Positivism, regulating its own life and controlling its own development.[13]

There are two rather curious features of the offspring of this unlikely marriage. The first is that levels of intelligence in the animal world and levels of consciousness in the human are taken to be comparable stages in an evolutionary development, stages, moreover, which form a chronological as well as a structural sequence. Biological and intellectual categories appear

[12] See below, Ch. 8.

[13] *Development and Purpose*, p. xix.

as successive historical phases. The second is that 'Humanity' or 'the human spirit' is treated as an entity to which a distinctive level of self-consciousness can be ascribed, and one which only appears as the final stage of development. In fact, varieties of this latter idea were common in late-nineteenth-century social thought, especially in Comtist-influenced circles.[14] For Hobhouse, there were of course additional advantages to being able to present the prospect of Humanity 'controlling its own development' as an integral part of the evolutionary process.

For he did assume that 'along with knowledge would go control'. There was a deep-seated, almost Aristotelian, belief in a natural order evident here, to which I shall return in the final chapter. In his own account he simply argued that 'control extends in a kind of geometrical ratio with each new turn in the development of consciousness', and then, even more optimistically, that 'as the full meaning of the self-conscious mind worked itself out it was seen to imply a grip on those underlying conditions of life which, as long as they remain obscure, thwart human effort and distract man from that social collaboration which is necessary to the greatest efforts'.[15] There is more than a hint here of the Comtean vision of a perfected social science as the basis – the sufficient basis – for the full flowering of the social spirit.[16] Given a sufficiently rationalist account of human behaviour, the analogy of Humanity with the individual yields the conclusion that self-knowledge produces self-control for both.

This account also suggests that a particular view of rationality was embedded in Hobhouse's central category of 'mind'. To determine the

[14] 'The belief that one can legitimately speak of Man, or Mankind, or Humanity, as a unitary historical being, as that which transcends every individual...was a belief which was among the most distinctive tenets of 19th century thought.' Mandelbaum, *History, Man, and Reason*, p. 236.

[15] *Development and Purpose*, pp. xx–xxiii.

[16] Hobhouse always remained sympathetic to Comte (distinguishing, like so many fellow-travellers of Positivism, between the Comte of the *Cours* and the Comte of the *Politique Positive*, the latter being more of an embarrassment than anything else); see, for example, his high praise for Comte's sociology in his 'The Law of the Three Stages', *Sociological Review*, I (1908), 262–79. Personally, he was quite closely involved with the English Positivists. While at Oxford, he became friendly with F. S. Marvin, who, with two other of Hobhouse's friends, Sidney Ball and Gilbert Murray, founded a Comte discussion society; see W. M. Simon, *European Positivism in the Nineteenth Century: An Essay in Intellectual History* (Ithaca, N.Y., 1963), pp. 81–2; and Murray, *Unfinished Autobiography*, p. 83. Hobhouse later married J. H. Bridges' sister-in-law, and became very close to him, receiving from him, as he said, 'the cream of Comtism'. When Bridges died in 1907, Hobhouse edited the posthumous collection of essays, and in 1926 contributed glowing reminiscences of Bridges to S. Liveing, *A Nineteenth-Century Teacher, John Henry Bridges* (London, 1926), esp. pp. 165–6, 238–40. He often quoted Bridges' definition of Humanity, with evident approval: for example, *Morals* (1915 edn), p. 238, and *Metaphysical Theory of the State*, p. 115; and see p. 216 and n below. The Positivists themselves were more than usually keen to claim Hobhouse as one of their number (although there is no evidence that he ever belonged to the Positivist Church); see, or example, *Positivist Review*, XIV (1906), 284–5, and XV (1907), 37–40, for very favourable reviews of *Morals* by Frederic Harrison and F. S. Marvin respectively, or the claim of another Positivist (XVI (1908), 212) that 'there is no serious difference of principle between the writer [Hobhouse] and the Positivist school'.

sequence of the development of mind, of course, some verifiable indicator of its various levels was needed. As Hobhouse reported his own solution to this problem:

I came to take the correlation which is effected in consciousness between different portions of our experience or between different acts and purposes as the basis of a classification... If we utter a simple sentence we bring different words, and the words stand for ideas or elements of ideas, into relation. If we execute a purpose we bring a series of acts into relation with one another. It is by correlation that the mind introduces order and establishes its control.[17]

Working with this rather functional concept of rationality, Hobhouse claimed to discover in the facts of evolution a pattern of cosmic significance. On this basis, as he put it,

it was possible to conceive of evolution in general as a blind and even brutal process, dependent on the anarchical struggle for existence, but...to display one particular line of evolution, for which I afterwards found Mr Sutherland's expression 'orthogenic evolution', as a series of advances in the development of mind involving a parallel curtailment of the sphere of natural selection. The conclusion was clear that natural selection was not the cause of progress, if progress meant the advance of mind.[18]

The polemical intentions revealed in this last sentence were underlined by the whole invention of the idea of 'orthogenic evolution'. For Sutherland does not in fact seem to have used the term 'orthogenic'. Hobhouse had previously acknowledged this in *Mind in Evolution*, where he claimed that it was 'suggested' to him by Sutherland's use of 'aristogenic', which referred to 'those which make a true advance to complexity, which make a step, however small, on the path to a nobler type'.[19] 'Nobler' is itself a curious category for biology to employ, and the way in which Hobhouse used 'orthogenic' makes it clear that it was meant to refer to both the biological and the historical development of intelligence and substantive rationality. For biological evolution, strictly conceived, is a process not a direction, a general name for the operation of certain scientific laws over time, such as natural selection. 'Orthogenic evolution', on the other hand, looks much more like a biological label for a very selective history of mental effort, in which a constant mechanism is supposed to be at work in a way which is comparable to, but crucially different from, the function of natural selection in evolution generally. Hobhouse would hardly be the first social theorist to seek to recommend his conclusions by presenting them in the guise of the most prestigious science of the day, and from these later accounts his animating desire to secure the belief in Progress as the advance

17 *Development and Purpose*, p. xxiii.

18 *Development and Purpose*, pp. xx–xxi.

19 Alexander Sutherland, *The Origin and Growth of the Moral Instinct* (2 vols., London, 1898), I, pp. 28–9; cf. *Mind in Evolution*, p. 5.

of social cooperation emerges very clearly. But to understand why this seemed to be the problem to address, and why this particular kind of answer recommended itself, we need to go beyond Hobhouse's own account and to return to the controversies of the 1880s.

As I suggested in Chapter 1, the 'scientific' argument for Individualism enjoyed its greatest vogue in the 1880s, and it was associated above all with the name of Herbert Spencer, then 'at the zenith of his world fame as England's greatest philosopher'.[20] The philosophical establishment largely treated him with condescension, scorn or hostility, but this could not hide – indeed, it was to some extent a sign of – the anxiety aroused in such quarters by his immense influence. In fact, it was by no means the case that the ponderous volumes of the 'Synthetic Philosophy' itself yielded all the conclusions which were sometimes attributed to them: the centrality and persistence of the struggle for survival, in particular, were very often exaggerated in the presentations of his theory popularized and plagiarized by that diverse collection of politicians, journalists and propagandists who claimed to be his disciples. Indeed, to his political opponents, Spencer was important and dangerous as much for having spawned popular Spencerianism as for the actual teachings of his complex theory. In part, Spencer himself was to blame for the popular account of his theory, for in his political polemics he did not hesitate to deploy simplified versions of some of his central arguments. It was through his most celebrated venture into this form in *The Man Versus the State* – 'the most conspicuous work of recent years in defence of Individualism and in opposition to the growing tendency of state intervention'[21] – that the political consequences of his theory received particular attention in the mid 1880s. Here was a scientific demonstration that Progress in the natural and social world alike resulted from the free adaptation of individual to environment; the laws of evolution prescribed a policy of Individualism. This forceful statement of the way in which Progress was yoked to Individualism touched too vital a nerve in the prevailing system of beliefs to be ignored. As Hobhouse's fellow-Oxford-Collectivist, D. G. Ritchie, remarked in an attack on Spencer's book (in an article first published in 1886): 'His practical conclusions, coming with the weight of his authority, seem to require refutation on the part of those who seriously believe that Liberal, or at least Radical, politicians are now moving, however slowly, in the right direction. Mr

[20] Beatrice Webb, *My Apprenticeship*, p. 196. For a contemporary view of the 'wide popularity' of Spencer's 'scientific theory of man and the Universe', see W. S. Lilly, 'Our Great Philosopher', *Contemporary Review*, LV (1889), 753.

[21] Ritchie, *Principles of State Interference*, p. 3.

Spencer is perhaps the most formidable intellectual foe with whom the new Radicalism has to reckon.'[22]

Spencer's work did provoke a spate of refutations in the next few years, and reformers felt called upon to do battle with 'Mr Spencer and his legion of followers' for a long time to come.[23] But to appreciate why Hobhouse should have undertaken to support the case for greater Collectivism by reformulating the theory of evolution, we need to consider the availability of two alternative strategies which might at first sight seem more plausible. In so doing we shall need to consider the constraining effect on intellectuals of Hobhouse's generation of the dominant beliefs about those two quintessentially Victorian deities, Science and Progress, as well as the role of the more purely personal aspect of Hobhouse's own temperament.

The first possible alternative would be to sever the connection between evolution and Progress. The persuasiveness of the Social Darwinist case rested upon asserting the closest possible link between the two, but the connection is not a necessary one – that is, the belief in Progress is not logically tied to a theory of biological evolution (though aspects of the relationship are in certain cases bound to be intimate: a catastrophist or degenerationist evolutionary theory, for example, would set limits to the security or the extent of the future which Progress could expect). So one simple way to invalidate the Spencerian syllogism would be to declare that human social life was not subject to the laws which governed the evolution of the lower animals, and hence that Progress did not depend upon 'following' these laws. But in the intellectual climate of the 1880s this move had only a limited appeal.

To begin with, it was the belief in evolution which was held to be distinctive of this generation, and which appeared to them to constitute a qualitative leap in the history of thought. As Edward Pease (who was born in 1857) recalled:

> The young men of the time...grew up with the new ideas and accepted them as a matter of course...Our parents who read neither Spencer nor Huxley lived in an intellectual world which bore no relation to our own; and cut adrift as we were from the intellectual moorings of our upbringings, recognizing, as we did, that the older men were useless as guides in religion, in science, in philosophy because they knew not evolution, we also felt instinctively that we could accept nothing on trust from those who still believed that the early chapters of Genesis accurately described the origins of the universe, and that we had to discover somewhere for ourselves what were the true principles of the then recently invented science of sociology.

[22] Ritchie, *Principles of State Interference*, p. 3.

[23] Hobson, *Social Problem*, p. 146. There is a good discussion of the replies which Spencer provoked in America in Richard Hofstadter, *Social Darwinism in American Thought 1860–1915* (Philadelphia, 1944; 2nd edn Boston, 1955). The response to Spencer in England has not been studied systematically; see also below, n64 to Ch. 6.

In this respect, he noted, 'Herbert Spencer, then deemed the greatest of English thinkers, was pointing out in portentous phraseology the enormous significance of evolution.'[24] Given the prestige of the Darwinian achievement, Darwin's own statements were crucially important here. In his more guarded moments – and his mature life was composed almost exclusively of such moments – Darwin had been careful to emphasize that natural selection did not guarantee development in any one direction, nor did it imply any favourable evaluation of the outcome, and in *The Origin of Species* he had refused to commit himself about the place of man in this story. However, in *The Descent of Man* (1871) he had argued at length that man had been produced from lower animals, chiefly by means of natural selection, and certain passages in *The Origin* thus acquired a new significance. For example, at one point in the latter he reflected upon the continuous evolution of species over a vast stretch of time, and allowed himself the remark that 'we may look with some confidence to a secure future of equally inappreciable length. And as natural selection works solely by and for the good of each being, all corporeal and mental developments will tend to progress towards perfection.'[25] This became, for the rest of the century, one of the most quoted passages of that not very quotable book, for here was the great Darwin himself apparently underwriting the law of Progress. The precise details of how this took place could be argued over, and limits to the operation of natural selection itself were increasingly insisted upon, but in 1898 a writer in a reputable journal could still maintain: 'I do not know of any question whose solution would more greatly advance our knowledge of human society than the question how far and in what ways the law of selection acts amongst mankind.'[26]

Furthermore, the more general Victorian attitude to scientific 'laws' was involved in the persuasiveness of the Social Darwinist argument. Since the laws of science were conceived in a positivistic way as the universally operative causes of the movement or growth or whatever of phenomena, their dominion could not be escaped. To deny the operation of such laws in some department of life was widely interpreted as a denial of the claims of science itself, a reversion to a theological or metaphysical level of explanation.[27]

[24] Pease, *Fabian Society*, pp. 17–18, 27.

[25] Charles Darwin, *The Origin of Species* (pbk, with Introduction by J. W. Burrow, Harmondsworth, 1968 [first published London, 1859]), p. 459.

[26] Winthrop More Daniels, 'The Bearing of the Doctrine of Evolution on the Social Problem', *International Journal of Ethics*, VIII (1897–8), 205. In arguing over the details of man's development, few writers wished to be as precise as J. Allen Brown, author of *Palaeolithic Man in N.W. Middlesex: The evidence of His Existence and the Physical Conditions under which He Lived in Ealing and Its Neighbourhood* (London, 1893).

[27] For this rather brisk assertion I have drawn upon the excellent discussion in Ch. 1 of Frank Miller Turner, *Between Science and Religion: the Reaction to Scientific Naturalism in Late-Victorian England*

The best illustration of the difficulties likely to be encountered by any attempt to sever the union between evolution and Progress is provided, paradoxically enough, by an episode involving 'Darwin's Bulldog' himself, T. H. Huxley. In the decades following the publication of Darwin's theory, Huxley had been its most pugnacious champion, especially against its 'pre-scientific' clerical enemies, but he had also been critical of the attempt to draw Individualist political conclusions from it, above all as this attempt was carried out in the work of his close friend, Herbert Spencer. When he was invited to deliver the Romanes Lecture in 1893, he decided that the time was ripe for an authoritative repudiation of this whole idiom of evolutionary political moralizing. In accepting the invitation, he confided to Romanes: 'I have long had fermenting in my head some notions about the relations of Ethics and Evolution (or rather the absence of such as are commonly supposed) which I think will be interesting to such an audience as I may expect.'[28] In fact, the terms of the lectureship prevented him from making the targets of his criticism explicit, and his very efforts at concealment may have contributed to the mixture of misunderstanding and hostility with which the lecture was received. For although Huxley did not actually abandon the belief which had animated his scientific career, that natural selection was the essence of the cosmic process, he now contended in a famous passage that 'social Progress means a checking of the cosmic process at every step, and the substitution for it of another which may be called the ethical process, the end of which is not the survival of those who happen to be the fittest in respect of the whole of the conditions which obtain, but of those who are ethically the best'. This process demanded that man should reject rather than emulate the competitive aspects of the struggle for existence:

> Laws and moral precepts are directed to the end of curbing the cosmic process and reminding the individual of his duty to the community, to the protection and influence of which he owes, if not existence itself, at least the life of something better than a brutal savage. It is from neglect of these plain considerations that the fanatical Individualism of our time attempts to apply the analogy of cosmic nature to society.[29]

(New Haven, Conn., 1974); see also Reba N. Soffer, 'The revolution in English social thought 1880–1914', *American Historical Review*, LXXV (1970), 1938–64; and J. W. Burrow, *Evolution and Society: A Study in Victorian Social Theory* (Cambridge, 1966), Chs. 4 and 5.

28 T. H. Huxley to G. J. Romanes, 7 June 1892, in *The Life and Letters of Thomas Henry Huxley*, ed. L. Huxley (3 vols., London, 1900; 2nd edn 1903), III, p. 287. Huxley had attacked Spencer's deduction of extreme Individualism from the organic analogy as early as 1871 in 'Administrative Nihilism', *Fortnightly Review*, X (1871), 525–43. He had criticized the foundations of evolutionary ethics in general in 'The Struggle for Existence in Human Society', *Nineteenth Century*, XXIII (1888), 161–80, about which he wrote to a correspondent: 'I am afraid it has made Spencer very angry – but he knows I think he has been doing mischief this long time.' Huxley to Sir John Donnelly, 9 Feb. 1888, in *Life and Letters*, III, p. 55.

29 T. H. Huxley, 'Evolution and Ethics', repr. in *Evolution and Ethics*, ed. J. Huxley (London, 1943), quotation at p. 81.

The lecture provoked a squall of criticism, not least from the indignant exponents of scientific naturalism who supposed Huxley to have reneged on his former evolutionary convictions. Spencer himself wrote that Huxley's view was 'a surrender of the general doctrine of evolution in so far as its higher applications are concerned...and is practically a going back to the old theological notions, which put Man and Nature in antithesis'.[30] In the 'Prolegomena' to subsequent editions, and in his correspondence, Huxley tried to make his position clearer: 'There are two very different questions which people fail to discriminate. One is whether evolution accounts for morality, the other whether the principle of evolution in general can be adopted as an ethical principle. The first, of course, I advocate, and have constantly insisted upon. The second I deny, and reject all so-called evolutional ethics based upon it.'[31] But it is very revealing of the sway of 'the doctrine of evolution' in 'its higher applications' that Huxley was so widely taken to have attempted to uncouple evolution and Progress altogether. As his son ruefully remarked: 'On the one hand he was branded as a deserter from free thought; on the other, hailed almost as a convert to orthodoxy.'[32]

The literature of the 1880s and 1890s is packed with attempts to dismantle the Spencerian syllogism for religious, moral or political reasons, but most writers prudently tried to restate the lessons of evolution rather than to deny their relevance. Leslie Stephen upheld his own brand of evolutionary ethics by finding a system of 'tacit alliances' in the higher reaches of nature.[33] Kropotkin later in the decade provided a survey of the whole evolutionary process which emphasized the important role of 'mutual aid' the title under which his articles appeared as a book in 1902.[34] Henry Drummond asserted that the efficacy of altruism was 'the missing factor in current theories of evolution', and managed to combine this with the claim that evolution was the working out of the moral intentions of a subtle

30 Herbert Spencer to James A. Skilton, 29 June 1893, in David Duncan, *The Life and Letters of Herbert Spencer* (London, 1908), p. 336.

31 Huxley to Thomas Commons, 31 Aug. 1894, in *Life and Letters*, III, p. 303.

32 *Life and Letters*, III, p. 292. This volume contains much interesting material relating to the lecture's reception. Further examples of published reactions include *Oxford Magazine*, X (1892–3), 463; Leslie Stephen, 'Ethics and the Struggle for Existence', *Contemporary Review*, LXIV (1893), 157–70; Henry Drummond, *The Ascent of Man* (London, 1894). For a recent decoding of Huxley's message, see Michael S. Helfand, 'T. H. Huxley's "Evolution and Ethics": the politics of evolution and the evolution of politics', *Victorian Studies*, 20 (1977), 159–77.

33 Stephen, 'Ethics and the Struggle for Existence'; his evolutionary ethical theory had been given its fullest exposition in *The Science of Ethics* (London, 1882); see Noel Annan, *Leslie Stephen; His Thought and Character in Relation to His Time* (London, 1951).

34 Kropotkin, *Mutual Aid*. Kropotkin's work was also a good example of what Hobhouse was to find lacking in other contemporary attempts to restate evolution: 'a closer attention to animal psychology' was needed, he claimed when reviewing Kropotkin's book, since, for example, it would take 'more than a casual reference to Buffon to make one believe that a young rabbit owes obedience not only to its father but to its grandfather'. *Speaker*, 15 Nov. 1902.

creator, a combination of conclusions which won him an enormous audience.[35] All these writers – and many more – wished to attack the fatalism and Individualism of Spencer's conclusions, and to argue that 'the theory of natural selection (in the form in which alone it can properly be applied to human society) lends no support to the political dogma of laissez-faire'.[36] But they did so precisely by trying to specify the 'proper application' of evolution to human social life, not by denying its relevance altogether.

The second possible alternative would seem to be to deny that the advocacy of social reform depended upon the provision of a suitable account of Progress, evolutionary or otherwise. Again, the link is certainly not a logical one: policies of social reform are now generally proposed without even any mention of Progress, beyond the improvement which the reform is, by definition, intended to bring. This makes all the more striking the extent to which advocacy of radical measures in the late nineteenth century was intimately bound up with statements about Progress. Although it is one of the greater clichés of nineteenth-century historiography to say that the Victorians believed in Progress, the importance and function of these statements in this period still needs to be established.

A progressive philosophy of history had, of course, served a variety of moral and political needs earlier in the century, above all in reformers' struggles with nostalgic or sceptical conservatism.[37] A view of this kind played a prominent part in the writings of someone like Macaulay, for example, and for Mill 'the consideration, which great improvement in life and culture stands next in order for a people as the condition of their further progress?' was an overriding criterion in political argument.[38] But it was the latter part of the century that saw the idea so well and widely established that it 'dominated all thought'.[39] J. B. Bury's classic survey culminated in the decades in which he had himself come to maturity, for as he recalled, 'in the seventies and eighties of the last century the idea of Progress was becoming a general article of faith'.[40] As one observer put

[35] Drummond, *Ascent of Man*, esp. pp. 1–74. In less than three years, 28,000 copies were printed according to the title page of the 1897 printing.

[36] D. G. Ritchie, *Darwinism and Politics* (London, 1889), p. iii of the Preface to the 2nd edn (1891). In this edition he included two additional essays dealing with the question 'In what form, if in any, can the theory of Natural Selection properly be applied to the intellectual, moral and social development of man?'

[37] There is an excellent discussion of beliefs about Progress and the needs which they served in the earlier period, in Burrow, *Evolution and Society*, esp. Chs. 3 and 4.

[38] Quoted in J. M. Robson, *The Improvement of Mankind: The Social and Political Thought of John Stuart Mill* (Toronto, 1968), p. 223.

[39] The judgement of Morris Ginsberg, *Reason and Unreason in Society* (London, 1947), p. 298.

[40] J. B. Bury, *The Idea of Progress* (London, 1920), p. 346. Bury stopped his history at this point because he thought that the belief had become an 'orthodoxy', though he briefly referred to the enormous literature published on the subject 'within the last forty years' (p. 348).

it at the time, 'the idea of Progress has in effect established itself in such a way that in principle it is no longer contested by anyone, and the only question which remains to be pursued is that concerning the conditions in which it is realized'.[41] Yet it was a belief which both flowered and withered within Hobhouse's lifetime. The tone of the concluding pages of *The Idea of Progress* bears more than a slight resemblance to that of an obituary, and when in the same year (1920) Dean Inge launched an even more acerbic attack upon those aspects of the belief in Progress which he found distasteful, he denigrated them in Stracheyesque mode as 'the gods of Victoria's reign'.[42]

To the young men of the 1880s, however, there was no doubt that, as Hobhouse's Oxford friend and contemporary, Gilbert Murray, declared, 'Progress is a fact'.[43] And yet is was not obviously a single or simple fact, and its complexity is best captured by regarding it as a gestalt: Progress was the pattern into which the educated late-Victorian Englishman naturally fitted both his perceptions of the past and his expectations of the future. Unless challenged, this was usually implicit; there is, anyway, something wrong with spectacles which themselves occupy the field of vision. Economic and technological growth was certainly the most tangible manifestation of Progress, and the one which in the later part of the century could be most easily demonstrated.[44] But this was not the most important aspect: it was the, frequently related, assumptions of intellectual and moral advance which provided the fundamental motif of the pattern. Here the belief in the passage from egoism to altruism was prominent. 'The continuous weakening of selfishness and the continuous strengthening of sympathy' was hailed by many as 'the fundamental characteristic of social progress' (a view which Spencer endorsed, despite the reputation of his theory as a celebration of selfishness).[45] The moralism of the age welcomed and accentuated this emphasis: as L. P. Jacks later summarized the point, 'since our constitution is essentially moral, all progress that we can

[41] Quoted by Ginsberg in his *The Idea of Progress: A Revaluation* (London, 1953), p. 1.

[42] W. R. Inge, *The Idea of Progress* (Oxford, 1920), p. 30. It had by then become a commonplace to suggest, as John Morley did, that for many people Progress 'had taken the place of religion'; quoted in D. A. Hamer, *John Morley: Liberal Intellectual in Politics* (Oxford, 1968), p. 47. And note Mandelbaum's conclusion: 'If there had been any one factor which, more than others, has led to a revolutionary shift in twentieth-century thought and which has involved a break with those nineteenth-century movements which still dominated the earlier years of this century, it has been the loss of belief in Progress.' Mandelbaum, *History, Man, and Reason*, p. 369.

[43] Murray, *Unfinished Autobiography*, p. 113.

[44] And this despite the experience of the so-called Great Depression of the late 1870s and 1880s. All parties could find comfort in Marshall's demonstration that wealth per head of the population had been increasing throughout the century; Marshall, *Principles of Economics* (8th edn 1920), p. 729. Among those who quoted Marshall on this was Hobhouse, *Labour Movement*, p. 87.

[45] John Fiske, quoted in Bury, *Idea of Progress*, p. 372. (For Fiske's involvement in English intellectual life, see Hofstadter, *Social Darwinism*, p. 15). On Spencer and the advance of altruism, see Peel, *Herbert Spencer*, *passim*.

recognize as such must be moral also', and he affirmed his own belief in 'moral progress as an historical fact, as a process that has begun and is going on and will be continued'.[46] In general, however, it was the interdependence of the various aspects of Progress which gave it its commanding position. As another of Hobhouse's Oxford friends and contemporaries reflected much later: 'We had been brought up in the idea of a stable peace, an expanding commerce, a progressive and steady advance in well-being and right reason throughout the world.'[47]

It is important to recognize that the use of the term in political argument was both evaluative and descriptive. That is, there was a basic set of criteria for the application of the term, and so in practice a range of phenomena which it was acknowledged to describe, but the term also had such a favourable evaluative force that to describe something as being a case of Progress was *thereby* to commend it.[48] So to establish that a particular social development constituted an aspect of Progress was to give a *prima facie* justification of it. Specifying the constituent components of Progress was thus an inherently contentious enterprise, and a considerable part of the political argument of these years consisted in attempts on all sides to show that a particular course of action was continuous with, and constituted the next step in, the acknowledged facts of Progress. Where this was brought off successfully, the favoured development was legitimated in such a powerful way that it acted as an overriding argument in most discussions. Spencer's political theory relied heavily on deploying the force of the term in just this way: the laws of evolution demonstrate that Progress is uniquely the result of the unrestricted actions of free individuals, and so the restriction of the interference of the state is 'the vital principle of social progress', however unpalatable its immediate consequences may seem.[49] Not to have challenged this claim, but instead simply to have proposed measures of social reform without displaying their compatibility with and contribution to Progress would have been to surrender a monopoly on this powerful intellectual weapon to one's political opponents.

One could, of course, reject Spencer without rewriting him. The Idealism which prevailed at Oxford at this time did not encourage such an intimate involvement with the natural scientific approach to the development of mind: Green, as he once memorably declared, 'was not interested in

46 L. P. Jacks, 'Moral Progress' in F. S. Marvin (ed.), *Progress and History* (London, 1916), p. 134.

47 H. A. L. Fisher, *An Unfinished Autobiography*, ed. D. Ogg (London, 1940), p. 77.

48 The modern philosophical literature on 'evaluative-descriptive terms' derives primarily from the work of J. L. Austin, especially his *How to do Things with Words* (Oxford, 1962). The necessary distinction between 'meaning' and 'speech-acts' was developed in the classic article by J. R. Searle, 'Meaning and speech-acts', *Philosophical Review*, LXXI (1962), 423–32.

49 Spencer, *Man Versus State*, p. 181.

dogs'.[50] But Hobhouse's early allegiance to Spencer and the scientific method inclined him against such disdain. The 'social meaning' of Mill and Spencer for a young man in revolt against the orthodoxy, particularly the religious orthodoxy, of his parents' generation was important here. They had been his earliest heroes, and loyalty to their philosophy indicated support for the rationalist, secular, radical point of view with which he so proudly identified. Thus, at the beginning of his undergraduate career, as he later recalled, 'I rather innocently took Herbert Spencer's evolutionary views as the last word of science', and this respect for Spencer's attempt at a philosophy based on evolutionary science never left him.[51] 'Whatever the defects of his method,' he later wrote, 'in this respect Mr Spencer...seemed to me to have been justly inspired.'[52] In the intensity and persistence of Hobhouse's efforts to rework the theory of evolution, therefore, there was some of the passion of the intellectual parricide.

For, of course, Spencer's political conclusions and the allegedly pernicious influence of his theory were anathema in the Collectivist circles in which Hobhouse increasingly moved. At the same time, he was drawn into much closer contact with the intellectual legatees of Green and Toynbee, and through them, as we have seen, with a generally Idealist approach to moral and political issues.[53] This was the 'advanced' thought of the day, and though Hobhouse's relationship with Idealism was always ambivalent, the vocabulary of 'self-realization' and 'the common good' best expressed his moral commitment. His position was thus an inherently eclectic one. But in fact the attempt to combine aspects of evolutionism and Idealism was not unheard of in Oxford in the 1880s, and it helps us to place the formation of Hobhouse's theory in its appropriate context if we briefly consider the rather similar enterprises of two of his slightly older contemporaries from which he drew encouragement.

The figure who, in general terms, did most to pioneer the investigation of these issues was D. G. Ritchie (1853–1903), the 'most brilliant' of Green's pupils at Balliol in the late 1870s, a Fellow and, from 1881, a Tutor

50 'Four years before Hobhouse came to Oxford, I remember that Hastings Rashdall took me to hear T. H. Green lecture at Balliol. The lecture was an argument for human immortality, based on the statement that since we only know of the existence of our bodies from the testimony of our conscious mind, there is no *a priori* reason for believing that the dissolution of the body affects the continued existence of the conscious mind. Green asked for questions; I, being fresh from reading Darwin, asked him whether his argument applied to the conscious mind of a dog, and Green answered that he was not interested in dogs.' Graham Wallas, Review of Hobson and Ginsberg, *L. T. Hobhouse*, *New Statesman and Nation*, 25 April 1931. Hobhouse, Wallas went on, 'was intensely "interested in dogs"'.

51 'Philosophy of Development', p. 150. See also his obituary article on Spencer, *Manchester Guardian*, 9 Dec. 1903.

52 *Development and Purpose*, p. xviii.

53 See above, Ch. 2.

at Jesus College.[54] Politically as well as philosophically he drew his inspiration from Green, but was keen to push beyond his master's ambiguous pronouncements on 'state-intervention'; in the language of the day, he was proud to call himself a 'Socialist'. As one friend recalled: 'The problem of "the function of the state" was no matter of academic casuistry to him; its solution determined his attitude to every contemporary political measure.'[55] He was a well-known supporter of radical causes in Oxford, and, for a while, a member of the Fabian Society.[56] As a philosopher and teacher what 'gave him a definite field of his own' was that he was 'one of the very first among academic teachers to come to close quarters with modern biological or pseudo-biological theory in its relation to social ethics', and he made 'a special study of the Lamarckian and Darwinian theories in biology'.[57] Spencer was his main target in this work because, as he put it in the late 1880s, 'there can be no doubt that the formulae of evolution (as expounded by Spencer) do supply an apparent justification to the defenders of unrestricted *laissez-faire*...and a plausible weapon of attack against those who look to something better than slavery or competition as the basis of human society'.[58] Ritchie did not wish to dispute the relevance of evolutionary theory to such political debates; on the contrary, he asserted the need for a more careful statement of the theory partly in order that its consequences for 'social ethics' could be more clearly established. He always insisted that cultural and intellectual improvements 'are transmitted in the *social inheritance* of the race and are not dependent on heredity in the biological sense', a point well worth insisting on in England in the 1880s and 1890s.[59] As Latta noted, 'Ritchie continually insisted on the importance of the "social factor" in mental development, not merely with regard to the higher or more complex mental processes, but in connection with the most elementary forms of cognition.'[60] At the same time his basic philosophical allegiance was to a modified neo-Hegelianism. He never produced a systematic account of the blending of these two traditions; in his essays he concentrated upon philosophical and political criticism, but these certainly earned him a wide audience, his

[54] For information on Ritchie, see the Memoir of him by Latta, prefixed to *Philosophical Studies*. The description of him is by his contemporary at Balliol, J. H. Muirhead: see Muirhead, *Reflections*, p. 95.

[55] W. J. Ashley quoted in *Philosophical Studies*, p. 9. 'He was a Socialist, and had the strongest belief in state action wherever possible' was Latta's recollection (p. 7).

[56] See his reviews and reports of his papers in *The Oxford Magazine* in the 1880s – e.g. 13 Feb., 13 May, 11 Nov. 1885, and many more.

[57] *Philosophical Studies*, p. 8.

[58] Ritchie, *Darwinism and Politics*, pp. 9–10.

[59] D. G. Ritchie, 'Social Evolution', first published *International Journal of Ethics* (1896), and repr. in D. G. Ritchie, *Studies in Political and Social Ethics* (London, 1902), pp. 7–8.

[60] *Philosophical Studies*, p. 34.

Darwinism and Politics, in particular, being frequently cited. It is noteworthy that as late as 1913 Hobhouse still pointed to the example set by Ritchie in insisting that 'the factor of consciousness...would influence the course of development'.[61]

The friend and colleague who provided Hobhouse with an example of pursuing his moral and philosophical interests into actual work in experimental psychology was Samuel Alexander (1859–1938).[62] Alexander was elected a Fellow of Lincoln in 1882 and seemed destined for the familiar philosophical career of the young Greats Tutor. But already 'his mind was turning towards an approach to philosophy which could be related to the empirical sciences, and, particularly to psychology and biology'. He became acquainted with J. Burdon-Sanderson, first Professor of Physiology at Oxford, and started to work in his laboratory. 'The seriousness of his interest is evidenced by the fact that...he resigned [his Fellowship] in 1888 in order to study psychology', and indeed studied for a period in Munsterberg's laboratory in Germany.[63] He, too, was brought into contact with Hobhouse (one of whose examiners he had been in 1887) by a range of shared interests – his work on physiology and psychology, his conception of moral progress, his involvement with Toynbee Hall, and so on.[64] Once their friendship was established, their philosophical cooperation became close, and Alexander later read and made extensive comments upon the draft of *The Theory of Knowledge*.[65] In general terms Alexander 'was seeking ways of trying to transpose some of the philosophy of Bradley and Bosanquet on to a realist basis, and to relate it to a strong interest in experimental psychology and neurology'[66] – which is a passable description

[61] *Development and Purpose*, p. xx. Hobhouse had also quoted Ritchie on this point, *Labour Movement*, p. 92. The circumstantial evidence strongly suggests that Ritchie and Hobhouse were in close contact at Oxford: apart from their political and intellectual interests, they had friends in common and were members of the same societies – e.g. Ritchie gave a paper to the Oxford Philosophical Society on 'Natural Selection in Relation to Mental Evolution' in 1890, and it is very probable that Hobhouse took part in the 'long and animated discussion' which followed; *Oxford Magazine*, 29 Jan. 1890. See also letters from Alexander in Latta's Memoir, *Philosophical Studies*, pp. 17, 32. But I do not wish to minimize the differences between Hobhouse and Ritchie, especially in philosophy where Ritchie was always a much more committed Idealist, and was, for example, critical of Hobhouse's 'chivalrous attempt to defend Mill against the fierce onslaught of Mr Bradley'; *Philosophical Studies*, p. 163.

[62] On Alexander, see his *Philosophical and Literary Pieces*, with a Memoir by J. Laird (London, 1939), and the Foreword by Dorothy Emmett to the re-issue of his *Space, Time and Deity* (repr. 1966 [first published London, 1920]).

[63] *Space, Time and Deity*, p. vii.

[64] *Philosophical Pieces*, pp. 14–17. Alexander, like Hobhouse, was at this time an enthusiastic follower of Mazzini, whose *The Duties of Man* he called 'one of the most important, truest, most spiritual works on politics this century has seen', *Oxford Magazine*, 22 April 1885. Laird also quotes an (anonymous) testimonial letter of 1893 from a group who claimed that they had been led from philosophy to psychology by Alexander; *Philosophical Pieces*, p. 17.

[65] See the many (barely legible) letters about it from Alexander in the Hobhouse Papers for 1895 and 1896, and Hobhouse's revealing letter of thanks of 14 Feb. 1896, Alexander Papers.

[66] Emmett's description, *Space, Time and Deity*, p. ix.

of Hobhouse's philosophical aspirations at this time. Alexander's first book, *Moral Order and Progress* (1889), was an attempt to describe the moral ideal in evolutionary terms whilst doing justice to the insights of Green and the Idealists. As he wrote in the Introduction: 'I have come to the ideas, borrowed from biology and the theory of evolution, which are prevalent in modern ethics, with a training derived from Aristotle and Hegel, and I have found not antagonism but, on the whole, fulfilment.'[67] The core of his argument was that a form of evolutionary progress had taken place in morals, and he proposed 'comprehensiveness' as the major criterion of such advance. His substantive values emerged in the application of this criterion. For example:

> the principle of democracy, which we are engaged at the present time in working out, contains an element of universality in respect of the civil and political status of persons, while at the same time it accentuates the solidarity of man in respect of the more ordinary social duties. This process of universalization may become more complete, and there is therefore nothing impossible in the dream of a political ideal which should comprehend mankind, as the social or humanitarian ideal already does.

He was also anxious to emphasize that the political implications of Green's teaching were quite consistent with the findings of evolutionary biology: 'Free service to a whole which is in continual progress is nothing but the analogy of animal life pushed forward one stage further...We have here in the domain of ethics that love of man for a higher and larger order than himself which morality represents as solidarity with society – a continuously progressive society of free individuals.'[68] Neither Ritchie nor Alexander pursued this subject in quite the same way as Hobhouse, and in their later work they all diverged quite sharply. But in the intellectual situation of the 1880s, particularly at Oxford, it was a theoretical issue with a strong claim on the attention of those who identified with radical political causes.

There were also more profound psychological sources of the deep involvement of this generation of reformers with the idea of Progress. They repeatedly invoked it to provide a sense of meaningfulness and significance which they seemed to find necessary to sustain political effort. Of course, it would sap the energies of even the most zealous radical to feel that his activities simply resembled those of Sisyphus, and no doubt even more discouraging models sometimes suggest themselves. But the intensity and scope of the late-Victorian search for reassurance far transcended this recognizable emotional response. To want a reasonable prospect of success in any specific enterprise is one thing; but to need to feel that one's activities

67 *Moral Order and Progress: An Analysis of Ethical Conceptions* (London, 1889), p. viii. As a dissertation, the book had been awarded the T. H. Green Moral Philosophy Prize in 1887.

68 *Moral Order*, pp. 391–3; 410; 412–13.

are in line with a global pattern of improvement is a far more taxing requirement. The implicit assumption of directional laws in history certainly intensified this demand, and the still fairly recent deprivation of the comfort of a Christian teleology may have contributed an additional element of insistence to the search for a higher purpose. At all events, for this generation of intellectuals the choice, as far as their subjective state was concerned, seemed to be between the buoyant conviction of being in the van of history, and the enervating despair of the spectator helpless in the face of a process of cosmic futility. Reflecting on this theme, William Clarke concluded: 'Whatever else may be or may not be, it is certain that reason is in the world, that it has a telos which must partake of its own nature; else why concern ourselves with rational action at all?' Social reform, argued Clarke, would seem 'a mad delusion' without this belief in a 'higher purpose'.[69] The young Charles Buxton expressed the point more politically when he wrote, 'If I did not believe that the world is advancing ever nearer to the ideals of the best men...I should be a conservative...The real foundation of liberalism is the belief in the higher world than the world around us of palpable facts.'[70] And, as we have seen, Hobhouse himself felt that to be 'a radical or socialist or anything reforming' it was necessary to have this kind of guarantee about the long-term prospects of social improvement.[71]

The subjective basis of this dependence of social reform upon the reassurance of Progress can be illustrated in detail by looking at lectures in which two prominent followers of T. H. Green addressed themselves to the anxieties of the reforming intellectual class more generally. With the singularly revealing title of 'The Ultimate Value of Social Effort', D. G. Ritchie began by explicitly asking his South Place Ethical Society audience how, in the absence of orthodox religious beliefs, one could justify one's efforts at social and moral improvement when they were challenged by the pessimist.[72] His answer was that 'the hopelessness of the pessimist in the face of suffering comes from his utter disbelief in social progress and in all attempts to remedy this suffering by improving the conditions under which men live'. This attitude is possibly understandable in 'the Oriental ascetic or mystic', to whom 'there is nothing new under the sun – no

[69] Quoted in Weiler, 'William Clarke', 86. Beatrice Potter, when a young social worker, expressed a similar anxiety in her diary: 'How can one raise these beings to better things without the hope of a better world, the faith in the usefulnesss of effort?' *My Apprenticeship*, p. 283. One of Hobhouse's Oxford contemporaries later wrote of his aspirations of that period: 'I wished to bring about an improved social order and direct our activities to an end great enough to give them a dignity and a meaning.' Hewins, *Apologia*, I, p. 15.

[70] Quoted in V. De Bunsen, *Charles Roden Buxton* (London, 1948), p. 32.

[71] See the letter of 1914 to Margaret Llewellyn Davies, quoted in Hobson and Ginsberg, *L. T. Hobhouse*, p. 65, and cited above, Ch. 3, text at n98.

[72] The lecture was originally delivered in 1889, and repr. in his *Studies in Political and Social Ethics*.

forward movement – no meaning in politics, no meaning in history'. What is needed if one should feel the pull of this despair – as at times Ritchie did himself[73] – is faith. 'The refusal to despair of human society upon this earth, and the endeavour to make human life better by social or political reforms implies *faith* in humanity and in Progress.' This faith is based upon 'knowledge of the past' and on 'the social instinct'. To deny the efficacy of that instinct 'is only possible to those who (like Oriental mystics) are ignorant of social development, or (like their Western imitators) ignore it'. Furthermore, the evidence of history proved that humanity had now reached the point where 'the personal gratification of the individual cannot exclude but must include the realisation of social well-being'.[74] Here, a proper understanding of social development provides not only a persuasive political argument for Collectivist reforms, but also a subjective defence against the anomie and depression which were so readily produced by contemplating the futility of swimming against the tide of history.

Addressing another Ethical Society in the 1890s, J. S. Mackenzie recognized that 'there are few words more freely used in our time than Progress'.[75] But, he asked, are there not 'certain doubts which suggest themselves as to the nature and value of human progress, which it seems of some importance to consider?' For example, has Progress been merely 'mechanical' (a favourite term of condemnation with writers of this school), and not the result of genuine advance in human character, or, again, have the achievements of particular periods, such as classical Greece, been imitated but never surpassed? Although he felt capable of dispelling these particular worries – like so many of the Idealists he particularly emphasized what Green had called 'the extension of the area of the common good' as the line of advance in modern times – he admitted that 'doubt may still be thrown on [the] permanence' of Progress. Though such doubts 'may be set aside as idle fears, they have a tendency, when once presented, to recur with a haunting persistence, and if we yield to them, to land us at last in a state of abject pessimism'. The language of this remark is revealing of the personal experience behind it – the 'haunting persistence' of doubts,

[73] See Latta's Memoir, *Philosophical Studies*, p. 16, for Ritchie's emotional reliance on the idea of Progress. The deep feeling with which he presents the case for pessimism at the beginning of this lecture suggests that it was a mood with which he was personally very familiar. 'Perhaps no-one,' he suggested with conviction, 'save those of a singularly fortunate natural temperament and exceptionally happy surroundings, no-one, certainly, who has reflected much on human life, can have escaped at least a temporary feeling' of this kind of despair. But, he warned, we must not let 'our own personal tendencies to doubt and despair' drive us to religious or irrationalist 'mysticism'; we must justify our 'humanist' view. *Philosophical Studies*, p. 176.

[74] *Philosophical Studies*, pp. 191, 181. As he remarked in the Preface to this volume, it is only possible to 'discuss practical questions of political and social ethics... provided that one may take for granted that faith in the value and meaning of human society and human history which is implied in all serious political and social effort' (p. iv).

[75] 'The Idea of Progress', *International Journal of Ethics*, IX (1898–9), 195–213.

the 'abject pessimism' which results if they are 'yielded' to (the emphasis upon the role of the will is very characteristic), and so on. Such depression had practical consequences, for, as he went on to explain, all that we do in the present is bound up with our hopes for the future:

> Hence, any doubt about the future of human life is inevitably a doubt about the present as well. If we lose our confidence in what men are to be, we lose also to a large extent our confidence in our present interests and duties... If we lose faith in mankind, we necessarily lose faith in ourselves and the significance vanishes from all our deepest interests and obligations.

This was particularly the case in view of what Mackenzie took to be 'our deepest interests and obligations' – social reform. 'Could any of us really be content to think that the efforts that are being made for human advancement are mere "fool's play" and "make-believe"? Could any of us bear to believe that the evils of which we are conscious in our present state would never be in any degree removed or mitigated?' The answer was self-evident, and he concluded, in a significant phrase, that 'the doubt as to the reality of Progress is one that cuts at the very root of human life'.[76]

How then were these doubts to be countered, given the imperative need to do so? To begin with, they 'might no doubt be partly removed by simply confronting them with the facts of experience'; history, that is, is an encouraging study. But Mackenzie was representative in wanting even greater assurance, since mere empirical observation of the facts of history is 'always liable to be upset by others'. A more reliable guarantee of future Progress could perhaps be found in the laws of evolution, but he quickly dismissed this as leading to the callous submission of present well-being to the operation of an inexorable evolutionary process, however beneficent, as advocated by Spencer. Mackenzie commended the criticisms of Spencer made (covertly) by Huxley in his Romanes Lecture, though he felt, in common with every other writer on this subject, that Huxley had attempted to establish a too radical disjunction between the ethical and the cosmic processes. A less arbitrary ground for optimism was needed. However, having reached this point, Mackenzie's argument petered out.[77] He repeated the Idealist's bromide that personal happiness was bound up with social well-being, and emphasized that effort on behalf of the common good was bound up with optimism about the future. 'The doubt that paralyzes effort is that as to the possibility of improvement'. but 'we must not suppose that [Progress] will come of itself': hope and effort go together.[78]

When we turn to Hobhouse, this psychological connection is crucial, for

[76] 'Idea of Progress', 198–9, 200–1.

[77] He was possibly handicapped in dealing with the evolutionary argument by the fact that the two scientific authorities he cited most frequently were Aristotle and Browning.

[78] 'Idea of Progress', 206, 213.

in his case temperament was fate. Although this is not a biographical study, some discussion of his character is relevant at this point because it constitutes part of the explanation of the nature of Hobhouse's theory. In mood, he oscillated between buoyant optimism and energy, and fits of cosmic gloom and depression in the manner of the classic manic-depressive. 'Throughout his life there were periods of immense and enthusiastic activity broken by periods of moody depression and slackness of will.'[79] It is particularly interesting to notice that while in his major published works optimism is the dominant note, in his occasional writings and even more in his private letters doom and despondency predominate. It is clear that the programmatic, almost wilful, optimism which he built into his theory was, at least in part, a response to his personal needs, a reassurance that things were not as bad, or not always going to be as bad, as they seemed. What J. A. Hobson said of Hobhouse in the twenties held true at most times: 'His real conviction was that we were "going through a bad time", but that the permanent factors in the making of human history were unassailable in their working for a wiser and a better world.'[80] Certainly in his reflections on the state of the world, particularly the current political situation, he often seemed to be on – or beyond – the point of despair, a mood which generated the fiercely ironical prose of much of his best journalism.[81]

This tension between temperament and theory pervades his writing about Progress. Even in his 1913 Preface when he is stating the case for Progress most forcibly, he admits feelingly that 'scepticism is abundantly possible, and it is easy to assert that there have been earlier epochs when religion was purer, social life better organized, men and women on the whole happier, industry devoted to the production of more beautiful objects than sky-scrapers, factory chimneys, gigantic hoardings and aniline dyes'.[82]

[79] Hobson's account, in Hobson and Ginsberg, *L. T. Hobhouse*, p. 94. The evidence is fragmentary and much of it now probably irrecoverable, but it certainly suggests that Hobhouse had manic-depressive tendencies. Nearly all of his very large output was written in brief intensive spells, and from his undergraduate days onwards, his friends spoke of his 'working in his usual steam-engine style'; quoted in Hobson and Ginsberg, *L. T. Hobhouse*, p. 18. His depressive periods seem to have been even more intense and frequently prevented him from working. At various points in his correspondence he refers to his 'psychological trouble' (e.g. to Barbara Hammond, 4 Sept. 1907, Hammond Papers), and he several times had to have treatment for breakdowns resulting from overwork or other nervous causes, beginning with his long convalescence in the autumn of 1887 (see Ch. 2 above). His depressions were exacerbated by various physical ailments later in his life, and after 1914 in particular this obviously contributed to the by then almost endemic gloominess of his views.

[80] Hobson and Ginsberg, *L. T. Hobhouse*, p. 69.

[81] In 1900, C. R. Ashbee noted in his diary, after spending a holiday with a very gloomy Hobhouse: 'The pessimism of the younger radicals has in it something almost tragic...and as for Leonard Hobhouse, he seems to me like a man who is pursued by a spectre. Restless, humorous, brilliant, earnest, with an irony that just saves itself from the [word illegible] that has burnt the wings of too many weaker men in their times.' Journal, Jan. 1900, Ashbee Papers.

[82] *Development and Purpose*, p. xxi, but in fact his work abounds with such passages.

As this passage suggests, he felt that nostalgia for the (selectively remembered) past which is so often found in those whose need to believe in Progress is strongest: he always displayed the symptoms of what might be called the 'jam yesterday...syndrome'.[83] At times, the contemplation of the modern world, the product of Progress to some extent, drew from him a bitterness and melancholy worthy of the great misanthropes of history. But he realized only too well the support for obscurantism and irrationalism which could be drawn from such pessimism, from concentrating on the weaknesses and failures of human effort or on the difficulties of consistent rationalism. It was then that the support of a theory of Progress was most needed, a theory, moreover, which would not be discredited by the short-term disasters and temporary set-backs to which the world was all too prone. Hobhouse could not bear to walk the tightrope of reforming politics without the security of a metaphysical safety-net, and it was the tension within his own personality which gave such an intensity to his persistent and single-minded efforts to create one.

[83] Consider in this connection the perceptive remark of Hobhouse's son: 'Father was immensely conservative in some ways, and would not take up with a reversal of the old order of things. Thus, though he was very fond of whist, he refused to learn bridge and he despised golf. He had the traditional instincts of the traditional county family, and these not being able to intrude on his thought, used to come out in little ways in his habits.' Quoted in Hobson and Ginsberg, *L. T. Hobhouse*, p. 90. As he grew older, his attachment to various features of his Victorian upbringing became more pronounced; he hated motor-cars with a fierce passion, and he deplored the innovations of 'modernism' in the arts. On his continuing identification with the intellectual and moral world of the second half of the nineteenth century, see below, Ch. 8.

6: SOCIAL DARWINISM AND SOCIAL SCIENCE

In the last chapter, I discussed Hobhouse's general strategy for challenging the Spencerian amalgam of biology and politics and affirming his own account of Progress. In the first part of this chapter, I shall look at his tactics as he worked out his plan in actual controversy in his writings of the 1890s and early 1900s. His earliest skirmishes against the scientific argument for Individualism are fairly brief and are overshadowed by his largely moral advocacy of the case for Collectivism. As he develops his own evolutionary theory, however, he is able to draw upon it for the ammunition necessary to sustain more extended engagements. In the second part of the chapter, I shall discuss the relationship of this kind of writing to the contemporary understanding of sociology, and show how Hobhouse's work was seen to coincide with the conception of sociology which was gaining ascendency at that time, and which is most fully displayed in the discussions of the newly formed Sociological Society.

In *The Labour Movement* (1893) Hobhouse complements his treatment of the economic, political and moral arguments with a brief discussion of 'the scientific arguments for Individualism. The chief of these arguments is the application to human progress of ideas derived from the organic world at large.'[1] In expounding this argument, he did not indicate a strictly Spencerian position: that is to say, he concentrated upon the direct application in a normative way of natural selection to society, without distinguishing between Spencer's emphasis on the inheritance of acquired characteristics, and the then recently publicized argument of Weismann that only genetically inherited factors could be transmitted.[2] He did not discriminate between them, since he took the political conclusions drawn from each to be identical. As he recalled in 1913, 'it was not until Weismann insisted upon the all sufficiency of Natural Selection' that the Social

[1] *Labour Movement*, p. 90.

[2] For a brief view of the debate between these two schools, see the numerous articles in *The Contemporary Review* beginning with G. J. Romanes ('Weismann's Theory of Heredity', *Contemporary Review*, LVII (1889), 686–99, which refers to 'the recently published translations of Prof. Weismann's essays on heredity and allied topics'); and carrying on into the mid 1890s, with Spencer conducting a drawn-out rearguard action. Weismann's articles were collected in *Essays on Heredity and Kindred Biological Problems*, I (Oxford, 1889), and Spencer's in *A Rejoinder to Professor Weismann* (New York, 1894).

Darwinist argument 'assumed its extremer form. But the social implications of Natural Selection were already apparent before Weismann's work acquired its ascendency, and were so far accepted by Mr Spencer as to be made the basis of an uncompromising economic individualism.'[3]

It was this composite argument, therefore, whose conclusions Hobhouse summarized.

> The natural result of the struggle is the survival of the fittest, which is the means of the gradual evolution of higher from lower forms. So in human life...in this way by slow degrees we attain to a higher type...Happiness and perfection are reached by men and by other organisms when they are thoroughly well adapted to their environment, and the supreme law of progress is that the ill-adapted being should be left to die.[4]

By way of reply, Hobhouse is at this stage only able to put pressure on the criteria for the application of the term 'fit'. Thus, he wrote: 'Now we fully agree with the evolutionists in their main position. It is desirable that the fit should succeed and the unfit fail...But who are the unfit? "Those who are ill-adapted to their environment", say the evolutionists. Quite so.' The lineaments of the argument are all too familiar. But what, asks Hobhouse, 'is the environment of man? The society of other men. Then who is the fit man? Clearly the man who is best adapted for social life.' The argument here begins to be Socratic in its sophistry as well as its style. For, asks Hobhouse rhetorically, who is this man? 'Is he the bold unscrupulous man of force, the exacting, the merciless, the ungenerous?... Or is he the merciful and generous man of justice, whose hardest fights are fought for others' lives, who would rather, with Plato, suffer wrong than inflict it, and who will lay down his life to serve mankind?'[5] Hobhouse is here juxtaposing those moral qualities of altruism and a sense of service, the ideals of the 'Oxford Movement' of the 1880s, with a caricature of the qualities associated with success in commercial competition. Such rhetoric was no substitute for refutation, and the real issue – the extent to which man is subject to the uncontrollable operation of wider biological laws – is ducked. It was uncontentious to conclude that the second type of man 'is fittest morally to survive in a society of mutually dependent human beings. And that the morally fittest shall actually survive and prosper is the object of good social institutions.' Here was that characteristic tendency to reduce social problems to moral questions, and then to appeal to an ethical ideal so widely defined that it was unobjectionable. He did approach the central issue when he declared: 'It is almost superfluous to point out the ambiguity of the word "fit"' (not least because this theme

[3] *Development and Purpose*, pp. xvi–xvii.

[4] *Labour Movement*, pp. 90–1.

[5] *Labour Movement*, p. 91.

had been so well explored, as he acknowledged, by D. G. Ritchie), but he did not pursue the point.[6]

In effect, Hobhouse was replacing biological with moral criteria: 'If we wish to preserve the morally fit, we must make submission to moral laws the main condition of success. Then the two meanings of fitness coincide. The morally fit become the best fitted to survive.' Here, the assertion that men must attempt to control their collective social life in accordance with their own standards of value is not actually dependent on accepting the organic analogy at all. He has simply retained the vocabulary of 'fit' and 'survive' (though of course it is arguable that most of the so-called Social Darwinists, including Spencer, also specified the criteria of fitness in terms of morally desirable social qualities). At this stage, Hobhouse is obviously trying to legitimate his own political values by appropriating the prestige of the evolutionary argument: 'A due regulation of economic conditions would provide for physical as for moral health, and far from scorning the teachings of biology, would use them to promote the evolution of a nobler species. The evolutionist argument thus correctly understood makes straight for collective control.'[7]

Such juggling with the components of the biological analogy was a commonplace in the controversies of the 1880s and 1890s. The first hint of what was to become Hobhouse's distinctive contribution was in his article on 'The Ethical Basis of Collectivism'. Since the aim of this article was to show that Socialism, correctly understood, was the practical application of the highly prized values of altruism and cooperation, Hobhouse was more vulnerable than a certain sort of hard-nosed Socialist to the evolutionists' claim that competition was the law of life.[8] So, in the vein of Drummond, Kropotkin, and a host of less popular contemporary writers, he began by complaining that 'it has been the mistake of many modern Evolutionists to eliminate love from consideration, and to leave hate, rivalry and competition as the sole spring of movement in organic life'. What he particularly wished to emphasize was that the increasing complexity of the higher organisms involved a proportionate increase in integration and interdependence: the point was Spencerian even if the conclusion which he wished to draw from it was not. Thus, he insisted that

> from the lowest stages of organic life upward to civilized man, there is an advance of integration which is constantly replacing the struggle of isolated atoms by the harmonious

[6] *Labour Movement*, p. 92. See Ritchie, *Darwinism and Politics*, Ch. 1.

[7] *Labour Movement*, pp. 92, 93.

[8] On this article, see above, Ch. 2. The Fabians, by contrast, increasingly adopted the language of 'Nationalist Social Darwinism', and even flirted with Eugenics. There is a useful discussion of this whole connection in Semmel, *Imperialism and Social Reform*; and in Searle, *Quest For National Efficiency*, esp. Chs. 3 and 4.

concurrence of interdependent parts...The loss of a limb matters little to the starfish, and not as much as might be supposed to the limb...But always as we mount the animal scale, we come to a closer organization, in which, as between the myriads of living units which constitute the body, competition is reduced to very narrow limits, the health of the whole is essential to the life of each, and the cells secure their own maintenance by cooperating in the support of the entire body.[9]

Here, 'cooperation' is at best a metaphor: at worst, it is a piece of verbal legerdemain. No one had ever asserted that an animal's hind-leg was engaged in the struggle for existence against its fore-leg, and to emphasize the greater complexity of the higher organisms – which is to state a tautology if 'higher' is used in its strict taxonomical sense of 'structurally and functionally more complex' – says nothing, logically, about the presence or absence of competition between separate organisms. But this is to underline the fact that, at one level, Hobhouse is still arguing from within the assumptions of the biological analogy. For, as he went on to say:

In the relations of animals and of human beings to one another, a somewhat similar development can be traced. Social life at any stage is a more or less organized structure as the case may be, and Progress consists in the development of organization. At every stage competition is the law of unorganized, cooperation of organized life.[10]

So, within the terms of the analogy, the conclusion is that the direction of social progress is towards greater organization (although whether this was to be produced by spontaneous cooperation or deliberate collective control – which was, after all, what was at issue – remained undetermined by this argument alone).

In fact, it soon becomes clear that Hobhouse's understanding of the concept of an 'organic society' owed more to Green than to Darwin: 'The true conception of an organic society is one in which the best life of each man is, and is felt to be, bound up with the life of his fellow-citizens.' His argument is designed to demonstrate that this 'is a natural deduction from all that we know of those evolutionary forces which make for progress'. There is a suggestion of circularity in this demonstration, but the central point upon which Hobhouse insists is that 'correlation of the individuals of a species may be one among other methods by which a type may be preserved'. Hobhouse construed this point in a very particular way: 'The natural organ of such organization is what at least in its higher developments we call the moral intelligence, in virtue of which the individual makes the goal of this social group, and ultimately of the whole species to which he belongs, an object of supreme interest to himself.'[11] If, therefore, this capacity was increasingly evident as one ascended the natural scale (as Hobhouse asserted rather than, at this stage, demonstrated), then there was

[9] 'Ethical Basis', 144. [10] 'Ethical Basis', 144. [11] 'Ethical Basis', 145–6.

a progressive development within evolution. Thus, in a passage in which the sequence of sentences is particularly revealing, he concluded:

> What we call progress in evolution, or the evolution of higher types, we take to be identical with the advance of organisation. History, if it has a meaning, is a record of the process by which elements of value and rational purpose have come to make themselves good by organised coherence. What we call the progressive organisation of life is, therefore, for us an evolutionary process, and the only evolutionary process of value.[12]

The 'therefore' in the final sentence is a rather transparent attempt to make the disparate elements of the argument hold together, a drop of poor-quality logical glue. For it is by now pretty obvious – certainly further analysis could only labour the point – that Hobhouse is still deploying a rather makeshift assemblage of arguments. To begin with, he is accepting some form of the organic analogy.[13] Within this framework, he wants to stress the *evolutionary* role of cooperation and altruism. But although popular Social Darwinism of the 1880s tended to neglect this, it was something which Spencer had been at some pains to establish as a feature of the higher stages of evolution. As ever, Hobhouse does not distinguish Spencer's own complex arguments from those of the vulgar Spencerians. His concern, of course, was to extract a rationale for Collectivism from his own account. He insists that it is 'the rational organisation of life', that is, the conscious attempt to control the common life, which emerged as the progressive development in the higher reaches of evolution, and this was a process in which 'elements of value and rational purpose have come to make themselves good' in history, an immanent teleology which is certainly not to be derived from biology *tout court*. In this way he tries to substantiate his claim that 'there is no greater or more common blunder than to treat Natural Selection as essentially an agent of Progress', and to conclude that 'the true line of social progress' consists in 'the development of that rational organisation of life in which men freely recognise their interdependence, and the best life for each is understood to be that which is best for those around him. The attempt to shape our social customs and institutions in this spirit is the aim and principle of Collectivism.'[14]

The end of the 1890s saw a decline in Hobhouse's optimism about, and perhaps even a tempering of his enthusiasm for, Collectivism, and his reliance on this assertive use of the evolutionary argument diminished correspondingly. For a while, he became more concerned with the role of Social Darwinist ideas in bringing about the 'reaction' which he saw as

[12] 'Ethical Basis', 146.

[13] Throughout, he accepts the utility of inferences from animal behaviour: thus, one sentence begins: 'If the fulness of animal vigour is to be attained...', and the next: 'If a satisfactory social life is to be attained...' (148).

[14] 'Ethical Basis', 147, 149.

characterizing these years.[15] In a series of articles on the subject written in 1901–2, he identified 'the doctrine that human progress depends upon the forces which condition all biological evolution' as 'the primary intellectual cause of the reaction'. It was Darwin who, unwittingly, had

> provided a philosophy for the reaction. Darwin himself, indeed, was conscious of the limitations of his own hypothesis, and was aware that the development of the moral consciousness in man involves from the first a suspension of the blind struggle for existence. But those who have applied Darwin's theories to the science of society have not as a rule troubled themselves to understand Darwin any more than the science of society.

As a result – and here we see the level of discussion which Hobhouse was concerned with –

> what has filtered through into the social and political thought of the time has been the belief that the time-honoured doctrine 'might be right' has a scientific foundation in the laws of biology. Progress comes about through a conflict in which the fittest survives. It must, therefore, be unwise in the long run – however urgent it seems for the sake of the present generation – to interfere with the struggle.[16]

However, to this old caricature of popular Spencerianism a new distinction had to be added. There are the theory's 'most logical exponents' who apply it 'to the relations of individuals in society', but there are now also, in an age dominated by imperial questions, those who apply the theory to nations, for whom 'progress might be thought of as resting on the struggle not of individuals, but of communities'.[17]

Hobhouse is here referring to 'Nationalist' or 'External' Social Darwinism, and his polemics against this group of writers is a good indication of how he continued to engage with the 'biological theory of society' in each of the new forms it assumed.[18] Benjamin Kidd and Karl Pearson were the best-known exponents of this view, although the growth in importance of imperial questions in the late 1890s produced a large number of writers willing to find a justification for imperialism in biology.

Benjamin Kidd's *Social Evolution* was a source-book for much of this propaganda.[19] Lamenting that there was 'no science of human society properly so called', Kidd claimed that the remedy was to recognize that 'all departments of knowledge which deal with social phenomena have their

[15] On this, see above, Ch. 3.

[16] 'The Intellectual Reaction', *Speaker*, 1 Feb. 1902.

[17] 'Intellectual Reaction'. He scoffed at the inconsistency of a theory in which 'it is the business of the individual to be a loyal and law-abiding subject of the state', and yet 'it is the business of the state merely to advance itself and trample down all who cross its path'. These are, of course, precisely the terms in which he criticized a very different theory, Bosanquet's Idealist political philosophy.

[18] See below, pp. 201ff, and p. 248 for Hobhouse's objections to Eugenics and later versions of biological social theory. 'External' and 'Internal' Social Darwinism are Semmel's terms.

[19] Benjamin Kidd, *Social Evolution* (London, 1894). The book displayed a combination of speculative history and pseudo-science which made it a best-seller – it ran to nineteen printings in the first four years, according to Halévy (*Imperialism and the Rise of Labour*, p. 19).

true foundations in the biological sciences'. Man had evolved from lower species, and 'in following his evolution in society, we find him in like manner subject to laws which have governed the development of the lower forms of life'. What these 'laws' revealed was that 'Progress everywhere from the beginning of life has been effected in the same way and is possible in no other way. It is the result of selection and rejection...Where there is Progress, there must inevitably be selection, and selection must in its turn involve competition of some kind.' But this struggle was now between races, 'the rivalry of nationalities', and 'one after another, races and civilisations appear to be used up in the process as it proceeds'. Internal social solidarity gave the nation its best chance of success, but such solidarity could not be achieved by rational persuasion. Only some supra-rational belief such as religion was adequate to the task. Indeed, 'a preponderating element in the type of character which the evolutionary forces at work in human society are slowly developing would appear to be the sense of reverence', and what most needed to be encouraged in the modern state was 'a sense of single-minded and simple-minded devotion to conceptions of duty'.[20] Needless to say, Kidd's combination of biologism, anti-rationalism, and incipient militarism did not endear him to Hobhouse, even although he was advocating a kind of Collectivism.[21]

Karl Pearson's writings never enjoyed the popularity of Kidd's, but they carried the weight of Pearson's much greater scientific authority. As Professor of Applied Mathematics and Mechanics at University College, London, and author of *The Grammar of Science* (1892), one of the most widely read of that Victorian genre of evangelizing scientific text-books, Pearson's advocacy of the elevating effects 'of the struggle of tribe against tribe, of race against race' could not be ignored.[22] Holding 'the scientific view of a nation', he was an early and rabid supporter of imperialism. A nation, he argued, was 'an organised whole', which was 'kept up to a high pitch of external efficiency by contest, chiefly by way of war with inferior races, and with equal races by the struggle for trade-routes and for the sources of raw material and of food supply'. Once again, the status of Progress as an overriding argument was involved. As Pearson said rather defensively in a lecture in 1900:

This dependence of Progress on the survival of the fittest race, terribly black as it may seem to some of you, gives the struggle for existence its redeeming features; it is the fiery crucible

[20] Kidd, *Social Evolution*, pp. 1, 26, 33–5, 286, 287.

[21] See, for example, Hobhouse's review of Kidd's second book, *The Principles of Western Civilization*, *Manchester Guardian*, 26 Feb. 1902; also *Morals* (1915 edn), p. 595. For their confrontation at the Sociological Society see below. For similar criticisms by Hobson, see his 'Mr Kidd's Social Evolution', *American Journal of Sociology*, 1 (1895).

[22] On Pearson, see Semmel, *Imperialism and Social Reform*, Ch. 2, and E. S. Pearson, *Karl Pearson: An Appreciation of Some Aspects of his Life and Work* (Cambridge, 1938).

out of which comes the finer metal. When wars cease mankind will no longer progress, for there will be nothing to check the fertility of inferior stock; the relentless law of heredity will not be controlled and guided by Natural Selection.[23]

In his *Speaker* articles Hobhouse did not undertake a detailed refutation of this theory, but contented himself with noting 'its effect on contemporary thought'. This effect included 'the increased belief in physical force, the discrediting of appeals to considerations of justice, the belief that strength proves superiority'; indeed, Hobhouse, like many other Liberal reformers, before and since, felt that 'belief in race itself is necessarily of a reactionary tendency, and such belief is fostered by modern biology'.[24] Finally,

to all this must be added a certain pseudo-scientific fatalism, a belief that great political and social changes are not to be grasped or foreseen by the mind of man, nor to be seriously affected by the changes which the statesman can make in institutions, but proceeds rather by occult physical laws, which, even when detected, can no more be altered than the law of gravitation itself.

Inequalities and injustices were not only to be left untouched by this passivity, but they 'are now declared to be essential to the progress of civilisation itself'.[25]

This, for one of Hobhouse's political persuasion, was a telling indictment, but hardly a refutation: more was needed than criticism of this sort. Later in the same year, he reviewed *Imperialism: A Study*, the classic anti-imperialist tract written by his friend and colleague J. A. Hobson. He was, quite naturally, full of praise for the book, both for its explanation of imperialism, and for the ethical standpoint from which imperialism was condemned. But when the original articles from which the book was made up had appeared in *The Speaker* in 1901, Hobhouse had confided to Hammond that he found them 'just a little disappointing',[26] and now he expanded upon this 'one point of criticism' in a revealing way. 'Mr Hobson,' he wrote, 'deals with the evolutionary theory, which is used as a basis for imperialism very effectively, it is true, but without, as it seems to the present writer, going to the root of the matter.' He indicated the Nationalist variety of Social Darwinism to which he was referring, and went on: 'Mr Hobson's reply is, in effect, that with the advance of civilisation the struggle for existence is transmuted. It repeats itself on a higher plane,

[23] Repr. in Karl Pearson, *National Life from the Standpoint of Science* (2nd edn 1905 [first published London, 1901]), pp. 26–7, 46. This last passage is also quoted in Gertrude Himmelfarb, *Victorian Minds* (New York, 1968), p. 320.

[24] 'Intellectual Reaction'. For an interesting discussion of the extent to which theories of race influenced late-nineteenth-century social thought, see G. W. Stocking Jnr, *Race, Culture and Evolution* (New York, 1968), particularly Ch. 10. The political uses of biological theories of race in America at this time are dealt with in Ch. 9 of Hofstadter, *Social Darwinism*.

[25] 'Intellectual Reaction'.

[26] Hobhouse to Hammond, 26 Nov. 1901, Hammond Papers.

as a rivalry of ideas, a competition in social excellence. This is good and true enough, but, at least to the present reviewer, it appears that there is a more far-reaching reply.'[27] Although Hobson had dealt at some length with 'the Scientific Defence of Imperialism', he had relied on a tone of sustained irony at the expense of these arguments, rather than making any positive attempt to establish what the relation actually was between evolution and social theory.[28] What Hobhouse felt was required was an actual account of this relationship which could replace the one then currently advocated by Pearson, Kidd, and their followers. 'A true theory of evolution', wrote Hobhouse, was the necessary starting-point, and this 'begins with the distinction of progress or orthogenic evolution from evolution in general'. He outlined once more – though now, note, using his new scientific term 'orthogenic evolution' (which he here equates with Progress) – his theory of how all living organisms develop towards greater organization and 'a more complex and complete cooperation of the parts that remain distinct'. He concluded, in a significant passage:

In human society a similar development constitutes the advance of civilisation...Hence social progress aims at unity but must repose on freedom. This result is in close accord with Mr Hobson's conception of Internationalism, and it is only mentioned here as indicating that *a philosophic theory of evolution leads us to results which justify and support the application of humanitarian principles to political affairs.*[29]

It was precisely this 'philosophic theory of evolution' that Hobhouse had set out a few months earlier in *Mind in Evolution*, and it is to 'that very remarkable book',[30] the most technical of all of Hobhouse's writings, that we must now turn.

For historians of the social sciences, *Mind in Evolution* has always been a problematical work, not easily categorized within the subject-divisions of any of their disciplines.[31] At first sight, it reads like a hybrid, sired by a monograph on animal psychology out of a text-book on evolution. In the Preface, Hobhouse himself said that in the book 'a hypothesis is propounded as to the general trend of mental evolution, and an attempt is made to test this hypothesis as far as animal intelligence and the generic distinction

[27] 'Democracy and Empire', *Speaker*, 18 Oct. 1902.

[28] See J. A. Hobson, *Imperialism: A Study* (3rd edn 1938 [first published London, 1902]), pp. 153–95; also Porter, *Critics of Empire*, Ch. 7.

[29] 'Democracy and Empire' (my emphasis). Cf. *Democracy and Reaction*, pp. 116–18.

[30] Graham Wallas, 'L. T. Hobhouse Memorial Address', *Economica*, IX (1929), 248.

[31] This puzzlement is very evident in, for example, Fletcher, *Making of Sociology*, II, esp. p. 130; see also the same author's *Instinct in Man* (repr. 1968 [first published London, 1957]), p. xxii. Owen, characteristically, simply does not discuss it: *L. T. Hobhouse, Sociologist*. Hearnshaw restricted himself to speaking of Hobhouse as one of the 'pioneers of British comparative psychology', though he also had to record that Hobhouse was 'only incidentally a psychologist'. L. S. Hearnshaw, *A Short History of British Psychology 1840–1940* (London, 1964), p. 101.

between animal and human intelligence are concerned'.[32] Accordingly, the first two-thirds of the book consist of a series of chapters on 'Organic Adaptability', 'Reflex Action', 'Instinct', and so on, in which Hobhouse carefully summarized the findings of contemporary work in animal psychology, relying mostly on Thorndike, Romanes, and Wesley Mills.[33] Scattered throughout these chapters are detailed accounts of the experiments which Hobhouse himself had carried out in an attempt to test the reasoning ability of a variety of animals. His contention was that most writers – particularly Thorndike, the leading authority of the day on animal psychology[34] – had underestimated or misperceived the nature of animal intelligence. By means of a series of rather homely experiments – many of them centering on the erratic domestic behaviour of Jack, his dog, and Tim, his cat – Hobhouse had tried to show that under certain circumstances some animals can make what he called 'a practical judgement', that is, they can draw upon a general inference from experience to perform a complex action which could not be accounted for by instinct or imitation alone.[35] This, he claimed, went to suggest that the characteristic feature of the operation of mind – the correlating of experience, whether to carry out actions, make statements, or construct ideas – is present in varying degrees in the higher animals, and is not peculiar to man. On the basis of this, he constructed a unilinear evolutionary sequence: at the lowest level, the adjustment of action to the ends of the individual or of the species is wholly instinctive, a pattern of inherited behaviour which is itself determined by the operation of natural selection; but as we ascend the animal scale, instinct is increasingly modified by learnt behaviour, until, in man, we reach the stage where self-conscious intelligence is a potentially determining factor in a great part of behaviour. It is this sequence that he described as 'orthogenic evolution'.[36]

However, the book does not end at this point, for he then goes on to examine the development of mind within the human species, which, he argues, constitutes the continuance of the orthogenic line. But his method is, in this section, not experimental, nor even, on the whole, empirical: it is teleological, with just enough history included to give plausibility to the sequence of human development which he posits. The teleology is implicit in his initial assumption that 'orthogenic evolution must consist in the

[32] *Mind in Evolution*, p. v.

[33] E. L. Thorndike, *Animal Intelligence* (New York, 1898); G. J. Romanes, *Mental Evolution in Animals* (London, 1883) and *Animal Intelligence* (London, 1881); Wesley Mills, *The Nature and Development of Animal Intelligence* (London, 1898).

[34] For a brief account of Thorndike's theories concerning the intelligence, or the lack of it, to be found in the animal kingdom, see the Supplement to *The Psychological Review* for June 1898.

[35] *Mind in Evolution*, Chs. 6–10.

[36] On this term, see above, Ch. 5.

unfolding of all that there is of latent possibility of mind, the awakening of its powers, the development of its scope'. The 'powers' and 'scope' of mind are then rather briskly identified with instrumental rationality: 'The whole process of Orthogenic Evolution consists in the gradual replacement of instinct by reason, and it is the final goal of man to do precisely what is ascribed to Instinct above – to bring all the experience of the race to bear in organising the whole life of the race.'[37] The terminal point of the development of mind, therefore, is the Utopia of the rationalist, where Humanity as a whole acts in accordance with rational principles. For if 'the work of intelligence is to correlate the permanent underlying conditions of racial development with its ideal goal', then the conclusion that may be drawn is that

> race experience, race maintenance, and race future are still the determining factors, but all now fall within the scope of the Reason, and purposes equally with methods are transformed accordingly. It is not the maintenance of the type, but its perfection which is sought: not mere adaptation to circumstances, but the domination of the rational spirit in the world.[38]

This is presented as an inference from the results of scientific experiments on the nature of animal intelligence. Faced with this development of the argument, it is no longer plausible to describe the work simply as 'a pioneering effort' in experimental psychology; a further characterization is needed, one capable of capturing the book's point in terms of the contemporary debate.

A helpful starting-point is provided by a series of articles which Hobhouse wrote in the following year in which he set out his conclusions in a form more palatable to the general public.[39] In the first of these, he commented upon the dominance of biology in the thought of the age, which was due, above all, to the immense prestige of the Darwinian triumph. The mode of explanation characteristic of biology, he complained, is the genetic, the tracing back of all things to their origins, the reducing of the higher to the lower.

> The study of mind, on the contrary, takes us at once to the highest thing that evolution has produced, and when we compare the different phases of mental growth, we get into the way of judging the lower by the higher, and viewing the process in relation to the result. In other words, if evolution is ever to be understood as the working out of a purpose, it must be through the investigation of the way in which its noblest work develops and comes to perfection.[40]

'Highest', 'purpose', and 'noblest' are revealing words. The implication of the passage is that only if evolution is regarded in this way can those

[37] *Mind in Evolution*, pp. 5, 9.

[38] *Mind in Evolution*, pp. 371–2.

[39] 'The Diversions of a Psychologist', *Pilot*, v (Jan. to April 1902), 12–13, 36–7, 126–7, 232–3, 344–5, 449–51.

[40] 'Diversions of a Psychologist', 12–13.

aspects which man values and strives after be given their due prominence. This is also the implication of the way in which Hobhouse referred to general evolution – as opposed to 'orthogenic evolution' – in the opening chapter of the book. 'Evolution,' he began, 'is a natural process moving without regard to human judgements of what is good or bad, right or wrong.' And again,

> In natural selection as such there is nothing whatever to prove that the individuals who prevail over others in the struggle for existence must necessarily be in any way 'higher' in the sense which we human beings attach to that word...The worst type very often survives, and evolution is not always upwards. It is not even normally upwards.[41]

In making this apparently uncontentious statement, he was aligning himself with Huxley, and attacking evolution's 'exponents who are often also its apostles', by whom 'evolution is used as synonymous with progress'. But Hobhouse eschewed Huxley's much criticized antithesis between the 'cosmic process' and the 'ethical process'. Instead, he looked for 'at least one upward line in the evolutionary tree', and an answer to the questions 'Is there development in the true sense? Is there progress or the evolution of a higher type?' Unlike Huxley (or, at least, unlike the general interpretation of his Romanes Lecture), he tried to find, by means of an analysis of the 'cosmic process' itself, an ethically congenial significance in evolution. Part of the 'point' of the book is thus to show, as he had put it elsewhere, 'while evolution is not the same thing as progress, there is such a thing as progress in evolution'.[42]

Moreover, this conception of evolution also gave a significant – and, to a social reformer, a congenial – role to self-conscious effort, for 'as soon as the past and present evolution of man are understood as the opening stages of a much nobler growth, as soon as that further growth becomes sufficiently understood to operate upon standards of morality and conceptions of social effort, evolution becomes conscious and full of purpose'. The goal to which this purpose was directing itself would be found in that 'perfect development' of mind 'to which it moves forward with that orderly unrolling of powers which we find in organic growth'.[43] It was, of course, this version of the organic analogy that gave credibility to this whole way of thinking about humanity, and which legitimated the use of phrases like 'natural laws of development', 'the path of growth', and so on.[44] Hobhouse only pursued this analogy for as long as it suited him to do so: the limits

[41] *Mind in Evolution*, pp. 1, 2.

[42] *Mind in Evolution*, pp. 1, 4; 'Ethical Basis', 145.

[43] *Mind in Evolution*, p. 397.

[44] For perceptive analyses of the role of the organic analogy in nineteenth-century thought, see Burrow, *Evolution and Society*; Peel, *Herbert Spencer*, Ch. 7; Mandelbaum, *History*, *Man*, *and Reason*, esp. pp. 57–9; Robert Nisbet, *Social Change and History: Aspects of the Western Theory of Development* (New York, 1969), esp. pp. 137–208.

of its usefulness had now been reached. The problem was that 'an organic growth in the ordinary sense follows a strictly determinate course', but 'if the development of humanity were fixed in this way, there would be no need of intelligence', and one would be back with the assumed passivity of Spencerianism. It was important to conclude, therefore, that 'human development was not fixed in this sense'; intelligence 'can alter the course by which it reaches its goal at its pleasure'. Since, in the development of man, 'there comes a stage when conception [*sic*] of the perfected growth seizes upon him, and makes him intelligently work towards it', human effort, so informed, is essential to Progress. And if it is objected that man's efforts have so far achieved very little in this direction, that is because 'it is only in modern times...that the threads begin to be drawn together to weave the larger purpose'.[45] Once again, as with all such theories, the present has to be endowed with a peculiar significance so that a qualitative leap into the freedom of the future may be assumed.[46]

The second aspect of 'orthogenic evolution' which Hobhouse emphasized, was its moral content. For as he put it with uncharacteristic succinctness, 'Self-consciousness of this kind is not attained by scientific theory alone. It rests on a spiritual truth, and must be applied by a moral force.' The reason for this, he explained, was that a central feature of the self-conscious stage is that Humanity becomes aware of its essential oneness, but 'a race devoid of moral feeling could not appreciate its own unity, which is essentially a moral truth'. Accordingly, 'along with the intellectual development of which we have spoken, must therefore go a certain evolution of ethical conceptions'. ('Must', it should be noted, is imperative because the ideal of a self-conscious humanity, as Hobhouse has construed it, demands such a development; this is, again, the teleological argument.) What 'we should expect to find at the highest stage of development' is 'that comprehensive harmony of conduct' in which nothing is left out 'that is permanently necessary or desirable in the formation of human character'.[47] Indeed,

> if we follow out this doctrine into all that it implies, we are led to think of an ethical system which will be guided by the conception of the human race as a whole, bound together by

[45] *Mind in Evolution*, pp. 399, 402.

[46] As Hobhouse noted in 1906, his particular version of this assumption was shared by Kidd, who also saw purpose 'emerging' and 'self-conscious development as the turning point in Evolution'. *Morals* (1915 edn), p. 595. It seems to have been a widely shared assumption: for example, J. H. Muirhead said in reviewing Kidd's *Principles of Western Civilization*: 'He rightly interprets the significance of the present age as springing from the fact that for the first time in history, this purpose has risen into clear consciousness, and promises to become an operative motive in public and private life.' *Hibbert Journal*, 1 (1902), 154.

[47] *Mind in Evolution*, pp. 337, 352. It is worth noting, by way of illustration of the 'moral consensus' which, I have argued, Hobhouse was able to assume, that he did not feel called upon to answer the question 'Who is to decide what is desirable in the formation of human character?'

> the ties of a common nature, and capable under ascertainable conditions of a future for which all earlier evolution is preparatory.[48]

In this way, universalistic humanitarianism is presented as the moral aspect of the stage of self-conscious development, the goal towards which 'orthogenic evolution' is moving. Thus, it was also part of the 'point' of *Mind in Evolution* to provide the scientific foundations for that 'philosophic theory of evolution' which would 'justify and support the application of humanitarian principles to political affairs'.

A minor aspect of the work which is important in the present context is that in it we see Hobhouse, for the first time, wrestling with the idea of the social sciences as the systematization of Humanity's self-consciousness. Towards the end of the book, he drew one of his many analogies between the human and non-human world. Just as a botanist studies the development of a plant species and seeks to understand the laws whereby it reaches that perfection of form which we recognize in, for example, the rose qua rose: so, argued Hobhouse,

> does the sociologist with the human species: he treats it as something that has evolved and is evolving, and he seeks to discover what further developments it holds in germ. In this way, the study of growth, human evolution, is to the humanitarian spirit, what botany is to the gardener, who would not only bring the flowers that he has to the summit of their perfection, but would seek to derive from them new and more beautiful varieties.[49]

It is clear that Hobhouse is positing an analogy, not an identity here: the suggestion that one member of the human species stands in relation to it as the gardener does to the roses (a different species) destroys any explanatory power the comparison might have had if otherwise used. That is, Hobhouse is not suggesting, as Spencer did, that the laws governing the development of botanical species are identical to and continuous with those operating on the human species. But even as a metaphor it disguises the teleological assumptions which are never far from the surface of Hobhouse's theory. For, in the passage quoted, how does the sociologist/gardener obtain his idea of the 'perfection' of the human species? Without some, necessarily normative, criteria of selection, it could not be obtained by mere empirical inspection of the evidence of human history: a conception of the ideal is needed to convert the study of history into the study of the 'growth' of the potential which 'it holds in germ'. In order to bring individual members of the species to 'the summit of their perfection', the 'humanitarian spirit' must be presumed to have privileged access to this ideal. Only when this is granted does sociology become (to use the term by which Tylor

[48] *Mind in Evolution*, pp. 352–3. He explicitly deals with humanitarianism as the latest stage of the development on pp. 347–55.

[49] *Mind in Evolution*, p. 351.

had characterized anthropology thirty years earlier) 'a reformer's science',[50] providing the reformer with evidence of the line of 'natural' human development, and, thereby, guidance in which branches to prune and which to encourage.

The particular interest of this passage for our present purpose is that it is the first time that Hobhouse refers to this activity as 'sociology'. This, as I suggest in the following section, was very much bound up with the increasing fashionableness of the term at the turn of the century, as well as with the development of Hobhouse's own thinking on the matter. Still, it seems that at last the entrance will take place of the long-awaited hero of the story – Hobhouse the Sociologist. This impression is strengthened when we see that in revising his *Speaker* articles for publication as a book – *Democracy and Reaction* (1904) – he included an entirely new chapter entitled 'Evolution and Sociology'. However, a closer examination of the chapter seems to suggest that what Hobhouse chose to discuss under the title of 'Sociology' implied a very idiosyncratic usage of the term.

In the previous chapter, as in his *Speaker* article, he had already 'traced the reaction on its intellectual side to the biological concept of evolution as its principal source', but nonetheless he was now of the opinion that 'it will be well to discuss it a little more fully, and consider whether a truer theory may not be found to take its place'. His particular anxiety at this point was the way in which such 'biologising' threatened to establish a monopoly over the fashionable enterprise of sociology.

> Volumes are written on sociology which take no account of history, no account of law, nor of ethics, nor of religion, nor of art, nor of social relations in their actual development, and, above all, have no consistent standard of value by which to measure the progress of which they speak. And their utterances are held to be the verdict of 'science' to which the mere student of society must yield.[51]

As he had complained in the previous year, there was in the 'half-formed science' of current sociology, 'too lavish a use of metaphor and strained biological analogy', for 'to take biological generalities and to bring social processes under biological conceptions is to build a cloud building'.[52] This was, he said, citing Comte, a form of materialism, and 'this lapse into materialism is precisely what has befallen the science of society in our own time'.[53] In this chapter he repeated his usual criticisms, but also indicated the intimate connection he had come to see between sociology and Progress.

[50] E. B. Tylor, *Primitive Culture* (2 vols., London, 1871), II, 410.

[51] *Democracy and Reaction*, pp. 96, 98–9. Cf. 'Intellectual Reaction'.

[52] 'Sociology in America', *Speaker*, 11 July 1903. In a review earlier in the year of Lester Ward's *Pure Sociology*, he had emphasized the need to 'liberate the science of society from the grip of the biologists'. *Manchester Guardian*, 28 April 1903.

[53] *Democracy and Reaction*, p. 98. This was precisely the criticism made by Bosanquet (*Philosophical Theory*, pp. 20–1).

'The theory that human progress depends upon the struggle for existence,' he began, 'claims recognition as a scientific truth. But though a theory of the progress of society, we do not find that it is based on the science of society.' Instead, inferences and analogies are drawn from the 'laws of evolution'. He then made a very revealing claim: 'The justification of any breach of ethics by the "laws of evolution" ceases to be valid as soon as it is understood that those "laws" have no essential tendency to make for human progress.'[54] Thus stated, the implication would seem to be that if these 'laws' *did* have 'an essential tendency to make for human progress', then they could be used to 'justify' any such 'breach of ethics' (Progress in such cases being an overriding argument). This would make it all the more important for Hobhouse to argue that the moral behaviour which he valued was actually among the criteria for the application of the term 'Progress' (in which case Progress could not, 'by definition', be used to override these values). Following a brief summary of *Mind in Evolution*, he claimed to have shown that it was 'the guidance of life by rational principles' which constituted 'the essence of orthogenic evolution'. So the 'application of ethical principles to the social structure, to national and international politics' is 'merely the effort to carry [this] one step further'. He lamented that 'it has been the misfortune of our time' that the prevalence of the biological theory of society had obscured this point about 'the essentials of progress'.[55] Sociology should be the corrective of this, but, as he had put it the previous year, what 'general sociology needs as its basis is not, primarily, biology, but above all things history – not the school history of political events, but the broad history of ideas, beliefs, customs and institutions', for only in this way could the facts of Progress be established.[56] Sociology, thus conceived, would then contribute to that 'truer view of evolution' which 'exhibits the attempt to remodel society by a reasoned conception of social justice as precisely the movement required at the present stage of the growth of mind'. Drawing on this argument, he is able later in the book to refer casually to 'the problem of progress, or what is the same thing, of social justice'.[57]

[54] *Democracy and Reaction*, pp. 96, 101.

[55] *Democracy and Reaction*, pp. 116, 117–18. His enumeration of what 'the spirit of progress' was achieving in the modern world indicates concretely the sort of thing Hobhouse had in mind: 'The doctrine that the government should be the servant rather than the lord of the people, which meant that political interests must yield to the common good; that all classes were entitled to equal treatment, which subordinated political privilege to moral justice; that restraints on liberty should be limited by the demonstrable needs of social welfare, which recognized the moral claims of the human personality to make the utmost of its powers', and so on (pp. 117–18).

[56] 'Sociology in America'. Here was another unacknowledged point of contact with Spencer, who had at one point complained of 'the ordinary historian who, thinking of little else but the doings of kings, court-intrigues, international quarrels, victories and defeats...asserts that there is no social science'. *Autobiography* (2 vols., London, 1904), II, p. 253.

[57] *Democracy and Reaction*, pp. 118, 226.

Despite its title, then, this chapter does not in fact deal with something which corresponds to the intellectual enterprise now called sociology. However, before assuming that Hobhouse was again attempting to adorn his political polemics with a purely personal interpretation of an imposing scientific word, we must examine in some detail the contemporary usage of the term. For what such an examination suggests is that far from using the word idiosyncratically, Hobhouse was exemplifying a general fashion. And the fact that the sort of work which he was doing at this time – as part of his long-drawn-out struggle with Social Darwinism – was very generally being described as 'sociology', led him to a crucial involvement with the newly formed 'Sociological movement'.

In England in the second half of the nineteenth century, the term 'sociology' was most frequently used to refer to the ambitious attempt to discover the laws of social development; it was identified with, above all, the grand system of Comte, inventor of the word, and, more importantly, with the work of Herbert Spencer. Occasionally it was used as an alternative to 'social science', though its advocates were prone to insist on a distinction between them on the grounds that the latter term 'has been at once rendered indefinite and vulgarised in common use, and has come to be regarded as denoting a congeries of incoherent details respecting every practical matter bearing directly or remotely on public interests, which happens for the moment to engage attention'.[58] Its advocates, however, were not numerous, though several influential figures were prepared to concede that much was to be hoped for from it in the future; for the present, it was frequently confused with Socialism, and was almost synonymous with exaggerated claims, arrived at in an *a priori* manner, about the direction of social change.

Spencer was the chief culprit here, and was largely responsible for the *odium academicum* visited upon sociology for so long in English universities. Spencer had defined the subject-matter of sociology at its simplest as 'the order among those structural and functional changes which societies pass through',[59] but the relation of this apparently historical enterprise to actual empirical historical research was not obvious, either in Spencer's programmatic statements on the subject or in his practice of it in the ponderous tomes of *The Principles of Sociology*. 'I take but little interest in what are called histories, but am interested only in Sociology, which stands related to these so-called histories much as a vast building stands

[58] J. K. Ingram, 'The Need for Sociology', Presidential Address to Section F of the British Association for the Advancement of Science, 1878, repr. in Abrams, *Origins of British Sociology*, quotation at p. 192.

[59] *The Study of Sociology* (London, 1873), p. 71.

related to the heaps of stones and bricks around it.'[60] The most fruitful approach, Spencer suggested in both precept and example, was for the sociologist to pursue the parallels suggested by the organic analogy, and in this way to discover 'the mutual dependence of many of the functions which taken together make up the social life'.[61] His inveterate habit of finding a justification for Individualism in all his studies made the association of sociology with Socialism less plausible, but hardly improved its scientific standing.

It was clear, however, that if it was to be established as the science of society, then it would have to conform to the standards expected of a science, that is, to be able to subsume the observed details of social phenomena under the operation of a few general laws, and 'to determine approximately their connection as causes and effects'.[62] The sense of social crisis so widely commented upon in the 1880s gave added urgency to the search for such a science. On the one hand, there was the intensification of efforts to obtain reliable contemporary social data, as shown most notably in the work of Booth, Rowntree and the Webbs, but also in the multiplication of government statistics brought about by civil servants like Llewellyn Smith.[63] On the other hand, there was an almost frenetic search for guidance in social action, guidance which, at the most fundamental level, it was felt that only the laws of social development could provide. Hence the appeal of Social Darwinist theorizing, which reached the peak of its popularity in England in the mid and late 1880s.[64] As Henry Drummond remarked, 'To discover the *rationale* of social progress is the ambition of this age', rightly emphasizing that there was 'a yearning desire, not from curious but for practical reasons, to find some light upon the course'.[65]

[60] Spencer, *Autobiography*, II, p. 185. Note also his complaint that 'the ordinary historian' overlooks 'the mutually dependent structures which have been quietly unfolding while the transactions he writes about have been taking place'. *Autobiography*, II, p. 253. Cf. n56 above.

[61] Quoted in Peel, *Herbert Spencer*, p. 176. Although Spencer's exclusive dependence upon the biological model was emphasized by his contemporaries, it is played down by Peel (e.g. pp. 173–4, 178–80), but even he allows that in *The Principles of Sociology* social functions are 'all compared at great length to their organismic analogues' (p. 181).

[62] Taken from G. Shaw Lefevre's definition of a science in his speech to the 1884 conference of the National Association for the Promotion of Social Science (*Transactions*, 27 (1884), 1).

[63] This is now well documented: in addition to the standard studies of Booth and Rowntree, see Anthony Oberschall (ed.), *The Establishment of Empirical Sociology* (New York, 1973); E. P. Hennock, 'Poverty and social theory in England: the experience of the 1880s', *Social History*, I (1976), 67–91. On the development of government statistics see Harris, *Unemployment and Politics* and Davidson, 'Llewellyn Smith'.

[64] This is necessarily an impressionistic judgement on my part, and is obviously open to correction by more thorough research. There is still no equivalent for England of Hofstadter's excellent study: a useful introduction is R. J. Halliday, 'Social Darwinism: a definition', *Victorian Studies*, XIV (1971), 389–405, but, as he at one point seems to acknowledge (402), his definition, which equates Social Darwinism with Eugenics, is too restrictive and idiosyncratic to be useful historically. Gertrude Himmelfarb, by contrast, operates with a definition of the term which is generous to the point of vacuity; 'Varieties of Social Darwinism' in her *Victorian Minds*.

[65] Drummond, *Ascent of Man*, p. 3.

It was as part of the debate over the source and nature of such guidance that 'sociology' became a vogue word. As always in such cases, there was some competition between rival points of view to appropriate the prestige of this newly fashionable term by defining it in terms of one's own preferred approach, and it was, very obviously, used in a variety of ways. The most marked division, frequently reflecting political differences, was between those who wished to equate it with the application of biological theory to society and those who did not. The latter group, however, had to reckon with this equation: they could not ignore it.

Once again, Spencer was the main point of reference.[66] In fact, by the late 1890s he no longer took a very active part in these controversies personally, and other writers were already proffering more 'modern' (which usually meant less Lamarckian and less Individualistic) versions of the biological theory. Kidd helped sustain the popularity of this approach. 'By those sciences which deal with human society', he had written, 'it seems to have been forgotten that in that society we are merely regarding the highest phenomena in the history of life, and that consequently all departments of knowledge which deal with social phenomena have their true foundations in the biological sciences.' He particularly emphasized that the recognition of this truth would have a 'transforming effect...in the department of sociology'.[67]

It is an indication of Kidd's prominence that he was asked to write the article on 'Sociology' for the tenth edition of *The Encyclopaedia Britannica* in 1902.[68] This was the first time there had been a separate article on the subject in the encyclopaedia, itself an example of the increased attention being paid to sociology at the end of the century. Kidd indeed announced in this article that sociology had recently become a science (he had lamented its failure to do so in 1894, but perhaps wished to suggest that the success of his own book had done something to remedy this). It had done so by freeing itself from the old way of regarding society 'simply as a medium for the conscious realisation of human desires along the line of least effort in the associated state', that is, as a branch of Utilitarian political theory.

[66] Cf. Abrams' remark: 'Modern British sociology was built, more than anything else, as a defence against Spencer. It is in this sense that his influence was decisive.' *Origins of British Sociology*, p. 67.

[67] *Social Evolution*, pp. 26ff. Kidd himself suggested some examples of what this transformed science could do: 'The first prominent feature we have everywhere to notice in groups and associations of primitive men is their military character. In whatever part of the world savage man has been met with, he is engaged in continuous warfare.' And again: 'As we watch the growth of the great powers of Antiquity...we find that it is made under the same conditions of stress and conflict ...Ancient Rome was a small city-state which grew to be mistress of the world by a process of Natural Selection, its career from the beginning being a record of incessant fighting' (pp. 40, 43).

[68] Commenting upon the backwardness of sociology in England, the American sociologist Albion Small later referred to 'the *sciolistic electicism* represented by Benjamin Kidd, which the editors of the *Encyclopaedia Britannica* mistook for sociology'. *American Journal of Sociology*, 30 (1924–5), 218.

Instead, in the 'sociological' view, 'the development of human society is regarded as the product of a process of stress, in which progress results from Natural Selection along the line, not of least effort in realising human desires, but of the highest social efficiency in the struggle for existence of the materials of which society is composed'. Sociology, or 'the science of social evolution' would have

> to be considered according to this view as the science of the causes and principles subordinating the individual to a process developing by inherent necessity towards social efficiency, and therefore as ultimately overruling all desires and interests in the individual towards the highest social potentiality of the materials of which society is composed.[69]

Sociology was in this way defined as the theoretical basis of Nationalist Social Darwinism, a view not peculiar to Kidd. The same volume contained an essay by Karl Pearson on similar lines, where the biological approach to all social and political subjects was recommended: 'it was a great step' in nineteenth-century thought, he wrote (pre-empting further debate on the subject), when 'the theory of the state became biological'.[70] In the context of the controversy over 'National Efficiency' which surrounded the Boer War, the claims of sociology to reveal the biological foundations of success in the social struggle commanded respectful attention.[71]

There were, however, many who rejected this 'crude biological sociology', as Hobson called it,[72] and who agreed with Drummond that 'the first step in the reconstruction of sociology will be to escape from the shadow of Darwinism'. But the way in which Drummond completed that sentence revealed that Darwin's shadow was long, and not so easily escaped: 'or rather to complement the Darwinian formula of the struggle for life by a second factor which will turn its darkness into light' – that is, not to reject the biological analogy, but to modify one of its terms. In this way, sociology could claim its true position among the sciences, as Drummond pointed out in a passage which reveals something of the all-embracing but vaguely defined role which sociology was expected to fill. 'The vacant place is there awaiting it; and every earnest mind is prepared to welcome it, not only as the coming science, but as the crowning science of all the sciences, the Science, indeed, for which it will one day be seen every other science exists.'[73] Even Hobson, though scathing in his attack on the 'Scientific Defence of Imperialism', implied that sociology should redraw the biological analogy, such was its polemical purchase. He rebuked the 'school

[69] Benjamin Kidd, 'Sociology', *Encyclopaedia Britannica*, XXXII (1902), p. 694.

[70] Karl Pearson, 'The Function of Science in the Modern State', p. vii.

[71] Especially with regard to the sudden anxiety over the physical degeneracy of the race which was provoked by the recruiting commission's report. See Searle, *Quest for National Efficiency*, Chs. 2 and 3; also Samuel Hynes, *The Edwardian Turn of Mind* (Princeton, 1968), pp 61–2.

[72] *Imperialism*, p. 187.

[73] Drummond, *Ascent of Man*, p. 57.

of biological sociologists' for their 'shortsightedness' in the 'exclusive attention they pay to the simpler forms of struggle', but only to insist that sociology should recognize that the 'true test of the efficiency of nations' was to be found in 'the higher forms of fight, and the more complex intellectual and moral weapons which express the higher degree of national differentiation'.[74]

Among those who were favourable to the idea of sociology, the most thoroughgoing rejection of the biological approach came from the Positivists who were much exercised at the turn of the century to maintain the principles of the Founder's science against the 'unreasonable encroachments from biology'.[75] They welcomed the new popularity of the subject, expressing the hope that 'the new interest aroused in sociology...may rescue that science from the usurpation of the biologists',[76] but the English disciples of Comte never really managed to market their Master's product successfully enough to perform this rescue themselves, and in particular they were unable to offer a political dividend in the way that the Social Darwinists could.

That this was what reformers looked for in sociology may be briefly illustrated by the example of Hobson, writing at the end of the century on *The Social Problem*. Much of the book was an attack, from the Ruskinian standpoint that 'there is no wealth but life', upon the failings of political economy when faced by complex social questions. Throughout his life, Hobson argued for the subordination of the narrowly economic to wider social and ethical considerations, and always protested against a 'purely mechanical treatment' of 'a distinctively organic problem'.[77] Capitalizing on the current fashion, Hobson gave a new name to this old attitude.

Every one of the separate questions into which the social problem breaks must be informed by special flows of ordered fact from channels of historic enquiry: but the gathering of these questions back into their unity, which is so necessary in order to understand their organic interaction, and, therefore, to deal safely and profitably with any of them, will transcend the study of 'history', and will belong to a 'sociology', which cannot be deferred on the ground that 'it is so difficult', because no social conduct can be rationally ordered without it.[78]

[74] *Imperialism*, pp. 188–92.

[75] See, for example, the series of articles by J. H. Bridges, *Positivist Review*, III (1895), 45, 110, 124, 143 (the quotation is at 147). Even Bridges, however, could not ignore the polemical purchase of biological language, and in an article of the previous year had justified the Positivist position on international morality by saying, 'Thus, by the law of Natural Selection, advantages and ultimate success are given to those societies that observe the rules of justice; disadvantage and failure are the ultimate fate of those who violate them.' *Positivist Review*, II (1894), 138.

[76] H. Gordon Jones, *Positivist Review*, XIII (1905), 41.

[77] *Social Problem* (1901), p. 59. For the persistence of this theme see Hobson, *Confessions of an Economic Heretic* (1938).

[78] *Social Problem*, p. 284. Note the assumption that to understand the social problem one looks to *history*.

And in a chapter entitled 'The Need of a Sociology', he treated sociology as both a catch-all and a cure-all.

If our hopes of social progress rest more and more upon the capacity of societies for the conscious interpretation of social utility, the education of this consciousness through sociology is of supreme importance. This education must involve a close and accurate intellectual replica of the entire intricacy of the social processes. The science of sociology thus conceived implies the correlation of a great number of groups of specialist students devoted to the investigation of biological or psychical facts, or their relations at some particular point or from some special focus.[79]

This was a theme to which Hobson returned frequently in the next thirty-five years, but he never again tied it so specifically to something called sociology. Partly this was because by then sociology was to be recognized as something rather different from this sort of Ruskinian social economics, and so such claims became less plausible; and partly it was because the fashion passed. But at that particular time it was a persuasive claim that 'the arts of social progress, depending upon the answers to the question "what are the probable net social results over different periods of time of particular changes in social institutions achieved by such and such methods at such and such a pace?" can safely rest on no other basis than this scientific sociology'.[80]

As ever, of course, there were those critics of sociology who, as Hobhouse later recognized, 'deny that it is a science at all'.[81] Leslie Stephen, for example, was emphatic that 'there is no science of sociology properly scientific – merely a heap of vague empirical observations, too flimsy to be useful in strict logical inference'.[82] Equally, it was not difficult to show that sociology had failed to come up to expectations regarding the solution of pressing social problems. So easy was it, that 'this inadequacy of modern sociology to meet the practical problems of our time has become a byword'.[83] However, criticism is often more revealing than advocacy where the accepted understanding of terms is at issue, and it is worth looking at

[79] *Social Problem*, pp. 261–2. On the next page he appeared to qualify his optimism about the power of the discipline: 'Sociology may furnish a true art of social progress: but whether, or how far, a given society will practice that art will depend upon the force which the moral bond of association exercises upon individuals.' But he then went on to suggest that even that was something sociology could deal with: 'Whatever stress may be laid upon moral choice, it is clear that such a science of sociology as is here advocated will have importance in as much as it can educate the social desires of individuals, by enforcing through plain causal revelations the true results of social and unsocial conduct. It can thus release what might be termed the potential forces of sociality in individuals, and economise them for social work.' (p. 263). Its relevance to the New Liberal emphasis upon 'community' is plain here.

[80] *Social Problem*, p. 262.

[81] In his 1907 Inaugural Lecture, repr. in *Sociology and Philosophy*, quotation at p. 3. For the views of the Idealists, the most prominent group of academic critics of sociology, see below, pp. 196–7, and, at much greater length, Collini, 'Sociology and Idealism', 19–47.

[82] Quoted in Kidd, *Social Evolution*, p. 5.

[83] Drummond, *Ascent of Man*, p. 57.

a couple of the more important of these criticisms in some detail. Its two most influential academic critics were probably Henry Sidgwick and Bernard Bosanquet, both, of course, in the very front rank of English philosophers of the time. Although they approached the questions from contrasting philosophical standpoints, they revealed, both in what they attacked and what they took for granted, an interesting area of agreement.

The setting for Sidgwick's first major assault on sociology was his Presidential Address to the Economic Science and Statistics Section of the British Association in 1885, in which he dealt with the (largely) Positivist claim that political economy needed to be studied in the context of 'the social organism as a whole and of the fundamental laws of its development', that is, 'as a duly subordinated branch of the science of sociology'.[84] Sidgwick's central strategy in contesting this claim was to enquire whether 'the sociology which professes this prevision is really an established science'. Taking the 'three most elaborate and ambitious treatises of sociology' in the three major European languages – Comte's *Politique Positive*, Schäffle's *Bau und Leben des Socialen Körpers*, and Spencer's *Sociology* (which presumably referred to the *Principles of Sociology*, possibly in conjunction with the *Study of Sociology*) – he pointed out that 'they exhibit the most complete and conspicuous absence of agreement or continuity in their treatment of the fundamental questions of social evolution'.[85] His objection (at least in this essay) was not to concentration on social evolution as such, for he accepted that sociology would have achieved its self-prescribed goal 'if we could ascertain from the past history of human society the fundamental laws of social evolution as a whole, so that we could accurately forecast the main features of the future state with which our present social world is pregnant'.[86] But this was far from being

84 Henry Sidgwick, 'The Scope and Methods of Economic Science', repr. in his *Miscellaneous Essays and Addresses* (London, 1904), pp. 170–99. Sidgwick took as his text J. K. Ingram's Presidential Address of 1878 (cited above, n58) in which this claim had been advanced. Abrams asserts that 'Sidgwick's argument...became the orthodox basis for resistance to sociology – above all for academic resistance'. *Origins of British Sociology*, p. 82.

85 'Scope and Methods', pp. 192–3. There was nothing eccentric about Sidgwick's selection of these three figures as representative of sociology at the time: three years later, Durkheim made the same selection in his Inaugural Lecture at Bordeaux (Lukes, *Emile Durkheim*, p. 278), while 'at the turn of the century, sociology meant for Weber an inflated approach vainly claiming the status of a master science in pursuit of the empirical and normative laws of social life. At best it meant the three-stage evolutionary scheme of Auguste Comte, the mechanistic similes of Herbert Spencer, or the organicist analogies of Albert Schäffle.' Reinhard Bendix and Guenther Roth, *Scholarship and Partisanship: Essays on Max Weber* (New York, 1970), p. 37.

86 Elsewhere, Sidgwick made clear that he was sceptical of the legitimacy of the aspiration itself; in this he was an exceptional, and exceptionally acute, critic of the historicist assumptions of the age. See his essays 'The Theory of Evolution in its Application to Practice', *Mind* (1876), and 'The Historical Method', *Mind* (1886). His criticisms were repeated in their most general form in a series of lectures on 'Philosophy and Sociology' given at Cambridge in the late 1890s – another sign of the vogue for the subject – and repr. in the posthumously published *Philosophy: Its Scope and Relations* (London, 1902), Lectures VI–XI.

the situation in the three works under consideration. For 'each philosopher has constructed on the basis of personal feeling and experience his ideal future in which our present social deficiencies are to be remedied', and, worse still, 'the process by which history is arranged in steps pointing towards his Utopia bears not the faintest resemblance to a scientific demonstration'. In view of the congruence of each writer's conclusions with his political preferences, his examples were well chosen. 'Guidance, truly, is here enough and to spare: but how is the bewildered statesman to select his guidance when his sociological doctors exhibit this portentous disagreement?' Again, he accepted that this was the role which sociology should play, but only once it had become an established science. It would become such 'when, for positive knowledge, it can offer us something better than a mixture of vague and variously applied physiological analogies, imperfectly verified historical generalisations, and unwarranted political predictions': when, that is, 'it has succeeded in establishing on the basis of a really scientific induction its forecasts of social evolution'.[87]

Before the end of the century, Sidgwick repeated substantially similar criticisms in two further articles, indicating that in his opinion this happy event was still some way off. What disturbed him was the increasing number of moral and political nostrums which were being peddled as the conclusions of the 'science of sociology'. In 1894 he took, as examples of this, two books published in that year – Kidd's *Social Evolution* and Charles Pearson's *National Life and Character*.[88] The crucial question, he suggested, which would have to be answered before any credence could be given to their recommendations, was 'Can we ascertain from past history the fundamental laws of social evolution as a whole?'[89] Kidd, in particular, had assumed that this could be done, and Sidgwick feared that the sales of the book indicated that a very large number of people believed that it was Kidd who had done it.[90] Sidgwick had little difficulty in lampooning what passed for reasoning in Kidd's work, and was particularly severe on the book's pseudo-scientific use of biology and biological concepts. 'In all such

87 'Scope and Methods', pp. 192, 193, 194–5, 198.

88 Not to be confused with Karl Pearson's *National Life from the Standpoint of Science*, published in 1901.

89 'Political Prophecy and Sociology', first published *National Review* (1894), repr. in his *Miscellaneous Essays*, quotation at p. 224.

90 On the success of Kidd's book – and, by implication, on the prevalence of such literature in general – Sidgwick perceptively noted that it exemplified the 'historical and evolutionary method'. 'When this attitude of mind is widely prevalent among educated persons generally, innovators whose social and political ideals are really in their inception quite unhistorical, are naturally led to adopt the historical method as an instrument of persuasion. In order to induce the world to accept any change that they desire, they endeavour to show that the whole course of history has been preparing the way for it...It is astonishing how easy it is plausibly to represent any desired result as the last inevitable outcome of this operation of the laws of social development.' 'Political Prophecy', pp. 218–19.

phrases,' Sidgwick perceived, 'an essentially vague analogy is strained to produce a false semblance of definite knowledge.' His conclusion, therefore, was that 'Mr Kidd has left the science of society where he found it – unconstructed as far as the laws of social development are concerned.'[91]

Writing again in 1899, he made clear that this was still the case, but now concentrated on another aspect of the question, 'The Relation of Ethics to Sociology'. What brought him to write on this was the fact that 'ideas of sociology have more and more tended to penetrate and pervade ethical discussion'. Writing as Britain's most eminent living moral philosopher, he viewed this with some alarm, all the more so in view of the lack of agreement about sociology. 'There is, as far as I know, no chair of sociology in any English university; it is not formally included in any academic curriculum; there is no elementary manual of English manufacture by which a student may learn to pass an examination in sociology with the least possible trouble.'[92] Sidgwick's characteristically academic concern was that in this situation sociology, like any new intellectual fashion, provided a cloak for all manner of opportunist charlatanism. But even if one assumed a more developed science, how could this affect ethics? Sidgwick allowed that there could be a sociology of ethics, for 'community of thought and sentiment – a common stock of ideas and convictions about the universe, its ground and end and human destiny' was 'the most essential social relation which binds human beings together on this plane of their life', and could, therefore, be legitimately studied by the science of society.[93] What worried Sidgwick was the increasing tendency to reverse this relation and to claim that sociology could yield moral conclusions. He agreed that for all but the most extreme ethical intuitionist, sociological findings could narrow the area of ethical disagreement, but he was adamant that sociology *per se* could not provide moral injunctions; normative conclusions could not be derived from factual assertions.[94] But what, he asked – going, as ever, straight to the heart of the matter – if the sociologist can demonstrate the 'natural' line of development for man? Surely 'it may be said, the moralist must adopt this sociological end as his ultimate ethical end, since otherwise he would be setting up an ideal opposed to the

[91] 'Political Prophecy', p. 233.

[92] 'The Relation of Ethics to Sociology', *International Journal of Ethics*, x (1899), repr. in *Miscellaneous Essays*, quotations at pp. 249, 250.

[93] Sidgwick's conclusion here reads like a programme note for Hobhouse's *Morals in Evolution*, to be published seven years later: 'Sociology undoubtedly comprehends in its subject-matter the study of morality as a social fact, and this study must include morality as a whole, the principles accepted in any age and country no less than the accepted and current applications of the principles to particular concrete problems of conduct.' 'Relation of Ethics to Sociology', p. 260.

[94] For his strict separation between 'is' and 'ought' see his contribution to the Symposium on 'Is the Distinction between "Is" and "Ought" Ultimate and Irreducible?', *Proceedings of the Aristotelian Society*, II (1892), 88–107.

irresistible drift of the whole process of life in the world, which would be obviously futile'. Such evolutionary naturalism was widely accepted, but not by Sidgwick:

> The argument that if he declines to accept it, he places himself in opposition to the process of nature, is only forcible if we introduce a theological significance into our notion of nature, attributing to it design and authority: and this introduction of theology carries the sociologist beyond the limits of his special science.[95]

He singled out Spencer for attack on these grounds, and attributed his success to the widespread belief 'that, in spite of appearances to the contrary, the world now in process of evolution is ultimately destined to reveal itself as perfectly free from evil and the best possible world'. The evolutionary optimism represented by Spencer was, he suggested, to be found in 'an even more extreme though vaguer form in a good deal of popular discourse about progress', in which, as he had put it earlier, a state of affairs 'is believed to be good because it is coming, quite as much as it was believed to be coming because it was good'.[96] Although such beliefs were beneath his philosophical contempt, Sidgwick had to admit that they accounted for the current vogue of evolutionary sociology, and he emphasized that when sociology became a fully established science, it would, while retaining social evolution as its central concern, dispense with such illegitimate moralizing.

While Sidgwick at least appeared to be sympathetic to the aims of sociology in principle, the other leading critic, Bernard Bosanquet, seemed, at first sight, opposed to the very idea of such a science. In *Mind* for 1897, and again in Chapter 2 of his *Philosophical Theory of the State* (1899), he presented a critique from the point of view of philosophical Idealism, in both places emphasizing that such a critique seemed called for in view of the great claims being made at that time in the name of sociology. Again, the picture given of contemporary sociology was of a rigidly positivistic science. Had not the inventor of the term said that 'the sociologist as such was to ask himself...in the language of physical science, what are the laws and causes operative among aggregations of human beings, and what are their predictable effects?' In particular, the 'more special analogy of the living organism' had come to dominate social thought, but this had brought with it a bias towards 'the explanation of the higher, by which I mean the more distinctly human phenomena, by the lower, or those more readily observed or inferred among savage nations, or in the animal world'.[97] Not

[95] 'Relation of Ethics to Sociology', p. 263. Here, as so often, Sidgwick is restating Mill; see Mill's essay, 'Nature', *Three Essays on Religion* (London, 1874), esp. pp. 64–5.

[96] 'Relation of Ethics to Sociology', pp. 268–9; 'Political Prophecy', p. 218.

[97] Bosanquet, *Philosophical Theory* (4th edn 1923), pp. 17, 19, 20. Chapter 2 of this work, 'Sociological Compared with Philosophical Theory', is a revision and extension of 'The Relation of Sociology to Philosophy', *Mind*, N.S.VI (1897), 1–8.

only, complained Bosanquet, was such reductionism bound to distort the evidence, but it could not possibly provide an adequate principle of explanation. In 1899 he was encouraged by recent developments in sociology (particularly as evidenced in the work of Tarde, Durkheim and Giddings): 'that a science of man must be a science of mind seems no longer disputable' was his conclusion, and thus sociology was increasingly being resolved into a 'psychological science'. Nonetheless, he still insisted that the 'positive bias of sociology is not transcended simply by this resolution'.

Throughout, Bosanquet's was the characteristically Idealist claim that human actions could only be properly understood in the context of the whole of human purposes and ends. 'The only unity that can really afford an explanation, that can correlate this irregular fragment of fact with the whole to which it belongs, is the living mind and will of society in which the phenomenon occurs.' We understand the full significance of an action only by perceiving what the agent of the action has it in him to become. This teleological approach, Bosanquet pointed out, perhaps a little smugly, was that adopted by philosophy (by Idealist philosophy, anyway): 'That is to say, it recognises a difference of level or of degree in the completeness and reality of life, and endeavours to point out when and how, and how far by social aid, the human soul attains the most and best that it has in it to become.' It was a mistake, said Bosanquet, to think that there could be such a thing as a 'social fact' or an 'economic fact' which was not in some way the creation of human action, and hence of mind; regarded in any other way, they remained 'dumb facts'. Bosanquet recognized that there was already the beginnings of a 'sociological movement', and he exhorted would-be practitioners of the new science to take 'at least a teleological attitude, testing social phenomena by the quantity and quality of life which they display'.[98]

In criticizing sociology from their very different philosophical standpoints, Sidgwick and Bosanquet revealed much about the prevailing understanding of the term. First, both recognized, and deplored, that sociology 'may be briefly described as an attempt to make the study of human history scientific by applying to it conceptions derived from biology, with such modifications as their new application requires' (as Sidgwick had defined it in his 1899 essay). Secondly, both agreed that interest in this new study had recently acquired a fresh intensity, and that the blooming of different varieties of this still rather exotic growth was a hopeful sign. The third area of agreement may at first seem to be one of sharp disagreement. For Sidgwick, the inductive discovery of the laws and direction of historical change was the goal towards which he hoped to see sociology progress; for Bosanquet, it was the relating of the phenomena of social life to a conception

[98] *Philosophical Theory*, pp. 40, 49, 43, 48.

of how 'the human soul attains the most and best that it has in it to become'. But a conception of sociology as the endeavour to show that society was developing towards the fulfilment of human potential as a result of the advance of mind could in fact go a long way to satisfying both these aims. Moreover such a conception would also meet the (increasingly expressed) need for an alternative to the reductionist biological sociologies then dominating the field. A certain philosophical eclecticism would be involved in the construction of such a theory, but, as Hobhouse was to discover, this was not necessarily an obstacle to its obtaining wide acceptance. These points are borne out by an examination of the richest source of evidence on this question, the *Papers* of the Sociological Society, which also merit attention as being the setting of Hobhouse's earliest performance in the role of sociologist.[99]

In May 1903, a miscellaneous group of people assembled in London to form a Society for 'the promotion and organization of those studies which are increasingly pursued under the title of Sociology' (a significant and accurate piece of phrasing), and, accordingly, a circular was sent out to 'teachers of Philosophy, History and Economics' in the universities, and to 'a few selected representatives of relevant scientific groups and practical interests, and to a few foreign sociologists'.[100] This list of recipients itself embodied certain assumptions which were soon to become explicit – namely, that teachers of a variety of disciplines were or ought to be interested in sociology, that there were foreign sociologists but no indigenous examples, at least by that name, and that the aims of sociology embraced those of certain 'practical interests'. Over fifty people responded to this circular, bringing with them a diversity of conceptions of sociology to match their diversity of backgrounds.[101] However, some further points of

99 An understanding of these debates is necessary to a proper interpretation of Hobhouse's programmatic statements about sociology, in a way which is similar to the relationship between the *Verein für Sozialpolitik* and some of Weber's famous methodological pronouncements. The contrast between Hobhouse's and Weber's statements on such matters as the '*wertfrei*' nature of sociology is, of course, very striking: the explanation of the differences is complex, but one crucial element would be the fact that, as contemporaries noted, 'the biological school has obtained little hold in Germany'. Anonymous review of C. Bouglé, *Les Sciences Sociales en Allemagne* in *Mind*, N.S. VI (1897), 426.

100 *Sociological Papers*, I (1905), in which is included the introductory pamphlet 'The Sociological Society' (quotation at pp. 11–12). The names of those who had taken this decision indicate the background of the Society: V. Branford, J. Bryce, M.P., Dr C. M. Douglas, M.P., Dr A. C. Haddon, C. S. Loch, Dr R. D. Roberts, Prof. Sully, E. J. Urwick and J. Martin White. The name of each member of the General (Provisional) Committee was followed by his title or description, which reveals a far greater variety even than the above list. Members ranged from 'the vicar of Ashmansworth, Hants.' to 'the Chairman, Public Libraries Committee, Woolwich', and included one gentleman who filled the two, presumably related, roles of 'President, Society for the Study of Inebriety' and 'Coroner for North-East London'.

101 Abrams remarks, without citing a reference, that in the three volumes of the Society's *Papers*, 'There are sixty-one definitions of the nature and aims of sociology.' *Origins of British Sociology*,

agreement did emerge from their initial discussion. One was their desire to avoid the concentration on practical questions which had absorbed the National Association for the Promotion of Social Science earlier in the century – 'the discussion of interesting specialities...as to the construction of drains and chimney pots' as one of them said, of 'Drink, Drainage, and Divorce' as another put it.[102] Secondly, and in more general terms, they agreed that sociology should be a science, and so should produce 'laws'; and, thirdly, that these laws should yield some guidance on matters of social reform. However, the content which they gave to these formal aspirations tended to be governed by their own pre-existing interests and attitudes. There was a further point on which some of the speakers, mostly the academics, were agreed, which was that sociology was not to be a specialist science alongside, say, anthropology or ethnology, but 'a science coordinating the other sciences which are designated social sciences'.[103] To regard sociology in this way, as some kind of synthesis of the specialist social sciences, was both a reflection of current usage, and an expression of the aspiration that a science might be founded which would reduce to order the by now bewildering array of facts and theories about society and its development. For there was a further assumption upon which they were agreed, but which was so taken for granted that no one felt the need to argue it: and that was that sociology would be an evolutionary science, and that the laws it discovered would be the laws of social development. Whatever other disagreements emerged at the meeting, it was uncontentious to assume that sociology ought to be the science of Progress.[104]

p. 3. The counting had actually been done by C. L. Tupper, *Sociological Review*, I (1908), 210. The aims particularly included support for well-established philanthropic causes. For example, T. C. Horsfall, 'President of Manchester and Salford Association for the Improvement of the Homes and Surroundings of the People', declared that 'Manchester, in common with all other manufacturing towns in Great Britain, is destroying the best qualities of our race, merely [*sic*] from ignorance of the conditions necessary for human welfare. I believe that nothing else could do so much to ensure that those conditions shall be established as the appointment of an able and zealous and well-trained man to a chair of Sociology at the Owens College.' (*Sociological Papers*, I; p. 14 of introductory pamphlet.) Similarly, Canon Barnett, disappointed at the diminishing impact of Toynbee Hall, also welcomed the Society. 'The call of East London is for more accurate knowledge of social conditions. Society...needs the knowledge necessary for scientific treatment by philanthropists and public bodies.' The merit of the Society was that it would make possible that 'understanding of social causes and effects which only patient investigation can give'. Quoted in Pimlott, *Toynbee Hall*, p. 102.

102 *Sociological Papers*, I; introductory pamphlet, pp. 19, 22.

103 *Sociological Papers*, I; introductory pamphlet, p. 21. Or, as the anthropologist A. C. Haddon, said: 'What we now require is a bringing together of the biologists, anthropologists, historians, economists and philosophers, who are interested in the origin, distribution and working of all social institutions.'

104 The statement drawn up on the 'Scope and Aims of the Society', for example, which was certainly intended to represent only those points on which there was general agreement, assumed without qualification that sociology was to study social evolution, for 'the conception of social evolution involves a clearer valuation of the conditions and forces which respectively hinder or help development, which make towards degeneration or progress'. *Sociological Papers*, I; introductory pamphlet, p. 31.

The mood of the meeting was one of cautious enthusiasm and every speaker emphasized the need for differences to be put aside in the pursuit of a greater goal. Benjamin Kidd, however, remarked upon the reservations one might have on that score 'when one looks round the room and sees the representatives of so many warring schools of opinion, often holding ideas and ideals mutually antagonistic, and even mutually destructive'. Kidd made his own contribution to this antagonism in his speech supporting the foundation of the Society. 'The more one studies the development of societies and of civilisations,' he declared,

the more one comes to perceive that it is the social factor which is in the ascendant in the evolution of the race, and that it is as a member of an effective type of society that man is principally made subject to the law of Natural Selection. The study of human progress is consequently mainly the study of the causes and principles contributing to social efficiency in the largest sense. This is equivalent to saying that it must be mainly sociological.[105]

Hobhouse was not the man to let such propaganda for a rival political view pass unchallenged, and he rose to second the motion that a committee be formed. He suggested that the present time was appropriate for an attempt to 'revive' sociology, explaining his use of this word by saying that sociology's first efforts at generalization early in the century had since been subject to much disintegrating criticism, 'and the result had been that the theoretical side of the science had incurred an undue and unjust amount of discredit'. He went on:

People ceased to believe in any scientific theory of society, but the vacuum thus created was only too readily filled. The empty mind, swept clear of all scientific methods, was speedily filled with seven devils of sciolism. The pseudo-scientific treatment of the questions affecting the bases of social ethics was never more popular than at present, and to it was largely due the deterioration of moral form in the discussion of public affairs, which was admitted and deplored by nearly all thinking men. In endeavouring to reconstitute sociology in its true position, the Society would, therefore, be doing something to meet a great practical need.[106]

Once again we see that Hobhouse's anxiety is over the effect of the biological – 'pseudo-scientific' – treatment of social and ethical questions on the general level of public discussion: it is anxiety over a moral and political question. His assumption is that such a pernicious influence will be countered by a properly conceived sociology, that sociology is something which *by its very nature* will constitute a rejection of the biological theory, and will thus meet 'a great practical need'. Such a definition of sociology was both widely accepted, and, at the same time, an accurate description of Hobhouse's own work.

It was certainly consistent with the position taken in a statement drawn

[105] *Sociological Papers*, I; introductory pamphlet, p. 24.
[106] *Sociological Papers*, I; introductory pamphlet, pp. 27–8.

up by the organizing spirit of the Society, Victor Branford (and printed in Volume One of the *Papers* 'at the special request of Hobhouse himself').[107] In an attempt to attract as wide a field of support as possible, Branford had adopted a generously ecumenical approach.[108] Sociology, he wrote, was to provide a synthesis of specialist studies, and as such would have two purposes:

The first of these two purposes is a speculative one – the understanding and interpreting of that unfolding drama of social evolution in which we are all interested as spectators and as participants. The second purpose is practical – the utilisation of our knowledge, gathered and unified from its manifold sources, for the directing, as far as may be, and in part controlling of this evolutionary process. The first task of sociology – as pure science – is thus the deliberate, systematic, and ever-continuing attempt to construct a more and more fully reasoned social theory – a theory of the origin and growth, of the structures and functions, of the ideals and destiny of human society. The second task of sociology – as applied science – is the construction of principles applicable to the ordering of social life in so far as concrete problems can be shown to come within the range of verifiable knowledge.[109]

Such a description could embrace most of the aspirations represented at the Society, though, of course, at a level of generality that left the conflicts between them unmediated.[110] Consider, for example, his claim that it is 'among the supreme problems of the sociologist to work out the conditions of normal evolution under which each type may develop to its highest perfection'; and again, 'to enquire what are the social conditions that make for such individual realisation is the ceaseless quest of applied sociology'.[111] From one point of view, this could look like a merger between evolutionary sociology and the political philosophy of self-realization, and possibly even a takeover bid. However, it could also seem to apply to quite opposite positions, such as the definition of Eugenics given by its patriarch, Francis Galton, in the first article published in the *Papers*:

Eugenics is the science which deals with all influences that improve the inborn qualities of a race; also with those that develop them to their utmost advantage...the aim of Eugenics

[107] According to Branford, 'The sociological work of Leonard Hobhouse', *Sociological Review*, XXI (1929), 273. He claimed that 'to the ideas and proposals in that statement Hobhouse gave his hearty adhesion' (273). The statement was entitled 'On the origin and use of the word sociology; and on the relations of sociological to other studies and to practical problems'.

[108] He claimed that 'each one of the sciences that directly deals with the phenomena of man is gradually organising and orienting itself towards a sociological position', though he had to admit that these were 'numerous influential groups of philosophers, scientists and critics' who denied the existence or even the possibility of such a discipline. *Sociological Papers*, I, 10, 11.

[109] *Sociological Papers*, I, 15–16.

[110] This applied to political as well as to methodological differences, insofar as they can be distinguished here. Thus, 'the principles applicable to the ordering of social life' would look very different when specified by a Socialist and by a C.O.S. worker. Nonetheless, it is always revealing of accepted assumptions to see *which* banalities the rhetoric relies upon.

[111] *Sociological Papers*, I, 24.

is to represent each class or sect by its best specimens; that done, to leave them to work out their own common civilisations in their own way.[112]

This is an important example because the year 1904, and the first discussions of the Society, marked the launching of Eugenics as a national campaign in which, in Galton's own words, it was to be 'introduced into the national conscience like a new religion'.[113] Galton himself, now over eighty, gave several papers to the Society expounding his theory; he also endowed a Research Fellowship in the University of London, from which developed the Eugenics Laboratory, and promoted the Eugenics Education Society with its series of popular lectures. Karl Pearson became his most prominent disciple and propagandized for the immediate political application of the theory.[114]

To Hobhouse, this was the old 'biological heresy' in new dress, and much of his subsequent writing on sociology takes the form of a sustained polemic against Eugenicist social theory.[115] Hobhouse was present at the meeting at which the first of Galton's papers was delivered in May 1904, and immediately perceived its possibly pernicious social consequences. In the discussion there had been, he noted, much scepticism over the preciseness and usefulness of the available scientific data on heredity. He suggested that these data were as yet inadequate as a basis for legislative proposals, whereas 'it is fairly obvious that we can affect the environment of mankind in certain definite ways', for which task, he declared rather optimistically, we can draw upon 'the accumulation of considerable tradition as to the way in which a given act will affect the social environment'. But, characteristically, he was willing to see one point in favour of Eugenics. 'The bare conception of a conscious selection as a way in which educated society would deal with stock is infinitely higher than that of Natural Selection with which biologists have confronted every proposal of sociology.' Any 'intelligent handling' of the question was better than 'submitting to the blind forces of nature', though he repeated that our ignorance of genetics and the absence of 'criteria of conscious selection' meant that such action was not at present a practicable proposition.[116]

This exchange was itself representative of the pattern of the Society's

[112] *Sociological Papers*, I, 45–6.

[113] *Sociological Papers*, I, 50.

[114] See, for example, Galton's *Essays in Eugenics* (published by the Eugenics Education Society, London, 1909), and Karl Pearson's *The Groundwork of Eugenics* (London, 1909). Galton had, of course, been pursuing his researches for several decades; he had published his *Inquiries into Human Faculty and its Development* as early as 1883. The controversy over Weismann's discoveries brought him increased public attention, but he, and Eugenics, only acquired a large following after 1904.

[115] As late as 1924, he was repeating the same criticisms; see Ch. 5 of *Social Development*, esp. pp. 111–15. His most extended criticism is in *Social Evolution*, Ch. 3 of which also appeared as 'The Value and Limitations of Eugenics', *Sociological Review*, IV (1911), 281–302.

[116] *Sociological Papers*, I, 63.

discussions, in which the speaker propounded his own definition of the aims and methods of sociology, and his audience, by way of criticism, briefly exercised their own hobby-horses.[117] In the course of this, certain general points emerged with regard to contemporary expectations of sociology.

To begin with, sociology was widely assumed to be conceptually linked to social reform. J. M. Robertson, historian and Liberal M.P., commenting on a paper on 'Civics' by Patrick Geddes, stressed that the social conditions of cities were a political problem to the solution of which sociology could usefully contribute. 'The question for the sociological student of history is: "How has this inequality of wealth and of service arisen and how is it to be prevented in the future?" That is the problem we have to study if we wish to make sociology a vital interest. A definition of progress is really the first step in sociology.' There is more involved here than simply seeing sociology as useful in social reform: it is assumed that sociology is the theory of Progress, and that social reform, the creation of the conditions of the next step in that Progress, is practical sociology.[118] *The Westminster Gazette*, applauding the Society's efforts to establish sociology in England, wrote: 'Such a study is essential to rescue not only politics but the whole field of social reform, from the dominion of charlatans, sciolists or short-range opportunists'; while the *Daily Chronicle* announced that 'sociology alone' could provide the necessary 'intellectual support' for 'the academic theorist, the fact-grubber, the politician, the moral teacher or clergyman, the social reformer of every sort'.[119] It was hardly surprising that, as Branford noted, there was 'a certain popular confusion of Sociology with Socialism'.[120]

The second question much discussed at the Society was that of the status of sociology among the other social sciences. The most widely held view, as we have already seen, was that sociology should in some way unite and synthesize the specialist social sciences. But how? And what, in practice,

[117] Most speakers only did so on the appropriate occasion: for example, Ebenezer Howard, founder of the Garden Cities Association, went for a brief canter during a discussion of Civics. However, Lady Welby (authoress of *What Is Meaning?*) ignored such niceties, and even when absent sent in written contributions emphasizing that the most urgent task was 'the training of all girls for the resumption of a lost power of race motherhood which shall make for their own happiness and well-being, in using these for the benefit of humanity'. Here was the real task of sociology, 'to prepare the minds of women to take a truer view of their dominant natural impulse towards service and self-sacrifice. They need to realize more clearly the significance of their mission to conceive'. *Sociological Papers*, I, 76, 78. This was an early, and unusual, version of the charge that British sociology is conceptually weak.

[118] *Sociological Papers*, I, 123. Another example of the assumption of this connection was E. W. Bradbrook's commendation of Frederic Harrison as his successor as President of the Society: 'By his eloquent advocacy of every movement tending to social progress, and his untiring labours for the public good, he has acquired a lasting claim on the gratitude of sociologists.' Quoted, *Sociological Review*, II (1909), 190.

[119] In both cases, the issue of 19 April 1904. Quoted, *Sociological Papers*, I, 289–92.

[120] *Sociological Papers*, I, 20.

would this conception entail about the actual subject-matter of the discipline? It was all very well to say, as so many of the speakers did, that sociology should stand to the social sciences as philosophy does to the sciences in general; but, as J. A. Hobson remarked, 'this improved systematisation is not the direct and primary object of the advance in the substance of sociology. In a word, sociology does not *consist* in the methodology of the social sciences.'[121] In what, then, did it consist? By definition, of course, it was held to consist in the scientific treatment of social phenomena. But this was precisely the ground covered by the specialist social sciences. Was sociology, hailed as *scientia scientiarum humanarum*, to be no more than the office-boy for these other disciplines, sweeping up the few scraps of social subject-matter which they neglected? Obviously not, and any self-styled 'science' has to furnish its credentials in the form of scientific laws, the 'discovery of sociological laws' being spoken of by several members as constituting the goal of the discipline.[122] Given the unanimity (sometimes implicit) of the Society on the need for sociology to be an evolutionary science, it was clear in which direction the sociologist would have to look for such laws – to the past, to the evidence of man's evolution so far; in short, to history. 'Sociology,' declared J. M. Robertson, 'is the science of history.' Or, as one of the Society's correspondents put it: 'Sociology...is identical with history scientifically treated. For history is not only political history as the historians generally think. The *science* of history is usually named philosophy of history. Therefore, sociology is the same as philosophy of history, if this is not metaphysically dealt with, but empirically.'[123]

Both these statements, obviously, put the matter in a polemical way, but consider the definition offered in a spirit of cool detachment by another correspondent, J. B. Bury (newly appointed as Regius Professor of History at Cambridge): 'Sociology, I should say, is concerned with two closely related subjects, the evolution of societies, and the relations of interdependence among the various social phenomena, which themselves form the subjects of special sciences.'[124] This was an adequate description of what was actually being attempted under the name of sociology, and the two subjects Bury referred to were 'closely related' because the evidence of these 'relations of interdependence among the various social phenomena' was to be looked for in 'the evolution of societies'. Indeed, it was not a bad description of the way in which the Society's members assumed that they should improve upon the work of sociology's founders, Comte and Spencer, to say that they hoped to deal with the philosophy of history

121 *Sociological Papers*, I, 212. Cf. 199, 200, and a host of speakers in the discussions reported on 204–59.

122 E.g. *Sociological Papers*, I, 212.

123 *Sociological Papers*, I, 214, 217.

124 *Sociological Papers*, I, 224.

'empirically' rather than 'metaphysically'. When they commented, as they so often did, on the great expansion of the specialist social sciences in the previous fifty years, it was invariably the historically oriented disciplines they mentioned – anthropology, archaeology, ethnology, comparative religion, comparative jurisprudence, and so on. The aspiration towards a general sociology was towards that account of social evolution which would combine these narrower studies into a coherent whole.

This ensured that the conflict between the biological theorists and their opponents, the third feature of note, continued undiminished. Thus, for Galton sociology should follow Eugenics, for 'it is now practically certain...that the physical characters of all living beings, whether men, other animals, or plants, are subject approximately to the same hereditary laws'.[125] and so, as one of his followers graphically put it: 'The legislator must...as far as possible conform to the principles of the stock-breeder.'[126] In more general terms, there were always those who, like H. Bernard, asserted that 'the driving back of all social problems to biology for their intelligent appreciation and solution is...the philosophic method'.[127] On the other hand, there were rather more speakers who agreed with J. H. Bridges that though sociology rests on biology, 'it is not to be conceived in biological terms', or, as Hobhouse put it, one should not treat 'the science of society as if it were a department of the science of biology'.[128] The third volume of *Papers* neatly highlighted this clash by printing both a paper by G. Archdall Reid on 'The Biological Foundations of Society', in which the usual Eugenics proposals were put forward as deductions from the laws of life;[129] and a paper by J. Arthur Thomson (himself a distinguished biologist but a disciple of Geddes) in which he attacked 'the fallacy of regarding sociology as no more than a recondite branch of biology', and the consequent fallacy of regarding 'the human societary group [as] no more than a crowd of mammals'.[130] This continued conflict meant that for many, particularly the organizing spirits of the Society like Branford, and its chief financial supporter, J. Martin White – both enthusiastic followers of Geddes – sociology became identified with the

[125] *Sociological Papers*, I, 85.

[126] Quoted, without reference, in Abrams, *Origins of British Sociology*, p. 127.

[127] *Sociological Papers*, III, 39.

[128] *Sociological Papers*, II, 219, 223.

[129] Reid had earlier published a book – *Alcoholism: A Study in Heredity* (London, 1901) – in which he asserted that a tendency to drunkenness was an hereditary disease, only to be cured by the political extermination of such infected stock. See the very hostile review by Hobhouse ('Biology and Temperance Reform', *Speaker*, 16 Nov. 1901), where he again complained that 'the whole theory of natural selection in its extreme form is being applied by many critics of the day loosely and mischievously to public affairs', and rightly observed: 'With a certain school the theory has become a mere fetish, a talisman which to name is to resolve all difficulties.'

[130] *Sociological Papers*, III, 159.

refutation of biological social theory. Hobhouse was again articulating a widespread assumption when he complained that at present 'you have the attempt to deal with the science of society as if it were a department of the science of biology', and immediately continued: 'The object of the Sociological Society is [*sic*] to protest against that method of treatment, by insisting on the historical study of social phenomena.'[131]

Very much related to this was the final significant feature of these discussions – the concentration upon Progress. As Durkheim and Fauconnet put it in their article which the Society reprinted from the *Revue Philosophique* for 1903, 'Progress is *the* social fact, *par excellence*.'[132] Thus, the investigation of Progress, its causes, its manifestations, and the grounds for belief in its continuance, lay at the heart of the sociological enterprise. Indeed, 'what really constitutes the most important part of sociology', according to one speaker, 'is the theory of human progress'.[133] Of course, for the biological sociologists this was no problem at all. As C. W. Saleeby put it: 'The establishment of organic evolution is the establishment of the truth that Progress is possible since Progress has occurred' – one need only examine the laws which have governed man's Progress from the apes to ascertain how he may progress yet further.[134] It was incumbent upon those who rejected this formula to show that their sociology could provide an equally convincing account of Progress. Part of the difficulty of this enterprise was that, having abandoned the biological criterion, it was no easy matter to come up with a substitute. As Geddes observed, 'We are all for Progress, but each defines it in his own way.'[135] From where could the sociologist derive a fresh standard of Progress once he had rejected 'most developed'? In a discussion of 1904, Hobhouse suggested an answer, which both revealed the connection between sociology and some of his own deepest anxieties, and indicated the direction he hoped sociology would take. The discussion was on that well-worn subject 'the relation of ethics to sociology', in the course of which Hobhouse said:

> Ethics ought legitimately to come into sociology at a certain stage. For if we treat sociology as an investigation into human development, the supreme question will be, 'What is the tendency of that development? Is there a lower and a higher in it? Is evolution a process making for the betterment, perfection and happiness of mankind, or a mere grinding out of the mechanical mill of existence of forms of life, one no better than another, the outcome of blind forces, and destitute of any characteristics which can fill us with hope for the future of society?' That question is always before us. It must always be in the back of our minds, if not in the front of our minds. But before we can answer, or even ask this question in a scientific spirit, we must know what we mean by higher and lower; and for this purpose we must have a philosophically thought-out standard of value as a test by which we can

131 *Sociological Papers*, II, 223.
132 *Sociological Papers*, I, 264.
133 *Sociological Papers*, III, 230.
134 *Sociological Papers*, III, 30.
135 *Sociological Papers*, I, 113.

appraise the different stages of evolution. In that sense, then...ethics is necessary to sociology.[136]

This makes it very clear that the sociologist does not simply allow his own moral values to make a post-factum appraisal of his scientific findings: but rather, since the essence of sociology is the investigation of Progress, the ethical evaluation of the phenomena is necessarily an inherent part of the enterprise. Not to 'appraise' the 'different stages of evolution' in this way, suggests Hobhouse, is to hand the question of Progress over to the biological theorists, with all the unacceptable consequences which that implies.

However, Hobhouse emphasized that the ethical judgement was not one arbitrarily superimposed on the whole process of social development. He quoted approvingly the speaker's remark that 'The ethically right must be sociologically possible, must be consistent with the conditions and laws of social development.' It is the second clause here which is most significant.[137] Not only must a moral recommendation be susceptible of fulfilment, it must also in some way fall into line with the whole trend of social evolution. For it is not enough simply to ensure that a hypothetically desirable action or set of actions is within the bounds of possibility as set by the social conditions at the time in question. A further two-way guarantee is sought – that what is good is also likely to be what is coming, as well as (for this is implied in the statement) that what is coming is likely to be good.[138] Spencer's criteria may have been rejected, but the same Spencerian search for certainty about the future is evident here.

Sociology, thus conceived, was committed to a search for the laws of social development. Hobhouse emphasized this when, as Chairman of one of the meetings, he introduced a paper by J. H. Bridges on 'Some Guiding Principles in the Philosophy of History'. Hitherto, he said, the Society had

[136] *Sociological Papers*, II, 188. Cf. the discussion of Hobhouse's later views on this issue below, Ch. 7.

[137] See the slightly different treatment of this point by Burrow, *Evolution and Society*, p. 273, and by Clarke, Introduction to *Democracy and Reaction*, p. xxiii. It is not, I think, that Hobhouse wants the ethically right to be a practical possibility *and* that he wants some grounds of optimism about the future: if the ethically right is sociologically possible that is, by definition, an assurance about Progress, since 'sociologically possible' was taken by Hobhouse, and others, to *mean* 'consistent with the conditions and laws of social development'.

[138] Cf. Branford in an earlier discussion: 'The sociological evolutionist is primarily concerned with origins, but ultimately and supremely with ideals. And, through the formulation of its larger generalisations as ideals, sociology may hope to achieve the necessary return from theory to practice.' *Sociological Papers*, I, 202. In such a passage it is hard to distinguish evolutionary sociology from evolutionary ethics. Also at work here, of course, was the widespread historicist assumption that, as Popper phrased it, 'only such plans as fit in with the main current of history can be effective'. Karl Popper, *The Poverty of Historicism* (London, 1957), p. 49. But many evolutionary theorists aspired to combine this with the optimism so blandly stated by the latest – and last? – of their number: 'We must accept the direction of evolution as good simply because it is good.' C. H. Waddington, *Science and Ethics* (London, 1942), p. 17.

dealt with 'side-issues', but they were now to approach 'the central citadel of sociology. . . the fundamental question of the origin, nature, development, and future of society'. He went on:

What we have to do is to discover the essential life of society, as it flows on in one continual stream through the period of recorded time. Through that period we have a continuous movement of human affairs. It must be possible to investigate that movement, to see whether there is a current in any direction, or in changing directions, so that we may form a probable opinion as to the whence and the whither, as to how it comes about and whither it is flowing.[139]

The assumption that there will be '*one* continual stream' observable in human history, through which '*society*' flows, may at first seem a very peculiar sociological idea; but if we remember that the search is for the path of Progress, this will seem less eccentric. For there cannot be Progresses; the essence of the concept is that it describes the *general* development (singular) observable, and predictable, in human history. The development may not all take place within one society or within one area of human life, nor need it be an unbroken advance: but having surveyed all such advances and regressions in all areas, it was still the overall, cumulative picture that was being referred to by the term 'Progress'. So, given the assumption that there would be discoverable directional 'laws' under such movements, it was natural to concentrate on establishing *the* line of social evolution from which the direction of Progress could be ascertained. If, as Acton said, 'Progress is the religion of those who have none',[140] then sociology was to be the theology of the new religion, at once a scientific theodicy and an inquiry into the grounds of faith.

[139] *Sociological Papers*, II, 221, 223.
[140] Quoted in Himmelfarb, *Victorian Minds*, p. 179.

7: SOCIOLOGY AS A VOCATION

In the last two chapters I have dealt with the development of Hobhouse's evolutionary theory as it grew out of his disputes with Social Darwinism, disputes which were fundamentally moral and political. I have argued that the intellectual enterprise which he thus became engaged in was widely recognized by contemporaries as a case of the newly fashionable 'sociology', and that far from intending to develop a theoretical sociology in the modern sense, Hobhouse had the role of sociologist thrust upon him. In the summer of 1907 he was offered the newly founded Martin White Chair of sociology in the University of London, the first (and for a long time the only) Chair of sociology in Britain. The offer came at a critical stage in his life. At the age of forty-two, he had resigned his short-lived editorship of the *Tribune*, with no obvious career in front of him, a succession of rather unsatisfactory jobs behind him, and a wife and three young children very much with him. He had just suffered one of his periodic nervous breakdowns and was in the pit of one of his more frequent depressions. 'The Martin White Chair was definitely offered me about a month ago,' he wrote moodily in September 1907. 'In the preliminary negotiations I had accepted, but, on finding that the contract was not complete and that my formal acceptance was still required, I hesitated. In the interval all the psychological trouble had deepened, and I hardly felt fit to undertake any responsibility. I shall see a doctor in a week or two, and then decide. This holiday has been a total failure'.[1] With this conspicuous lack of enthusiasm Hobhouse finally accepted, and in September 1907 became Britain's first professor of sociology.

He thereby stepped into a place in text-book histories of sociology and is now generally included in most teams of 'Founding Fathers' of the subject.[2] Accordingly, his 'contribution' has to be identified, and so we are told that he was a 'master of the developmental sociology of non-industrial societies', or else that 'Hobhouse's sociology as a whole is

[1] Hobhouse to Barbara Hammond, 4 Sept. 1907, Hammond Papers.

[2] As early as 1912 Albion Small, the general manager of American sociology, could report that 'Professor Hobhouse is in his own right in the front rank of the sociologists of the world'. From a review of Hobhouse's *Social Evolution and Political Theory* in *American Journal of Sociology*, 17 (1911–12), 547. For a representative selection of 'Founding Fathers' see Raison (ed.), *Founding Fathers*.

concerned with the influence of intellectual developments upon social institutions'.[3] But viewed in this perspective, much of Hobhouse's professedly sociological writing appears odd, irrelevant or simply unintelligible.[4] In this chapter, therefore, I shall try to reappraise the main features of Hobhouse's sociology by analysing it within the terms of the context established in earlier chapters.

I do not intend to provide any detailed summary of the content of Hobhouse's avowedly sociological writing, since it is rather the general nature of his conception of the discipline and its relation to his political theory which is relevant to my argument. Moreover, since I think it can be shown that the main features of his sociology were already established by 1907, even if not explicitly presented as such, further chronological analysis of his work would involve a good deal of repetition. Instead, I propose in this chapter to adopt the following strategy: in the first part I shall look in some detail at *Morals in Evolution*, Hobhouse's major 'sociological' achievement and the work which, it can be argued, provides the basis for all his subsequent accounts of social development. In the second part of the chapter I shall deal analytically with the three questions which any treatment of Hobhouse's sociology must answer: (1) What was his account of the nature and methods of sociology, and how did he distinguish it from related disciplines? (2) What was his view of the relationship between 'descriptive' and 'normative' statements in sociology – why, that is, did he so strongly and persistently insist that sociology must include an ethical evaluation of the phenomena which it studies? (3) Why did he concentrate almost exclusively on questions of social development, and particularly the development of pre-literate societies, and to what extent did he successfully establish criteria by which such development could be measured?

Since this chapter is not arranged chronologically it may be helpful to begin by briefly noting the sequence of Hobhouse's sociological writings during this period. *Morals in Evolution* was published in 1906: it made his reputation in the field and possibly earned him the Martin White Chair in the following year. His Inaugural Lecture and his Inaugural Editorial for the newly founded *Sociological Review* were both written in late 1907, and they provided him with a unique opportunity to pronounce authoritatively on the new discipline.[5] In the following years he was deeply

[3] MacRae, *Ideology and Society*, p. 45; T. B. Bottomore, *Sociology: A Guide to Problems and Literature* (2nd edn 1971 [first published London, 1962]), p. 239.

[4] E.g. Owen, *L. T. Hobhouse, Sociologist*, *passim*.

[5] Abrams thinks that the editorial was 'as near to an agreed manifesto as any group of British sociologists have ever produced'. Abrams, *Origins of British Sociology*, p. 247. It is true that Hobhouse was attempting to justify the *Review* as a forum for a variety of social scientists, but it should be noted that there were some groups to whom the olive branch was deliberately not extended.

involved in journalism and in the political developments inaugurated by the only government of his lifetime from which he expected much.[6] In his lectures at Columbia in the spring of 1911 (published as *Social Evolution and Political Theory*) he renewed his attack on the latest variant of the biological theory of society – Eugenics – and briefly summarized his view of sociology. His theory of social development was sketched in *Development and Purpose* in 1913, and in 1915 appeared *The Material Culture and Social Institutions of the Simpler Peoples*, his most extensive attempt to establish empirically levels of development for pre-literate peoples. It was also about this time that he began his long analytical article on 'Sociology' (published in 1920) which is said to have marked something of a watershed in his thinking about the nature of the subject.[7] Thereafter, between 1918 and 1924, he published the four volumes of his curiously entitled 'Principles of Sociology', at least three of which would now be classed as moral or political philosophy.[8] In the twenties, he also contributed to various encyclopaedias and collective volumes. I shall only deal with these later writings insofar as they throw light on the main themes established in the earlier works, or where their innovations are particularly revealing of the tendency of Hobhouse's sociological thinking. But it is his initial account of social evolution which continues to structure his later theory, and it is with the major expression of that account as set out in *Morals in Evolution* that we must begin.

Later sociologists have seen this book as Hobhouse's 'major work' as a sociologist, and as 'a decisive landmark for British sociology',[9] but a brief analysis of its structure suggests how remote it is from the characteristic concerns of modern sociology. After two introductory chapters, Volume One contains seven chapters describing ethical ideas as they are revealed in customs, institutions and laws from the 'lowest societies' (an ambiguous term to be considered further) to the beginning of the twentieth century – that is to say, not philosophical or moral statements, but the ethical assumptions expressed in the various forms and institutions of social life: in, for example, different judicial procedures or in the position of women in different societies. In Volume Two, he deals with ethical reasoning, that is, the justification given for the various practices he had examined in Volume One, together with the statements of ideals upon the basis of which

[6] In 1908–9 he did write the first version of what was only published in 1921 as *The Rational Good* 'in amplification of a sketch of ethical theory contained in my *Morals in Evolution*'. *The Rational Good: A Study in the Logic of Practice* (London, 1921), p. 8.

[7] According to Branford, the article was 'written, revised and finished by Hobhouse in the early years of the war'. 'Sociological work of Leonard Hobhouse', 276.

[8] *The Metaphysical Theory of the State* (1918); *The Rational Good* (1921); *The Elements of Social Justice* (1922); *Social Development* (1924).

[9] Bottomore, *Sociology*, p. 239; Abrams, *Origins of British Sociology*, p. 130.

these practices were criticized. These included a variety of moral codes, broadly conceived, particularly those of the various religions, as well as the more systematic contributions of philosophy. The first four chapters survey the 'early' stages of mythological and religious moral teaching; Chapter 5 is a brief exposition of Confucian ethics, Chapter 6 a rather longer treatment of the Greeks, and Chapter 7 a much longer survey of modern ethics which concludes with a concise exposition of his own moral philosophy.

To restore the work to a more illuminating interpretative context we need to take seriously Hobhouse's own characterization of it as a contribution to 'a branch of evolutionary science' wherein he would produce 'a morphology of ethics comparable to the physical morphology of animals and plants'.[10] *Morals in Evolution* completes the enquiry begun in *Mind in Evolution*. There he had propounded 'a hypothesis...as to the general trend of mental evolution' and attempted 'to test this hypothesis as far as animal intelligence and the generic distinction between animal and human intelligence are concerned'. He noted that he would deal with 'the higher development of the human mind in society' in a later work, adding that although it was convenient to make this division, 'at the same time, evolution is a single continuous process, the different phases of which are only seen in their true significance when treated as parts of the whole to which they belong'.[11]

Thus, in *Mind in Evolution* he had argued that the growth of intelligence leads to the modification of instinct by means of learnt behaviour. He now goes on to claim that the development of this tendency which is peculiar to human society is that this experience is expressed in terms of 'rules of behaviour', and 'the fact that they arise and are handed on from generation to generation makes social tradition at once the dominating factor in the regulation of human conduct', 'the modelling of each generation by the heavy hand of the past'.[12] It is important to notice how, on the one hand, this is presented as part of a general theory of mental evolution ('orthogenic evolution'), in which there is a continuous development of 'regulation by intelligence' from the lowest animal to the most recent stages of human history; and how, on the other hand, it is at the same time a denial that human Progress is to be seen as taking place in the same way as 'progress by natural selection' in the animal world. To insist that, as he later put it, 'progress is social not racial',[13] was, therefore, to insist that it was a

[10] *Morals*, I, p. v.

[11] *Mind in Evolution*, p. 5. See above, Ch. 6, p. 179–84.

[12] *Morals*, I, pp. 14, 16. He also notes that it is through such 'custom' that the shared meanings necessary to society are transmitted: 'Without such rules we can scarcely conceive society to exist, since it is only through the general conformity to custom that men can understand each other, that each can know how the other will act under given circumstances and without this amount of understanding the reciprocity, which is the vital principle of society, disappears' (p. 12).

[13] *Social Evolution*, p. 39.

mistake to look for Progress in accumulated improvements in human stock, as both Spencerians and Eugenicists did in their different ways. In spelling out this argument, he also revealed the underlying point of the book very clearly:

If...there is ethical progress (and whether there is such is after all our main question), it is to be found not in the development of new instincts or impulses or in the disappearance of instincts that are old and bad, but rather in the rationalization of the moral code which, as society advances, becomes more clearly thought out and more consistently and comprehensively applied. For as mental evolution advances, the spiritual consciousness deepens, and the ethical order is purged of inconsistencies and extended in scope.[14]

Thus, it very soon emerges that the point for Hobhouse of 'a study in comparative ethics' (the book's subtitle) undertaken as part of a more general evolutionary theory was to establish the reality of moral progress.

Both the general approach and the details of the book reflect Hobhouse's obsession with this question. To begin with, the comparative method, as has since frequently been noted, tended to reinforce the prevailing historicist and ethnocentric assumptions which had given rise to it. It depended upon structural classification (in terms of level of 'civilization', or complexity of social structure, or technology or whatever) being taken as a chronological (or at least developmental) classification, existing 'primitive' societies being assumed to provide evidence about earlier stages of existing civilized societies.[15] Hobhouse's morphology was, therefore, also a scheme of development.[16] This is evident, for example, in his initial attempt to correlate types of morality with types of social organization, since he argues that his three types of 'the social bond', though in part ideal-typical constructions, are generally to be found in historical sequence. Given that his three types – kinship, authority and citizenship – are, at least in the latter two cases, forms of *political* classification, and thus are bound to express certain very general moral attitudes, it is hardly surprising that he does find an overall correlation. Moreover, 'citizenship' was such a favourably evaluative term (and was described by Hobhouse in an idealized way) that the progressiveness of the development could hardly be doubted.[17] This was also the case with his arrangement of moral codes in the second

[14] *Morals*, I, p. 34.

[15] On the assumptions underlying this approach, see the studies cited above, Ch. 6, n44. Some of these assumptions have outlived the demise of the comparative method; they seem, for example, to be present in our current category of 'modern' society, in so far as many contemporary societies are deemed not to be 'modern'.

[16] This was oddly reflected in the heading of his first chapter: in the Contents it was listed as 'The Scope and Method of Comparative Ethics', but the title actually printed at the head of the chapter is 'General Characteristics of Ethical Evolution'.

[17] There is a discussion of 'citizenship' during this period in Richter, *Politics of Conscience*, Ch. 11. It is interesting to compare Hobhouse's trilogy with Weber's – traditional, charismatic and bureaucratic – which are explicitly types of *authority*. Note also the different evaluation of modern society expressed in 'citizenship' from that expressed in 'bureaucracy'.

volume, since within this explicitly chronological framework he places his own theory, which is presented as an improved version of 'modern humanitarianism', at the end of the sequence. The nature of his own Neo-Aristotelian moral theory thus informs his view of the sequence and is presented as its natural outcome. For, assuming that 'the moral standard of man is based on the character of man',[18] this kind of theory is prone to see moral advance as a matter of clarifying and extending basic conceptions of human nature. In this way moral progress is assimilated to intellectual progress, with rationalization and universalization as the means of advance. So again, viewed in the context of a theory of mental development, it is not difficult to present moral change as moral progress. As Hobhouse put it in a review of Westermarck's similar volume, 'thus understood, ethical history appears as a necessary phase in the total process of orthogenic evolution'.[19]

In the details of the work, too, the moral standpoint underlying this view of Progress emerges very clearly. Consider for example his exposition of his third type of the 'social bond', citizenship. The essence of this form, he says, is that it reverses the previous relationship between authority and the people, making the former the servant of the latter: government is the pursuit of the common good within the bounds of individual rights.[20] His gloss on this notion is pure T. H. Green, with a dash of Gladstone thrown in: not only does the state provide each man with the conditions for 'the realization of what is in him' insofar as 'by developing certain sides of ourselves, far from injuring or cramping, we stimulate and assist the similar development of others', but also 'this same principle once pushed through annuls, ethically speaking, the distinction between citizen and foreigner' (who is 'morally seized of the same rights and duties'), so 'the fully developed state...must also find itself in definite ethical relation to humanity as a whole'.[21] His observation that this is the form of social union which preponderates 'among peoples of the highest civilization' would be Panglossian were it not in fact a recommendation in the form of a tautology.

Obviously, such a range of material could only be surveyed selectively, but the nature of the selection is revealing. Hobhouse explicitly accepted the long-standing categorization into 'savage' – those peoples who had

[18] *Morals*, I, p. 16.

[19] Review of Edward A. Westermarck's *Origin and Development of the Moral Ideas* (2 vols., London, 1906–8), *Sociological Review*, II (1909), 403.

[20] It is further evidence of my earlier point about Hobhouse and the New Liberals assuming full democracy in Britain that he adds here: 'In the societies which have advanced furthest in this direction, all classes are admitted finally to a share or voice in the government.' *Morals*, I, p. 68.

[21] *Morals*, I, pp. 70–1, 72. Note the normative use of 'fully developed'. The recommendation embodied in it is then spelt out: 'The future of the state is bound up with internationalism...If progress continues, it must consist in the quickening into active life of those germs of internationalism which the best statesmen of the nineteenth century helped to bring into a precarious existence' (p. 76).

little formal social structure or political organization, and who practised only limited cultivation and production; 'barbaric' – the more organized and settled but still essentially pre-literate peoples; and 'civilized'. These latter were arranged in chronological sequence: they were taken to begin with the Babylonian and Egyptian empires, which gave place to Jewish, Greek, Roman and Arab civilizations; the civilizations of China and India were assumed to be more or less coeval with these, though they invariably received much less attention. From that point on civilization was identified with Europe, but even here Hobhouse was systematically selective. The Middle Ages is largely glossed over and Eastern Europe receives very short shrift. The tendency is to concentrate on reform in nineteenth-century England. For example, in the section dealing with 'The Treatment of the Helpless', he begins with the protection such people receive in the extended family of primitive society, goes on to contrast Greek and Christian attitudes to the poor, moves directly from that to the state provision for the destitute in Tudor England, and concentrates on nineteenth-century attempts to go beyond charity 'by organic reform in the economic structure of society'.[22] Evidence which did not illustrate the rise of 'the distinctively ethical viewpoint' was ignored.

In other places, his political and moral opinions are boldly stated. In discussing the development of public justice, for example, he argues that although civilized societies now have a legal system which in essence is founded upon 'the ethical conception', still there was some evidence that 'the power of the purse' meant in practice that ordeal by money had been substituted for ordeal by person.[23] Elsewhere, he expresses his approval of the recently established Hague tribunal as a laudable advance towards 'the actual realization of internationalism'. In this connection he commends Cobdenism for its contribution to international peace, but criticizes it for failing to provide a justification for European intervention to rescue the Armenians from persecution by the Turks; in this respect he found Gladstonianism 'better'.[24] Such judgements occur throughout the book.[25] It was no part of Hobhouse's conception of his task to refrain from them since they were, as he always argued against the Social Darwinists, essential to any assessment of Progress.

It should by now be clear, without labouring the point any further, that the Gestalt of Progress structured Hobhouse's elaborate assembly of empirical evidence. What still needs to be pointed out is that this was more

22 *Morals*, I, p. 363.

23 *Morals*, I, pp. 111, 117. He also criticized even the best of modern legal systems for not being sufficiently 'reformatory'.

24 *Morals*, I, pp. 279, 278.

25 E.g. I, p. 22 on 'barbarous practices'; p. 215 on the 'abuse' of divorce; II, pp. 254–7 eulogizing the achievements of 'humanitarianism', and so on.

than simply an optimistic review of historical development: it was dependent throughout on an implicit teleology. Despite being decked out with the regalia of biological evolutionary theory, Hobhouse's theory of 'orthogenic evolution' was, as I have already suggested, inspired by a conception of the self-realization of rational humanity. As with so many nineteenth-century theorists who spoke of the pattern of history on the analogy of the growth of the individual, Hobhouse's treatment of 'humanity' as an entity with a single history facilitated this intellectual conjuring trick. Thus, magic is believed in at a certain 'stage of psychological development' in the growth of 'Humanity'; his explanation for obedience to moral rules in primitive society is 'the puerile fear' of retribution; the early Hebrew religion is taken as 'the adolescence' of monotheism, from which we move on to its 'full development'; with the Greeks we get the beginning of reasoning about morality and so pass beyond 'the naive imagery of the childish mind'; the 'whole course of history' is one 'wherein mind grows... to an adult vigour', and so on.[26] He is quite explicit about imputing this progressive development to 'Humanity'. 'Humanity is a growing organism,' he writes at one point, and again 'the essence of its growth is that Humanity becomes conscious of itself, that is to say more and more aware of the conditions upon which its happiness and progress depend, and so capable of self-direction'.[27] 'Humanity', however, is not strictly equated with the whole of the human race. He approvingly quotes Bridges' Positivist definition, where Humanity is described as consisting in 'those parts of each man's life... which are social, which have converged to the common good'.[28] This was what Hobhouse unblinkingly identified as 'the "best" in human nature', that 'which contributes to the harmony and onward movement of society'. So the exercise of moral self-direction in the service of the common good could be presented as the phase of 'maturity', the natural outcome of the cycle of growth described in historical terms.[29]

[26] *Morals*, I, pp. 27, 53, 127, 180, 241.

[27] *Morals*, II, p. 234.

[28] Quoted in *Morals*, II, p. 238. It is a passage of which Hobhouse was very fond and quoted often (e.g. *Metaphysical Theory of the State*, p. 115). The full quotation indicates what Hobhouse found appealing in this definition. It is a mistake, says Bridges, to think that 'by Humanity we mean the same thing as the human race. We mean something widely different. Of each man's life, one part has been personal, the other social: one part consists in actions for the common good, the other part in actions of pure self-indulgence, and even of active hostility to the common welfare. Such actions retard the Progress of Humanity, though they cannot arrest it: they disappear, perish and are finally forgotten. There are lives wholly made up of actions such as these. They form no part of Humanity. Humanity consists only of such lives, and only of those parts of each man's life, which are impersonal, which are social, which have converged to the common good.' J. H. Bridges, *Essays and Addresses* (London, 1907), p. 86.

[29] I think one could argue that Parsons' demonstration of how the late-Victorian ideal of 'character' was universalized in Marshall's economics could be extended to Hobhouse's 'sociology' and indeed to a great deal of the 'social science' of the period. See Talcott Parsons, *The Structure of Social Action* (New York, 1937), Ch. 4.

Moreover, success is guaranteed by a further metaphysical assumption. After all, this development might, on the face of things, seem to stand a more than equal chance of being subverted by other tendencies than those which contribute to 'the harmony and onward movement of society'. But Hobhouse's assumption of harmony as the form of substantive rationality forestalls this possibility. 'Evil is not a positive force,' he declares. 'Evil is merely the automatic result of the inorganic.' This assertion provides the grounds for a cosmic optimism:

> Hence the working of that retributive principle in history whereby whatever is evil, being inorganic, conflicts with itself and perishes 'by its inherent badness', while the elements of goodness, of rational harmony, in the long run support and further one another, and this upon the whole at an accelerating rate in proportion as they have already acquired organic union. Here is that internal inherent strength on which the spiritual order depends for its ultimate victory.[30]

This was not an argument which Hobhouse invoked very often (and it does not sit well with his frequent anti-fatalist assertions that 'progress is not something that goes on of itself by an automatic law or an inherent tendency of things').[31] But by thus extending the concept of the rational until it embraced the cosmic order, Hobhouse created a fail-safe device which would ultimately guarantee Progress. Once again, the search for a reassurance of the reality of Progress is revealed as Hobhouse's most fundamental concern.

This cosmic scheme seems to assign no role to human efforts, a question which is notoriously difficult for those who are at once radicals in politics and historicists in theory. It is here that Hobhouse's moral philosophy relies upon his conception of sociology. As an objectivist in morals, he takes the task of ethics to be the finding of 'rational grounds for the moral judgement', and a course of action is 'justified by reason' if 'its aims alone give harmonious and coherent meaning to our practical efforts and our conception of the good'.[32] What meets these requirements, he declares, are the rights and duties which derive from the recognition that 'each man

[30] *Morals*, II, p. 281. Cf. the discussion of Hobhouse's metaphysics below, Ch. 8.

[31] *Morals*, II, p. 280. Cf. *Development and Purpose*, p. xxi: 'I was never one of those who think that the general fact of progress may be readily assumed, or that mankind constantly advances to higher things by an automatic law which can be left to itself.' But, of course, to accept that progress is not 'automatic' or 'constant' is compatible with a belief that it is nonetheless the general and inevitable course of things, and provides an easy way of accommodating the otherwise embarrassing evidence of 'regression'.

[32] *Morals*, II, pp. 215, 217, 219. Hobhouse was familiar with, but a consistent critic of, the non-objectivist moral theories of his day. To the claims of one such theory he replied: 'The rationalist will not wholly admit that the moral judgment merely issues an order and does not state a truth. On the contrary it either asserts or implies that one cause is "right" or "good" or "better" than another, and in so doing it appears to be founded on the real relations of things.' *Morals*, II, p. 217. See also his reviews 'Two Typical English Moralists', *Speaker*, 23 Nov. 1901; and 'Henry Sidgwick on his Contemporaries', *Speaker*, 24 Jan. 1903.

is a member of a spiritual whole to which he owes service' (a doctrine whose Idealist ancestry he was here willing to acknowledge); a course of action, he seems to suggest, can then be read off accordingly. 'If this conclusion is correct,' he announces with triumph, 'the problem of finding the principles of a rational moral order, resolves itself into that of formulating the nature and supreme purposes of the whole to which man belongs.'[33] The difficulties of traditional moral philosophy are thus resolved into questions of metaphysics – or rather, for their immediate solution as Hobhouse envisaged it, into sociology.

For what rational self-understanding is to the individual, sociology, the systematization of society's self-understanding, is to humanity as a whole. What has been lacking in previous ethical systems, Hobhouse argues, is 'a conception of the collective social life of humanity emerging and maturing under conditions which it is the supreme object of practical wisdom to ascertain and understand'. The earliest traces of such an idea are to be found in 'the historical sociology' of such writers as Vico, Montesquieu, and, above all, Comte, who understood that 'Humanity is a growing organism, and the problem of the thinker is to understand the laws of its growth, and to adjust the code of conduct which his disciples are to preach to the needs of the present place.'[34] Once again, *knowledge* is made the guarantee of right conduct, and with Humanity's growth to maturity, such knowledge increases: it is as part of this growth that we get 'the scientific adjustment of the relations of man to man – sociology'. He repeated the statement heard so often in the discussion of the Sociological Society that it was 'a science in its infancy'. For that very reason, he suggested, it held out great hope for the future:

> the mere attempt to deal with public questions in the spirit of science implies an advance ethical as well as intellectual. At any rate, it is on the possibility of controlling social forces by the aid of social science as perfectly as natural forces are controlled at present by the aid of physical science, that the permanent progress of humanity must depend.[35]

Moreover, sociology is not only expected to provide the basis for action in this way, but also to answer the question of 'whether there is any broad and general tendency in historical evolution giving meaning and value to the long tragedy of human development'.[36] As it appears in this work,

[33] *Morals*, II, pp. 222–3.

[34] *Morals*, II, p. 234.

[35] *Morals*, II, pp. 280–1. Even in the course of this rhetorical flourish, he cannot resist the old refrain: 'The struggle for existence is not as such a force that makes for betterment...There is nothing in the scheme of organic evolution to determine that the higher type should prevail', and so on.

[36] *Morals*, II, p. 160. This passage continued: 'Has the actual course of human evolution on the whole been from lower to higher, and if so, is this movement based on something permanent in the nature of things or in the forces which move the human mind? On the answer to this question, in which as it were all the results of science, or morals, of statesmanship, are summed up and weighed in the balance, our whole attitude to life, to social affairs, I would add to ethics and to religion, must very largely depend. It is on the impartial investigation of the facts of mental and moral life that

sociology is, to borrow William James' description of Pragmatism, very much 'a new name for old ways of thinking'.

The ultimate value of sociology for Hobhouse always lay in its role as a theodicy, in its potential capacity for reconciling the ways of evolution to man, and this is the framework for all his later sociological writing. However, he was never content with his formulations, and constantly revised his statement of the theory. Moreover, and more importantly as far as his account of the nature of sociology was concerned, his own institutional position and the more general trend towards professionalization, both in Britain and to a much greater extent in Europe and America, exerted pressure on him to refine his definitions and demarcations of the discipline. In so doing, he laid down the lines which theoretical sociology was to follow in Britain for several decades.[37] At the same time, he thereby incorporated his own long-standing concerns about Progress into the professional task of the new discipline.

At first, Hobhouse did not greatly concern himself with defining sociology; he was content to utilize the term for his own polemical purposes and to follow the fashion in applying it to inquiries into 'the fundamental questions of the origins, nature, development and future of society'.[38] Even in *Morals* he was not greatly exercized by the vagueness of the field thus delimited; he still accepted a basically Comtean conception of sociology as the scientific study of the developmental laws of society which formed the necessary and final intellectual conditions for controlling it.[39] But in both his pronouncements of 1907 he was speaking *ex cathedra*, and so had to address himself to the controversies over the nature of the new discipline. In his Inaugural, he represented it as the synthesis of the special social sciences (which all were agreed had flourished in the late nineteenth century): 'All these enquiries are contributory to sociology, but none of them exhausts a science which has the whole social life of man as its sphere.' The form of the synthesis was not to be some set of general analytical categories which would provide a coherent conceptual framework for these 'special studies', but a very concrete 'conception of a general social evolution'.[40] In his Editorial, which was an elaborate exercise in extending

the answer must ultimately rest, and this consideration gives to the most tedious and minute investigation in these fields an inestimable value in the sight of those who determine their attitude to these great issues not by guess-work but by science.'

37 In Donald MacRae's opinion, Hobhouse 'clarified once and for all the vocabulary of sociology in Britain'; 'it was Hobhouse who made sociology at L.S.E. and therefore in Britain'. 'Leonard Trelawny Hobhouse 1864–1929', *L.S.E. The Magazine of the London School of Economics*, 43 (1972), 10.

38 Quoted in *Sociological Papers*, II, 221. Cf. above, Ch. 6, text at n139.

39 E.g. *Morals*, II, pp. 279–80.

40 *The Roots of Modern Sociology*, repr. in *Sociology and Philosophy*, pp. 3, 18.

the olive branch to the heterogeneous collection of members who had conflicted at the Sociological Society, there was an added advantage to pressing the claims of general sociology as the synthesis of the special social sciences, and he announced that the *Review* would 'seek to touch each specialism at the point where it comes in contact with General Sociology'. But the nature of this 'General Sociology' is elusive and to say that 'to the sociologist "nothing that is human is foreign"' is hardly to delimit a field of study.[41] For Hobhouse, however, the task of sociology was already clear: 'The main problem of Sociology at the present day is to build up the great Comparative Science which alone can put the theory of social evolution on a firm basis.' And the point of such studies is clearly spelt out: 'All contribute to the general enquiry into the nature, conditions and possibilities of human progress and to understand their contributions is the work of sociology.'[42]

Any conception of sociology, I would argue, must wrestle with the intractable problem of distinguishing its field from that of history, particularly one like Hobhouse's which describes its field in concrete historical terms. At various times Hobhouse faced himself with the question: 'In what respect a descriptive formula of social evolution would differ from a comprehensive social history',[43] and the essence of his reply was that sociology dealt with historical material but not in a historical way. That is, he repeated that 'we want to determine the orbit, if orbit there be, of human social evolution. This I take to be the prime object of sociology', but such a task 'carries us outside the conception of history as a narrative' and so 'the method by which it is to be approached is a social morphology...a systematic arrangement of social types'.[44] This approach certainly enabled Hobhouse in his institutional role as leader of an emerging academic community to provide an organizing conception of the discipline,[45] and of course it was one which was to have an enduring influence on British sociology. Morris Ginsberg ensured that it remained

[41] His example did not help: 'Thus, Economics is logically a branch of Sociology and every economic truth is a sociological truth. But there are economic investigations which would be best suited to the *Economic Journal*, and others – such as touch most nearly the general life of the people – that would find an appropriate place in the *Sociological Review*.' Editorial, repr. in Abrams, *Origins of British Sociology*, quotation at p. 258. The phrase in parentheses fails to provide any viable criterion for distinguishing the separate fields, and Hobhouse was never to develop the kind of sociological critique of economics which the first sentence promises.

[42] Editorial, p. 259.

[43] *Social Evolution*, p. 108.

[44] *Social Evolution*, pp. 118, 108. Here, as so often, Hobhouse is paying tribute to biology's status as the paradigmatic successful science of the century. In adopting this method, he argues, 'we are merely following precedent. It would seem that the foundation of any sound evolutionary theory is always a morphology', and he then spends four pages showing how this was the basis of Darwin's achievement.

[45] His main course of lectures at the L.S.E. was on 'Social Evolution', in which he emphasized 'social morphology as the basis of social evolution'. *L.S.E. Calendar*, 1908–9, entry under 'Sociology'.

the dominant approach until at least the 1940s.[46] But it can be seen as in fact a fundamentally *ahistorical* approach in which the historicity of phenomena is subordinated to criteria of selection and arrangement deriving from a structural morphology.[47] Moreover, in Hobhouse's 'studies in correlation' there is no explanatory theory of historical change, and their potential for generating sociologically fruitful studies of social change is thereby limited.[48]

The difficulty of formulating a distinctive and programmatic account of sociology was obviously one which continued to worry Hobhouse. Victor Branford recalled how just before the war Hobhouse 'had been wont to speak despondently about his own lectures on sociology, complaining of his failure to get the field of studies and research clear. And he went so far on one occasion as to indicate some thought of resigning the chair.' What, according to Branford restored Hobhouse's confidence was the composition of the long article on 'Sociology' for *Hastings' Encyclopaedia of Religion and Ethics* in the early years of the war.[49] In fact, this article does not suggest that Hobhouse radically revised his conception of the subject, but he did attempt to define its field more analytically (possibly in response to the attempts of an increasing number of authors of sociology text-books to do the same).[50]

[46] One of the best-known examples of Ginsberg's many programmatic statements upon these lines was 'The Problems and Methods of Sociology' in F. Bartlett, M. Ginsberg, E. J. Lindgren and R. H. Thouless (eds.), *The Study of Society* (London, 1939; 6th imp. 1961).

[47] Criticisms along these lines have of course long been made of the comparative method and social evolutionism generally. For a summary of such criticisms see Kenneth Bock, *The Acceptance of Histories: Towards a Perspective in Social Science* (New York, 1957), and Mandelbaum, *History, Man, and Reason*, Chs. 5–7.

[48] An example of an explicit attempt to apply Hobhouse's scheme which, I would argue, reinforces my point, is T. Brennan, E. W. Cooney, and H. Pollins, *Social Change in South West Wales* (London, 1954).

[49] Branford, 'Sociological work of Leonard Hobhouse', 276. It seems to me very likely that Branford, who was not close to Hobhouse, misjudged the importance of these remarks, since Hobhouse was always prone to sound despondent about all his activities when in one of his frequent gloomy moods. Since, as I suggest, the article itself also does not mark such a change of thinking as Branford claims, it would seem that those, like Abrams, who have accepted Branford's testimony, have greatly exaggerated the extent to which this marked a 'turning-point' in Hobhouse's sociological thinking (*Origins of British Sociology*, p. 133).

[50] Hobhouse lists a selection of such works in the Bibliography to the article. I would speculate that R. M. MacIver was the most important influence on Hobhouse's thinking about sociology during this period. There is some circumstantial evidence in support of this – for example, MacIver during this period was external examiner at the L.S.E. and recorded talking frequently about sociology with his acquaintances there (R. M. MacIver, *As a Tale that is Told* (Chicago, 1968), p. 65). Hobhouse may well have read his *Community: A Sociological Study* in the long period between its completion (mid 1914) and its publication (1917); he acknowledged his obligation to it, and although he did not adopt MacIver's slightly eccentric terminology, he seems to follow MacIver's analysis in several ways – for example, see MacIver on the distinction between 'society', 'community' and 'association', and his pronouncement that 'in the wider sense sociology includes the special social sciences. In the narrower sense, as a distinctive study it investigates all those social relations which are too broad or deep or complex to fall within the scope of any one of the specific social sciences.' *Community*, p. 50.

He begins by announcing that 'sociology is the study of human society, which means in its most general sense the tissue of relations into which human beings enter with one another'.[51] He recognizes that this does not exactly narrow the field, but then introduces the distinction between 'society' – as, apparently, a relational term signifying human interaction and its consequences – and '*a* society' as a particular, limited structure of such relationships. He goes on to say, rather oddly in the light of his repeated assertions to the contrary elsewhere, that 'the formation of societies – their growth, structure and decay, their inner history and their mutual relations – constitutes the principal part of the study of society but not the whole'. He does not make clear what such a description omits, beyond saying that all forms of social relationship need to be studied, not just that selection of them which are held to constitute the structure of a society. The rather peculiar premise needed to make sense of this point, a premise which he seems to endorse on the next page, is that *a* society is constituted by a set of *organized* social relationships. Thus he concludes: 'Ideally the complete subject of sociology is the entire field of these social relationships organized or unorganized'. But the use of 'ideally' signals the fact that Hobhouse recognizes unresolved difficulties in this prescription. Above all, the fact that these social relationships constitute a 'seamless web' means that there is no immediately obvious way of distinguishing the field of any special social science, and so he still has his old problem that 'the existing sum of sociological knowledge includes all the scientific studies of all these departments of society. The ideal sociology which has yet to be created would be the synthesis correlating and correcting their results.'[52] (Not surprisingly, it always remained his view that this ideal sociology had 'yet to be created'.) In fact, his introduction of an analytical dimension into his conception of sociology did not enable him to specify its field any more rigorously or to formulate any more feasible programme for research. 'In the meantime' he fell back on 'the immediate task of the sociologist': 'to discuss and expose the central conceptions from which a synthesis may proceed, to analyze the general character of society, examine the action of social development and distinguish the permanent factors on which society rests and from which social changes proceed'. On this view, 'the investigation of the nature and determining conditions of social development' remained the *raison d'être* of the enterprise.[53]

Furthermore, his reference to a distinction between 'permanent factors'

[51] 'Sociology', *Hastings' Encyclopaedia of Religion and Ethics*, XI (New York, 1920); repr. in *Sociology and Philosophy*, quotation at p. 23.

[52] 'Sociology', pp. 24, 25, 27. As usual, in inveighing against those approaches which exaggerate one aspect of the social whole, he takes the opportunity to snipe at *politically* objectionable targets, such as political economy, Marxism, and 'theories of race and of the struggle for existence' (pp. 25–7).

[53] 'Sociology', p. 27.

and those which, presumably, are merely transient suggests that his understanding of 'the general character of society' will encourage a particular, ahistorical, account of social development. In fact, it depends upon a psychological essentialism which, when combined with Hobhouse's optimistic metaphysic, reinforces the teleological tendencies of his theory. For he seems to regard only harmonious activities as genuinely 'permanent factors', remarking at one point that 'a certain ultimate community of aims and character underlies those relations between men which are continuously active and permanent'.[54] Although less harmonious activities are included in sociology's subject-matter, they surely become inessential as far as the main features and direction of social change are concerned. From the outset, the assumptions which Hobhouse brings to his sociology predispose him to find the criteria of development in those aspects of social life which bespeak increasing harmony and cooperation.[55]

In his later writings Hobhouse does not add very much to this account of the nature of sociology. In his much used text-book *Social Development: Its Nature and Conditions*[56] he still assigns sociology the immodest role of discovering (or rather confirming) the meaning of life by establishing the facts of Progress.[57] He did make further efforts to distinguish the operation of 'the social factor' which it was sociology's more specific professional task to study, but retained a fairly positivistic distinction between 'mind' and 'society'. That this is the case despite his initial remark that 'the mental systems actually operative in society constitute a distinctively social product' is made clear by his examples. For instance, he offers by way of illustration: 'a man wishes to satisfy his needs, and will put a certain energy into the task. These are psychological characters. In virtue of them he makes goods and sells them at a price. The price is a social product'; or more

[54] 'Sociology', p. 23.

[55] His account of social development is discussed in the last section of this chapter. One can note here his passing use of the organic growth metaphor in this context: 'How far in such order [i.e. a "settled" social order] the development of individuals is subject to restraint, how far it is full, harmonious and free, are questions to which the answer must differ from case to case, and in each case it tells us how far that community is in the full sense a completely developed organism.' 'Sociology', p. 50.

[56] London, 1924. All quotations are from the Unwin University pbk edn, with Foreword by Morris Ginsberg, 1966.

[57] In one notable passage, sociology appears as the antidote even to Macbeth's despair: in 'social evolution as a whole' he declaims: 'Empires rise and fall; creeds and institutions flourish and decay; whole civilizations have their exits and their entrances upon the stage. Is there any unity or significance in the drama as a whole? The one thing certain is that the play is not played out, is so far from being played out that we cannot even say what act we are in at this moment of history, though it would seem to be one of the critical stages of the piece. Furthermore, we are not spectators merely, but actors, and our living interests are deeply engaged. Can we under all these difficulties form any notion of the plot? Are we sure that there is a plot at all, and that our play is not a tale told by an idiot signifying nothing? These as I conceive the subject are the questions which sociology has to resolve.' *Social Development*, p. 31.

briefly: 'rational curiosity again is a personal characteristic; science is a social product'.[58] His conceptual scheme does not enable him to see the 'needs' or the 'curiosity' as themselves 'social products', specified and fostered by the 'cultural system' of the society in which they appear. In fact, even in his 1927 essay on 'Sociology' in the collaborative volume on *The Mind*, in which he gave probably his most Idealist account of sociology, he still retains the (unworkable) distinction in which minds are the subject-matter of psychology and their interaction the subject-matter of sociology. Once again he argues that 'the social fabric...rests on mind, and owes its development to the development of mind', but once again in facing the question of whether therefore 'psychology and sociology should not collapse into one science' he draws the distinction between them in the same positivistic way.[59] Actually, this does not seem to have struck Hobhouse as a particularly problematic issue; for him, the primary task was to establish that human society could not be understood in purely biological terms, and the attempt to meet this need created a sufficient role for sociology.

Indeed, in both works he very quickly goes on from the analysis of 'the social factor', to an exhortation on the theme of 'however much mind-factors may penetrate social life, they will not direct society unless they are in some fashion united in pursuit of a common end'. Warming to his real enthusiasm, he declares that in 'ordinary folk' there is 'a potential basis of response to the demands of the common good, ready to be enlisted in support of those who make plain what its demands are'. Thereafter, the essay becomes yet another orchestration of Hobhouse's enduring themes. There is a brief polemic against the newly christened 'social biology' from Malthus to the Eugenicists; there is a plea for internationalism; there is a summary of 'orthogenic evolution', a sketch of reality as both 'mind' and 'mechanism', and a reiteration that 'rational impulse is that which moves to comprehensive harmonious system'. The essay concludes by proclaiming the significance of this account of evolution: 'It is clear that mind as we know it holds a position of central importance in the entire evolutionary process', and this is 'a result which must affect our whole conception of reality, and, therewith, our ethical and religious beliefs'. Moreover, it also has a very general but unmistakable political significance, for it shows that mind's 'greatest work has been done in cooperation, and that the task immediately before it is to make cooperation more comprehensive and more secure'.[60]

[58] *Social Development*, pp. 210–11.

[59] It does nothing to diminish the somewhat parochial and time-bound impression which his account suggests at this point that his example of a sociological phenomenon is 'so simple but important a fact as that I can get a reasonably good tea of a simple kind for sixpence in the Strand'. 'Sociology' in R. J. S. McDowall (ed.), *The Mind* (London, 1927), p. 301.

[60] 'Sociology' in *The Mind*, pp. 302–16. On his opposition to 'social biology', see below, p. 248.

In thus moving from the definition of sociology through polemics against social biology and on to that set of moral and metaphysical questions which cluster about Progress, the essay neatly recapitulates, in reverse order, the development of Hobhouse's intellectual career.

On the question of the relation between 'facts' and 'values' in his sociology, the second theme to be examined, Hobhouse's position appears extremely odd when viewed from the perspective of the modern debate about the value-neutrality of the social scientist. For he seems to hold neither the view, associated with the orthodox professional doctrine, that moral or political evaluation should play no part in sociological studies, nor the view, associated with the critics of that orthodoxy, that, given the ultimate invalidity of the fact/value distinction, such evaluation is inevitable and should be made explicit.[61] Thus Hobhouse always insists that 'sociological thinking must start with a clear-cut distinction between the facts of social life and the conditions on which society actually rests and the ideal to which society should conform'; but equally he always claims that both are to be included in sociology, that it must 'embrace a social philosophy and a social science', and that the former is not something 'added' to sociology, but is a constitutive part of it.[62] Once again, I think that Hobhouse's views regain their intelligibility when their roots in the debates about Progress are restored to view.

This is most economically done by reconsidering his contribution to a discussion at the Sociological Society in 1904 (cited in Chapter 6 above), for this adumbrated the essentials of his later view. He insisted that

> Ethics ought legitimately to come into sociology at a certain stage. For if we treat sociology as an investigation into human development, the supreme question will be, 'What is the tendency of that development? Is there a higher and lower in it? Is evolution a process making for the betterment, perfection and happiness of mankind, or a mere grinding out of the mechanical mill of existence of forms of life, one no better than another, the outcome of blind forces and destitute of any characteristics which can fill us with hope for the future of society?' That question is always before us. It must always be in the back of our minds, if not in the front of our minds. But before we can answer or even ask this question in a

[61] As a result, most commentators have found it difficult to cope with his views on this point. Owen, for example, characteristically takes refuge in repeating Hobhouse's own words (without acknowledgement), somewhat lessening their intelligibility in the process (Owen, *L. T. Hobhouse*, pp. 72–4). But even Abrams finds his position rather baffling, and complains that Hobhouse's 'own substantive contribution to sociology was limited' by his views on this question (Abrams, *Origins of British Sociology*, pp. 135–6). Parsons attempts to make sense of Hobhouse's view 'that the normative grounding of judgements of value should be part of the task of sociology' by assuming that he believed 'that there is in the last analysis no basic difference between empirical science and philosophy', although in fact Hobhouse's position is based precisely upon the maintenance of this distinction. Talcott Parsons, Review of *Sociology and Philosophy*, *Sociological Enquiry*, 43 (1973), p. 86.

[62] Editorial, p. 251; 'Sociology', p. 29; see also *Social Development*, p. 92.

scientific spirit, we must know what we mean by higher and lower; and for this purpose we must have a philosophically thought-out standard of value, as a test by which we can appraise the different stages of evolution. In that sense, then...ethics is necessary to sociology.[63]

In later works, he continued to insist on this point, though sometimes in more careful language: sociology is the study of Progress and if it is to avoid the fallacies of the Social Darwinist argument it must have a standard of value by which to appraise the development which it establishes. Not to do so would be to provide an incomplete refutation of rival accounts of Progress, and he always emphasizes that Social Darwinism only managed to obtain any purchase because, in the first place, the distinction between evolution and Progress was obscured, but also because, secondly, no coherent conception of the ethical end was deployed to reveal the deficiencies of the Social Darwinist assimilation of social progress to biological growth.[64] In particular, he frequently pointed out that many of the terms involved, such as 'higher' or 'more developed' 'carry a "eulogistic" suggestion' and enable demonstrations of change to masquerade as 'proof that the struggle for existence is the condition of every advance towards better things in the life of society'. The remedy is to develop a sociology which explicitly includes a philosophical analysis of the ethical end: then 'we shall not, for example, speak of one type as "higher" than another merely because it is later. Still less shall we go on to argue that the higher type always takes the place of the lower, and that therefore all is working for the best in this best of all possible evolutionary schemes.'[65]

There were certain variations which Hobhouse played upon this basic theme. One was that when he was attacking the other school of social philosophy which he claimed based unacceptable political conclusions upon a mistaken approach to this question – the Idealists – he was much more prone to insist on the rigid distinction between facts and values in social science. This is true from his earliest polemics in *Democracy and Reaction* to his full-fledged attack in *The Metaphysical Theory of the State* (and beyond).[66] Not only did he argue that the very existence of a social science depended upon contesting the Idealist claim that society could only be understood philosophically, but he also took what he saw as Idealism's confusion of the ideal and the actual to be the converse error to that of the Social Darwinists. That is to say, in his view the Idealists emphasized

[63] *Sociological Papers*, II, 188. See above, Ch. 6, text at n136.

[64] E.g. 'Sociology', pp. 30–1; *Social Development*, pp. 90–4.

[65] 'Sociology and Ethics', *Independent Review*, XII (1907), 324–5. This was his reply to Bertrand Russell's hostile review article on *Morals*, discussed below.

[66] *Democracy and Reaction*, pp. 77–84; *Metaphysical Theory of the State*, esp. Chs. 1 and 5; *Social Development*, pp. 13, 90–4, 179–82; 'Sociology' in *The Mind*, esp. the attack on Bosanquet, pp. 286–92.

the ideal to the point of seeing the actual as the realization of the ideal, whereas the Social Darwinists presented the actual in such a way that it took the place of the ideal. Correspondingly, therefore, the emphasis in his position was different: in criticizing the Idealists he accentuated the difference between facts and values in sociology in order to argue that an analysis of the concept or 'nature' of the state (the ideal) was no substitute for the study of the facts of existing society (the actual); in criticizing the Social Darwinists he combined facts and values in sociology in order to show that what was coming to be (the actual) was not to be mistaken for what ought to be (the ideal). As ever, what is at the root of Hobhouse's hostility to both these theories is his allegation, from the standpoint of political radicalism, that by presenting the actual as ideal they legitimate the status quo and thereby serve the interests of conservatism.[67]

Hobhouse also had two other arguments which he sometimes used in support of his claim about the necessary place of ethics in sociology. One, which he only rarely relies upon explicitly, is that although 'one of the conditions of human association' is not the same thing as 'an element in the ethical ideal', there are, he claims, 'circumstances in which the two come very nearly to the same thing'. For

> if the condition is a vital and unalterable condition of human life, if science proves that the social life cannot subsist without it, and if moral philosophy regards the maintenance of the social life as a necessary part of its ideal, then the scientific truth is at once translatable into a moral command.[68]

The clause about moral philosophy prevents this from being a straightforward example of the long-standing confusions about 'obeying' the 'laws' of nature, but there is a suggestion of a subtler form of circularity in the argument. The problem is revealed when he says 'if right conduct is truly social conduct the results of sociology cannot be indifferent to the moral philosopher'.[69] The suggestion is that 'social life' in the first quotation will be defined in terms of an aggregate of 'truly social conduct' (as we shall see, Hobhouse certainly defines social development in terms of an increase of such conduct); but if that is the case, then a 'vital and unalterable condition' of such life already has a normative element smuggled into it. In effect, the criterion by which Hobhouse identifies some conditions as 'vital and unalterable' (and elsewhere as 'permanent') is precisely the extent to which they contribute to the realization and maintenance of a 'healthy' and 'progressive' (and hence desirable) form of social life.

The second argument, which Hobhouse uses much more frequently and

[67] This was a staple of Hobhouse's lesser political writings, and Hobson frequently assaults these theories for exactly the same reason; see, for example, his essay on 'The Higher Tactics of Conservatism' repr. in *Crisis of Liberalism*, esp. p. 187.

[68] Editorial, 252–3.

[69] Editorial, 252.

explicitly to justify the involvement of ethics in sociology is much more akin to that employed by modern exponents of this view. Its weak form is that since it is 'the web of purpose' which is the 'distinctive feature' of sociology's subject matter, the sociologist will frequently want to ask how far such purposes attain their ends:

> whence our fundamental question about the interaction of distinct purposes and the purposes of separate personalities is how far they tend to frustrate or to further one another, how they conflict or harmonize. But to raise this question is at once to revert to the old ethical problem of the individual and the common good.[70]

And so, he argues, moral analysis of our conception of the common good will have to form part of our sociology. But it is more revealing of Hobhouse's concerns than of the logic of the social sciences to claim that the 'fundamental question' must be about the 'common good'. It is hard to see why 'human purposes' should uniquely demand this unless one already had Hobhouse's fixation on increasing harmony as the form of social development.[71]

The strong form of this argument is that the very language of the sociologist is, in modern terms, 'value-laden', so that he is unavoidably if not always consciously evaluating, from his own moral standpoint, the material which he studies. Hobhouse wavers rather over whether this is *necessarily* the case or is simply very *likely* to be so. Thus, at one point he says that the sociologist '*cannot*...wholly divest himself' of his moral responses in his scientific work, and elsewhere that 'we, as investigators, are naturally and *inevitably* charged with prepossessions and interests similar to those that we dissect'.[72] Normally, however, Hobhouse does not seem to want to make the point this strongly (and he certainly has no theory of, for example, ideology, with which to underpin it), and he is usually content to claim that social science is '*often* found to be indirectly recommending one thing and deprecating another', or that 'the employment of "eulogistic" and "dyslogistic" terms in social affairs is *almost* unavoidable'.[73] The fact is that this last distinction was probably of little importance to Hobhouse. His interest lay in using the abundant evidence that so-called sociologists had covertly recommended where they claimed simply to describe to support his main point that the ethical standard should be explicitly treated as such within the confines of sociology.

In this way Hobhouse hoped that sociology could both attain the respectability of science and at the same time answer 'the question of

[70] Editorial, 253–4; cf. *Social Development*, p. 37.

[71] This is discussed below; here one may simply quote his own conception of 'a fully developed social life as a harmonious realization of human capacity'. *Social Development*, p. 92.

[72] Editorial, 253; 'Sociology and Ethics', 324 (my emphases in both cases).

[73] 'Sociology and Ethics', 324 (my emphases); cf. *Metaphysical Theory of the State*, pp. 12–16.

supreme interest' about Progress. In 1907 he recognized that sociology was standardly reproached with 'confusing questions of value with questions of fact – questions of what ought to be with questions of what has been, is or will be', and in his role of professional leader he was committed to trying to remove this stain upon its public face.[74] But he never accepted the view urged with increasing force in the next twenty years 'by the more rigid exponent of sociology as a science' that 'the facts of science are one thing and the ends of man quite another'.[75] To Hobhouse, this looked like a renunciation of the very *raison d'être* of sociology, and indeed in his later years he tended to complain that as it became more specialized and professionalized it 'produces valuable special studies, but it does not give us a Sociology. It yields no theory of the nature and development of society as a whole, it gives no account of the general trend of civilization, and answers none of the questions about progress or retrogression.'[76] Of course it is only when we recognize that this is what Hobhouse looked to sociology for that we can understand how he could give his last four books the collective title of 'The Principles of Sociology' when three of them are about moral and political philosophy and the fourth treats social development as part of 'that unresting impulse of mind to the fulfilment of its being'.[77] Finally, it may be worth remarking that insofar as the professional orthodoxy on this question derives from Weber, as it largely does, it is based upon a thoroughgoing critique of just the kind of position Hobhouse maintained. For among Weber's chief targets in 'The Meaning of "Ethical neutrality" in Sociology and Economics' were 'our many colleagues who believe that they can analyze social change by means of the concept of "progress"', and at the end of his careful discrimination of senses of the term, he concluded: 'I still regard the use of the term "progress"...as very unfortunate.'[78]

[74] 'Sociology and Ethics', 323. In his first year at the L.S.E. he gave a course on 'Sociology and Ethics', but thereafter seems mostly to have lectured on 'Sociology' separately from 'Social Philosophy'. *L.S.E. Calendar*, 1908–10; 1919–21.

[75] *Social Development*, p. 37.

[76] Introduction to F. Müller-Lyer, *The History of Social Development*, trans. E. C. and H. A. Lake (London, 1920), p. 5.

[77] In fact, it seems to me questionable whether this conception of them as a series was much more than a publisher's device. It was certainly retrospective in that three of the four volumes had appeared before they were ever described as such, and it is clear that Hobhouse never planned them as a series – *The Metaphysical Theory of the State* is very much a *pièce d'occasion*, and *The Rational Good* was first drafted in 1908–9. Even in *Social Development*, where he does mention a 'little series', he only refers to two of the other three. Branford later recollected that Hobhouse in a letter had described the volumes as constituting 'his presentment of the principles of sociology', though even this may have been in part an allusion to the way in which his mature theory provided an alternative to Spencer's famous *Principles of Sociology*. Branford, 'Sociological work of Leonard Hobhouse', p. 277.

[78] Edward A. Shils and Henry A. Finch (eds.), *Max Weber on the Methodology of the Social Sciences* (Glencoe, Ill., 1949), pp. 27, 39.

In turning to the third and final theme of this analysis – Hobhouse's account of the criteria of social development – we reach what has been taken to be his major substantive contribution to the social sciences.[79] As will by now be clear, my interpretation of the general role of this topic in Hobhouse's thought is rather different, and in this section I shall simply try to show how he arrived at his account of social development, and how from the start the way in which his categories were framed ensured that his inquiries would culminate in the demonstration of Progress.

A revealing source here is Hobhouse's exchange with the most scathing critic of the account of ethical development given in *Morals in Evolution* – Bertrand Russell. The basis of Russell's criticism was the claim – which his friend and colleague G. E. Moore was in the process of making into an orthodoxy – that a moral standard, and hence an estimation of Progress, could not be derived from social evolution or the history of morality, but depended upon a judgement grounded independently of them.[80] He recognized that Hobhouse did not attempt this derivation in any simple or explicit way, 'yet one cannot doubt that he regards his anthropological data as merely means to an end, namely to his conclusion as to ethics and politics'. That, Russell presumed, was the rationale of tracing 'the development of moral ideas from the rudest savages to the present day, or perhaps rather farther' (a shrewd reference to Hobhouse's teleology), and

> to call these changes 'evolution' or 'growth' or 'development' is to assume that we know that the changes constitute a progress, i.e. that we know which stages are better and which worse. But if we already know this, it is merely an unnecessary *detour* to deduce it from the course of events.[81]

In his reply, Hobhouse once again explicitly dissociated himself from the crude evolutionary naturalism for which sociology had become a byword.[82] He endorsed much of Russell's reasoning whilst denying that it constituted a criticism of his book. But he still wanted to claim, more

[79] By, e.g., MacRae, *Ideology and Society*, pp. 132–3; or Fletcher, *Making of Sociology*, II, p. 221.

[80] Bertrand Russell, 'The Development of Morals', *Independent Review*, XII (1907), 204–10. He concedes that 'the study of past moral systems' might have a negative usefulness: 'It instils wholesome doubts and promotes a careful examination of our views, and this may suggest grounds *against* many cherished ethical dogmas; but it is quite incapable of giving grounds *for* any opinion as to what is desirable. Such an opinion can only validly come from our own perception of what is good, not from the distilled essence of the views of previous ages' (p. 207).

[81] 'Development of Morals', 209, 204, 210. Cf. Burrow, *Evolution and Society*, p. 273 where this point is made in almost exactly the same way. Russell was only ten years younger than Hobhouse, but on this question the difference between them represents, I would suggest, a fundamental shift away from the moral outlook which Burrow so splendidly describes to a more agnostic position which only became at all common after the First World War.

[82] He acknowledged that in the view of many contemporary critics there are 'certain errors of which all sociologists are guilty. The writer is a sociologist, therefore he is guilty of them', and he protested with his usual irony that 'as a sociologist, it is already proved that I secretly hold that all change is development, all development an advance to better things, and the course of development the test of truth'. 'Sociology and Ethics', 322, 327.

cautiously, that moral philosophy and the history of morals 'are by no means unrelated'. Having outlined several forms of this relation which stopped well short of the deduction of the one from the other (and in the process accepting a rather more limited view of their relation than his book suggested), Hobhouse could not resist, in the final pages, pressing the connection a little further. Conceding that 'the historical development of society involves retrogression and stagnation as well as advance', he continued:

> But as in evolution generally we can trace what has been called the 'orthogenic line', the one movement among many which does carry us forward, so it is in particular with human history. There is an onward movement discernible among the many changes that are valueless or worse, and this we may identify with the growth of mind of which the development of thought is one expression.

Once again, we can see that Hobhouse is not in fact content to see whether history has advanced towards an independently specified standard of the ideal: he always tries to guarantee the right answer by smuggling an element of value into his initial categories. Why else is the 'growth of mind' to be singled out as 'an onward movement'? It is obviously not purely temporal since it is precisely in order to distinguish 'advance' from mere change that he formulated the concept of 'orthogenic evolution' in the first place. So, given that there is an implicit criterion by which movement 'forward' is distinguished, it is strictly tautological to go on to say that 'in this development, though in no other, it becomes broadly justifiable to say that the more advanced stage is also the higher and more true'.[83] By treating the development of morals as a part of the growth of mind, moral progress is underwritten with a cosmic guarantee.

Thus Russell's criticism, though valid as far as it went, did not touch the heart of Hobhouse's enterprise. Hobhouse did not attempt to derive his morality from the process of evolution, since as he showed elsewhere he was always prepared to justify his ethics in more traditional philosophical terms. He is thus not, strictly speaking, to be included in the school of 'evolutionary naturalists' in ethics.[84] His formative and enduring concern was rather to establish beyond the possibility of refutation the reality of human Progress, and to demonstrate that its essential character or mechanism, far from being in conflict with the moral and political values

[83] 'Sociology and Ethics', 330–1.

[84] This has been recognized by the school's historian, who observed that, although Hobhouse attempted 'a natural history of morals', his was 'a Rationalist, not an Empiricist ethic', and so 'though the empirical part of Hobhouse's ethics is similar to the ethics of Evolutionary Naturalism, there are metaphysical elements added by him which distinguish his theory from that which makes evolution the fundamental explanatory principle'. W. F. Quillian, *The Moral Theory of Evolutionary Naturalism* (New Haven, Conn., 1945), pp. 25–6. Of course, it is arguable that most evolutionary naturalists did not *derive* their ethics from evolution, but merely justified them in terms of it.

which he cherished, is actually constituted by their progressive realization. Among the tasks which this ambition imposed upon Hobhouse was that of formulating a coherent account of actual social development which could then be shown to correlate with moral advance. The simple typology of the social bond upon which he had relied in *Morals* did not meet this need since it failed really to establish historical development. Mere history, on the other hand, neither dealt with the anthropological material nor furnished criteria of development. As Hobhouse saw it, the task was one for sociology, and a social morphology was the tool for the job.

He first spelt out this role for sociology, as I indicated very briefly earlier, in his 1911 Columbia lectures. Having argued that the problem was to 'form a closer definition of progress, and then compare it with the actual course of evolution', he devoted a lecture to each half of the problem. In the first, he assumed that 'a life which is completely social – which fully realizes the social capacities of man – is good, and that if we use the phrase social development as a short expression for the accomplishment of such a life, social development is good'. The form of social development is presented as 'a development of individuals in harmony' involving 'a fuller vitality' and 'the realization of mental or spiritual capacity'.[85] It is worth emphasizing that this account of social development forms part of the conception of Progress in this work, since it is later to reappear in somewhat altered form on the other side of the distinction. In these lectures, he then goes on to compare this conception with 'the ascertained facts of social evolution itself'. He accepts that 'we cannot reduce the study of social evolution to a simple narrative', and so argues that 'our method must be not so much historical as comparative. It must consist in a review of the multifarious forms of human achievement, with a view to scientific classification', the goal being the drawing up of 'a social morphology'. However, he did not attempt this here, and contented himself with looking at one (politically very congenial) example – the development of 'the principles necessary to social cooperation and in particular the growth of government and its relation to liberty'.[86] Nonetheless, it was clear that the aim of sociology could only be realized if a social morphology could be produced, and since this implied an account of genesis,[87] the pressing need was for a way of establishing the sequence of social development.

[85] *Social Evolution*, pp. 80, 83, 91. Another of his restatements of the idea of the common good is lurking behind this: he sees this harmonious development as a good 'in which all members of a society can share. It is such that its pursuit by one, far from hindering, positively promotes its pursuit by another.' (p. 92).

[86] *Social Evolution*, pp. 111, 118, 125.

[87] Hobhouse made this explicit: 'We are seeking not merely to classify, but to classify in such a way as to throw light on genesis. That is to say, we want to exhibit institutions in an order in which they might be conceived as growing up. This is what is meant by saying that we want our classification to be a morphology.' *Social Evolution*, pp. 119–20.

This is the context in which to see the book by which Hobhouse has always been best known to anthropologists, *The Material Culture and Social Institutions of the Simpler Peoples*.[88] This was an attempt to establish statistically a correlation between levels of material culture (technology, food production, and so on) and other features of the social life of those societies for which there was no historical record. Hobhouse conceded that no 'absolute order of development' could be established, but argued that, on the basis of a morphology, a general trend could be demonstrated.[89] The reason why 'material culture' was taken as the basis for correlation was, as Ginsberg later acknowledged, 'because it afforded the best indication of the level of intellectual development, and our aim was then to inquire how the mental is related to the social structure'.[90] In this way, the book was a contribution towards the realization of Hobhouse's more general ambition of portraying the course of social development as part of the larger movement of 'orthogenic evolution'. But although the method used provided a rough guide to levels of development where historical evidence was not available, Hobhouse was obviously not willing to make 'material culture' the sole criterion of advance. Moreover, it would be difficult to formulate the results arrived at by this method in such a way as to enable the comparison with the ethical ideal to be made, and the case for Progress depended upon the positive outcome of this comparison. At all events, it would seem that shortly after completing this book, Hobhouse switched his attention again to trying to provide a more analytical set of categories by which to measure social development.

In this way he arrived at his well-known set of criteria of development, first worked out in the encyclopaedia article on 'Sociology', and revised and expanded in *Social Development*. In the former, he laid down that societies could be said to differ on 'three principal points, and it is by such differences that we measure their development', the three points being '(a) the efficiency of their operation, (b) their scale or scope, (c) the basis or principle of their organization'. The first he defined in functionalist terms

[88] L. T. Hobhouse, G. C. Wheeler and Morris Ginsberg, *The Material Culture and Social Institutions of the Simpler Peoples: An Essay in Correlation* (London, 1915; repr., with Introduction by Morris Ginsberg, 1965]). See, for example, the references to it in John J. Honigmann (ed.), *Handbook of Social and Cultural Anthropology* (Chicago, 1973), esp. pp. 356–8. It is the only work of Hobhouse's mentioned in Marvin Harris, *The Rise of Anthropological Theory* (London, 1969), pp. 33, 612, though it is amusing to see that Harris gives it such prominence because of its 'materialism'.

[89] *Material Culture*, pp. 2–5. He repeated that 'what may be called a social morphology of this kind, that is to say, the ascertaining and classification of the actual forms of any institution known to exist, may be regarded as the first step towards the introduction of order into the field of comparative sociology' (p. 3). Hobhouse never satisfactorily achieved this classification, and one of the last pieces he wrote was a fresh survey of the greatly increased literature on primitive societies: 'The Simplest Peoples', first published (in German) in the *Zeitschrift für Völkerpsychologie und Soziologie* (1929), and repr. in *Sociology and Philosophy*, pp. 109–66.

[90] Introduction to *Material Culture* (1965 edn), p. ix.

as the success of a community in meeting its needs or goals whatever they may be. The second was seen in terms of size and extent (and revealed Hobhouse's leanings towards internationalism), but also in terms of whether the community 'cover a larger or smaller sphere life or activity'. The third was another covert restatement of the idea of the common good: advance means a growth in spontaneity and freedom, but 'the problem of freedom is not that of dispensing with all guidance and all restraint, but that of finding the lines upon which the manifold social qualities of man can develop in harmony, with the result that the restraints involved are voluntarily accepted and self-imposed'. So his conclusion is expressed in the formula: 'the most developed community would be that which effectively achieves the most complete synthesis of the widest range of human activity, including within its membership the largest number of human beings, but in such wise as to rest most completely upon their free cooperation thus expressing the whole of their vital energies as far as these are capable of working together in harmony'.[91] If the genesis of these criteria in the working out of Hobhouse's long-standing moral and political commitments has been successfully established, further analysis of the ways in which they retained their 'value-laden' character should now be otiose. In *Social Development* he revised them slightly, subdividing the last into two – 'freedom' and 'mutuality' – but in his definitions the echoes of the rhetoric of the New Liberalism are still plainly audible. 'By freedom is meant scope for thought, character and initiative on the part of members of the community, by mutuality service of an end in which each who serves participates.' And in each case, of course, he arrives at the unsurprising conclusion that 'social development thus conceived corresponds in its concrete entirety to the requirements of rational ethics'.[92] In later years, critics of Hobhouse's sociology tended to complain that he 'defines "social development" in a manner that sways uncertainly between the concept of evolution and that of progress'.[93] But in the light of the foregoing analysis of the genesis of this definition, one is tempted to say that Hobhouse would not have considered that he was creating a sociology capable of fulfilling its promise *unless* he had defined social development in this way.

[91] 'Sociology', 50–5.

[92] *Social Development*, pp. 78, 88. Cf. 'Sociology', 56: 'Thus we arrive at the result that in fundamental principle development in social organization, considered in its fullness, coincides with ethical development as conceived by a rationalistic system.' Since he allowed that 'partial developments may diverge from ethical requirements in any degree', the proposition was in effect unfalsifiable.

[93] R. M. MacIver and C. Page, *Society: An Introductory Analysis* (London, 1949), p. 610.

Part Four: Harmony

8: PHILOSOPHY AND THE WILL TO BELIEVE

The foregoing chapters should suggest some doubt as to whether it is now particularly illuminating to label Hobhouse as a 'Liberal' or a 'sociologist' at all, at least without considerable qualification. In order to underwrite his severely moral conception of politics, he constructed an essentially teleological account of Progress as the advance of rationality, and hence, given his Greenian assumptions, as the advance of altruism and cooperation also. The substantive content of this theory has been indicated in the previous chapters. At various points its philosophical foundations have been exposed to view, and although I do not intend to provide any systematic or extensive account of Hobhouse's contribution to philosophy, the final stage of the argument involves demonstrating very briefly how the whole construction was underpinned and informed by a quasi-Idealist metaphysics which is made explicit in his most ambitious philosophical writings, and in particular how 'harmony' and 'Progress' are again revealed as Hobhouse's central organizing concepts.

It must be remembered that Hobhouse was a philosopher by both training and inclination, and though he was only so by profession for the first ten years of his career, he always thought of himself primarily as a philosopher, at least in a broad conception of that role. Philosophy was 'the divine subject', and in reply to Scott's repeated offers of a permanent full-time appointment at the *Manchester Guardian*, he reiterated that 'philosophy has the first claim on me'.[1] After he had left Oxford, it was largely pushed into the background by his many other commitments, but never permanently so, and in the 1920s it was again to absorb most of his

[1] Hobhouse to J. L. Hammond, 26 Nov. 1901, Hammond Papers; Hobhouse to Scott, 4 Feb. 1901, Scott Papers. Hobhouse had earlier told Scott that the continuation of the existing arrangement at the *Guardian* 'depends exclusively on my power of getting on with philosophy' (9 Nov. 1898). It is interesting that at this time when Hobhouse was writing *Mind in Evolution* he should still refer to his work as 'philosophy'.

energies.[2] Moreover, his philosophical views underwent some very important changes during this period. In recent years, historians of political theory and of sociology have tended to describe him as an 'empiricist',[3] but once again I would argue that a more careful examination of the chronological development of his thought suggests that this description, too, is misleading.

It is certainly true that as an undergraduate, Hobhouse was not converted to the prevailing Idealism. This was partly due to the associations of the scientific method with the secular radicalism with which he identified at this date.[4] In part, too, it may have been due to the peculiar bias of the philosophy teaching at Corpus, where Thomas Case expounded his own brand of 'Physical Realism'.[5] At all events, having embarked on the empirical study of mental evolution in a philosophical climate far from sympathetic to empiricism, 'it was necessary to justify the empirical method', Hobhouse later recalled, 'to examine the foundations of knowledge', and he worked on this 'for several years...before beginning the systematic study of evolution'.[6] He published his first articles on induction, unfashionably defending Mill, in *Mind* in 1890–1.[7] His allegiance to Mill was always a good example of the mingling of philosophical and political elements in his loyalties: he later complained, for example, that since Mill's death there had been a return 'to earlier ways of thinking which are at bottom incompatible with Progress and are naturally associated with a theological and political reaction', and this always remained a source of his antagonism to Idealism.[8]

One of the ways in which Idealism had contributed to this reaction was

[2] See blow, pp. 249–50. The Chairs which he was repeatedly offered in America, including at Harvard and Yale, were almost always in philosophy; in 1929 he was invited to deliver the William James lectures. Hobson and Ginsberg, *L. T. Hobhouse*, pp. 59–60.

[3] E.g. Weiler, 'New Liberalism of L. T. Hobhouse', 143: 'In the strict sense, Hobhouse was philosophically an empiricist not an Idealist'; or Fletcher, *Making of Sociology*, II, p. 123: 'Throughout his work, Hobhouse was emphatically an *empiricist*...Hobhouse's sociology was ...*never* "philosophical" in any cloudy, metaphysical, "normative", non-empirical sense.'

[4] See above, Ch. 5.

[5] The title of his most important book published in 1888. See John Passmore, *A Hundred Years of Philosophy* (pbk edn, Harmondsworth, 1968 [first published London, 1957]), p. 240. For Case's hostility to Idealism, see his letter of 9 Aug. 1889 to another Corpus undergraduate, E. K. Chambers, on Lotze: 'What nonsense his philosophy is!...How long is metaphysics to be topsy-turvydom?'; or the notes of his 1892 lectures on the history of the scientific method (Bodleian Library, Oxford, Mss. Top. Oxon. d. 453–5). I am grateful to the staff of the Bodleian for helping me to find these less than well-known materials.

[6] *Development and Purpose*, p. xxvi.

[7] 'Experimental Certainty', *Mind*, O.S. XV (1890), 251–60; 'The Principle of Induction', *Mind*, O.S. XVI (1891), 80–91; 'Induction and Deduction', *Mind*, O.S. XVI (1891), 507–20.

[8] 'The Early Essays of J. S. Mill', *Manchester Guardian*, 9 Feb. 1897. Compare the terms in which he later praised Mill: 'If he cares about the theory of Universals, it is not, at bottom, as an intellectual problem, but because he saw in a false theory a basis of obscurantism, and a means of resisting the march of knowledge.' 'John Stuart Mill', *Nation*, 14 May 1910.

in its scorn of 'common-sense' knowledge and its disdainful criticism of the foundations of science. 'In such a state of things the sinister interests in the commonwealth of knowledge see their chance. The popular essayist tells us that there is really nothing to speak of that we can know with certainty. One belief is on the whole as untrue as another, and therefore why not keep to that which is recommended to us by authority as best suited to our needs?'[9] Hobhouse had no wish to defend empiricism as an epistemological theory, but he insisted strongly that 'the philosophy of the future must make its account with science'.[10] Thus he argued that the so-called 'English school' 'from Bacon and Locke to Mill and Spencer', despite its 'many defects and limitations', did at least have 'the merit of dealing, or attempting to deal, in a sympathetic spirit with the problems and methods of the sciences'. At the same time, Hobhouse was not willing to dismiss 'the higher conceptions by which Idealism has held so firmly', and he announced his conviction that 'what is genuinely highest, we have good reason to think, must also be truest, and we cannot permanently acquiesce in a way of thinking which would resolve it into what is lowest'. What was needed, therefore, was 'an unprejudiced attempt to fuse what is true and valuable in the older English tradition with the newer doctrines which have now become naturalized among us. In betaking ourselves to Lotze and Hegel, we need not forget what we have learnt from Mill and Spencer'.[11]

This was the need that Hobhouse tried to meet with his massive enquiry into the foundations of knowledge, published early in 1896 as *The Theory of Knowledge: A Contribution to Some Problems of Logic and Metaphysics*. Although it was intended to be an argument for a modified 'realist' epistemology, the book was widely taken to be an attack on the prevailing Idealism. This was not so far wide of the mark, since it had been the publication in 1893 of Bradley's *Appearance and Reality*, in which all claims to knowledge short of the Absolute are argued to involve self-contradiction, which provided Hobhouse with the necessary foil against which to set off his own views. What these were, he explained succinctly in a letter to Samuel Alexander:

> My position is this. Grant that knowledge is valid, it is no doubt possible that it should not deal with or refer to ultimate reality. But on what ground is this suggested? As I understand on the ground of certain alleged difficulties or contradictions in so interpreting knowledge. Such [word illegible] are the difficulties in the conception of external reality, of the self, and again inherent difficulties as to the judgement if taken as reference to reality.

[9] *Theory of Knowledge* (1896), p. viii. Hobhouse had been particularly enraged by the way in which such shallow scepticism had been used to bolster conservatism by the Tory philosopher-statesman, A. J. Balfour; see esp. *Theory of Knowledge*, p. 618n.

[10] *Development and Purpose*, p. xvii.

[11] *Theory of Knowledge*, pp. viii–ix.

Now these difficulties I claim to have met in detail at various portions [*sic*] of my book. Grant (for the sake of argument) that I am successful in so doing and the grounds on which knowledge has been denied to be of reality disappear. The point is are (e.g.) Bradley's απορια as to predication, relation, quality etc. genuine contradictions? If so the thought which is built on them cannot be valid of ultimate reality. If not, if they are only as I contend dialectical puzzles, there can be on this ground no objection to my realism. You may say this only removed objections, and knowledge at least *may* have a merely relative validity. But this also I provide for by enquiring what reality is – what we mean by this term. I reply as you know that the primary meaning of a real fact is something given or apprehended. If therefore knowledge as a whole is a structure based upon the apprehended order and legitimately formed, its content is true of reality. The question of legitimacy then alone remains and this is the question of validity treated under that head.[12]

Hobhouse had acknowledged his debt to 'my friend Mr F. H. Bradley, whom I have been compelled to single out for criticism simply because his statement of views I wish to combat is the most powerful to be found', and upon publication he wrote to reassure Bradley: 'I am criticising the book not you.'[13] In the following month, Bradley sent Hobhouse several long letters detailing his objections to Hobhouse's arguments, but he padded them with praise.[14] However, his public response was less kind. He added an Appendix to the second edition of *Appearance and Reality* in 1897 in which he replied to his critics, treating Hobhouse as one of the most important. His comments were couched in that apparently polite but devastatingly ironic tone which he reserved for those unfortunates who seemed incapable of understanding the simplest argument – 'Mr Hobhouse seems to me (I suppose mistakenly) to be arguing...', and so on. He was particularly scornful of Hobhouse's defence of Mill: 'But I am not persuaded after all that Mill must have been a prophet because he has at last found a disciple to build his sepulchre.'[15] When four years later Hobhouse gloomily reflected that he had failed to get his own work 'even taken seriously', it may well have been this contemptuous dismissal which still irked him, since his book had in fact been quite favourably reviewed.[16]

[12] Hobhouse to Samuel Alexander, 1 Feb. 1896, Alexander Papers.

[13] *Theory of Knowledge*, pp. ix–x; Hobhouse to F. H. Bradley, 25 Feb. 1896, Bradley Papers.

[14] This is evident from Hobhouse's replies: Hobhouse to Bradley, 25 Feb., 3 and 24 March 1896. Bradley's letters to Hobhouse have not survived.

[15] *Appearance and Reality* (2nd edn 1897), pp. 618–19, 596; see also pp. 565, 594–5, and 614–16. The claim that 'Bradley himself saw little at issue between them' (C. M. Griffin, 'L. T. Hobhouse and the idea of harmony', *Journal of the History of Ideas*, XXXV (1974), 649) is not supported by this or any other evidence.

[16] Hobhouse to Scott, 16 March 1901, Scott Papers. For example, Bosanquet called it 'a valuable criticism of the Idealist position', 'Systematic Philosophy in the United Kingdom in the Year 1896', *Archiv für systematische Philosophie*, III (Berlin, 1897), 123; or the long and generous review by J. S. Mackenzie, *Mind*, N.S. V (1896), 396–410. Arthur Sidgwick reported that in Oxford the book was 'much thought of': Sidgwick to Scott, 20 Nov. 1896; and J. H. Bridges wrote to Hobhouse to tell him that Shadworth Hodgson and the 'London Realists' of the Aristotelian Society thought well of it: Bridges to Hobhouse, 29 Nov. 1896, Hobhouse Papers.

This episode no doubt contributed to his hostility to 'Oxford Idealism' – a hostility which Bradley may have come to reciprocate[17] – and to the sense of distance from the philosophical establishment generally which he exhibited thereafter. Thus, in an article of 1902, after firing an opening salvo about how 'philosophy in England has sympathised with the general reaction, of which indeed it has been in part the cause', he could write:

> The whole movement may be said to have ended in a blind alley in the work of Mr Bradley. The brilliance of Mr Bradley's great metaphysical work made it for some years the dominating influence in the philosophic world, but it was a brilliance that dazzled rather than illuminated, and as soon as men recovered the use of their eyes they were sure to see that the effect of *Appearance and Reality* was in the main destructive.[18]

In *The Theory of Knowledge* Hobhouse had been particularly concerned to differentiate between 'primitive apprehension' and the more complex 'judgement', and thus although he granted that the latter was integral to our *knowledge*, he was careful to 'distinguish our position from that of Kant and his present-day followers. The understanding makes knowledge but it does not make nature.'[19] For the most part he remained within the limits of such epistemological issues, but there were already signs of a desire for more ambitious metaphysical construction. He contended that 'so far as mere logic can give us any suggestion on the matter' it led us to assume that reality must be a harmonious whole. Moreover, he argued that 'no truth can be final or complete which is not in harmony with the whole of our nature', and that 'in this harmony the body of scientific truth already formed would find its place, not overthrown but completed and fulfilled'. 'True faith as opposed to false,' he observed gnomically, 'is in one word the anticipation of a harmony which shall be complete', and he concluded with the rousing declaration that each addition to our knowledge brings us nearer to 'the goal of all effort, the right understanding of the whole of things as they are in their inmost nature'.[20] In his efforts to wrestle with such metaphysical questions Hobhouse was led closer to a recognizably Idealist position which gave explicit philosophical statement to certain recurrent patterns in his thought.

Hobhouse himself later recognized how his thought had been developing during this period. 'For a long time I did not imagine the function of

[17] Bradley's response to Hobhouse may have been partly political in inspiration. It was well known that 'in political matters he was deeply conservative or reactionary. The mere mention of Gladstone's name enraged him...Bradley was the implacable enemy of all utilitarian or liberal teaching; he could not abide pacifism or generalized humanitarian sentiment, and any belief in the natural equality of man or in the inviolability of life (whether political or religious in inspiration) he regarded as "sentimental", "degenerate", and "disgusting".' R. Wollheim, *F. H. Bradley* (London, 1959), p. 14.

[18] 'Philosophy in England', *Speaker*, 13 Dec. 1902.

[19] *Theory of Knowledge*, p. 594.

[20] *Theory of Knowledge*, pp. 587, 620, 621, and 623.

philosophical criticism to be anything but critical and negative. It was not until much later that I came to think that it might yield certain sound generalisations as to the nature of reality.' He had initially taken 'mechanical causation' to be 'the ultimate category of science', and was 'at first opposed to anything like a theistic or teleological interpretation of reality as a whole'. This was his position when writing *The Theory of Knowledge.*

Not long after the book was published, however, some new considerations occurred which convinced me that this was an error, and that however much I might object to the form of their reasoning there was an element of substantial truth on this head in the reasoning of the Idealists. The result was to suggest that by mechanical reasoning from a purely empirical starting-point a candid thinker would be led to admit an element of purpose in the system of Reality.[21]

Already in 1896 he was writing to Bradley to say that he felt 'a great and growing respect for Hegel', and in his paper to the Aristotelian Society of the following year on 'Some Problems of Conception' he cited Hegel (in German) extensively.[22] In 1901 he concluded *Mind in Evolution* with a brief adumbration of the idea of a 'conditioned purpose' working itself out in and forming reality.[23] But as Bosanquet noted at the time, this was still an 'equivocal' answer to the question of 'in what sense if at all reality is teleological', and 'therefore perhaps the author has not moved towards Idealism so much as might appear in comparison with his former work'.[24] Hobhouse was still moving in that direction, however, and in describing his development much later he concluded:

I arrived...at a conception of the Rational which brought me back into unexpected contact with Idealism. This 'organic' view of rationality, which...has come to be for me the basis of knowledge, ethics, and even in a sense of Reality, is due mainly, I believe, to Dr Bosanquet, though it would not be fair to father my interpretation of it upon him.[25]

In its fully developed form, this 'organic view' of reality made its appearance in 1913 in *Development and Purpose*, Hobhouse's equivalent to Spencer's *First Principles* and the *summa philosophica* of his system.

Part One of the book is a summary of his account of the development of mind; that is, he deals both with the biological evolution of intelligence from the lower animals, and with the historical development of intellectual

[21] *Development and Purpose*, pp. xviii, xxvi.

[22] Hobhouse to Bradley, 5 March 1896, Bradley Papers; his paper was published in *Mind*, N.S. VI (1897), 145–63.

[23] *Mind in Evolution*, pp. 402–6.

[24] 'Jahresbericht über "Philosophy in the U.K. for 1901"', *Archiv für systematische Philosophie*, VIII (Berlin, 1902), 506. Bosanquet noted that in the conclusion of *Mind in Evolution* Hobhouse had treated developing reality as a process in time rather than as a process which included time, and was open to Idealist criticisms on this score. By 1913 Hobhouse could write: 'In the more ultimate sense in which Reality is not in time, but time is in Reality...' *Development and Purpose*, p. 351.

[25] 'Philosophy of Development' (1924), p. 150.

activity through a presumed chronological sequence (as discussed in Chapter 5 above). Throughout, he speaks of 'mind' as the substantive entity whose progress he is tracing, an entity which bears more than a casual resemblance to the '*Geist*' of the Hegelian system. In Part Two he undertakes a transcendental analysis designed to show that knowledge of reality itself, even understood in purely mechanical terms, presupposes an element of purpose which is in the process of realizing itself. Thus, the conclusions of each part are presented as mutually reinforcing: 'From two opposite starting-points we have arrived at the conception of a conditional purpose as constituting the core of the world-process.'[26] I do not intend to look at the argument in detail; the reasoning involved does not seem to be irresistibly persuasive. Nonetheless, for the purposes of interpretation, this book – 'the work he valued most highly'[27] – sheds revealing light on three important facets of his thought: first, the extent to which his theory rested upon a teleological conception of reality which was heavily Idealist in origin; secondly, the way in which this involved something of a rapprochement with religion; and thirdly, how it also accentuated the tendency of Hobhouse's theory generally to concentrate on the potential for harmony at the expense of analysing the actuality of conflict.

His own summary of his previous work on social evolution makes clear the extent to which it is already an implicit teleology; for example, he posits as the highest stage of mental evolution that wherein men so 'conceive of the heightened claims of personality as to make them not disruptive of the social order but working constituents of social harmony', and then aims to show how man has progressively approached this realization of his true nature.[28] He now situates this merely terrestrial development in a wider metaphysical framework. The conclusion he draws from his transcendental analysis is that reality is 'a system of elements conditioning and conditioned by a principle of organization leading up to an ultimate harmony', and that 'the actual constitution of things at any given time must be determined by the element in that harmony which each one of them is to contribute'. He thus arrives at a perspective very similar to that of Absolute Idealism: 'Everything that exists must be conceived as determined by, as owing its existence and character to, the contribution it has to make directly or indirectly to the ultimate harmony of the whole.' This is then claimed to be consonant with the nature of mind which is in the process of realizing itself, so that 'the fuller realization of the potentialities of mind [is] effect

[26] *Development and Purpose*, p. 368.

[27] Barker, 'Leonard Trelawny Hobhouse', 545.

[28] *Development and Purpose*, p. 195. Cf. p. 200: 'The realisation of such an order would involve the full development of personal capacity, and such development, when shared in common partnership, is the substance of a noble and happy life. The furtherance of such a life has a claim on man through that element in his nature which we may call, indifferently, rational or spiritual.'

and cause of a more extended harmony'. The story of mental evolution is, therefore, part of a larger teleology: 'The human mind is a germ for whose maturity provision is already made.'[29] Although Hobhouse never accepted the epistemological case for Idealism, and although his hostility to what he took to be its reactionary political and social consequences remained undimmed (indeed, it was intensified by the war), there can be no doubt that at the most fundamental level his own theory came to rest upon a recognizably Idealist metaphysics.

Moreover, although he did not follow Green in speaking of an 'eternal consciousness', he did consider 'mind, as we know it empirically, whether in the individual or in the group' to be 'the product...and a true constitutive part of the permanent mind' (or, as he less happily described it in other passages, 'central mind').[30] Here, as he recognized, he was approaching a belief which could be called religious, akin to that de-christianized humanist deism which enjoyed such a vigorous life among English intellectuals during this period, especially in its Positivist and Ethical Society forms.[31] In Hobhouse's case, this was a belief which he had only slowly come to accept. In the 1880s, in the full flush of oedipal antagonism, he had been 'a firm agnostic',[32] and in his paper to the Aristotelian Society of 1903 he was still scornful of those who

> restate the old belief in metaphysical terms, alleging truth of idea where it is no longer possible to plead truth of fact and using the ambiguities of abstract terms as a cover, behind which by moving rapidly from one meaning to another the direct conflict with brutal fact may be indefinitely evaded.

But he was already willing to postulate a 'spiritual order having its very imperfect manifestation in the life of humanity', and acknowledged the need to believe in 'a wider, a higher and a nobler reality than anything which we actually see or touch'.[33] In the conclusion to *Morals in Evolution* he was more positive: he contended that his findings about Progress provided

> the germ of a religion and an ethics which are as far removed from materialism as from the optimistic teleology of the metaphysicians, or the half naive creeds of the churches. It gives a meaning to human effort, as neither the pawn of an overruling Providence nor the sport of blind force. It is a message of hope to the world, of suffering lessened and strife

[29] *Development and Purpose*, pp. 348–9, 363, 362n, 271.

[30] *Development and Purpose*, pp. 371, 368.

[31] The plethora of societies formed around such beliefs are discussed in detail in Warren Sylvester Smith, *The London Heretics 1870–1914* (London, 1967). The original statement of principles of the London Ethical Society was representative in its affirmation that 'the moral and religious life of man is capable of a rational justification and explanation apart from authority and tradition'. Quoted in Smith, *London Heretics*, p. 125. As far as I have been able to discover, Hobhouse never actually joined any of these societies, though broadly sympathetic to them: many of his close friends belonged to them, Hobson being a particularly faithful member of the South Place Ethical Society.

[32] See above, Ch. 2, text at n18.

[33] 'Faith and the Will to Believe', *Proceedings of the Aristotelian Society*, VI (1903), 87, 104.

assuaged, not by fleeing from reason to the bosom of faith, but by the increasing rational control of things by that collective wisdom, the εἷς ξυνὸς λόγος which is all that we directly know of the Divine.[34]

In 1913 he spoke more freely of 'a greater Spirit', and argued that 'if, as we now conclude, a purpose runs through the world-whole, there is a Mind of which the world-purpose is the object'. He did not venture into genuinely theological speculation; he was content to claim that 'God is that of which the highest known embodiment is the distinctive spirit of Humanity', but also to insist, conversely, that the experience of human nobility, love and goodness indicated the fundamental reality of 'a spiritual power'.[35]

The third aspect of Hobhouse's thought for which *Development and Purpose* provides notable evidence is the way in which, in the face of the recurrent temptations to doubt and despair, his theory offered ever-widening circles of reassurance. Each embraced the discordant elements of the narrower sphere in a harmony which was both ideal and actual. Thus, when faced by the fact that individuals seem destined to be torn by conflicting desires, he takes comfort in the fact that 'harmony tends to fulness of life, to *complete* development of personality'. He had to concede that 'there remain the cases of monstrosity, of cruelty, treachery and aggravated lust', but blandly asserted that they 'are more and more clearly reducible by psychological investigation to pathological growths, by which the normal mental structure is obsessed and distorted'.[36] Still, even a society composed exclusively of 'normal' harmonious personalities may seem bound to face discord and conflict: but 'for the rational man there is no harmony within the self unless as a basis of harmony with other centres of experience and feeling, and the realisation of any one self is regarded only as an item in the development of society, that is, in a Common Good'. Not surprisingly, he finds that 'the net movement' of social evolution in this respect has been 'to contribute the appropriate conditions for the realisation of the ethical ideal'.[37] Still, as Hobhouse again had to recognize, the fact that civilization had advanced this far was no guarantee that it might not regress or even

34 *Morals*, II, p. 284.

35 *Development and Purpose*, pp. 365, 371. In 1925, reflecting on the life and recent death of his wife, he was moved to declare in a letter to the Hammonds: 'I'll say here definitely that it [?made] me believe in what most people call God – I will say a spiritual element fundamental in Reality. I don't believe that a being like Nora came about by the random collocation of "genes" and the ramifications of physical heredity. She doesn't stand by herself. She comes out of the great far-reaching spiritual impulse which is striving to expression through all the limiting conditions of mechanism...For my part, I fear deceiving myself, which would be unworthy of her, if I accept anything definite as a consolation...All these thoughts have been forming in my mind gradually for 30 years....' Hobhouse to J. L. and B. Hammond, 19 Oct. 1925, Hammond Papers.

36 *Development and Purpose*, p. 199 (my emphasis); 368. Cf. *Rational Good*, pp. 91, 104.

37 *Development and Purpose*, pp. 170, 226.

perish altogether in the future. 'Only if mind should one day reach the point at which it could control all the conditions of life could this danger permanently be averted.' That mind should control 'all' the conditions of life and 'permanently' avert the danger of regression might seem a rather stiff requirement. However, at this high point of his optimism, Hobhouse was willing to claim

that it is precisely on this line that modern civilization had made its chief advance, that through science it is beginning to control the physical conditions of life, and that on the side of ethics and religion it is forming those ideas of the unity of the race, and of the subordination of law, morals and social constitutions generally to the needs of human development which are the conditions of the control that is required.[38]

Finally, if all else failed – which it was prone to do with alarming frequency, as Hobhouse gloomily recognized – the rationality of reality itself could still be relied upon. He admitted that 'in the position here adopted, the conception of reason is no doubt considerably widened', and such a conception might seem embarrassingly close to the 'optimistic teleology of the metaphysician' which he had earlier derided. But now this view of reason met the need: 'It is the conscious expression of that impulse to harmony which dominates the entire evolution of Mind, and the rationality of the process is the guarantee of its ultimate success.'[39] In his search for reassurance, Hobhouse was clearly taking no chances. After all, a belief in Progress established by mere induction must necessarily be something of a wager against the future: nasty surprises cannot be ruled out. Hobhouse hedged his bets, however, and made sure that he only tossed with his own double-headed metaphysical coin. The concluding sentences of the book eloquently reveal the needs which the whole Panglossian construction was designed to meet, for

if it is sound, it does settle the fundamental questions – whether the life of man is full of hopeful purpose or void of meaning, whether he can recognize in the constitution of things something that meets his hopes and answers to his aspirations, whether he can make for himself a religion without self-deceit, whether he can finally improve the condition of his race by effort or is doomed always to fall back from every apparently forward step, whether he can trust to his reason or must admit the ultimate futility of thought, whether the spirit of human love is justified of her children or blood and iron must continue to rule the world. To all these questions the conclusion here reached supplies a definite and positive answer.[40]

[38] *Development and Purpose*, pp. xxii–xxiii.

[39] *Development and Purpose*, p. xxix.

[40] *Development and Purpose*, p. 372. This was no doubt why, until the recent revival of scholarly interest in Hobhouse, his work seems mainly to have survived as devotional reading in the lesser colleges of India and certain campuses of the American Midwest.

EPILOGUE: THE STRANGE DEATH OF MORAL ENGLAND

Development and Purpose was published in 1913, not an auspicious year in which to argue for the certainty of cosmic Progress. To Hobhouse, the First World War was, as his son observed, 'a shattering blow' which 'struck directly at the whole foundation of his thought'; he later said himself that it had made an old man of him.[1] In one of his early wartime dialogues, Hobhouse recognized, with a redeeming irony, how vulnerable his position now appeared. He pictures himself as saying: 'But, after all, we always knew that such a war was one of the things to be reckoned with...' 'Such a war?' his fictional interlocutor exclaims: 'Do you mean that you, with your evolving ethics, wouldn't at any time have confidently maintained, on the basis of comparative sociology and psychology and ethnology and at least five other elaborately constructed sciences, that anything like the present war had become historically impossible?'[2] In fact, at a more mundane level, he had been increasingly alarmed at the development of the international situation before 1914; once the war had begun, his jeremiads turned into obituaries. 'All one's hopes for social and political progress are shattered once and for all...We may write *Finis* to our work, and hope that civilization may rise again elsewhere.' To Graham Wallas he wrote: 'As to political and social progress, they will be names without a meaning for our time...I cannot look forward.'[3] But it would be a long recitation indeed which included all such declarations of despair by the ageing Hobhouse. Already in September 1914, he had to write contritely to Emily: 'What you say about myself is quite true. I am and always have been too ready to think that all is lost. I will try not to think so.' This was a promise which he spectacularly failed to keep in the next few years. Late in the war, the ever more sanguine Scott gently chided him: 'Surely you are much too gloomy.' To Hobhouse, the idea of being *too* gloomy was barely conceivable. 'My anticipations, pessimistic as [?they] are, are always wrong by not being pessimistic enough.'[4]

1 Quoted in Hobson and Ginsberg, *L. T. Hobhouse*, p. 91.

2 'The Soul of Civilization', first published *Contemporary Review*, Aug. 1915, and repr. in *Questions of War and Peace* (London, 1916), quotation at p. 11.

3 Hobhouse to Emily Hobhouse, 8 Aug. 1914, Hobhouse Papers; Hobhouse to Graham Wallas, same date, Wallas Papers.

4 Hobhouse to Emily Hobhouse, 12 Aug. 1914, Hobhouse Papers; Scott to Hobhouse, 28 March 1918, Scott Papers; Hobhouse to Emily Hobhouse, 4 Jan. 1920, Hobhouse Papers.

In seeking to explain the catastrophe, he characteristically looked not primarily to the political situation and diplomatic manoeuvring of the pre-war years, but rather to long-term intellectual changes. In so doing, he revealed the way in which some of his own deepest sympathies were for what he recalled as the stable moral world of the late-Victorian era. The essence of the contrast with present tendencies, as he now saw it, was that 'the Victorian age believed in law and reason. Its sons have come in large measure to believe in violence, and in impulse, emotion or instinct.' In 1915 he singled out Nietzsche and Bergson as the intellectual progenitors of this change, with Syndicalism and Anarchism as its extreme manifestation in politics, and the 'Modernist' movement in literature and the arts as its aesthetic expression. In fact, it is in his aesthetic judgements – which in his case, of course, turned largely on moral judgements – that Hobhouse's antipathy to some of the most distinctive intellectual developments of the twentieth century is most evident. He disapproved of what he saw as the obsession with subjectivity and self-assertion in modern art: for such an artist, he sneered, the external world seems to exist

> only to excite in him emotions, often apparently of indescribably painful character and tangled meaning, which he proceeds to transfer to canvas. The picture need be no more like the original than a tree is like the painful internal sensation to which it apparently gives rise in some painters. The artist's business is ever the same – to express himself in his moving and changeful moods, and despise alike nature and the critic. If he aims at anything it should be violence. If he despises anything on principle is should be beauty. If he persistently abhors anything it should be repose. Noise is to be the note of music; glaring contrast and flaunting incongruity of painting.[5]

It is always hard to distinguish nostalgia, philistinism, and moral conservatism in such judgements; in Hobhouse's case, the third element is particularly evident in his account of the figure whom he chooses to represent the virtues of the earlier period. For he returns to George Eliot in part for the 'Realism' of her technique, but even more for the way in which the best of her novels, such as *Middlemarch*, provide 'a justification of all that it was then usual to sum up in the word altruism'. The mood of the present generation involved, it seemed to Hobhouse's jaundiced wartime sensibilities, 'an extraordinary exaltation of the human will, and in particular of those elements underlying the will which man shares with the animal world, emotion, impulse, instinct. Instead of submitting them to reason, conscience and law, we are bidden rather to confide ourselves to them and let them carry us withersoever they will.' George Eliot, by contrast, 'upholds the traditional virtues, she insists on order and obedience. She is permeated by the sense of a law of life, and the conviction that those

[5] *The World in Conflict* (London, 1915), pp. 29, 46.

who hold by it resolutely will win through, will save their own souls, and bring in others with them.'[6]

This despondent sense that the march of history was proceeding rapidly in the wrong direction was the dominant note of the last decade of Hobhouse's life. Towards the end of the war he reflected gloomily, 'the future, anyway you take it, is dark', and the twenties brought little light.[7] In politics he continued to hanker after a union of 'progressive' forces, the old ideal of a party of 'brains and numbers', with the Liberals supplying most of the first and Labour almost all of the second. In practice, however, neither party now seemed very willing to follow this script. Hobhouse's own disaffection from the Liberal rump became more pronounced, especially after 1924. Confined to his sick-bed, he ruminated to Scott:

> My difficulty about the Liberal Party lies further back than yours. I doubt if it any longer stands for anything distinctive. My reasons are on the one side that moderate Labour – Labour in office – has on the whole represented essential Liberalism, not without mistakes and defects, but *better* than the organized party since C-B's death. [Campbell-Bannerman had died in 1908.] On the other side the Liberal party, however you divide it up, never seems any better agreed within on essentials. Of the present fragment part leans to the Tories, part to Labour, part has nothing distinctive, but is a kind of Free Trade Unionist group. The deduction I draw is that the distinction between that kind of Labour man who does not go whole hog for nationalization on the one side and the Liberal who wants social progress on the other is obsolete. I myself have always felt that it was unreal and that if we divided parties by true principles, the division would be like this

Communist	ordinary Labour	Bad Liberal	Diehards
Theoretical Socialist	Good Liberal	ordinary Tory	

> But traditions and class distinctions kept many good Liberals outside Labour. Now Labour has grown so much that it tends to absorb them and to leave only the 'bad' Liberals who incline to the Tories and a mass of traditional Liberals who can't desert a party of that name.[8]

The Liberal Summer School movement was an attempt to draw upon such intellectuals as could be persuaded to take part in the perennial task of providing the party with a programme, and Hobhouse participated spasmodically. Although he attended some of the meetings of the committee which eventually produced the 'Liberal Yellow Book', he reported in February 1927: 'I told them I was not a member of the Liberal Party.'[9]

6 *World in Conflict*, pp. 35, 41, 35. He was here returning to a writer whom he had celebrated as a moral and aesthetic radical in his youth; see '"George Eliot" as a Novelist', *Marlburian*, XVII (1882), 21–3.

7 Hobhouse to Emily Hobhouse, 6 Jan. 1918, Hobhouse Papers.

8 Hobhouse to Scott, 7 Nov. 1924, Scott Papers.

9 Quoted in Hobson and Ginsberg, *L. T. Hobhouse*, p. 67. On the Liberal Summer School movement and Hobhouse's participation in it, see John Campbell, 'The Renewal of Liberalism: Liberalism without Liberals', in Gillian Peele and Chris Cook (eds.), *The Politics of Re-appraisal* (London, 1975). Hobhouse was particularly concerned to argue for the merits of the recently ended Wages Board system. See also his contribution, 'The Regulation of Wages' in Robert Cecil *et al.*, *Essays in Liberalism* (London, 1922).

Unlike several other erstwhile New Liberal intellectuals, however, he never actually joined the Labour Party. This was not due to any diminution in his sympathy for radical causes. In part, it was the familiar hostility to a class-based party. 'The constitution of the Labour Party binds it tight to the Trade Unions and the sectional selfishness, a most serious defect,' he complained in 1924. His own continuing concerns are indicated in his remark about the Liberal Industrial Council: 'I want to see whether individualism or the common good will get its way with these committees.'[10] Nor did he have a very high opinion of the Labour leadership: even in 1929, though welcoming the Labour victory, he confessed that he was 'sorry the Liberals did not get more seats, as I think (I know it's blasphemy) they carry more brains to the square inch than Labour, most of whose men are merely dull and terribly afraid of their permanent officials'.[11] He had lamented to his sister in 1925: 'I wish I thought any good would come of political changes, but I don't really think Labour has much in the way of ideas', and Hobson was surely right to conclude that Hobhouse's 'disillusionment with existing parties, organizations, and methods' meant that 'his political and economic attachments became weaker in his later years'.[12]

He continued in lonely eminence as the sole professor of sociology in Britain, though even at the L.S.E. there was no great enthusiasm for his abstract and evolutionary conception of the subject. Beveridge, the Director of the School after 1919, interpreted 'social science' in a strongly positivistic way, and deployed his resources to foster more empirical and quantifying studies; 'social biology' was his pet project, against which Hobhouse protested vigorously, ever suspicious of the old Social Darwinist heresy reappearing in fashionable academic disguise.[13] Though Ginsberg remained devoted to him, and though many students later recalled him as an impressive teacher, it is noticeable that Hobhouse did not really found a 'school' in sociology, or produce a generation of graduate students committed to propagating his views (compare, in this respect, the impact of such colleagues as Malinowski or Laski). Perhaps Albion Small, the doyen of American sociology, saw the problem when reviewing the final volume of Hobhouse's so-called 'Principles of Sociology'. 'It is doubtful', he began with an exaggerated flourish, 'if all the living philosophers and

[10] Hobhouse to Scott, 16 Nov. 1924, Scott Papers; Hobhouse to Margaret Llewellyn Davies, n.d., quoted in Hobson and Ginsberg, *L. T. Hobhouse*, p. 67.

[11] Hobhouse to Margaret Llewellyn Davies, June 1929, quoted in Hobson and Ginsberg, *L. T. Hobhouse*, p. 67. See also above, Ch. 3, pp. 90–1, 100.

[12] Hobhouse to Emily Hobhouse, 17 May 1925, Hobhouse Papers; Hobson and Ginsberg, *L. T. Hobhouse*, p. 63.

[13] There is now a good discussion of this episode in José Harris, *W. H. Beveridge: A Biography* (Oxford, 1977), Chs. 11 and 12; Beveridge thought Hobhouse's work was insufficiently 'scientific' (p. 287). Hobhouse briefly criticized 'social biology' in his essay on 'Sociology' in *The Mind* (1927), esp. p. 307.

sociologists combined command prestige among American sociologists equal to that of Professor Hobhouse.' (Even allowing for the exaggeration, what this suggests about the judgement of early-twentieth-century American sociologists is rather alarming.) But whereas, he continued, American sociologists actually practised their trade, Hobhouse was still explaining how it might be possible to do so; his work was read 'not for its sociology but for its pre-sociology'. The reason for this, Small suggested, was that 'it does not yet appear that the center of Professor Hobhouse's interest is in sociology rather than in general philosophy', and in a telling phrase he concluded: 'It is doubtful whether a commission of physical scientists would be able to discover that the method foreshadowed in these volumes is an advance in principle over T. H. Green's *Principles of Political Obligation*.'[14]

In fact, in the last decade of his life Hobhouse's interests increasingly reverted to philosophy. The philosophical implications of the fundamental changes in natural science that had taken place since the turn of the century particularly absorbed him, and he spent a long time revising *Development and Purpose* to take account of them.[15] But in philosophy, too, he was to some extent swimming against the tide. It was not so much that the positions which he had taken up in the 1880s and 1890s had been subjected to fatal criticism (as so often in the history of philosophy these were ignored rather than refuted); indeed, something quite similar to his kind of 'critical realism' formed the epistemological centre-piece of the new philosophical fashion set by Moore and Russell.[16] It was rather that a more austere conception of the professional business of the philosopher was taking hold. For Hobhouse, the task of philosophy was more than ever to deal with 'the one great central problem, that of life as a whole and the universe as a whole', but he had to recognize that this was a task which professional philosophers seemed less and less inclined to tackle. It was partly to meet this lack and to speak to the concerns of non-philosophers that in 1925 he helped to found, and became the first Chairman of, the British Institute

14 Albion Small, Review of *Social Development*, *American Journal of Sociology*, 30 (1924–5), 216–20. The rapid expansion and intellectual vacuity of early American sociology contributed to give Hobhouse a large and appreciative audience in the United States at this time; for some characteristic eulogies, see Owen, *L. T. Hobhouse, Sociologist*, Ch. 1. Two full-length studies and several articles, for the most part celebratory rather than critical, appeared on Hobhouse's work during the twenties: see particularly Hugh Carter, *The Social Theories of L. T. Hobhouse* (Chapel Hill, North Carolina, 1927), and J. A. Nicholson, *Some Aspects of the Philosophy of Hobhouse: Logic and Social Theory* (Urbana, Illinois, 1928).

15 He began revising the book in 1924; see Hobhouse to Oliver Hobhouse, 5 Nov. 1924, Hobhouse Papers. Ginsberg reported that Hobhouse 'devoted a good deal of his time to their [the developments in the natural sciences] study in the years before his death and intended to deal with them more fully on his retirement'. Hobson and Ginsberg, *L. T. Hobhouse*, p. 259.

16 See G. Dawes Hicks, *Critical Realism: Studies in the Philosophy of Mind and Nature* (London, 1938), p. xvi.

of Philosophical Studies. In his Chairman's Address he expressed his animating belief that 'the task of making knowledge coherent for our own generation (and thereby helping to make our lives healthy, sane and reasonable) is worth doing', and that in pursuing this task 'the study of philosophy can be of exceptional value'.[17] However, the trend to professionalization was already subverting this purpose: one of the earliest frequenters of the Institute was Gilbert Ryle, who, after a more severely professional career, recalled with some scorn the 'philosopher-missionaries' who had founded the Institute and who had been 'influenced by intermittent but rosy visions of some acts of edification and inspiration issuing out of the philanthropically-unbolted doors of our philosophy departments into the homes and hearts of the Comman Man'.[18] Even those who at the time were fairly sympathetic to Hobhouse's conception of philosophy complained of 'the way he will drag in half-sentimental, half-murderous "political" prejudices in philosophy', and some of his friends thought that his repeated failure to be elected to the British Academy in the early twenties was in part because 'he has always damaged his work by dragging in his own most disputable views about contemporary politics into his philosophy'.[19]

Above all, however, it was a change in moral attitudes in the broadest sense which gave the later Hobhouse his slightly beleaguered air. This is one of the most elusive yet fundamental kinds of change for the historian to try to capture and convey, an area of the past which remains relatively unexplored. The seductions of selective quotation have usually proved irresistible; faced with them, I can here only incite to virtue rather than practise it. But in the present case such change is too important to ignore, even if the evidence for it is as yet sadly impressionistic. Concentration on the war itself has no doubt led the suddenness and magnitude of this change to be exaggerated: there was obviously a good deal of iconoclasm in certain circles before the war, and many so-called 'Victorian' attitudes persisted long after it. Nonetheless, the generation of intellectuals which came to maturity in the twenties inhabited a somewhat different moral world from that of their parents' generation. The belief in Progress seemed not only less persuasive but also less necessary. The dominant moralism of the earlier age had been diluted: the values of 'character', of 'self-restraint', and of 'Duty' no longer had quite the same hold. The process of professionalization was squeezing the more overt kinds of moralizing out

17 Repr., *Journal of Philosophical Studies*, II (1927), 595–8. See also his Address of the following year, III (1928), 565–7.

18 Gilbert Ryle, 'Fifty years of philosophy and philosophers', *Philosophy*, 51 (1976), 386–7.

19 A. E. Taylor to Samuel Alexander, 27 June 1922 and 31 Dec. 1923, Alexander Papers. Hobhouse was finally elected in 1925, but as he rightly observed 'my compeers have mostly had it years ago'. Hobhouse to Emily Hobhouse, 15 July 1925, Hobhouse Papers.

of academic disciplines.[20] The new generation complained of the way their elders had 'turned everything into rhetorical abstraction', and they publicly scorned the imperatives of 'Discipline, Purity, Duty'.[21] Hobhouse was aware of the change: in explaining his political views to his own son, he concluded sadly, 'I don't expect you to agree to this but like to express... the idealism of the last generation.'[22] And in one of his blacker moods, he wrote to a friend: 'The unmitigated selfishness with which Shaw has indoctrinated his generation isn't going to make them happier. It's probably going to lead to the final world catastrophe which a generation bent on pleasure will never take the trouble to avert.'[23] The terms of reproach are characteristic: whatever one's assessment of the aspirations and achievements of Hobhouse and his contemporaries, no one could ever claim that they were 'a generation bent on pleasure'.

In 1914, however, Hobhouse was already fifty years old, and set in his intellectual ways. His post-war writing played a series of rather repetitive variations on the themes of his earlier work. The First World War is certainly not an event which is easily incorporated into a theodicy, and it is a sign of the very deep roots of Hobhouse's programmatic optimism that he managed it at all. In the revised edition of *Development and Purpose*, published in 1927, he spoke feelingly of the 'regret', 'doubt', and 'disappointment' which the war and its consequences induced, and so 'in revising the book...I found myself compelled to face very seriously the question whether the view of social development which it involves could any longer be maintained'.[24] In a letter written while he was working on

20 One surrender to the charms of selective quotation: in 1890 Alfred Marshall's *Principles of Economics* was widely praised for its 'moral tone'; in 1919 a reviewer of his *Industry and Trade* complained that its moralizing was 'out of place...in a scientific treatise'. Quoted in *Official Papers of Alfred Marshall*, p. 47.

21 Stephen Spender, *World Within World: The Autobiography of Stephen Spender* (London, 1951), pp. 7, 9. Spender's father, Harold Spender, Hobhouse's close friend and Oxford contemporary, was described as 'one of the best, perhaps the most typical, of that generation of Oxford men who went into active life at the end of the eighties, inspired by the humanitarian zeal for which Arnold Toynbee and Canon Barnett were then the most conspicuous prophets'. F. S. Marvin, Foreword to Harold Spender, *The Fire of Life*, p. 3. His son recalled (in a passage also quoted by Richter, *Politics of Conscience*, p. 376): 'If I had to play football, he impressed on me that this was to harden the the tissues of my character. His own accomplishments were to him difficulties surmounted with unflinching resolution at the cost of infinite pains. He spoke often in parables which illustrated the point that life was a perpetual confronting of oneself with vague immensities...My father's habit of mind created a kind of barrier between him and us, which asserted itself even in the most genuine situations.' *World Within World*, p. 5.

22 Hobhouse to Oliver Hobhouse, 29 Oct. 1924, Hobhouse Papers. He sadly informed Emily (4 Jan. 1920): 'The point of view of the new generation differs from ours.'

23 Hobhouse to Margaret Llewellyn Davies, Dec. 1928, quoted in Hobson and Ginsberg, *L. T. Hobhouse*, p. 69. It is clear that the 'generation' Hobhouse is referring to is that which was influenced by Shaw rather than that which was contemporary with him.

24 *Development and Purpose* (2nd edn, 1927), pp. xxxiii–xxxiv.

the revision, he had revealed his usual conflict between optimism and pessimism:

My mind is in three layers. The top layer accepts it as it stands and recognizes that at any rate I have done my best and put the argument as well as I could and am prepared to defend it. The second layer is sceptical. It says: 'Your argument was based upon a belief in modern civilization, but in fact modern civilization is going to pot. It is all going to be more and more machinery, more ugliness, more freedom for the motorist till there is none for the pedestrian, some form of class war to end in the triumph of Fascism, and probably an international war which will destroy urban life. At the best you can no longer think of any humanitarianism as the soul of social development, and so the linchpin is out of your argument'. When this stage is reached, I begin to think of cancelling the book and paying Macmillan's expenses. But there is a third layer which is less articulate, but says something to this effect: 'Your arguments are all pretty poor but your meaning's right. It is absolutely true that the world is neither mechanism nor spirit, but a spiritual struggle for wholeness or harmony in discordant parts, and the struggle makes evolution because it has a drive behind it which the inert mechanical parts have not. You'd betray your ideas if you gave up, because though a poor thing it is the best you can do. You don't express them well, but nobody else expresses them at all'. So it will go on – and there is a candid expression of the writer's frame of mind. But it is a bore to feel a doubleness of this kind and to feel in fact quite deeply and keenly in opposite ways.[25]

However, in his survey of the post-war world he still saw signs of advance in, for example, the position of women, the welfare of the working classes or the liberation of colonial peoples, which suggested that Progress had not ground to a complete halt. Even if the worst were to happen, as it seemed to Hobhouse always to be on the point of doing, and 'our civilized order' were to be 'broken up by intestine violence', still he was confident that Western civilization would leave a legacy of ideas 'sufficient...to define the direction in which the development of mind proceeds'. Once again, therefore, he is able to conclude:

whatever our hopes and fears for the present fabric of civilization, I have, after weighing the adverse evidence, come to the conclusion that the conception of human development as moving to a maturity of rational self-direction, at which point the process would assume a quite new character, may be legitimately retained.[26]

This idea appeared somewhat dated in 1927, and fifty years later it seems almost quaint. Nor have Hobhouse's other intellectual achievements worn much better. But his work is now attracting a considerable amount of attention from those interested in the history of social and political thought. It has become fashionable to explain the presumed 'weakness' of such theorizing in Britain during this period in terms of the 'individualism' of

[25] Hobhouse to Margaret Llewellyn Davies, n.d. [early 1927], quoted in Hobson and Ginsberg, *L. T. Hobhouse*, p. 259.

[26] *Development and Purpose* (2nd edn 1927), pp. xxiv–xxxvi.

its Liberal political theory and the 'positivism' of its sociology.[27] Now, there were certainly many contributions to these two activities other than Hobhouse's, but his have generally been seen as decisive in both cases; and although in some senses of those protean terms there were elements of individualism in his political theory and positivism in his sociology, it should by now be clear that these terms provide a wholly inadequate characterization of the central theoretical orientations of his work. In particular, they ignore the moral collectivism and the Idealist teleology which, as I have tried to show, lay at the heart of his thought. However, it should also be clear by now that it is no part of my intention to attempt to restore Hobhouse's reputation or to advocate a return to his methods. On the contrary, my aim has been to emphasize that his thinking was embedded in a set of assumptions which no longer demands our allegiance, and addressed to a range of problems which no longer commands our attention. Above all, his theories sustained and were sustained by a pattern of moral attitudes which enjoyed a special prominence during this period. Taken together, these considerations suggest the need to reassess the established accounts of social and political thought in Britain during this period, at least insofar as they depend, implicitly or explicitly, upon the prevailing interpretation of Hobhouse's work. They also suggest that we would do better to look elsewhere for illumination on our present concerns about the relationship between Liberalism and sociology.

27 I discuss some of the dubious assumptions underlying the conventional way of stating this question in 'Sociology and Idealism', 3–8.

BIBLIOGRAPHY

The place of publication is London unless otherwise specified.

MANUSCRIPT COLLECTIONS

Apart from the papers in the possession of Hobhouse's granddaughter, Mrs J. Balme, which contain mainly family material, and the Hobhouse–Scott correspondence in the *Guardian* Archives, I have traced no substantial collection of Hobhouse manuscripts. However, I list below all those collections I have consulted which contain items of his correspondence or other relevant material.

Samuel Alexander Papers (Manchester University Library)
C. R. Ashbee Papers (King's College, Cambridge)
F. H. Bradley Papers (Merton College, Oxford)
James Bryce Papers (Bodleian Library, Oxford)
J. S. Burdon-Sanderson Papers (University College, London)
Sir Henry Campbell-Bannerman Papers (British Library)
Courtney Collection ((Papers of Lord and Lady Courtney of Penwith) British Library of Political and Economic Science (L.S.E.))
Herbert Gladstone Papers (British Library)
J. L. and B. Hammond Papers (Bodleian Library, Oxford)
L. T. Hobhouse Papers (in the possession of Mrs J. Balme, Whitebridge Farm, Semley, near Shaftesbury, Dorset)
Sir Hubert Llewellyn Smith Papers (in the possession of Mr A. and Mr H. Llewellyn Smith, 1 Ockley Road, Streatham, London S.E.19)
F. S. Marvin Papers (Bodleian Library, Oxford)
Gilbert Murray Papers (Bodleian Library, Oxford)
H. W. Nevinson Papers (Bodleian Library, Oxford)
Lord Samuel Papers (House of Lords)

C. P. Scott Papers ((1) *Guardian* Archives, Manchester University Library; (2) British Library)
Bernard Shaw Papers (British Library)
Graham Wallas Papers (British Library of Political and Economic Science (L.S.E.))

NEWSPAPERS AND PERIODICALS

This list is confined to the titles of primary sources actually cited in references. Full details of secondary-source articles will be found in a separate section of the Bibliography, pp. 273–6.

American Journal of Sociology
Calendar of the London School of Economics
Contemporary Review
Daily Chronicle
Economic Journal
Economic Review
English Review
Fortnightly Review
Hibbert Journal
Independent Review
International Journal of Ethics
Journal of Philosophical Studies
Manchester Guardian
Marlburian
Mind
Nation
National Review
Nineteenth Century
Oxford Magazine
Pilot
Proceedings of the Aristotelian Society
Positivist Review
Progressive Review
Sociological Papers
Sociological Review
Speaker
Times
Transactions of the National Association for the Promotion of Social Science
Tribune

WORKS BY HOBHOUSE

Books

1893 *The Labour Movement* (2nd edn 1897; 3rd edn 1912; 3rd edn repr., with Introduction and notes by Philip P. Poirier, Brighton, 1974).
1896 *The Theory of Knowledge: A Contribution to Some Problems of Logic and Metaphysics* (2nd edn 1906; 3rd edn 1921).

1901 *Mind in Evolution* (2nd edn 1915; 3rd edn 1926).

1904 *Democracy and Reaction* (2nd edn 1909; 1st edn repr., with Introduction to 2nd edn appended, and Introduction and notes by P. F. Clarke, Brighton, 1972).

1905 (with J. L. Hammond) *Lord Hobhouse: A Memoir.*

1906 *Morals in Evolution: A Study in Comparative Ethics* (2 vols.; 2nd edn (1 vol. as subsequent edns) 1907; 3rd edn 1915; 4th edn 1923; 7th edn, with Introduction by Morris Ginsberg, 1951).

1911 *Liberalism* (repr., with Introduction by Alan P. Grimes, New York, 1964).

Social Evolution and Political Theory (New York).

1912 (with J. W. Headlam) *Special Report on Certain Tutorial Classes in Connection with the Workers' Educational Association* (Board of Education Special Report No. 2).

1913 *Development and Purpose: An Essay towards a Philosophy of Evolution* (2nd edn 1927).

1915 (with G. C. Wheeler and Morris Ginsberg) *The Material Culture and Social Institutions of the Simpler Peoples: An Essay in Correlation* (repr., with Introduction by Morris Ginsberg, 1965).

The World in Conflict.

1916 *Questions of War and Peace.*

1918 *The Metaphysical Theory of the State: A Criticism.*

1921 *The Rational Good: A Study in the Logic of Practice* (repr., with Foreword by Archibald Robertson, 1947).

1922 *The Elements of Social Justice.*

1924 *Social Development: Its Nature and Conditions* (repr., with Foreword by Morris Ginsberg, 1966).

1966 *Sociology and Philosophy: A Centenary Collection of Essays and Articles* (ed. Morris Ginsberg).

Articles

Hobhouse's output of articles and journalism during his writing life of forty years was enormous, and the list which follows is by no means comprehensive. It includes all the signed contributions (other than the *Manchester Guardian*) consulted for this study, and a selection of major items published after 1914.

1882 '"George Eliot" as a Novelist', *Marlburian*, XVII, pp. 21–3.

1883 'Mill and Mazzini: A Contrast', *Marlburian*, XVIII, pp. 81–4.

1890 'Experimental Certainty', *Mind*, O.S. XV, pp. 251–60.

1891 'The Principle of Induction', *Mind*, O.S. XVI, pp. 80–91.

'Induction and Deduction', *Mind*, O.S. XVI, pp. 507–20.

Review of George Howell, *Conflicts of Capital and Labour*, *Economic Review*, I, pp. 134–44.

1892 Review of C. B. Phipson, *The Redemption of Labour*, *International Journal of Ethics*, III, pp. 123–6.

1897 'Some Problems of Conception', *Mind*, N.S. VI, pp. 145–63.

1898 'The Ethical Basis of Collectivism', *International Journal of Ethics*, VIII, pp. 137–56.

1899 'The Foreign Policy of Collectivism', *Economic Review*, IX, pp. 197–220.

1901 'A Sane Imperialist', *Speaker*, 5, pp. 102–3.

'Biology and Temperance Reform', *Speaker*, 5, pp. 189–90.

'Two Typical English Moralists', *Speaker*, 5, pp. 216–17.

'Some Shattered Illusions', *Speaker*, 5, pp. 300–1.

'The Limitations of Democracy', *Speaker*, 5, pp. 359–60.

BIBLIOGRAPHY

1902 'Democracy and Liberty', *Speaker*, 5, pp. 388–9.
'Democracy and Nationality', *Speaker*, 5, pp. 415–16.
'Democracy and Imperialism', *Speaker*, 5, pp. 443–5.
'The Growth of Imperialism', *Speaker*, 5, pp. 474–5.
'The Intellectual Reaction', *Speaker*, 5, pp. 501–2.
'The Intellectual Reaction', *Speaker*, 5, pp. 526–7.
'The Diversions of a Psychologist' (6 articles), *Pilot*, 5, pp. 12–13; 36–7; 126–7; 232–3; 344–5; 449–51.
'Democracy and Empire', *Speaker*, 7, pp. 75–6.
'The New Darwinism', *Speaker*, 7, pp. 171–2.
'Philosophy in England', *Speaker*, 7, pp. 282–3.

1903 'Henry Sidgwick on his Contemporaries', *Speaker*, 7, pp. 421–2.
'Religions of the Ancient East', *Speaker*, 8, pp. 278–9.
'The Laws of Hammurabi', *Living Age*, XIX, pp. 250–3.
'Sociology in America', *Speaker*, 8, pp. 344–5.
'Faith and the Will to Believe', *Proceedings of the Aristotelian Society*, VI, pp. 87–111.

1904 'Hammurabi and Moses', *Speaker*, 9, pp. 432–3.

1905 *Towards a Social Policy: Suggestions for Constructive Reform* (a collection of articles repr. from *The Speaker*, and written by a committee consisting of C. R. Buxton, H. C. Fairfax-Cholmely, J. L. Hammond, F. W. Hirst, L. T. Hobhouse, J. A. Hobson, C. F. G. Masterman, J. H. Morgan, Vaughan Nash).
'Five per cent All Round', *Independent Review*, 5, pp. 37–52.

1907 'The Question of the Lords', *Contemporary Review*, XCI, pp. 1–11.
'The Constitutional Issue', *Contemporary Review*, XCI, pp. 312–18.
Preface to J. H. Bridges, *Essays and Addresses*.
'The Career of Fabianism', *Nation*, I, pp. 182–3.
'A Great Journalist', *Nation*, I, p. 572.
'Sociology and Ethics', *Independent Review*, XII, pp. 322–31.
The Roots of Modern Sociology (Inaugural Lecture, repr. in *Sociology and Philosophy*, pp. 3–19).

1908 Editorial, *Sociological Review*, I, pp. 1–12 (repr. in Abrams, *Origins of British Sociology*, pp. 247–60).
'The Law of the Three Stages', *Sociological Review*, I, pp. 262–79 (repr. in *Sociology and Philosophy*, pp. 59–79).
Review of J. S. Mackenzie, *Lectures on Humanism with Special Reference to Its Bearings on Sociology*, *Sociological Review*, I, pp. 305–6.
'The Prospects of Liberalism', *Contemporary Review*, XCIII, pp. 349–58.
'Idealism and Life', *Nation*, II, pp. 211–12.

1909 'The Mills of God', *Nation*, III, p. 200.
'Idealism and Life', *Nation*, III, pp. 374–5.
'The Lords and the Constitution', *Contemporary Review*, XCVI, pp. 641–51.
Review of Edward A. Westermarck, *The Origin and Development of the Moral Ideas*, *Sociological Review*, II, pp. 402–5.

1910 'John Stuart Mill', *Nation*, VII, pp. 246–7.
'The Contending Forces', *English Review*, IV, pp. 359–71.
Government by the People (People's Suffrage Federation pamphlet).

1911 'Workmen's Insurance and Employers' Liability', *Nation*, IX, pp. 763–4.
'The Harvest of Pessimism', *Nation*, X, pp. 499–500.
'The New Spirit in America', *Contemporary Review*, C, pp. 1–11.

1912 'The Prospects of Anglo-Saxon Democracy', *Atlantic Monthly*, LIX, pp. 345–52.
'The Mind of Conservatism', *Nation*, XI, pp. 151–3.
'The Moral Effects of the War', *Nation*, XII, pp. 253–4.
'Irish Nationalism and Liberal Principle' in J. H. Morgan (ed.), *The New Irish Constitution: An Exposition and Some Arguments*, pp. 361–72.

1913 'Equality of Income', *Nation*, XII, pp. 312, 383–4.
'The Historical Evolution of Property in Fact and in Idea' in Charles Gore (ed.), *Property, Its Duties and Rights Historically, Philosophically and Religiously Regarded*, pp. 1–33.
'The Right to a Living Wage' in *The Industrial Unrest and the Living Wage* (with Introduction by W. Temple), pp. 63–75.

1914 'The Mechanisms of the Soul', *Nation*, XIII, p. 889.
(with G. C. Wheeler and Morris Ginsberg) 'The Material Culture of the Simpler Peoples: An Essay in Correlation', *Sociological Review*, VII, pp. 203–31.

Major items after 1914

1915 'Science and Philosophy as Unifying Forces' in F. S. Marvin (ed.), *The Unity of Western Civilization*, pp. 162–79.

1918 'Are Physical, Biological and Psychological Categories Irreducible?', *Proceedings of the Aristotelian Society*, XVIII, pp. 62–71 (repr. in *Sociology and Philosophy*, pp. 285–93).

1920 Introduction to F. Müller-Lyer, *The History of Social Development*.
'Sociology' in *Hastings' Encyclopaedia of Religion and Ethics*, XI, pp. 654–65 (repr. in *Sociology and Philosophy*, pp. 23–57).
Introduction to Walter Willis, *Trade Boards at Work: A Practical Guide to the Operation of the Trade Boards Acts*.

1921 'Democracy and Civilization', *Sociological Review*, XIII, pp. 125–35.

1922 'The Regulation of Wages' in Robert Cecil *et al.*, *Essays in Liberalism*, pp. 165–75.

1924 'The Philosophy of Development' in J. H. Muirhead (ed.), *Contemporary British Philosophy*, 1st series, pp. 149–88 (repr. in *Sociology and Philosophy*, pp. 295–331).
'Competitive and Social Value', *Economica*, IV, pp. 278–90.

1926 Preface to Susan Liveing, *A Nineteenth-Century Teacher, John Henry Bridges*.
'The Place of Mind in Nature', *Proceedings of the Aristotelian Society*, supplementary vol. V, pp. 112–26.

1927 'Sociology' in R. J. S. McDowall (ed.), *The Mind*, pp. 282–316.

1929 'Comparative Ethics', *Encyclopaedia Britannica* (14th edn), VI, pp. 156–64 (repr. in *Sociology and Philosophy*, pp. 237–67).
'Comparative Psychology', *Encyclopaedia Britannica* (14th edn), VI, pp. 167–70 (repr. in *Sociology and Philosophy*, pp. 271–82).

1930 'Aristocracy', *Encyclopaedia of the Social Sciences*, II, pp. 183–90 (repr. in *Sociology and Philosophy*, pp. 191–206).
'Christianity', *Encyclopaedia of the Social Sciences*, III, pp. 452–61 (repr. in *Sociology and Philosophy*, pp. 169–88).

1931 'The Problem' in J. A. Hobson and Morris Ginsberg, *L. T. Hobhouse, His Life and Work* (repr. in *Sociology and Philosophy*, under the title 'Industry and the State', pp. 209–33).

1946 'Scott as Liberal and Humanist' in A. P. Wadsworth (ed.), *C. P. Scott 1846–1932: The Making of the 'Manchester Guardian'*, pp. 84–90.

1956 'The Simplest Peoples', *British Journal of Sociology*, VII, pp. 77–119 (first published in German in *Zeitschrift für Völkerpsychologie und Soziologie* (1929); repr. in *Sociology and Philosophy*, pp. 109–66).

Manchester Guardian and *Tribune*

The existing records of the *Manchester Guardian* do not, for various reasons, allow all of Hobhouse's contributions to be traced, although they do identify many unsigned pieces. Book reviews were often, but by no means always, signed; 'back-pagers' rarely so (a small selection of these is included in Hobson and Ginsberg, *L. T. Hobhouse*, pp. 292–353). Leading articles, both the 'long' and 'shorts', were, of course, never signed, and it is these which make up the bulk of Hobhouse's contribution. He was a full-time leader-writer from 1897 to 1902; thereafter he frequently and irregularly wrote leaders, especially after 1911 when he became a director of the paper. Some indication of the scale of his contribution is provided by Hobson's calculation that in 1902 alone Hobhouse wrote 322 articles for the paper (*L. T. Hobhouse*, p. 40). And Ayerst estimates that 'Scott and Hobhouse between them wrote nearly half the long leaders in 1916, and over half in 1918. In 1915 and 1917 they wrote well over a third' ('*Guardian*', pp. 377–8). Hobhouse frequently took charge of the editorial policy of the paper during Scott's absences. Sometimes Hobhouse would provide material and opinions which Scott would work up into an article. For all these reasons, it is impossible to disentangle the extent of Hobhouse's contribution to the *Guardian* during this period. The greater part of his writing for the newspaper was obviously of ephemeral interest. I have cited a few of the more important articles where it is clear, from internal or external evidence, that they were written by Hobhouse.

Similarly, there is no record of his contributions to the *Tribune*. He was full-time political editor from December 1905 to January 1907, and some of the leaders of this period clearly bear his stamp. But again, since he was working closely with like-minded colleagues during this period, it would be impossible to identify all the articles which were exclusively his.

OTHER PRIMARY SOURCES

Alexander, Samuel. *Moral Order and Progress: An Analysis of Ethical Conceptions* (1889).
—— *Space, Time and Deity* (1920; repr., with Foreword by D. Emmett, 1966).
—— *Philosophical and Literary Pieces* (with Memoir by J. Laird, 1939).
Angell, Norman. *The Great Illusion* (1911).
—— *After All* (1951).
Atkins, J. B. *Incidents and Reflections* (1947).
Balfour, A. J. *A Defence of Philosophic Doubt* (1879; 2nd edn 1921).
Barker, Ernest. *Political Thought in England 1848–1914* (1915; 2nd edn, 14th imp. 1947).
—— *Philosophy and Politics* (1934).
—— *Age and Youth: Memories of Three Universities, and Father of the Man* (1953).
Barnett, Henrietta. *Canon Barnett: His Life, Work and Friends* (1918).
Bennett, Arnold. *The Journals of Arnold Bennett* (2 vols., 1932).
Benson, E. F. *Sketches from Marlborough* (Marlborough, 1888).
Beveridge, Janet. *An Epic of Clare Market: Birth and Early Days of L.S.E.* (1960).
Beveridge, W. H. *The London School of Economics and Its Problems, 1919–1937* (1960).
Blease, Walter Lyon. *A Short History of English Liberalism* (1913).
Bliss, W. P. D. (ed.). *The Encyclopaedia of Social Reform* (1897; 2nd edn 1908).

Blunt, W. S. *My Diaries. Being a Personal Narrative of Events 1888–1914* (2 vols., 1919 and 1920).

Bonar, James. *Philosophy and Political Economy in Some of Their Historical Relations* (1893; 3rd edn 1922).

Bosanquet, Bernard. *The Civilization of Christendom, and Other Studies* (1893).

—— *The Philosophical Theory of the State* (1899; 2nd edn 1910; 3rd edn 1920; 4th edn 1923, repr. 1925 and 1930).

—— *Social and International Ideals: Being Studies in Patriotism* (1917).

—— *Some Suggestions in Ethics* (1918).

—— *What Religion Is* (1920).

—— (ed.). *Aspects of the Social Problem* (1895).

—— (See also under Muirhead, J. H.).

Bosanquet, Helen. *Bernard Bosanquet* (1924).

Bradley, F. H. *The Presuppositions of Critical History* (1874).

—— *Ethical Studies* (1876; 2nd edn Oxford, 1927).

—— *The Principles of Logic* (2 vols., 1883).

—— *Appearance and Reality* (1893; 2nd edn 1897).

—— *Essays on Truth and Reality* (Oxford, 1914).

Bridges, J. H. *Essays and Addresses* (1907).

Brown, Jethro. *Underlying Principles of Modern Legislation* (1912).

Bryce, James. *Address on the Aims and Programme of the Sociological Society* (1905).

Burrows, Herbert, and Hobson, J. A. (eds.). *William Clarke: A Collection of His Writings with a Biographical Sketch* (1908).

Bury, J. B. *The Idea of Progress* (1920).

Buxton, C. R. *et al. Towards a Social Policy: Suggestions for Constructive Reform* (1905).

Caird, Edward. *The Moral Aspect of the Economical Problem* (1888).

Cairnes, J. E. *Leading Principles of Political Economy* (1873).

Cecil, Robert *et al. Essays in Liberalism* (1922).

Chamberlain, J. *et al. The Radical Programme* (1885; repr., with Introduction and notes by D. A. Hamer, Brighton, 1971).

Chatterton-Hill, Georges. *Heredity and Selection in Sociology* (1907).

Chesterton, G. K. *Autobiography* (1936).

Churchill, Winston. *Liberalism and the Social Problem* (1909).

Coulton, G. G. *Fourscore Years* (Cambridge, 1943).

Darwin, Charles. *The Origin of Species* (1859; pbk, with Introduction by J. W. Burrow, Harmondsworth, 1968).

Dicey, A. V. *Lectures on the Relation between Law and Public Opinion during the Nineteenth Century* (1905; 2nd edn 1914).

—— *Memorials of A. V. Dicey, Being Chiefly Letters and Diaries* (ed. R. S. Rait, 1925).

Drummond, Henry. *The Ascent of Man* (1894).

Duncan, David. *The Life and Letters of Herbert Spencer* (1908).

Elton, Oliver. *C. E. Montague: A Memoir* (1929).

Ensor, R. C. K. (ed.). *Modern Socialism: As Set Forth by Socialists in Their Speeches, Writings and Programmes* (1904; 2nd edn 1907).

Escott, T. H. S. *England: Its People, Polity, and Pursuits* (1879; 2nd edn 1885).

Fairman, Frank. *Herbert Spencer on Socialism: A Reply* (1884).

—— *The Principles of Socialism made Plain* (with Preface by William Morris, 1888).

Fisher, H. A. L. *James Bryce* (2 vols., 1927).

—— *An Unfinished Autobiography* (ed. D. Ogg, 1940).

Flint, Robert. *Socialism* (1894).
Follett, M. P. *The New State: Group Organization the Solution of Popular Government* (New York, 1918).
Foxwell, H. S. *Irregularity of Employment and Fluctuations of Prices* (Edinburgh, 1886).
Galton, Francis. *Essays in Eugenics* (1909).
George, Henry. *Progress and Poverty* (1881).
—— *A Perplexed Philosopher: Being an Examination of Mr Herbert Spencer's Various Utterances on the Land Question with Some Incidental Reference to his Synthetic Philosophy* (1893).
Ginsberg, Morris. *Studies in Sociology* (1932).
—— *Sociology* (1934).
—— *The Unity of Mankind* (1935).
—— *Reason and Unreason in Society* (1947).
—— *The Idea of Progress: A Revaluation* (1953).
—— *On the Diversity of Morals* (1956).
—— *Evolution and Progress* (1961).
—— and Bartlett, F., Lindgren, E. J., Thouless, R. H. (eds.). *The Study of Society* (1939; 6th imp. 1961).
Gooch, G. P. *Under Six Reigns* (1958).
Gore, Charles (ed.). *Property, Its Duties and Rights Historically, Philosophically and Religiously Regarded* (1913).
Goschen, G. J. *Essays and Addresses on Economic Questions 1865–1893* (1905).
Green, T. H. *Liberal Legislation and Freedom of Contract* (Oxford, 1881; also in *Works*, III).
—— *Prolegomena to Ethics* (ed. A. C. Bradley, Oxford, 1883).
—— *Works* (ed. R. L. Nettleship, 3 vols., 1885–8).
—— *Lectures on the Principles of Political Obligation* (ed. Bernard Bosanquet, 1895).
Hammond, J. L., Hirst, F. W. and Murray, Gilbert. *Liberalism and the Empire* (1900).
Headley, F. W. *Darwinism and Modern Socialism* (1909).
Hetherington, H. J. W. and Muirhead, J. H. *Social Purpose: A Contribution to the Philosophy of Civic Society* (1918).
Hewins, W. A. S. *The Apologia of an Imperialist* (2 vols., 1929).
Hirst, F. W. *In the Golden Days* (1947).
Hobhouse, Stephen. *Forty Years and an Epilogue: An Autobiography 1881–1951* (1951).
—— 'Towards Harmony: A Century of Letters Mainly to His Family' (ed. R. W. Hobhouse, typescript, L.S.E. Library, 1965).
Hobson, J. A. *The Evolution of Modern Capitalism* (1894).
—— *John Ruskin Social Reformer* (1898).
—— *The Economics of Distribution* (New York, 1900).
—— *The Psychology of Jingoism* (1901).
—— *The Social Problem* (1901).
—— *Imperialism: A Study* (1902; 2nd edn 1905; 3rd edn 1938).
—— *The Crisis of Liberalism: New Issues of Democracy* (1909; repr., with Introduction by P. F. Clarke, Brighton, 1974).
—— *The Industrial System: An Enquiry into Earned and Unearned Income* (1909).
—— *Work and Wealth* (1914).
—— *Towards Social Equality* (1931).
—— *Confessions of an Economic Heretic* (1938).
—— and Ginsberg, Morris. *L. T. Hobhouse, His Life and Work* (1931).
Hobson, S. G. *A Pilgrim to the Left: Memoirs of a Modern Revolutionist* (1938).

Holmes–Laski Letters. *The Correspondence of Mr Justice Holmes and Harold J. Laski 1916–35* (ed. Mark de Wolfe Howe, 1953).
Huxley, T. H. *Evolution and Ethics* (Oxford, 1893; ed. J. Huxley, London, 1943).
—— *The Life and Letters of Thomas Henry Huxley* (ed. L. Huxley, 3 vols., 1900; 2nd edn 1903).
Inge, W. R. *The Idea of Progress* (Oxford, 1920).
Jevons, W. S. *The State in Relation to Labour* (1882).
Jones, Henry. *Idealism as a Practical Creed* (Glasgow, 1909).
—— *The Working Faith of the Social Reformer, and Other Essays* (1910).
—— *Old Memories: Autobiography* (1929).
—— and Muirhead, J. H. *The Life and Philosophy of Edward Caird* (Glasgow, 1921).
Keynes, J. M. *Essays in Persuasion* (1931; *Collected Works*, XI, 1972).
Kidd, Benjamin. *Social Evolution* (1894).
—— *Principles of Western Civilization* (1902).
Kirkup, T. *History of Socialism* (1892; 2nd edn 1906).
Kropotkin, Peter. *Mutual Aid: A Factor of Evolution* (1902; repr., with Introduction by Paul Avrich, 1972).
Langshaw, H. *Socialism and the Historic Function of Liberalism* (1925).
Laurie, A. P. *Pictures and Politics* (1934).
Liveing, Susan. *A Nineteenth-Century Teacher, John Henry Bridges* (with Preface by L. T. Hobhouse, 1926).
Lloyd Morgan, C. *Emergent Evolution* (1923).
Loch, C. S. (ed.). *Methods of Social Advance* (1904).
MacDonald, J. Ramsay. *Socialism and Society* (1905).
McDowall, R. J. S. (ed.). *The Mind* (1927).
MacIver, R. M. *Community: A Sociological Study* (1917; 4th edn 1970).
—— *As a Tale that is Told: The Autobiography of R. M. MacIver* (Chicago, 1968).
—— and Page, C. *Society: An Introductory Analysis* (1949).
Mackay, T. (ed.). *A Plea for Liberty: An Argument against Socialism and Socialistic Legislation* (with Introduction by Herbert Spencer, 1891).
McKechnie, W. S. *The State and the Individual: An Introduction to Political Science with Special Reference to Socialistic and Individualistic Theories* (Glasgow, 1896).
—— *The New Democracy and the Constitution* (1912).
Mackenzie, J. S. *An Introduction to Social Philosophy* (Glasgow, 1890; 2nd edn 1895).
—— *Lectures on Humanism, with Special Reference to Its Bearings on Sociology* (1907).
—— *John Stuart Mackenzie* (ed. H. M. Mackenzie, with Foreword by J. H. Muirhead, 1936).
Mackintosh, R. *From Comte to Benjamin Kidd* (1899).
Maine, H. S. *Ancient Law* (1861).
Mallet, Bernard. *British Budgets 1887–1913* (1913).
Marett, R. R. *Tylor* (1936).
—— *A Jerseyman at Oxford* (1941).
Marriott, J. A. R. *Memories of Four-Score Years* (1946).
Marshall, Alfred, *Principles of Economics* (1890; 8th edn 1920; 9th (Variorum) edn 1961).
—— *Memorials of Alfred Marshall* (ed. A. C. Pigou, 1925).
—— *The Official Papers of Alfred Marshall* (ed. J. M. Keynes, 1926).
Marvin, F. S. *Comte: The Founder of Sociology* (1936).
—— (ed.). *Progress and History* (1916).
Massingham, H. W. *H.W.M.: A Selection from the Writings of H. W. Massingham* (ed. H. J. Massingham, 1925).

Masterman, C. F. G. (ed.). *The Heart of the Empire: Discussions of Modern City Life in England with an Essay on Imperialism* (1901; repr., with Introduction by B. Gilbert, Brighton, 1973).
Mill, J. S. *Principles of Political Economy* (2 vols., 1848; Books IV and V, pbk, with Introduction by Donald Winch, Harmondsworth, 1970).
—— *On Liberty* (1859; pbk, with Introduction by Gertrude Himmelfarb, Harmondsworth, 1974).
—— *Collected Works* (Toronto, 1965–).
Milner, Alfred. *Arnold Toynbee: A Reminiscence* (1895).
Montague, C. E. and Ward, Mrs Humphry. *W. T. Arnold* (Manchester, 1907).
Montague, F. C. *The Limits of Individual Liberty: An Essay* (1885).
Morley, John. *The Life of Richard Cobden* (2 vols., 1879; 9th edn, 1 vol., 1903).
—— *Miscellanies* (4th series, 1908).
—— *Recollections* (2 vols., 1917).
Muirhead, J. H. *The Starting Point of Poor Law Reform* (1910; first published as *By What Authority?* 1909).
—— *The Platonic Tradition in Anglo-Saxon Philosophy* (1931).
—— *The Man Versus the State as a Present Issue* (1939).
—— *Reflections by a Journeyman in Philosophy* (ed. John W. Harvey, 1942).
—— (ed.). *Contemporary British Philosophy: Personal Statements* (1st series, 1924; 2nd series, 1925).
—— (ed.). *Bernard Bosanquet and His Friends: Letters Illustrating Sources and Development of His Philosophical Opinions* (1935).
Murray, Gilbert. *An Unfinished Autobiography* (1960).
Nettleship, R. L. *Philosophical Remains* (ed., with Biographical Sketch, A. C. Bradley, 1897; 2nd edn 1901).
Nevinson, H. W. *Changes and Chances* (1923).
—— *More Changes, More Chances* (1925).
—— *Last Changes, Last Chances* (1928).
—— *Visions and Memories* (ed. E. Sharpe, with Introduction by Gilbert Murray, Oxford, 1944).
Newbolt, Henry. *My World as in My Time* (1932).
Olivier, Sydney. *Letters and Selected Writings* (ed. Margaret Olivier, 1948).
Pearson, Karl. *Inquiries into Human Faculty and Its Development* (1883).
—— *National Life from the Standpoint of Science* (1901; 2nd edn 1905).
—— *The Groundwork of Eugenics* (1909).
Pease, E. R. *The History of the Fabian Society* (1916; 2nd edn 1925; 3rd edn 1963).
Pentland, Lady. *Rt Hon. John Sinclair, Lord Pentland* (1928).
Pethick-Lawrence, F. *Fate Has Been Kind* (1942).
Rae, John. *Contemporary Socialism* (1884; 2nd (rev.) edn, with new chapter on 'State Socialism', 1891; 3rd edn, with new chapter covering 1891–1900, 1901).
Reid, Andrew (ed.). *Why I am a Liberal* (1885).
Ritchie, D. G. *The Moral Function of the State* (1887).
—— *Darwinism and Politics* (1889; 2nd edn 1891; 3rd edn 1895).
—— *The Principles of State Interference* (1891).
—— *Darwin and Hegel, with Other Philosophical Studies* (1893).
—— *Natural Rights: A Criticism of Some Political and Ethical Conceptions* (1895).
—— *Studies in Political and Social Ethics* (1902).
—— *Philosophical Studies* (ed., with Memoir, Robert Latta, 1905).
Rockow, Lewis. *Contemporary Political Thought in England* (1926).

Romanes, G. J. *Darwin and after Darwin* (3 vols., 1894–7).
Rowntree, B. Seebohm. *Poverty: A Study in Town Life* (1901).
Sadleir, M. *Michael Sadler 1861–1943* (1949).
Saleeby, C. W. *Sociology* (1906).
—— *Parenthood and Race Culture: An Outline of Eugenics* (1909).
Samuel, Herbert. *Liberalism: An Attempt to State the Principles and Proposals of Contemporary Liberalism in England* (1902).
—— *Memoirs* (1945).
Shaw, G. B. *Collected Letters of George Bernard Shaw 1874–97* (ed. Dan H. Lawrence, 1965).
—— (ed.). *Fabianism and the Empire* (1900).
—— *et al. Fabian Essays in Socialism* (1889; 6th edn, with Introduction by Asa Briggs, 1962).
S[idgwick], A. and E. M. *Henry Sidgwick, A Memoir* (1906).
Sidgwick, Henry. *The Methods of Ethics* (1874; 7th edn 1907).
—— *The Principles of Political Economy* (1883; 2nd edn 1887).
—— *The Elements of Politics* (1891; 2nd edn 1897).
—— *Philosophy: Its Scope and Relations* (1902).
—— *Miscellaneous Essays and Addresses* (1904).
'Six Oxford Men'. *Essays in Liberalism* (1897).
Smith, Bruce, *Liberty and Liberalism: A Protest against the Growing Tendency toward Undue Interference by the State with Individual Liberty, Private Enterprise and the Rights of Property* (1887).
Sorley, W. R. *On the Basis of Ethics with Special Reference to the Theory of Evolution* (privately printed, 1884).
Spencer, Herbert, *Social Statics: Or the Conditions Essential to Human Happiness Specified, and the First of them Developed* (1851; 2nd (rev. and abridged) edn, printed with *The Man Versus the State*, 1892).
—— *Over-Legislation* (1854).
—— *The Study of Sociology* (1873).
—— *The Principles of Sociology* (1876; abridged, ed. S. Andreski, 1969).
—— *The Man Versus the State* (1884; repr., with *Social Statics*, 1892; repr., with Introduction by D. G. MacRae, 1969).
—— *The Principles of Ethics*, II (1893).
—— *Autobiography* (2 vols., 1904).
—— (See also under Duncan, David).
Spender, Harold. *The Fire of Life: A Book of Memories* (with Foreword by F. S. Marvin, n.d. [?1926]).
Spender, J. A. *Life, Journalism and Politics* (1927).
Stephen, Leslie. *The English Utilitarians*, I: *Bentham* (1900).
Sutherland, Alexander. *The Origin and Growth of the Moral Instinct* (2 vols., 1898).
Tillett, Ben. *Memories and Reflections* (with Foreword by P. Snowden, 1931).
Toynbee, Arnold. '*Progress and Poverty*': *A Criticism of Mr Henry George* (1883).
—— *Lectures on the Industrial Revolution in England* (1884; repr., with Introduction by T. S. Ashton, Newton Abbot, 1969).
Toynbee, Arnold J. *Acquaintances* (Oxford, 1967).
Toynbee, Gertrude (ed.). *Reminiscences and Letters of Joseph and Arnold Toynbee* (n.d. [?1910]).
Trevelyan, Charles P. *From Liberalism to Labour* (1921).
Tylor, E. B. *Primitive Culture* (2 vols., 1871).
Wallace, William. *Lectures and Essays on Natural Theology and Ethics* (ed., with Biographical Introduction, E. Caird, 1898).

Wallas, Graham. *Human Nature in Politics* (1908; 2nd edn 1910; 3rd edn 1920; 4th edn 1948).
—— *The Great Society, A Psychological Analysis* (1914).
—— *Men and Ideas* (ed. May Wallas, with Preface by Gilbert Murray, 1940).
Watson, J. *The State in Peace and War* (Glasgow, 1919).
Webb (née Potter), Beatrice. *The Cooperative Movement in Great Britain* (1891).
—— *My Apprenticeship* (1926; pbk, with Introduction by B. Jackson, Harmondsworth, 1971).
—— *Our Partnership* (ed. B. Drake and M. I. Cole, 1948).
—— *Diaries 1924–1932* (ed. M. I. Cole, 1956).
Webb, Sidney. *Socialism in England* (Baltimore, 1889; repr. London, 1893).
Webb, Beatrice and Sidney. *Industrial Democracy* (2 vols., 1897).
—— —— *Methods of Social Study* (1932).
Weber, Max. *Max Weber on the Methodology of the Social Sciences* (ed. Edward A. Shils and Henry A. Finch, Glencoe, Illinois, 1949).
Westermarck, Edward A. *The Origin and Development of the Moral Ideas* (2 vols., 1906 and 1908).
—— *Sociology as a University Study* (1908).
—— *Festskrift Tillegnad Edvard Westermarck* (Helsingfors, 1912).
Wilde, Oscar. *The Soul of Man under Socialism* (1891; repr., with *Intentions*, in *Collected Works* (1908; repr. 1969), VIII).
Wilson, Roland K. *The Province of the State* (1911).

SECONDARY SOURCES

Books

Abbagnano, Nicola. *Il Nuovo Idealismo Inglese e Americano* (Naples, 1927).
Abrams, Philip. *The Origins of British Sociology 1834–1914* (Chicago, 1968).
—— *Being and Becoming in Sociology* (Durham, 1972).
Adelman, Paul. *The Rise of the Labour Party 1880–1945* (1972).
Ahmad, Zeyauddin. *Social Philosophy of L. T. Hobhouse* (Patna, 1965).
Alpert, H. (ed.). *Robert M. MacIver: Teacher and Sociologist* (Northampton, Mass., 1953).
Anderson, M. *Noel Buxton: A Life* (1952).
Annan, Noel. *Leslie Stephen: His Thought and Character in Relation to His Time* (1951).
—— *The Curious Strength of Positivism in English Political Thought* (1959).
Antoni, Carlo. *From History to Sociology: The Transition in German Historical Thinking* (1962; first published in Italian 1940).
Austin, J. L. *How to do Things with Words* (Oxford, 1962).
Ausubel, Herman. *In Hard Times: Reformers among the Late-Victorians* (New York, 1960).
Ayerst, David. '*Guardian*', *Biography of a Newspaper* (1971).
Baillie, J. *The Belief in Progress* (1950).
Ball, Oona Howard. *Sidney Ball: Memories and Impressions of 'An Ideal Don'* (Oxford, 1923).
Banton, M. (ed.). *Darwinism and the Study of Society* (1961).
Barker, Bernard (ed.). *Ramsay MacDonald's Political Writings* (1972).
Barker, Michael. *Gladstone and Radicalism: The Reconstruction of Liberal Policy in Britain 1885–94* (Brighton, 1975).
Barnes, H. E. *An Introduction to the History of Sociology* (Chicago, 1948).
Barnett, S. (ed.). *A Century of Darwin* (1959).
Barry, Brian. *Political Argument* (1965).

BIBLIOGRAPHY

Barry, E. Eldon. *Nationalization in British Politics: The Historical Background* (1965).

Beales, A. C. F. *The History of Peace. A Short Account of the Organised Movements for International Peace* (1931).

Beales, H. L. *The Making of Social Policy* (1945).

Becker, Carl. *Progress and Power* (New York, 1936; 2nd edn, with Introduction by Leo Gershoy, 1965).

Beer, S. H. *Modern British Politics* (1965).

Beetham, David. *Max Weber and the Theory of Modern Politics* (1974).

Bellamy, Joyce M. and Saville, John (eds.). *Dictionary of Labour Biography* (3 vols., 1972–6).

Bendix, Reinhard and Roth, Guenther. *Scholarship and Partisanship: Essays on Max Weber* (New York, 1970).

Berlin, Isaiah. *Four Essays on Liberty* (Oxford, 1969).

Best, Geoffrey. *Mid-Victorian Britain 1851–75* (1971).

Blewett, Neal. *The Peers, the Parties, and the People. The General Elections of 1910* (1972).

Boardman, Philip. *Patrick Geddes: Maker of the Future* (Chapel Hill, North Carolina, 1944).

Bock, Kenneth. *The Acceptance of Histories: Towards a Perspective in Social Science* (New York, 1957).

Bottomore, T. B. *Sociology, A Guide to Problems and Literature* (1962; 2nd edn, 1971).

Brailsford, H. N. *The Life Work of J. A. Hobson* (1948).

Bramson, L. *The Political Context of Sociology* (Princeton, 1961).

Brennan, T., Cooney, E. W. and Pollins, H. *Social Change in South West Wales* (1954).

Briggs, Asa. *Seebohm Rowntree 1871–1954* (1961).

—— and Saville, John (eds.). *Essays in Labour History* (2 vols., 1960 and 1971).

Brown, Alan Willard. *The Metaphysical Society. Victorian Minds in Crisis 1869–80* (New York, 1947).

Brown, K. D. (ed.). *Essays in Anti-Labour History: Responses to the Rise of Labour in History* (1974).

Bullock, A. and Shock, M. (eds.). *The Liberal Tradition* (Oxford, 1956).

Burrow, J. W. *Evolution and Society: A Study in Victorian Social Theory* (Cambridge, 1966; 2nd edn 1970).

Butt, J. and Clarke, I. F. (eds.). *The Victorians and Social Protest* (Newton Abbot, 1973).

Caine, Sydney. *The History of the Foundation of the L.S.E.* (1963).

Carpenter, L. P. *G. D. H. Cole: An Intellectual Biography* (Cambridge, 1973).

Carter, Hugh. *The Social Theories of L. T. Hobhouse* (Chapel Hill, North Carolina, 1927).

Childe, V. Gordon. *Social Evolution* (1951).

Clark, T. N. *Prophets and Patrons: The French University and the Emergence of the Social Sciences* (Cambridge, Mass., 1973).

Clarke, P. F. *Lancashire and the New Liberalism* (Cambridge, 1971).

Clegg, H. A., Fox A. and Thompson, A. F. *A History of British Trade Unions since 1889*, I: *1889–1910* (Oxford, 1964).

Coats, A. W. (ed.). *The Classical Economists and Economic Policy* (1971).

Cockshut, A. O. J. *The Unbelievers: English Agnostic Thought 1840–90* (1964).

Cole, G. D. H. *A History of Socialist Thought* (4 vols., 1954).

Cole, Margaret. *The Life of G. D. H. Cole* (1971).

—— *The Story of Fabian Socialism* (1961).

Cullen, Michael J. *The Statistical Movement in Early Victorian Britain: The Foundations of Empirical Social Research* (Brighton, 1976).

Dangerfield, George. *The Strange Death of Liberal England* (1935; 2nd edn 1966).

Dawes Hicks, G. *Critical Realism: Studies in the Philosophy of Mind and Nature* (1938).

Deane, Herbert A. *The Political Ideas of H. J. Laski* (New York, 1955).

De Bunsen, V. *Charles Roden Buxton* (1948).
Dowse, R. E. *Left in the Centre: The I.L.P. 1893–1940* (1966).
Emy, H. V. *Liberals, Radicals and Social Politics 1892–1914* (Cambridge, 1973).
Ensor, R. C. K. *England 1870–1914* (Oxford, 1936).
Erikson, Erik. *Identity: Youth and Crisis* (1968).
Feinberg, Joel. *Social Philosophy* (Englewood Cliffs, N.J., 1973).
Fine, Sidney. *Laissez-Faire and the General Welfare State: A Study of Conflict in American Thought 1869–1901* (Michigan, 1956).
Fisher, John. *That Miss Hobhouse* (1971).
Fletcher, Ronald. *Instinct in Man* (1957; 2nd edn 1968).
—— *The Making of Sociology* (2 vols., 1971).
—— (ed.). *The Science of Society and the Unity of Mankind: A Memorial Volume for Morris Ginsberg* (1974).
Flew, A. G. N. *Evolutionary Ethics* (1967).
Flügel, J. C. *A Hundred Years of Psychology* (1933; 2nd edn, rev. D. J. West, 1964).
Forster, E. M. *Goldsworthy Lowes Dickinson* (1934).
Fraser, Derek. *The Evolution of the British Welfare State* (1973).
Fremantle, Anne. *This Little Band of Prophets. The Story of the Gentle Fabians* (1960).
Fruchon, Pierre. *F. H. Bradley, The Presuppositions of Critical History: Etude et Traduction* (Paris, 1965).
Fry, Anna Ruth. *Emily Hobhouse: A Memoir* (1929).
Giddens, Anthony. *Politics and Sociology in the Thought of Max Weber* (1972).
Gilbert, Bentley B. *The Evolution of National Insurance in Great Britain: The Origins of the Welfare State* (1966).
—— *British Social Policy 1914–39* (1970).
Ginsberg, Morris (ed.). *Law and Public Opinion in England in the Twentieth Century* (1959).
Girvetz, Harry K. *The Evolution of Liberalism: From Wealth to Welfare* (New York, 1950).
Gosden, P. H. J. H. *Self-Help: Voluntary Associations in the Nineteenth Century* (1973).
Grampp, W. D. *The Manchester School of Economics* (1960).
Grisewood, H. (ed.). *Ideas and Beliefs of the Victorians* (1949).
Gross, John. *The Rise and Fall of the Man of Letters: Aspects of English Literary Life since 1800* (1969).
Gurvitch, Georges and Moore, Wilbert E. (eds.). *Twentieth Century Sociology* (New York, 1945).
Haldar, Hiralal. *Neo-Hegelianism* (1927).
Halévy, Elie. *A History of the English People in the Nineteenth Century*, v: *Imperialism and the Rise of Labour (1895–1905)* (first published in French 1926; 1st English edn 1929; 2nd edn 1951).
—— *The Era of Tyrannies: Essays on Socialism and War* (1967).
Haller, John S., Jnr. *Outcasts from Evolution: Scientific Attitudes of Racial Inferiority 1859–1900* (Urbana, Illinois, 1971).
Haller, Mark. *Eugenics* (New Brunswick, N.J., 1963).
Hamburger, Joseph. *Intellectuals in Politics: John Stuart Mill and the Philosophic Radicals* (New Haven, Conn., 1965).
Hamer, D. A. *John Morley: Liberal Intellectual in Politics* (Oxford, 1968).
—— *Liberal Politics in the Age of Gladstone and Rosebery. A Study in Leadership and Policy* (Oxford, 1972).
Hammond, J. L. *The Growth of the Common Enjoyment* (1933).
—— *C. P. Scott of the 'Manchester Guardian'* (1934).
Harris, H. W. *J. A. Spender* (1946).

Harris, José. *Unemployment and Politics: A Study in English Social Policy 1886–1914* (Oxford, 1972).
—— *W. H. Beveridge: A Biography* (Oxford, 1977).
Harris, Marvin. *The Rise of Anthropological Theory* (1969).
Harrison, Brian. *Drink and the Victorians: The Temperance Question in England 1815–72* (1971).
Harrison, Royden. *Before the Socialists: Studies in Labour and Politics 1861–81* (1965).
Harvie, Christopher. *The Lights of Liberalism: University Liberals and the Challenge of Democracy 1860–86* (1976).
Havard, W. C. *Henry Sidgwick and Later Utilitarian Political Philosophy* (Gainesville, Florida, 1959).
Havighurst, A. F. *Radical Journalist: H. W. Massingham (1860–1924)* (Cambridge, 1974).
Hawthorn, Geoffrey. *Enlightenment and Despair: A History of Sociology* (Cambridge, 1976).
Hay, J. R. *The Origins of the Liberal Welfare Reforms 1906–1914* (1975).
Hearnshaw, F. J. C. (ed.). *Edwardian England* (1933).
Hearnshaw, L. S. *A Short History of British Psychology 1840–1940* (1964).
Henley, Dorothy. *Rosalind Howard, Countess of Carlisle* (1958).
Hetherington, H. J. W. *The Life and Letters of Sir Henry Jones* (1924).
Himmelfarb, Gertrude. *Darwin and the Darwinian Revolution* (1959).
—— *Victorian Minds* (New York, 1968).
—— *On Liberty and Liberalism: The Case of John Stuart Mill* (New York, 1974).
Hingston Quiggin, A. *Haddon the Head-Hunter* (Cambridge, 1942).
Hobsbawm, E. J. *Labouring Men, Studies in the History of Labour* (1964).
Hofstadter, Richard. *Social Darwinism in American Thought 1860–1915* (Philadelphia, 1944; 2nd edn, Boston, 1955).
Hollis, P. (ed.). *Pressure from Without in Early Victorian England* (1974).
Holloway, J. *The Victorian Sage: Studies in Argument* (1953; 2nd edn 1962).
Honigmann, John H. (ed.). *Handbook of Social and Cultural Anthropology* (Chicago, 1973).
Houang, F. *La Neo-Hégélianisme en Angleterre: La Philosophie de Bernard Bosanquet* (Paris, 1954).
Hughes, H. Stuart. *Consciousness and Society: The Reorientation of European Social Thought 1890–1930* (1959).
Hutchison, T. W. *A Review of Economic Doctrines 1870–1929* (Oxford, 1953).
Hyams, Edward. *The New Statesman: The History of the First 50 Years 1913–63* (1963).
Hynes, Samuel. *The Edwardian Turn of Mind* (Princeton, 1968).
Jha, N. *The Age of Marshall: Aspects of British Economic Thought 1890–1915* (1963; 2nd edn 1973).
Jones, G. Stedman. *Outcast London: A Study in the Relationship between Classes in Victorian Society* (Oxford, 1971).
Jones, Peter D'A. *The Christian Socialist Revival 1877–1914: Religion, Class and Social Conscience in Late-Victorian England* (Princeton, 1968).
Kitson-Clark, G. S. R. *Churchmen and the Condition of England 1832–85* (1973).
Koebner, R. and Schmidt, H. D. *Imperialism: The Story and Significance of a Political Word 1840–1960* (Cambridge, 1964).
Koss, Stephen. *Lord Haldane, Scapegoat for Liberalism* (New York, 1969).
—— *Sir John Brunner Radical Plutocrat 1842–1919* (Cambridge, 1970).
—— *Fleet Street Radical: A. G. Gardiner and the 'Daily News'* (1973).
Lane, Robert E. *Political Thinking and Consciousness: The Private Life of the Political Mind* (Chicago, 1969).

Laski, H. J. *The Decline of Liberalism* (1940).
—— *The State in Theory and Practice* (1941).
Lawrence, E. P. *Henry George in the British Isles* (East Lansing, Michigan, 1957).
Le Chevalier. *Ethique et Idéalisme: Le Courant Néo-Hégelien en Angleterre: Bernard Bosanquet et Ses Amis* (Paris, 1963).
Letwin, Shirley. *The Pursuit of Certainty* (Cambridge, 1965).
Lewis, H. D. *Freedom and History* (1962).
—— (ed.). *Contemporary British Philosophy*, III (1956).
Lichtheim, George. *A Short History of Socialism* (1970).
Lindsay, A. D. *The Modern Democratic State*, I (1943).
Lloyd, E. M. H. *Experiments in State Control* (Oxford, 1924).
Lofthouse, W. F. *F. H. Bradley* (1949).
Lubenow, W. C. *The Politics of Government Growth: Early Victorian Attitudes toward State Intervention 1833–1848* (Newton Abbot, 1971).
Lubove, Roy. *The Professional Altruist: The Emergence of Social Work as a Career 1880–1930* (Cambridge, Mass., 1965).
Lukes, Steven. *Emile Durkheim: His Life and Work. A Historical and Critical Study* (1973).
—— *Individualism* (Oxford, 1973).
Lynd, Helen Merrel. *England in the Eighteen-Eighties: Toward a Social Basis for Freedom* (New York, 1945; 2nd edn, London, 1968).
McBriar, A. M. *Fabian Socialism and English Politics 1884–1918* (Cambridge, 1962; repr. 1966).
Maccoby, S. *English Radicalism 1886–1914* (1953).
Macintyre, Alasdair. *Secularization and Moral Change* (1967).
—— *A Short History of Ethics* (1967).
McKendrick, Neil (ed.). *Historical Perspectives: Studies in English Thought and Society in Honour of J. H. Plumb* (1974).
McKibbin, R. I. *The Evolution of the Labour Party 1910–24* (Oxford, 1974).
MacRae, Donald G. *Ideology and Society: Papers in Sociology and Politics* (1961).
Magnus, P. *Gladstone* (1954).
Mairet, Philip. *Pioneer of Sociology: The Life and Letters of Patrick Geddes* (1957).
Mandelbaum, Maurice. *History, Man, and Reason: A Study in Nineteenth-Century Thought* (Baltimore, 1971).
Manning, D. J. *Liberalism* (1976).
Marshall, T. H. *Citizenship and Social Class, and Other Essays* (Cambridge, 1950).
—— *Social Policy* (1965; 3rd edn 1970).
Martin, David A. *Pacifism: An Historical and Sociological Study* (1965).
Martin, Laurence W. *Peace without Victory: Woodrow Wilson and the British Liberals* (New Haven, Conn., 1958).
Marwick, Arthur. *Britain in the Century of Total War: War, Peace and Social Change 1900–1967* (1968; pbk, Harmondsworth, 1970).
Masterman, Lucy. *C. F. G. Masterman: A Biography* (1939).
Matthew, H. C. G. *The Liberal Imperialists: The Ideas and Politics of a Post-Gladstonian Elite* (Oxford, 1973).
Metz, Rudolf. *A Hundred Years of British Philosophy* (first published in German 1935; trans. J. W. Harvey, T. E. Jessop and Henry Sturt, ed. J. H. Muirhead, 1938).
Midwinter, E. C. *Victorian Social Reform* (1968).
Mills, C. Wright. *The Marxists* (Harmondsworth, 1963).
Mills, Haslam. *The Manchester Guardian: A Century of History* (Manchester, 1921).

Milne, A. J. M. *The Social Philosophy of English Idealism* (1962).
—— *Freedom and Rights* (1968).
Mitchell, G. D. *A Hundred Years of Sociology* (1968).
Morgan, K. O. *The Age of Lloyd George: The Liberal Party and British Politics 1890–1929* (1971).
—— *Keir Hardie, Radical and Socialist* (1975).
Morris, A. J. A. *Radicalism against War 1906–14: The Advocacy of Peace and Retrenchment* (1972).
—— (ed.). *Edwardian Radicalism 1900–1914: Some Aspects of British Radicalism* (1974).
Mowat, C. L. *Britain between the Wars 1918–1940* (1955; repr. 1972).
—— *The Charity Organization Society 1869–1913: Its Ideas and Work* (1961).
Needham, Joseph. *Integrative Levels: A Revaluation of the Idea of Progress* (Oxford, 1937).
Nicholson, J. A. *Some Aspects of the Philosophy of Hobhouse: Logic and Social Theory* (Urbana, Illinois, 1928).
Nisbet, Robert. *The Sociological Tradition* (New York, 1966).
—— *Social Change and History: Aspects of the Western Theory of Development* (New York, 1969).
Nowell-Smith, S. (ed.). *Edwardian England* (Oxford, 1964).
Nozick, Robert. *Anarchy, State and Utopia* (New York, 1974).
Oberschall, Anthony (ed.). *The Establishment of Empirical Sociology* (New York, 1973).
Owen, John E. *L. T. Hobhouse, Sociologist* (with Introduction by Ronald Fletcher, 1974).
Parsons, Talcott. *The Structure of Social Action* (New York, 1937).
Passmore, J. A. *A Hundred Years of Philosophy* (1957; pbk, Harmondsworth, 1968).
—— *The Perfectibility of Man* (1970).
Pearson, E. S. *Karl Pearson: An Appreciation of Some Aspects of His Life and Work* (Cambridge, 1938).
Peel, J. D. Y. *Herbert Spencer: The Evolution of a Sociologist* (1971).
Peele, Gillian and Cook, Chris (eds.). *The Politics of Re-appraisal* (1975).
Pelling, Henry. *The Origins of the Labour Party 1880–1900* (1954; 2nd edn, Oxford, 1965).
—— *Popular Politics and Society in Late-Victorian Britain* (1968).
Penniman, T. K. *A Hundred Years of Anthropology* (1935; 3rd edn 1965).
Perkin, Harold. *The Origins of Modern English Society 1780–1880* (1969).
Pfannenstil, Bertil. *Bernard Bosanquet's Philosophy of the State* (Lund, Sweden, 1936).
Pierson, Stanley. *Marxism and the Origins of British Socialism: The Struggle for a New Consciousness* (Ithaca, N.Y., 1973).
Pimlott, J. A. R. *Toynbee Hall* (1935).
Pinker, Robert. *Social Theory and Social Policy* (1971).
Plamenatz, John. *Consent, Freedom and Political Obligation* (Oxford, 1938).
—— (ed.). *Readings from Liberal Writers, English and French* (1965).
Pocock, J. G. A. *Politics, Language and Time: Essays on Political Thought and History* (1972).
Popper, Karl. *The Poverty of Historicism* (1957).
Porter, Bernard. *Critics of Empire. British Radical Attitudes to Colonialism in Africa 1895–1914* (1968).
Quillian, W. F. *The Moral Theory of Evolutionary Naturalism* (New Haven, Conn., 1945).
Raison, Timothy (ed.). *The Founding Fathers of Social Science* (Harmondsworth, 1969).
Ramsey, I. T. (ed.). *Biology and Personality* (Oxford, 1966).
Rawls, John. *A Theory of Justice* (Cambridge, Mass., 1971).
Rees, J. C. *Mill and His Early Critics* (Leicester, 1956).
Rex, John (ed.). *Approaches to Sociology: An Introduction to Major Trends in British Sociology* (1974).

Richter, Melvin. *The Politics of Conscience: T. H. Green and His Age* (1964).
Ringer, Fritz. *The Decline of the German Mandarins: The German Academic Community 1890–1933* (Cambridge, Mass., 1969).
Robbins, L. C. *The Theory of Economic Policy in English Political Economy* (1952).
Roberts, Charles. *The Radical Countess: The History of the Life of Rosalind Countess of Carlisle* (with Preface by Wilfrid Roberts, Carlisle, 1962).
Roberts, David. *Victorian Origins of the British Welfare State* (New Haven, Conn., 1960).
Robson, J. M. *The Improvement of Mankind: The Social and Political Thought of John Stuart Mill* (Toronto, 1968).
Robson, R. (ed.). *Ideas and Institutions of Victorian Britain* (1967).
Robson, W. A. (ed.). *Man and the Social Sciences* (1973).
Rose, M. E. *The English Poor Law 1780–1930* (Newton Abbot, 1971).
Rowland, Peter. *The Last Liberal Governments* (2 vols., 1968 and 1971).
Ruggiero, Guido De. *The History of European Liberalism* (trans. R. G. Collingwood, 1927).
Ryan, Alan. *The Philosophy of John Stuart Mill* (1970).
—— *J. S. Mill* (1975).
Sabine, B. E. V. *A History of Income Tax* (1966).
Sabine, G. H. *A History of Political Theory* (New York, 1937; 4th edn, London, 1966).
Sahlins, M. D. and Service, E. R. (eds.). *Evolution and Culture* (Michigan, 1960).
Scally, Robert J. *The Origins of the Lloyd George Coalition: The Politics of Social Imperialism 1900–18* (Princeton, 1975).
Schneewind, J. B. *Sidgwick's Ethics and Victorian Moral Philosophy* (Oxford, 1977).
Schultz, H. J. (ed.). *English Liberalism and the State: Individualism or Collectivism?* (Lexington, Mass., 1972).
Schwartz, Pedro. *The New Political Economy of J. S. Mill* (1972).
Scott, Drusilla. *A. D. Lindsay: A Biography* (Oxford, 1971).
Searle, G. R. *The Quest for National Efficiency: A Study in British Politics and Political Thought 1899–1914* (Oxford, 1971).
Semmel, Bernard. *Imperialism and Social Reform: English Social-Imperial Thought 1895–1914* (1960).
Shannon, R. T. *Gladstone and the Bulgarian Agitation 1876* (1963).
Shehab, F. *Progressive Taxation* (Oxford, 1953).
Simey, T. S. *Social Science and Social Purpose* (1968).
—— and M. B. *Charles Booth: Social Scientist* (Oxford, 1960).
Simon, W. M. *European Positivism in the Nineteenth Century: An Essay in Intellectual History* (Ithaca, N.Y., 1963).
Skinner, A. S. *Adam Smith and the Role of the State* (Glasgow, 1964).
Sklair, Leslie. *The Sociology of Progress* (1970).
Smith, Paul. *Disraelian Conservatism and Social Reform* (1967).
Smith, Warren Sylvester. *The London Heretics 1870–1914* (1967).
Spender, Stephen. *World Within World: The Autobiography of Stephen Spender* (1951).
Spiller, G. *The Ethical Movement in Great Britain: A Documentary History* (1934).
Spinner, Thomas J., Jnr. *George Joachim Goschen: The Transformation of a Victorian Liberal* (Cambridge, 1973).
Stocking, G. W., Jnr. *Race, Culture and Evolution* (New York, 1968).
Sutherland, Gillian (ed.). *Studies in the Growth of Nineteenth-Century Government* (1972).
Swartz, Marvin. *The Union of Democratic Control in British Politics during World War One* (Oxford, 1971).
Taylor, A. J. *Laissez-Faire and State Intervention in Nineteenth-Century Britain* (1972).

Taylor A. J. P. *The Trouble Makers: Dissent over Foreign Policy 1792–1939* (1957).
—— (ed.). *Lloyd George: Twelve Essays* (1971).
Terrill, Ross. *R. H. Tawney and His Times: Socialism as Fellowship* (Cambridge, Mass., 1973).
Thatcher, David S. *Nietzsche in England 1890–1914: The Growth of a Reputation* (Toronto, 1970).
Thompson, F. M. L. *English Landed Society in the Nineteenth Century* (1963).
Thompson, Paul. *Socialists, Liberals and Labour: The Struggle for London 1885–1914* (1967).
—— *The Edwardians* (1975).
Thornton, A. P. *The Imperial Idea and Its Enemies: A Study in British Power* (1959).
Titmuss, R. M. *Essays on the Welfare State* (1958).
Turner, Barry. *Free Trade and Protection* (1971).
Turner, Frank Miller. *Between Science and Religion: The Reaction to Scientific Naturalism in Late-Victorian England* (New Haven, Conn., 1974).
Ulam, A. B. *The Philosophic Foundations of English Socialism* (Cambridge, Mass., 1951).
Van Doren, C. *The Idea of Progress* (New York, 1967).
Van Holthoon, F. C. *The Road to Utopia: A Study of J. S. Mill's Social Thought* (Assen, Holland, 1971).
Vincent, John. *The Formation of the British Liberal Party 1857–1868* (1966).
—— *Pollbooks: How Victorians Voted* (Cambridge, 1967).
Waddington, C. H. *Science and Ethics* (1942).
Wadsworth, A. P. (ed.). *C. P. Scott, 1846–1932: The Making of the 'Manchester Guardian'* (1946).
Warnock, Geoffrey. *English Philosophy since 1900* (Oxford, 1958; 2nd edn 1969).
Warnock, Mary, *Ethics since 1900* (1960).
Watkins, Frederick. *The Political Tradition of the West: A Study in the Development of Modern Liberalism* (Cambridge, Mass., 1948).
Watson, George. *The English Ideology: Studies in the Language of Victorian Politics* (1973).
Webb, R. K. *Modern England: From the Eighteenth Century to the Present* (1969).
Wiener, Martin J. *Between Two Worlds: The Political Thought of Graham Wallas* (Oxford, 1971).
Williams, Raymond. *Keywords: A Vocabulary of Culture and Society* (1976).
Wilson, Trevor. *The Downfall of the Liberal Party 1914–35* (1966).
—— (ed.). *The Political Diaries of C. P. Scott 1911–28* (1970).
Winch, D. *Economics and Policy: A Historical Study* (1969; 2nd edn 1972).
Winter, J. M. *Socialism and the Challenge of War: Ideas and Politics in Britain 1912–18* (1974).
Wolfe, Willard. *From Radicalism to Socialism: Men and Ideas in the Formation of Fabian Socialist Doctrines, 1881–1889* (New Haven, Conn., 1975).
Wolff, K. H. (ed.). *Emile Durkheim 1858–1917* (Ohio, 1960).
Wolff, Robert P. *The Poverty of Liberalism* (Boston, 1968).
Wolin, Sheldon. *Politics and Vision: Continuity and Innovation in Western Political Thought* (Boston, 1960).
Wollheim, R. *F. H. Bradley* (1959).
Wood, Ellen M. *Mind and Politics: An Approach to the Meaning of Liberal and Socialist Individualism* (Los Angeles, 1972).
Woodroofe, Kathleen. *From Charity to Social Work* (1962).
Young G. M. *Last Essays* (1950).
Zeitlin, Irving M. *Ideology and the Development of Sociological Theory* (Englewood Cliffs, N.J., 1968).

BIBLIOGRAPHY

Articles

Auld, John W. 'The Liberal pro-Boers', *Journal of British Studies*, XIV (1975), 78–99.

Bannister, R. C., Jnr. 'William Graham Sumner's Social Darwinism: a reconsideration', *History of Political Economy*, III (1973), 89–109.

Barker, Ernest. 'Leonard Trelawny Hobhouse 1864–1929', *Proceedings of the British Academy*, XV (1929), 536–54.

Bayliss, F. J. 'The Independent Members of the British Wages Councils and Boards', *British Journal of Sociology*, VIII (1957), 1–25.

Benn, S. I. and Weinstein, W. L. 'Being free to act, and being a free man', *Mind*, LXXX (1971), 194–211.

Bestor, A. E. 'The evolution of the Socialist vocabulary', *Journal of the History of Ideas*, IX (1948), 259–302.

Bock, Kenneth. 'Darwin and social theory', *Philosophy of Science*, XXII (1955), 123–34.

Bourn, J. D. 'Philosophy and action in politics', *Political Studies*, XIII (1965), 377–85.

Branford, Victor. 'The sociological work of Leonard Hobhouse', *Sociological Review*, XXI (1929), 273–80.

Brebner, J. B. 'Laissez-faire and state intervention in nineteenth-century Britain', *Journal of Economic History*, Supplement VIII (1948), 59–73.

Briggs, Asa. 'The Welfare State in historical perspective', *Archives Européennes de Sociologie*, II (1961), 221–58.

Bristow, Edward. 'The Liberty and Property Defence League and Individualism', *Historical Journal*, XVIII (1975), 761–89.

Brown, D. G. 'Mill on liberty and morality', *Philosophical Review*, 81 (1972), 133–58.

Brown, J. 'Charles Booth and labour colonies 1889–1905', *Economic History Review*, XXI (1968), 349–60.

—— 'Social judgements and social policy', *Economic History Review*, XXIV (1971), 106–13.

Clarke, P. F. 'The Progressive Movement in England', *Transactions of the Royal Historical Society*, 5th series, 24 (1974), 159–81.

—— 'The electoral position of the Liberal and Labour Parties, 1910–1914', *English Historical Review*, XC (1975), 828–36.

Coats, A. W. 'Political Economy and the Tariff Reform campaign of 1903', *Journal of Law and Economics*, XI (1968), 181–229.

Collini, Stefan. 'Idealism and "Cambridge Idealism"', *Historical Journal*, XVIII (1975), 171–7.

—— 'Hobhouse, Bosanquet and the state: philosophical Idealism and political argument in England 1880–1918', *Past and Present*, 72 (1976), 86–111.

—— 'Liberalism and the legacy of Mill', *Historical Journal*, XX (1977), 237–54.

—— 'Sociology and Idealism in Britain 1880–1920', *Archives Européennes de Sociologie*, XIX (1978), 3–50.

Collins, D. 'The introduction of Old Age Pensions in Great Britain', *Historical Journal*, VIII (1965), 246–59.

Cornford, James. 'Transformation of Conservatism in the late nineteenth century', *Victorian Studies*, VII (1963), 35–66.

Cromwell, Valerie. 'Interpretations of nineteenth-century administration: an analysis', *Victorian Studies*, IX (1966), 245–55.

Crouch, R. L. 'Laissez-faire in nineteenth-century Britain: myth or reality?', *Manchester School of Economic and Social Studies*, XXXV (1967), 199–215.

Dewey, C. J. 'Images of the village community: a study in Anglo-Indian ideology', *Modern Asian Studies*, 6 (1972), 291–328.

—— '"Cambridge Idealism": Utilitarian revisionists in late-nineteenth-century Cambridge', *Historical Journal*, XVII (1974), 63–78.

Emy, H. V. 'The impact of financial policy on English party politics before 1914', *Historical Journal*, XV (1972), 103–31.

Freeden, Michael. 'J. A. Hobson as a New Liberal theorist: some aspects of his social thought until 1914', *Journal of the History of Ideas*, XXXIV (1973), 421–43.

—— 'Biological and evolutionary roots of the New Liberalism in England', *Political Theory*, 4 (1976), 471–90.

Gallie, W. B. 'Essentially contested concepts', *Proceedings of the Aristotelian Society*, LVI (1955–6), 167–98.

Griffin, C. M. 'L. T. Hobhouse and the idea of harmony', *Journal of the History of Ideas*, XXXV (1974), 647–61.

Halliday, R. J. 'The sociological movement: the Sociological Society and the genesis of academic sociology in Britain', *Sociological Review*, 16 (1968), 377–97.

—— 'Social Darwinism: a definition', *Victorian Studies*, XIV (1971), 389–405.

Harrison, Brian. 'Religion and recreation in nineteenth-century England', *Past and Present*, 38 (1967), 98–125.

—— 'Animals and the state in nineteenth-century Britain', *English Historical Review*, LXXXVIII (1973), 786–820.

—— and Hollis, P. 'Chartism, Liberalism, and the life of Robert Lowery', *English Historical Review*, LXXXII (1967), 503–35.

Hart, Jenifer. 'Nineteenth-century social reform: a Tory interpretation of history', *Past and Present*, 31 (1965), 33–61.

Helfand, Michael S. 'T. H. Huxley's "Evolution and Ethics": the politics of evolution and the evolution of politics', *Victorian Studies*, 20 (1977), 159–77.

Hennock, E. P. 'Poverty and social theory in England: the experience of the 1880s', *Social History*, 1 (1976), 67–91.

Horn, P. L. R. 'The farm workers, the dockers and Oxford University', *Oxoniensia*, 32 (1967), 60–70.

Hume, L. J. 'Jeremy Bentham and the nineteenth-century revolution in government', *Historical Journal*, X (1967), 361–75.

Hutchison, T. W. 'Bentham as an economist', *Economic Journal*, 66 (1956), 286–306.

—— 'Economists and economic policy in Britain after 1870', *History of Political Economy*, 1 (1969), 231–53.

Kaufman, A. S. 'Wants, needs and liberalism', *Inquiry*, 14 (1971), 191–206.

Lee, Alan J. 'Franklin Thomasson and the *Tribune*: a case-study in the history of the Liberal Press', *Historical Journal* XVI (1973), 341–60.

Lummis, T. 'Charles Booth: moralist or social scientist?', *Economic History Review*, XXIV (1971), 100–5.

MacCallum, G. C. 'Negative and positive freedom', *Philosophical Review*, 76 (1967), 312–34.

McCloskey, H. J. 'Liberalism', *Philosophy*, 49 (1974), 13–32.

Macdonagh, O. 'The nineteenth-century revolution in government: a re-appraisal', *Historical Journal*, II (1958), 52–67.

Macintyre, Alasdair. 'The essential contestability of some social concepts', *Ethics*, 84 (1973), 1–9.

MacRae, D. G. 'Leonard Trelawny Hobhouse 1864–1929', *L.S.E. The Magazine of the London School of Economics*, 43 (1972), 9–10.

McWilliams-Tullberg, Rita. 'Marshall's "tendency to Socialism"', *History of Political Economy*, 7 (1975), 75–111.

Mariz, George. 'L. T. Hobhouse as theoretical sociologist', *Albion*, 6 (1974), 307–19.
Milne, A. J. 'The Idealist critique of Utilitarian social philosophy', *Archives Européennes de Sociologie*, VIII (1967), 319–31.
Mitchell, H. 'Hobson revisited', *Journal of the History of Ideas*, XXVI (1965), 397–416.
Mowat, C. L. 'Social legislation in Britain and the United States in the early twentieth century: a problem in the history of ideas', *Historical Studies*, VII (1969), 81–96.
Nicholls, David. 'Positive liberty 1880–1914', *American Political Science Review*, LVI (1962), 114–28.
Parris, H. 'The nineteenth-century revolution in government: a re-appraisal re-appraised', *Historical Journal*, III (1960), 17–37.
Parsons, Talcott. 'Wants and activities in Marshall', *Quarterly Journal of Economics*, XLVI (1931–2), 101–40.
—— 'Economics and sociology: Marshall in relation to the thought of his time', *Quarterly Journal of Economics*, XLVI (1931–2), 316–47.
—— Review of *Sociology and Philosophy*, *Sociological Enquiry*, 43 (1973), 85–7.
Petter, Martin. 'The Progressive Alliance', *History*, 58 (1973), 45–59.
Quinton, Anthony. 'Absolute Idealism', *Proceedings of the British Academy*, LVII (1971), 303–29.
Ricci, David M. 'Fabian Socialism: a theory of rent as exploitation', *Journal of British Studies*, IX (1969), 105–21.
Richter, Melvin. 'Intellectual and class alienation: Oxford Idealist diagnoses and prescriptions', *Archives Européennes de Sociologie*, VII (1966), 1–26.
Roach, John. 'Liberalism and the Victorian intelligentsia', *Cambridge Historical Journal*, XIII (1957), 58–81.
Rogers, J. A. 'Darwinism and Social Darwinism', *Journal of the History of Ideas*, XXXIII (1972), 265–80.
Rowbotham, Sheila. 'The call to University Extension teaching 1873–1900', *University of Birmingham Historical Journal*, XII (1969), 55–71.
Ryle, Gilbert. 'Fifty years of philosophy and philosophers', *Philosophy*, 51 (1976), 381–9.
Schneider, F. W. 'Fabians and the Utilitarian view of empire', *Review of Politics*, XXXV (1973), 501–22.
Schwartz, Pedro. 'J. S. Mill and laissez-faire: London Water', *Economica*, XXXIII (1966), 71–83.
Searle, J. R. 'Meaning and speech-acts', *Philosophical Review*, LXXI (1962), 423–32.
Shils, Edward A. 'Tradition, ecology and institution in the history of sociology', *Daedalus*, 99 (1970), 760–826.
Simon, W. M. 'Herbert Spencer and the "social organism"', *Journal of the History of Ideas*, XXI (1960), 294–9.
Skinner, Quentin, 'Meaning and understanding in the history of ideas', *History and Theory*, VIII (1969), 3–53.
—— 'Some problems in the analysis of political thought and action', *Political Theory*, 2 (1974), 277–303.
Soffer, Reba N. 'The revolution in English social thought 1880–1914', *American Historical Review*, LXXV (1970), 1938–64.
Swart, K. W. '"Individualism" in the mid nineteenth century (1826–1860)', *Journal of the History of Ideas*, XXIII (1962), 77–90.
Viner, Jacob. 'The intellectual history of laissez-faire', *Journal of Law and Economics*, III (1960), 45–69.

Weiler, Peter. 'The New Liberalism of L. T. Hobhouse', *Victorian Studies*, XV (1972), 141–61.

—— 'William Clarke: the making and unmaking of a Fabian Socialist', *Journal of British Studies*, XIV (1974), 77–108.

Weinstein, W. L. 'The concept of "liberty" in nineteenth-century English political thought', *Political Studies*, XIII (1965), 145–62.

Winter, J. M. 'R. H. Tawney's early political thought', *Past and Present*, 47 (1970), 71–96.

Wohl, A. S. '*The Bitter Cry of Outcast London*', *International Review of Social History*, XIII (1968), 189–246.

Woodard, C. 'Reality and social reform: the transition from laissez-faire to the Welfare State', *Yale Law Journal*, LXXII (1962), 286–328.

Unpublished dissertations

Clark, L. A. 'The Liberal Party and Collectivism 1886–1906' (Cambridge, M.Litt., 1957).

Davidson, Roger. 'Sir Hubert Llewellyn Smith and Labour Policy 1886–1916' (Cambridge, Ph.D., 1971).

Freeden, M. S. 'English Liberal Thought: Problems of Social Reform 1886–1914' (Oxford, D.Phil., 1972).

Griffin, C. M. 'A Critical Examination of L. T. Hobhouse's Political and Social Theories' (London, Ph.D., 1972).

Jones, K. T. 'The Political Philosophy of L. T. Hobhouse' (Wales, M.A., 1973).

Kaufman, A. S. 'Liberalism in Transition: The Political Philosophy of Leonard Trelawny Hobhouse' (Columbia, Ph.D., 1955).

Lee, Alan J. 'A Study of the Social and Economic Thought of J. A. Hobson' (London, Ph.D., 1970).

Mehta, V. R. 'T. H. Green's Ideas in Relation to His Time with Special Reference to His Social and Political Thought' (Cambridge, Ph.D., 1971).

Weiler, Peter. 'Liberal Social Theory in Great Britain 1896–1914' (Harvard, Ph.D., 1968).

INDEX

INDEX